Coordination among Schools, Families, and Communities

SUNY Series, Educational Leadership
Daniel L. Duke

Coordination among Schools, Families, and Communities

Prospects for Educational Reform

edited by
James G. Cibulka
William J. Kritek

STATE UNIVERSITY OF NEW YORK PRESS

Chapter 4 by Shirley Brice Heath and Milbrey W. McLaughlin was previously published in 1994 under the same title in *Educational Administration Quarterly* 30 (3), pp. 278–300. It appears here by permission of Corwin Press, Inc., a Sage Publications Company.

Chapter 7 by Mark A. Smylie, Robert L. Crowson, Victoria Chou, and Rebekah A. Levin was previously published in 1994 under the same title in *Educational Administration Quarterly* 30 (3), pp. 342–364. It appears here by permission of Corwin Press, Inc., a Sage Publications Company.

Chapter 8 by Carolyn Herrington was previously published in 1994 under the same title in *Educational Administration Quarterly* 30 (3), pp. 301–323. It appears here by permission of Corwin Press, Inc., a Sage Publications Company.

Chapter 9 by Hanne B. Mawhinney was previously published in 1994 under the same title in *Educational Administration Quarterly* 30 (3), pp. 324–341. It appears here by permission of Corwin Press, Inc., a Sage Publications Company.

Chapter 11 by Deborah A. Verstegen was previously published in 1994 under the same title in *Educational Administration Quarterly* 30 (3), pp. 365–390. It appears here by permission of Corwin Press, Inc., a Sage Publications Company.

Chapter 12 by Colleen A. Capper was previously published in 1994 under the same title in *Educational Administration Quarterly* 30 (3), pp. 257–277. It appears here by permission of Corwin Press, Inc., a Sage Publications Company.

Published by
State University of New York Press, Albany

© 1996 State University of New York

For information, address the State University of New York Press, State University Plaza, Albany, NY 12246

Library of Congress Cataloging-in-Publication Data

Coordination among schools, families, and communities : prosepcts for educational reform / edited by James G. Cibulka, William J. Kritek.
    p.   cm. — (SUNY series, educational leadership)
    Includes bibliographical references and index.
    ISBN (invalid) 0-7914-2857-7 (alk. paper). — ISBN 0-7914-2858-3 (pkb. : alk. paper)
    1. Community and school—United States.   2. Home and school—United States.   3. School management and organization—United States.   4. Educational change—United States.   I. Cibulka, James G.   II. Kritek, William J., 1940–   .   III. Series: SUNY series in educational leadership.
LC215.C58   1996
370.19'31'0973—dc20   95-8929
                                                                        CIP

10 9 8 7 6 5 4 3 2

Contents

v

Section II:
Organizational and Management Issues Surrounding Coordination

Section III:
Evaluation and Critiques of Coordination as a Reform

Introduction

William J. Kritek

Establishing coordination among schools, families, and communities has emerged as a major policy issue in the debate over the quality of education and how the restructuring of education should be accomplished. Whether as a component of various educational reform efforts, or as an issue presented starkly in its own right, coordination among schools, families, and communities is being reexamined and rethought by scholars and by policymakers at every level of government. The impetus for the renewed interest has its roots in two significant developments of the past twenty years: the worsening condition of the lives of millions of American children who are born into, and grow up in, poverty, and the decline of the United States as the preeminent economic power in the world.

Because of widespread racism and deliberate governmental policy regarding taxes and spending priorities and, according to some commentators (e.g., Murray 1984), because of the failure of the welfare state, a huge segment of the population has become economically poor. In its wake, continuous and pervasive poverty has spawned an underclass characterized by unemployment, a propensity for violence, dependency on drugs, and a breakdown of traditional family structures. While the status of poor and minority children has always been marginal, over the last two decades or so the economic condition of the poor has deteriorated even more. In big cities, the poor are concentrated in neighborhoods that have become breeding grounds for more and more problems—from severely undernourished young mothers to a culture of unemployment from which it is almost impossible to escape. In some rural areas, although the word *concentration* may be inappropriate, unrelenting poverty sometimes engulfs whole counties. In both urban and rural communities, the result is the same: a syndrome of underfinanced and inadequate schools, insufficient medical services, dependence on the welfare system, and frequent encounters with the police and the courts.

A report of the Carnegie Corporation of New York, as cited in an April 12, 1994, *New York Times* article, provides examples of the problem, based on 1990 census data:

— almost one-fourth of all American infants and toddlers, and over one-fifth of children under 18 live in poverty.

— more than one-fourth of all children are born to unmarried mothers;

— large numbers of American children are not immunized;

— an increasing number of young children grow up with firsthand experience of stabbings, shootings, and beatings.

The second development, the loss of economic preeminence, represented by importing high-quality products from other countries and exporting jobs to countries where labor is cheap, has resulted in the determination of government and business to reverse the tide. Business leaders have looked to techniques such as total quality management and downsizing in an effort to improve quality and make operations more efficient. Simultaneously, these leaders have identified the schools as a major part of the problem. Desegregation efforts seem to have done little to improve the educational opportunities available to city children. Entrenched bureaucracies and teacher unions seem more committed to the status quo than to finding ways to implement programs that ensure that children have access to, and profit from, a high quality education. Dating back at least to the much publicized slippage in Scholastic Aptitude Test (SAT) scores, and thrust on the nation's consciousness by the publication of *A Nation at Risk* in 1983, business has concluded that the inadequacies of our educational system have made it impossible for the United States to remain economically competitive with other countries.

As a result, business has added its considerable influence to efforts to improve the quality of education in the United States. Tightening up requirements for graduation, improving the teaching force, creating school-to-work initiatives, pushing for the use of the marketplace in the form of voucher plans and privately run schools, and, more recently, advocating for early childhood programs and services seem to constitute the business prescription for improving the quality of education. Politicians have moved in concert with business leaders both to improve the efficiency of government operations and to address the problem of the perceived low quality of the schools.

If an understanding of the dire circumstances in which many of our nation's children live is not enough, in itself, to spark concerted efforts to improve their condition, the loss of economic preeminence has resulted in the realization by government and business that something must be done about the poor quality of education, especially in our major cities, where many students drop out of school and many of those who graduate do so without marketable skills. Policy leaders have become aware, as Harold Hodgkinson (1985, 11) says, "that if large numbers of youth fail in school and work, the consequences for us all are severe."

Politicians and business leaders have rightly perceived the culture of poverty as a threat to the well-being of the entire country. While the most immediate concern of many citizens may be related to personal safety, policy makers are also aware of the huge drain on the economy caused by unused resources and the burden on taxpayers who are called on to pay for social services and the prison system. It is now obvious that revitalizing the economy will require a highly skilled work force and a dramatic increase in the number of people who are engaged in productive work. In essence, solving the economic problem will require solving the social problem caused by poverty and racism. Solving both will require a dramatic restructuring of public education and other social services in the United States.

Thus, the country has recently heard recommendations for far-reaching solutions, including the complete reinvention of the welfare and health care systems. Policies designed to address poverty directly are occasionally offered, including tougher laws regarding payment of child support, earned income-tax credits, and payment for job training. But calls for the total restructuring of the educational system have been particularly loud and insistent.

A new focus is developing in the arena of social policy, one aimed more at prevention than remediation, at investment in children, at designing structures that build and preserve families, and at changes that address the whole ecology in which children learn and develop (Bronfenbrenner 1979). It is clear that factors such as teenage pregnancy and pervasive poverty make it more and more unlikely that children will be able to take advantage of the opportunities available at school. In recent years, there has been a resurgence of interest in tapping the human resources available in every community and neighborhood—from families, schools, churches, voluntary organizations, and social service agencies to individual parents, teachers, community-based police, health care personnel, and social service workers. Scholars and policymakers have shown renewed interest in the concept of "social capital"—the set of norms, networks, and neighborliness that supports community and family development (Coleman 1987) and in "human capital investment" (Glazer 1993). It is in this context that school reform efforts have begun to focus on the coordination among schools, families, and communities.

THE EVOLUTION OF SCHOOL REFORM

In response to these problems and the demand for change, various reform efforts have been initiated in schools in an attempt to insure that students receive the type of education that will allow them to develop to their full potential and to become productive members of the workforce and competent citizens of a democratic society. The education restructuring movement has gone through a well-documented evolution from a concern about teacher competency and holding children accountable for learning the basic skills, to an interest in policies that insure that school decision making involves staff and takes place at the site level, to an understanding that all children need and deserve high quality curriculum and instruction, and finally to a more fundamental restructuring that seeks to involve parents and communities more centrally in the education of their children (Bacharach 1990). Each of these strands of the restructuring movement, not just the latest one, has had something to say about coordination among schools, parents, and communities.

The early effective schools research and the resulting recommendations for school policy, as articulated by Ronald Edmonds (1979), can be seen as a precursor of what eventually came to be known as the restructuring movement. This effort to improve city schools was fueled by a search for equity—a quest for ways to insure that students in those schools, primarily poor children of color, acquired the knowledge and skills attained by their more well-off peers. Because the early effective schools research was a reaction to the conclusions of the 1966 Coleman report, and was an effort to locate responsibility for school improvement squarely at the door of school people, Edmonds' five well-known correlates of effective schools pointedly omitted mentioning anything about parents or the community. But the idea of "effective schools" was too powerful, and the task facing schools was too complex, for the relatively simple Edmonds approach to endure without substantial elaboration. Almost immediately, additional "correlates" were suggested, including one that postulated the need for parental involvement in the schools.

In the new school effectiveness programs (e.g., Comer 1988; Levin 1988; and Slavin et al. 1992) not only is instruction stressed much more than in the Edmonds model, but involving parents in the education of their children and educating parents about their role in supporting the work of the school are key elements. What started out as a movement to change the schools eventually led to the need to find ways to reach out to, and involve, parents and families so the schools' efforts could be complemented. Indeed, Herbert Walberg (1984, 397) synthesized thousands of research studies and concluded that "the efficiency of the home in fostering learning has declined for several decades, but cooperative partnerships between the home and the school can dramatically raise educational productivity."

Following the publication of *A Nation at Risk,* the pressures to improve mounted on all schools and resulted in extending the concept of effective schools to every school whether serving rich, secondary students in the suburbs, or poor, elementary children in the cities. However, the first wave of reform was more heavily laden with not-so-subtle overtones from business: tighten up on teacher quality, get the students to work harder and longer, and demand greater accountability. These requirements were incorporated into the statutes of many states. At the same time, businesses and universities signaled their commitment to school improvement by establishing partnerships with elementary and secondary schools in an attempt to better prepare young people for the workplace or higher education. While some of the partnerships attempted to stimulate systemic change, most focused directly on teachers or students, e.g., recognizing and rewarding teacher initiatives, establishing student mentoring programs, or providing jobs for graduates.

The next wave of school restructuring added the dimension of improving school culture and school programs by involving the staff in school decision making and by a strong effort to professionalize teaching. Moving significantly beyond stressing the basics and tightening up requirements and qualifications, this wave counted on locally determined programs to provide high quality curriculum and instruction for all students. This push to site-based management drew some of its impetus from a similar development in business and industry. However, the fledgling site-based management initiatives soon were extended beyond the school walls to include a parental and community presence on local school councils. This development was similar to school reform efforts in the 1960s, which evolved from efforts to decentralize urban school systems administratively (although rarely to the school site) to the more radical political decentralization, giving parents and community members decision-making powers.

Building on this latter development, the succeeding third wave of the restructuring movement has had a more explicit connection to involvement of families and community. In Chicago, state legislation created local school councils, semiautonomous governing boards, made up of two teachers, six parents, and two community members in addition to the principal, for each school. These councils hire and fire the principal, determine the school improvement plan, and oversee the school's budget. In theory, at least, Chicago's schools should be more closely coordinated with families and the community.

The third wave of reform has also ushered in policies enabling families to choose the school of their choice from a menu of public and private options. Within the public sector, magnet schools and the movement to site-based management seem to suggest that schools will develop unique personalities and programs. Voucher plans, charter schools, and various choice programs that enable students to attend private schools extend the options even further. The mechanism of the marketplace, it is assumed, will enable these schools to be responsive to student and parental needs and wishes.

And the third wave has capitalized on the growing realization that changes that have occurred in the United States over the past twenty years have left many schools unable to accomplish their mission alone. Policies and structures that further coordination of schools and families with social service and health care agencies and with an array of other public and private groups are needed in order to take full advantage of the educative and developmental potential of each of these groups and of all the groups working together. The intent of this book is to describe and analyze the programs and policies that have been developed to establish this coordination.

COORDINATION OF SERVICES

We use the term "coordination" in the title of this book to convey the process of acting together toward a common goal. Other words are commonly used (e.g., cooperation, collaboration, integration, partnership) to describe the wide variety of linkages that are possible between and among schools, parents, and communities. Obviously, there are important differences among these words. For example, Shirley Hord (1986) distinguishes between collaboration and cooperation (the former a more complex process involving greater sharing of resources, control, and responsibility) and provides a useful synthesis of the research on collaboration among organizations. However, the terms are frequently used interchangeably, and processes linking schools, parents, and communities are almost always in flux, hopefully moving from some level of cooperation to some higher level of collaboration. We have chosen to use what we think is a more general term—coordination.

Schools have long been in the business of coordinating services for young people. The diagnosis of, and provision of services to, children with special educational needs is an example of the coordination of the work of various professionals. Many elementary school teachers try to coordinate their expectations with what is going on in the children's homes. Beyond that, schools serve breakfasts and lunches; they are the sites for vision and hearing testing, if not more comprehensive health clinics; they link young people to the workplace through various work-study programs; they are connected to colleges and universities through the curriculum and counseling; they offer before and after-school care programs; they refer children to social service and child protection agencies; they utilize the diagnoses of physicians in the planning of programs for children with disabilities. Indeed, the array of services provided or utilized by schools is so extensive that some educators and commentators claim that the schools have lost sight of their appropriate role and call loudly for a return to the school's primary mission of teaching and learning.

The idea that education is a tool for social progress and social remediation has a long history in the United States. American education reformers in the middle of the eighteenth century believed that "social stability and individual welfare" required universal access to public school. In the cities, in particular, they viewed the public schools as the answer to the problems caused by urbanization (Tyack 1981). Progressive reformers advocated many social functions for the schools, but they also sought to insulate schools from provincial, parochial, and political pressure in families and communities. Now, at the end of the twentieth century, it is evident that the schools acting alone are not a sufficient institutional response to address societal changes. The current thinking seems more akin to the African proverb that it takes an entire village to educate one child. A belief that was practiced the world over in simpler times, the concept of a village partnership to promote the development and learning of young people seems to be an idea that has been rediscovered for the twenty-first century.

The coordination of services for children and youth has become a major policy issue and initiative at virtually every level of government—federal, state, county, and city. In a 1991 report, the Committee on Economic Development observed that "policy leaders have begun to subscribe to a broader view of human-resource development. They are starting to view early-childhood development, education, social services, job training, and economic development as parts of an interdependent system of human investments, rather than as independent enterprises" (3). The first of the six national education goals, "By the year 2000, all children in America will start school ready to learn," conveys an implicit, if not explicit, acknowledgment that a broad array of agencies will have to contribute to its realization. Insuring readiness for school will require the active involvement of the family, the church, health-care providers, and social service agencies (Kagan 1990). Similarly, the sixth education goal for the year 2000, "Every school will be free of drugs and violence," will require the effort of the entire community if there is to be any hope of its accomplishment.

Many states have enacted statutes requiring some level of coordination of services for children and youth. In Ohio, for example, regional Family Councils have been mandated since 1987 to streamline and coordinate existing public services for families. In Stark County, Ohio, seven agencies representing education, health and human services, and the family court cooperatively spend categorical dollars in noncategorical services for children. The work of the Family Council is focused on a unified system of wrap-around services, on prevention, on "family-centered, culturally sensitive" services and supports, on affirming that the community is part of the solution, and that families are partners in defining issues and planning solutions (Stroul 1992).

The impetus for coordination of services, then, comes from a growing realization of the desirability of a holistic approach to child development and learning. In addition, parents have become frustrated by their inability to locate services they need, by not getting services when they need them, and by not having services available in a relatively convenient place. They are dismayed by the duplication in some areas and by the cracks in the system where no services are provided (Kirst and McLaughlin 1990). And they are alienated by the impersonality and dehumanizing maze of the welfare bureaucracy. Similarly, teachers and school administrators, as well as other service providers, are frustrated by their inability to put together a coherent program of services for children. It is not uncommon for teachers to become aware of some relatively straightforward parental need when working with a child and then be frustrated by an inability to locate the appropriate service. A patchwork of service boundaries, program eligibility criteria, and professional jargon hamper the best efforts of providers to bring services to those who need them. Coordination is hindered by many roadblocks, including categorical funding systems, strong norms of professional autonomy, and diverse organization philosophies. Robert Agranoff (1991) provides a list of coordinating mechanisms including case management, coapplication procedures, information sharing, partnership agreements, and location in a common setting that can help overcome some of these problems.

But there are other sides to this issue of coordination of services. While at least one segment of public opinion recognizes the tremendous need for improved services for families, another segment of opinion (sometimes espoused by the same individuals) recoils at the increased costs associated with providing those services. Their concern is with providing the services more efficiently. They point to the unseemly spectacle of agencies competing with one another for resources, apparently worrying more about building the agency than about serving clients. In part, the demographics of America at the end of the twentieth century make it politically more difficult to provide the care that children need.

> As other groups compete for resources, public expenditures for children may be cut back, and the tendency to consider children as special dependents who deserve protection from adult pressures may be reversed. In short, as society ages, it may become easier to ignore the special needs of children. (Richman & Stagner 1986, 177)

The growing unwillingness to use the property tax to support schools and other social programs must be added to these pressures for efficiency. The coordination of services, it is hoped, will reduce duplication and streamline and rationalize programs that seem entirely too chaotic.

While the push for coordination of services for children and families is held out as a possible means of accomplishing both the effectiveness and efficiency objectives, there is, as yet, very little data to give much support to either hope, although some evidence seems to indicate that coordination of services has produced real benefits. For example, some school-based health clinics have helped reduce teenage childbearing by more than 50 percent within three years and have contributed to raising the age at which young people become sexually active. Some preschool programs have evidence that their participants were less likely to drop out, become delinquent, become teenage mothers, or remain unemployed (Schorr 1993). However, coordination itself may have some costs in the form of additional staff and other resources. Further, improved effectiveness and efficiency may lead to greater utilization of services and thus greater total costs. On the other hand, while these services are expensive, it may also be possible to show that programs such as those that have a prevention emphasis reduce the need for additional services in the long run.

And there is still a third side to the issue of coordination of services for children and youth. This perspective questions the appropriateness of any additional social engineering and social control. If people are already overcontrolled by countless laws and regulatory agencies, it may be that they are actually protected in some measure by the gaps and looseness of coordination. To tighten up the system much more, even in the name of providing help, may, in fact, make it even more totalitarian than some people currently perceive it.

The literature dealing with coordination of services for children and families considers the issues identified above, but it remains diffuse. To date, we have a number of policy papers (e.g., Crowson and Boyd 1993), many initial reports of what is taking place in various parts of the country (e.g., Payzant 1992), a growing collection of guides for partnerships and coordinated efforts (e.g., Tushnet 1993), and scattered program evaluations (e.g., Wattenberg 1993). These reports, papers, guides, and evaluations have identified barriers to, and facilitators of, coordination and collaboration. They have contained suggestions and lists of "how-to's," often with conflicting recommendations. There is obviously a need for more case studies and more long-term studies of coordinated services programs. We need a greater understanding of the contexts in which coordination is taking place. We need better theoretical and conceptual frameworks to guide these studies. And we need more comprehensive evaluations of collaborative endeavors.

PLAN OF THE BOOK

As the foregoing discussion should have made clear, the topic of coordination among schools, families, and communities is extremely vast. All manner of school reforms might be encompassed within this rubric, for example, parental involvement in student learning, or school-to-work programs, or school choice, or school-based clinics. Having set this broader context, we have tried to confine the book's focus to addressing coordination of services for children and youth between and among schools, families, and community groups, and agencies. We view coordination as one strategy for dealing with a broad set of educational and social issues and problems. In the concluding chapter (see the summary below), we link coordination of services back to these bigger questions, although, to some extent, the individual chapters also address these concerns. By keeping our focus on coordination of services for children and youth, primarily from an educational perspective, we hope to strike a helpful balance between in-depth coverage of one reform strategy and discussion of its place in the larger context of educational and social reform.

The intent of this book, then, is to extend our understanding of the policy arena related to coordination of services for children and families. We have divided the chapters into four sections, but it will be evident that the content of many chapters could also have led us to locate them in one of the other sections.

Models of Coordination

We begin with a selection of papers that describes various models of coordination and collaboration. Each of these papers reports on field research conducted in one or two sites. Together they convey the wide array of possible venues for pursuing coordination and collaboration.

In the first chapter, Claire Smrekar describes the first year of two family-resource centers established under the 1990 Kentucky Educational Reform Act. These centers were designed as *school-based* centers for linking services. Smrekar documents the "uneasy alliance" of parents and teachers that is mediated by the Center. Interestingly, the centers have disconnected from the schools symbolically and physically in order to establish new and expanded channels of communication.

The case study provided by Bruce Wilson, Jaci Webb, and Dickson Corbett identifies students as the logical connection between the community and the school. Based on interviews of community and education professionals associated with a single elementary school, the authors found shared understandings about the kinds of people students should become. The authors identify the need for early discussions among community and school people to uncover and build on these "unseen commonalities."

Paul Heckman, Reed Scull, and Sharon Conley report on a case study of a foundation-funded project located in two schools involving university and school personnel designed to influence both formal (school), nonformal (after-school), and informal (family and community) educative experiences. The authors report that, although the inevitable conflict developed, shared meanings have emerged, and the coalition gained influence in the larger polity.

The last two selections in this first section extend the site of collaboration beyond the school to community-based programs. In the first, Shirley Brice Heath and Milbrey McLaughlin provide case studies of two community-based youth-serving organizations. They describe the programs of these organizations as highly educational, "authentic," and supportive of youth development and preparation for employment. They make explicit suggestions for collaborative partnerships with schools that would provide the "best of both worlds."

Finally, Rebecca Newman, and Lynn Beck document the extent of the problem of homeless children and describe a school for these children jointly sponsored by a county department of education and two private organizations. The findings of their study point to policies that facilitate or impede collaborative efforts such as this, and they document insufficient planning and evaluation and, in general, a lack of sufficient communication among the partners.

These five chapters provide a glimpse of the extensiveness of the arena of coordination and collaboration among schools, families, and communities. As a group, they point to the need for structures and processes that facilitate communication among groups that are not used to talking with one another, let alone planning and carrying out programs collaboratively. The chapters, in other words, point to the need to address organizational and management issues as coordination efforts are undertaken, which is the focus of the next section of the book.

Organizational and Management Issues

In the first chapter of this section, Robert Crowson and William Boyd use an institutional analysis framework to compare five cases of coordination of children's services. They identify four interorganizational domains of collaboration: the convening process, institutional interests and reward systems, institutional "conventions," and institutional environments. Potential collaborators need to address these four domains and build shared institutional structures that are responsive to the tasks that need accomplishing in these areas.

Mark Smylie, Robert Crowson, Victoria Chou, and Rebekah Levin focus on the role of the school principal in a coordinated children's service project in Chicago. Their case comes from the foundation-funded program called "The Nation of Tomorrow," which links families with the schools, child care and youth programs, and community health-care agencies. The case reveals that principals face pressure to open up the schools and take services out to the community and simultaneously face pressures to maintain organizational control and stability. The authors identify three fundamental statregies: compartmentalization, entrepreneurial activities, and control mechanisms involving commu-nication and reporting systems, micromanagement, gatekeeping, and influencing the work agenda.

Carolyn Herrington also focuses on the challenges collaborative programs create for school administrators. Based on interviews with principals and superintendents involved in initial projects, Herrington finds that the problems they encountered were not as severe as some have indicated and certainly not unsurmountable. While more serious problems may crop up when the projects move to full-scale imple-mentation, at least in the initial phases, the administrators did not find serious jurisdictional, technical, or administrative problems.

Hanne Mawhinney's ethnographic study of efforts to promote collaboration extends the array of venues of collaboration to Canada and to a high school. Like Crowson and Boyd, Mawhinney uses an institutional analysis framework to document change in light of the persistence of institutional patterns in the school. She concludes that the "institutionalization of collaboration is often dependent upon positive feedback from incremental adjustments."

Patrick Galvin's case study of a Minority Engineering Science Achievement Program also uses a theoretical framework to guide his discussion. In this case, the framework is agency theory and organiza-tional economics, and the focus is on organizational arrangements that are developed to achieve cost effectiveness and efficiency. Galvin calls attention to the costs of information, monitoring, and contracting that are not as apparent as line items on a proposal budget.

Finally, Deborah Verstegen relates the issue of coordination and collaboration of services to school finance and to policies that support equal opportunity to learn for all students. She identifies the need to align financing policies for schools and related community services.

The chapters in the second section identify a set of challenges that faces schools and program administrators who attempt to implement a program involving coordinated services. The program must struggle against pressures to maintain institutional patterns, there are costs associated with increased communication requirements, and, of course, there are funding issues that must be faced by organizations that are chronically underfunded. Coping with these challenges involves skill that goes beyond the specific programmatic expertise that administrators bring to the collaboration.

Evaluating and Critiquing Coordination and Collaboration

In the first chapter of this section, Colleen Capper brings a critical perspective to a case study of a neighborhood-based interagency collaborative project. This case illustrates clearly how collaborative teams can support families and neighbors in ways that support educational efforts. The neighborhood-based effort provides personalized and accessible service, but Capper alerts us to the possibility that coordinated services might constrain client choices and lead to increased "surveillance" and a decrease in privacy.

Gail Furman and Carol Merz provide a theoretical discussion of collaboration using a sociological framework. They observe that collaboration is a gemeinschaftlich strategy designed to increase community but note that collaboration can also have gesellschaftlich consequences by improving the bureaucratic efficiency of professionals serving clients.

Debra Shaver, Shari Golan, and Mary Wagner provide an evaluative study of 37 collaborative projects funded under California's Healthy Start Initiative. They describe the diverse ways communities operationalized the concept of collaboration for school-linked service and identify factors associated with early indicators of success. For example, they note the importance of good working relationships among members of the collaborative in order to resolve obstacles like conflicting policies, rigid regulations, and turf issues.

In the final chapter of this section, Maureen McClure, Bruce Jones, and Eugenie Potter provide an example of the difficulty and promise of collaboration. Using their collaborative authorship to illuminate issues in other collaborative efforts and in the evaluation of those efforts, they clearly demonstrate that individuals with common concerns may have quite different interpretations of events and situations and quite different understandings of how work should proceed. The use of multiple perspectives and multiple frameworks is clearly a necessity in evaluating collaboratives where participants will undoubtedly come with dramatically different viewpoints.

The chapters in this section call attention to the possibility of unanticipated, possibly negative, consequences as we pursue the coordination of services for children and families. Will we inadvertently strengthen bureaucracy as we strive for a more efficient delivery of services? Will the tensions between professionals and their clients merely be exacerbated? These chapters make it clear that any attempt to evaluate programs that coordinate services must be open to recording multiple perspectives and assessing multiple outcomes.

Conclusion

In the final chapter, James Cibulka summarizes the contributions of the authors by identifying four tensions that surface in the discussion and debate about coordination among schools, families, and communities. What is the proper role of the public school in regard to the mix of academic and social goals? What is the appropriate balance between lay and professional authority? What should be the nature of the welfare state in the twenty-first century? How are the competing values of efficiency, equity, choice, and responsiveness embodied in policies related to coordination of services? He concludes by observing that the movement to coordinated services is another indication of the decline in the professional-technical model of schooling. It is unclear how the four tensions in our political system will shape the nature of the coordinated services movement or its success.

SUMMARY

Coordination among schools, families, and communities to deliver services to children and youth raises the possibility of a radically changed educational landscape. In some ways, the changes have already begun. The inclusion of parents on site-based management councils, the training of parents to help their children with educational tasks, the cooperative programs with business and higher education, and the fledgling collaboration among professionals to serve children and youth more effectively have all contributed to opening up and democratizing the system. It is unlikely that the doors and windows will be closed, although there may be temporary shutters installed to keep out the threatening winds. The question then is how to preserve, strengthen, extend, and fine tune the experiments in coordination that have developed over the past few years. The studies that are represented in this book contribute to answering this question. They provide descriptions of a very diverse set of coordinated programs; they provide insight into program operation and management; and they raise, and begin to address, the philosophical and ethical issues that are involved.

REFERENCES

Agranoff, R. (1991). Human services integration: Past and present challenges in public administration. *Public Administration Review* 51(6): 533–542.

Bacharach, S. B. (1990). *Education reform: Making sense of it all.* Boston: Allyn and Bacon.

Bronfenbrenner, U. (1979). *The ecology of human development: Experiments by nature and design.* Cambridge: Harvard University Press.

Coleman, J. S. (1987). Families and schools. *Educational Researcher* 16(6): 32–38.

Comer, J. P. (1988). Educating poor minority children. *Scientific American* 259(5): 42–48.

Committee for Economic Development (1991). *The unfinished agenda: A new vision for child development and education.* New York: Committee for Economic Development.

Crowson, R. L., and W. L. Boyd (1993). Coordinated services for children: Designing arks for storms and seas unknown. *American Journal of Education* 101: 140–179.

Edmonds, R. (1979). Effective schools for the urban poor. *Educational Leadership* 37: 15–24.

Glazer, N. (1993). A human capital policy for the cities. *The Public Interest* 112: 27–49.

Hodgkinson, H. L. (1985). *All one system.* Washington, D.C.: Institute for Educational Leadership.

Hord, S. (1986). A synthesis of research on organizational collaboration. *Educational Leadership* 43: 22–26.

Kagan, S. L. (1990). Readiness 2000: Rethinking rhetoric and responsibility. *Phi Delta Kappan* 72(4): 272–275.

Kirst, M. W., and M. McLaughlin. (1990). Rethinking policy for children: Implications for educational administration. In *Educational leadership and changing contexts of families, communities, and schools,* ed. B. Mitchell and L. L. Cunningham, Eighty-ninth Yearbook of the National Society for the Study of Education, Part II, 69–90. Chicago: University of Chicago Press.

Levin, H. M. (1988). Accelerating elementary education for disadvantaged students. In *School success for students at risk,* ed. Chief State School Officers. Orlando, Fla.: Harcourt Brace Jovanovich.

Murray, C. (1984). *Losing ground.* New York: Basic Books.

Payzant, T. W. (1992). New beginnings in San Diego: Developing a strategy for interagency collaboration. *Phi Delta Kappan,* 74(2): 139–146.

Richman, H. A., and M. W. Stagner. (1986). Children in an aging society: Treasured resource or forgotten minority? *Daedalus* 115(1): 171–200.

Schorr, L. B. (1993). What works: Applying what we already know about successful social policy. *The American Prospect* 13: 44–54.

Slavin, R. E., N. A. Madden, L. J. Dolan, et al. (1992). *Success for all: A relentless approach to prevention and early intervention in elementary schools.* Arlington, Va.: Educational Research Service.

Stroul, B. A. (1992). *Profiles of local systems of care.* Washington, D.C.: Georgetown University Child Development Center.

Tushnet, N. C. (1993). *A guide to developing educational partnerships.* Washington, D.C.: U.S. Department of Education, Office of Educational Research and Improvement.

Tyack, D. B. (1981). Governance and goals: Historical perspectives on public education. In *Communities and their schools,* ed. D. Davies, New York: McGraw-Hill.

Walberg, H. J. (1984). Families as partners in educational productivity. *Phi Delta Kappan,* 65(6): 397–400.

Wattenberg, E. (1993). *Learning to sing from the same sheet of music: A study of family preservation integration projects for high-risk, school-age children and their families in Minnesota.* Minneapolis: University of Minnesota, Center for Urban and Regional Affairs.

I

*Models of Coordination:
Implications from Field Research*

Chapter 1

The Kentucky Family Resource Centers: The Challenges of Remaking Family-School Interactions

Claire Smrekar

INTRODUCTION

An increasing number of states and localities have recently developed initiatives designed to address fragmentation issues in the delivery of social services for children and their families. Many of these efforts have targeted public schools as the nexus for linkages among education, health, employment, and recreation agencies. The impetus for greater coordination and collaboration among human service agencies is driven by a growing realization that many children face a complex set of overlapping and interrelated problems; changes in family patterns, demographics, and economic realities have created discontinuities between the needs of students and the abilities of both schools and families to meet them. Households of two working parents, single parents, or transient family members predominate across many parts of the nation. Today, one in five children lives in poverty. Many of these families are desperately poor, with incomes less than half the federal poverty level. More and more families, dispirited and discouraged by the conditions of their lives, struggle to survive in communities where poverty, unemployment, alienation, and violence are commonplace. The old patterns of effective institutional commitment and smooth transition between family and school have begun to unravel. These conditions demand new conceptualizations of integration

3

of systems and services as resources for children and their families. An ecological perspective reinforced by a better understanding of the context of children's lives is expected to result in improved care and enhanced student performance.

In addition to these compelling arguments, the notion of using schools as the linchpin for family services resonates with systemic education reform efforts aimed at addressing school, community, and state-level demands and expectations. Schools provide the organizational context for the most sustained and ongoing contact with children outside the family setting. This unique position can be utilized to establish a process of problem identification and treatment. While highly variable in program scope and administrative scale, these efforts reflect the broad appeal of service and organizational integration as a tool for addressing the multiple needs of students and their families. Illustrative models range from nationwide initiatives to city- and county-led projects, to more modest individual site experiments, including the following: Cities in Schools program is involved in 217 local school sites and features coordinated health, educational, and social services delivered to students enrolled in public schools; the New Jersey Department of Human Services funds 29 school-based projects, which offer employment counseling, drug and alcohol abuse counseling, health services, and recreation services; the Annie E. Casey Foundation's "New Futures" grants to the cities of Dayton, Pittsburgh, Little Rock, and Savannah support a case management system to provide an array of social services to students and their families.

The policy debates and implementation strategies associated with school-linked social services tend to focus on the politics of inter-organizational linkages, the competition for power and autonomy, and the struggles over turf (e.g., see Boyd and Crowson 1993; Cunningham 1990; Kirst 1991; Wilson 1989). Whereas the politics undergirding horizontal and vertical linkages across schools and social services in New Jersey and the New Futures sites have been examined extensively, connections between families and schools have received relatively less attention, despite the critical changes in traditional roles and relationships that school-linked social service arrangements imply.

The importance of addressing family-school linkages rests with a set of sweeping assumptions regarding the roles of administrators, teachers, and parents under this model of social service delivery. Programs aimed at enhancing students' abilities to succeed in school by providing them and their families with greater access to social services are linked to certain expectations regarding enhanced levels of understanding, familiarity, and communication between parents and school officials. A traditional school asks teachers to think about what happens to their students in the *classroom;* a school linked to a social service delivery system asks teachers and administrators to go further, to think about what happens to their students when they go *home.* Linking schools with social services demands a reorientation for both families and schools to a set of relationships that exceed the tenuous, negotiated parameters demarcating professional and private spheres.

This paper presents data from the initial year of a three-year qualitative study of the Kentucky Family Resource Centers (FRC) to explore two central themes: (1) the impact of family resource centers on family functioning and student engagement; and (2) the relationship between the nature of family-school interactions and the role and function of school-linked integrated services.

THE KENTUCKY FAMILY RESOURCE CENTERS: A BACKGROUND

The Kentucky Education Reform Act of 1990 (KERA) establishes a system for statewide coordination of child serving agencies through a school-based collaborative arrangement. Family resource centers (to serve children up to age twelve) and youth services centers (to serve children age twelve and older) are charged with developing relationships and programmatic linkages among agencies that serve children and families, including social services, health department, social insurance, employment services, mental health workers, juvenile justice, and colleges and universities (Interagency Task Force on Family Resource and Youth Services Centers 1990). Specifically, the legislation calls for the family resource centers to connect families with the services necessary to meet basic needs, including:

- full-time child care for two- and three-year olds

- after-school child care for children ages 4–12

- health and education services for new and expectant parents

- education to enhance parenting skills

- support and training for child day-care providers

- health services or referrals

Unlike other state initiatives designed to promote interagency collaboration and coordination that target a particular locality or district, the Kentucky plan calls for *statewide* involvement through the public school system. While other state and local plans are typically aimed at enhancing the effectiveness, efficiency, and accountability of the *systems* designed to serve children and their families, the Kentucky plan makes an important distinction by focusing on enhancing the lives of the *individuals* served by the system:

> The school-based Kentucky Family Resource and Youth Services Centers are efforts to promote the flow of resources and support to families in ways to strengthen the functioning and enhance the growth and development of the individual members and the family unit. This method of focusing on families and on relationship-building is an effective and proven way to enhance children's ability to learn and grow. (Interagency Task Force on Family Resource and Youth Services Centers Final Report 1990, p. 13)

Family resource centers are located in or near schools with at least 20 percent of the student population eligible for free school meals. The size of an FRC grant is equal to the total number of students eligible for free lunch, multiplied by $200, up to a maximum grant award of $90,000.[1] As of the 1994–95 school year, 455 family resource and youth service centers have been established in the state of Kentucky (Cabinet for Human Resources, Commonwealth of Kentucky).

Centers are staffed by a Center Coordinator with the assistance of an Advisory Council comprised of parents, school staff, community members, and local service providers.[2]

METHODOLOGY

Semistructured interviews were conducted over a twelve-month period with teachers, the principal, and the center coordinator from each of four elementary school-based family resource centers in Kentucky, two located in a large urban district, and two located in small rural communities. The interviews focused on patterns of family-school interactions, the nature of family needs and community resources, and the role and impact of family resource centers. The inclusion of four sites was based upon the following conditions: (1) the design and intent of the family resource center program to meet local needs; (2) the subsequent high variability across family resource center programs, e.g., *within sector* differences driven by differences in economics, culture, and social service resources; and (3) the interest in examining these organizational and contextual differences and their impact on families and schools. Sites selected for the study reflect statewide differences in school, center, and community-level conditions, including population size and dispersion (urban versus rural), physical location of family resource center vis-à-vis the school, and professional background of the center coordinator (education versus social service).

Interviews were conducted at the school site, audiotaped with participants' permission, and transcribed. Four to six teachers were interviewed from each school to include a cross section from both lower- and upper-primary levels. Each interview lasted approximately one hour. All the teachers interviewed for the study had had at least one referral experience with the family resource center at their school. Center coordinators were "shadowed" over the course of the twelve-month study and interviewed at repeated intervals (four to six times) during this time. Some of these interviews took place in a car between home visits, while others took place at the school/center site. In addition to interviews, formal and informal interactions involving families and center/school officials were observed, including home visits, conferences, and center-sponsored workshops. Relevant documents related to program goals and activities were collected and examined. These included the annual grant proposals and year-end summaries submitted to Kentucky FRC program officials, promotional and informational materials such as center brochures and service announcements, advisory council meeting minutes, centers' budget and service reports, and other internal memoranda.[3]

THE SETTING: PORTRAIT OF TWO SCHOOLS

The data presented in this paper are drawn from two of the four centers in the study, one located in Louisville, and the other in a rural community in southern Kentucky.

Horace Mann Elementary School

Horace Mann Elementary School[4] in Louisville, Kentucky, sits at the edge of one of Louisville's poorest neighborhoods. Built in 1903, the limestone and brick structure rises two stories above the asphalt staff parking lot that doubles for the students' playground. A chain-link fence around the perimeter of the lot/playground buffers the school's hillside boundary from the busy boulevard traffic below. Despite the encroachment of modern medical buildings and concrete parking structures on the school's eastern and southern edges, and the slicing intersection of city streets on the other, this impressive stone and pillar edifice stands as a kind of steady reminder of the structure's historical relevance and resilience.

Mann Elementary serves 428 students (58 percent white, 42 percent black) in grades prekindergarten through fifth and provides additional services through Head Start, special education, and Chapter 1 programs. Approximately 92 percent of the students at Mann qualify for free or subsidized meals. Two-thirds of the students ride a bus to school from neighborhoods within three miles of the school. Many of the black students at Mann live in apartments in a public, subsidized housing complex about a mile from school. Other students and their families rent older, single-story, so-called shotgun houses that were built in the 1920s using a long and narrow style of residential architecture. Most of these homes in the community around Mann have fallen into disrepair.

Horace Mann Family Resource Center

The family resource center at Horace Mann opened two years ago in a meeting room just off a corridor from the main office. While the center has a separate entrance from the main office, visitors do not enter unnoticed. For security reasons, all persons must first gain access to the school building by pushing a button at the front door of the school; since there is no automatic release, someone must come down from the office to open the door. The family resource center is marked by a stop sign-size, yellow and blue nylon banner. The room conveys both the warmth of a family room and the order of an organized classroom. There are children's books and brightly colored wood animals and toys on top of the file cabinet and artwork covering the walls. The Apple computer screen saver features a running message: Welcome to the Horace Mann Family Resource Center. The walls are a soft pink, washed white by the light streaming through the double-frame windows. A tweed sofa against the wall and a round table and chairs in the center dominate the room.

The center coordinator, Janice Spain, sits at her executive-style desk only when using the telephone; she uses the round table for all other business to avoid the sitting-at-the-head-of-the-table image of authority: "I don't want our parents to feel challenged; I want them to feel like we are their advocates." She has worked to make her center a "warm and fuzzy place to be" and encourages students to come by for hugs and warm words of encouragement. Spain's community service background serves her well in fundraising and soliciting in-kind donations (T-shirts, food baskets) from merchants and in organizing multiagency programs on such topics as self-esteem, cultural awareness, and drug abuse. Mrs. Spain is a former school teacher, community center director, and summer camp coordinator. When she talks about her style of work, she emphasizes the importance of individual character:

> I think anybody can be successful if you are not afraid of people. You have to be a people person. That's how I spent my first 6 months—was going door to door meeting people. . . . I have a big mouth, and I'm not afraid to knock on any door.

Griffith County Elementary Schools

Griffith County is typical of rural counties in southern Kentucky. The population for the entire county is about 15,000, of which half reside in the central town of McKinley. After tobacco and soybean farming, the primary industries in Griffith consist of a handful of small manufacturing plants (printing, diapers) near the outskirts of town. The Griffith County Courthouse and other government offices are located in the old town square in McKinley, surrounded by mature, shady sugar maple and shingle oak trees; several attorneys' offices, a local bank, bookstore, and a Dollar General Store line the quiet streets fronting the town square. No more than a minute's drive from the square, and all within a mile of each other, are the three public schools that serve the elementary schoolchildren of Griffith County.

The three Griffith County public elementary schools combined serve over 1,500 students from prekindergarten through fifth grades, of whom 90 percent are White and 10 percent Black. About one-third of the students are eligible for free or reduced lunches. While most students live within a 3-mile radius of the County square, the majority of these ride a bus to school. Many of the students who are middle class live with their families in modest 3-bedroom homes valued at between $40,000 and $60,000. Lower-income housing is provided by a public housing apartment complex on the north side of town and a trailer park on the west side that rents individual singlewide trailers for $75 to $100 a week.

Griffith County Family Resource Center

In a trailer some 150 yards from the back of one of Griffith County's elementary schools, the family resource center in this rural community stands in deliberately sharp contrast to the one in inner-city Louisville. The partition separating the secretary's desk from the coordinator's space muffles the sound of computer keyboards and telephone calls; these are cramped, no-frill work areas. The coordinator, Mark Hoyt, is a former high school teacher and coach. He spends much of the day in his minivan making home visits and transporting students and their parents to dental offices, hospitals, social insurance offices, and school. Hoyt walks the corridors and classrooms of each of Griffith's three elementary schools several times each week, often visiting with teachers to let them know the outcome of a referral, and chatting briefly with school children, most of whom he knows (as well as their siblings) on a first name basis. He views his job as that of an advocate for children and their families and uses the physical separation of the center from the schools to punctuate the point:

> If I'm part of the building, I'm part of the problem. I don't know what coordinators are doing if they're not making home visits. I need to know what the family needs are, not just hear about them. It's a hands-on approach. My job is to build trust and to offer something to people so that they will come to us. I'm not a guidance counselor, and I'm not a social worker. I'm not here to judge, but to help. (coordinator, Hoyt)

Family Life, Family Needs

The explicit design and intent of Kentucky's family resource centers rests with providing the assistance and support with the resources necessary to improve family functioning. With an eye toward removing barriers or impediments to children's learning, the FRCs function to intervene in family lives in ways which will enhance student learning by promoting student engagement in schooling. The implications of these expanded roles and relationships for schools and families include a shift from a model of education based upon separate spheres with blurry boundaries to an ecological perspective of family life that considers the human context of need and locates the school as the nexus for expanded interventions. The rationale for this effort is clear: students and their families do not live in social isolation; rather, they function within cultural, economic, and geographical communities that are bridged by schools.

As noted earlier, the Kentucky FRC program targets schools in which at least 20 percent of the school population is eligible for free or reduced meals. After this baseline definition of need is established, the Kentucky program, similar to other school-linked social services initiatives, assumes a direct and seminal role for teachers in identifying students and families in need and in making the appropriate referral to the school-based family resource center coordinators. Consequently, an initial test of the integrity of the FRC program is the way in which teachers' identify and understand students needs and family lives. How much do teachers know about their students and students' family lives? How are the images of family life communicated to teachers, and how do home life issues manifest in school life?

Interviews with teachers at Horace Mann in Louisville and the elementary schools in Griffith County indicate that teachers' knowledge of student lives, however accurate, is directly related to the willingness of students to share information with teachers. Younger elementary school children are particularly apt to share and confide with or seek reassurance from their teachers, often telling teachers "more than their parents want them to tell." Teachers construct a composite of the context of students' lives by piecing together the incomplete and abbreviated images drawn by their students in seeking explanations for students who suddenly "act out," have repeated and unexcused absences, or seem withdrawn and distracted. The portraits teachers draw of family life are often disturbing and disillusioning to them, as this teacher recalled:

> I hear lots of stories about drug and alcohol use and abuse. They are really worried about it. After a long weekend, they come in and talk about a big family get together, and so and so and their kids came over, and there is lots of drug use and stories where real scary things happen. (teacher, Mann)

Several teachers described the trauma many students suffered after a former Mann student was shot and killed at the subsidized housing complex near school:

> A lot of them have a siege mentality. They talk about being out and knowing what to do when they hear those loud bang sounds. Their parents have coached them to fall down on the ground. I think, generally, the home life of these kids is pretty shocking for many people. (teacher, Mann)

While the nature of family problems glimpsed by teachers in rural southern Kentucky is somewhat less violent than those in inner-city Louisville, the serenity and order of closely knit, small communities like Griffith have been ruptured by demographic shifts and disturbing social trends, including the repeated human tragedies associated with drug traffic and abuse, as this principal described:

> We are dealing more and more with the type of problems that the more urban area schools have dealt with in earlier times. We are now facing things like that—dealing with students that are a result of parents being on drugs at the time that they were born, broken homes, single-parent homes, problems like that. (principal, Griffith County)

Often, the sketches teachers and principals draw of students and their family lives are refined with repeated observations of students' appearance, pattern of interactions, mood, and general demeanor. With a state-mandated cap on class size in the primary elementary grades in Kentucky at twenty-four, teachers report a high degree of confidence in their ability to detect even subtle changes in their students' behavior or appearance.

> When a child comes to school the next day and they are dirty and they still have last night's dinner around their mouth because they haven't had breakfast yet, so you know it's still last night's dinner around their mouth, their needs are not being met. (teacher, Mann)

Despite the satisfaction that may come from knowing that young children often reveal to adults certain elements of their lives (lack of food, clothing, health needs, abuse) that may be attended to by schools through the combined efforts of a teacher and a family resource center, serious questions arise regarding the students who remain silent. Even when teachers are informed or are able to recognize signs of need or distress, it is often at a point of critical intensity. As both teachers and family resource center coordinators acknowledge, these conditions translate into constant crisis management: attempting to work with students, families, and social service agencies under acute pressures and constraints and when the consequences of delay or error can mean a serious illness, permanent disability, eviction, or prison.

It is under these conditions that the Kentucky family resource centers are functioning to establish new and expanded roles between families and schools. As the next section illustrates, the family resource centers are responding to the crisis management mode by moving schools from an organizational emphasis on problem-*identification,* to a schoolwide focus on problem *solving.* In the process, the statewide initiative is creating a camp of vocal advocates.

VOCAL ADVOCATES

When teachers and principals were asked about their impressions of the family resource centers in their schools, many described the relief of "having an extra set of legs" to make a home visit to a parent who has no telephone, of "having somebody I can call and get help to remedy a situation" when a child has lice or requires eyeglasses. A teacher in Griffith County said simply: "I don't want to lose it. I love it." Many teachers acknowledged that the problems now being addressed by resource center coordinators have existed for some time, but, with limited resources and no additional staffing, these issues were either left to Band-Aid solutions or left alone. Before resource centers, problems were identified and blame assessed, but corrective action was often limited and ineffective. Teachers had difficulty knowing whom to contact to make a report of suspected child abuse or what organization to ask for help in purchasing a student's eyeglasses. There was little time to call and no way to expedite the often frustrating delays with intake workers at the social service agencies. The worlds of teachers and social service agencies seemed utterly incompatible. Consider the frustration echoed by several teachers interviewed for this study:

> We do not have a nurse in this school system. We do not have a social worker that works this school system. So either the teacher sees that this is carried out, and, 9 times out of 10, the teacher doesn't have time to go through every folder to see if that child passed an eye test. Is this why Johnny's not learning? Is this why he is not hearing what I'm saying? Is this why he is such a behavior problem? There's not time to do that. There is not the manpower to do that. You don't have anybody who goes into the school and does that. (teacher A, Griffith)

> Q. So then what happens?

> The child goes without unless you, yourself, as a teacher, or you have someone like the family resource center that can step in and say, okay, we know somebody over here, we know the way to get glasses. If the teacher has to do that leg work, then where's the teaching? (teacher B, Griffith)

Resource centers allow schools to shift this organizational emphasis on problem identification to problem solving by establishing a clear
intent to intervene in ways necessary to improve family functioning
and remove barriers that impede student learning. The problems identified by teachers are communicated to the center coordinator through
a written referral, short note, or conversation (e.g., during a teacher's
prep period or lunch break). From this initial point of intake, the coordinator assumes the role as the school's point person for coordinating a strategy that addresses the family-related problem. Thus, the
roles of teachers have not changed, only response patterns have. The
relationships established between coordinators and social service agencies provide the conduit for immediate response previously lacking in
most school-social agency interactions. The center coordinators provide more than a ready referral list; they often have the crucial personal contacts in social service offices that are critical for expediting an
investigation of child abuse at Child Protective Services, reducing the
paperwork for a parent enrolling in a federal Job Opportunities and
Basic Skills (JOBS) program or finding affordable child care for a single
parent through the local United Way. As the center coordinator at
Mann explained:

> We can move some of the barriers a little easier. Clout in the sense that
> a mother will call up for a physical from the health center and get it
> in three weeks. We can call up and say, "This is the Mann Family
> Resource Center; our child is out of school. We need this appointment
> now." Sometimes it doesn't work, but a lot of times it does.

And, as far as assisting teachers:

> When you have 90 percent at risk, you have a lot of problems, and
> they (teachers) could not necessarily teach the child, do those lesson
> plans, get the glasses for the kid, follow-up on why the child doesn't
> have the glasses. That we can do. And usually very quickly, and the
> child doesn't have to miss school. (coordinator, Mann)

But what does all this have to do with school achievement? How
will improving access to social services and enhancing problem-
solving techniques for schools improve student engagement? What
linkages between family life and school life are the Kentucky family
resource centers assuming? Are these assumptions valid? When asked
these questions, teachers and principals responded by identifying a

critical connection between student self-esteem and learning. Their observations echo the argument advanced in establishing Kentucky's family resource centers in which students' social, emotional, and physical well-being, including the provision of such basic needs as food, clothing, shelter, and parental love and nurturing, are linked with the ability to learn and achieve.

> Everything is linked. The ones that say, "I'm a failure," that's hard to erase, but by making them feel good about themselves: "I'm dressed. I've got shoes on. Nobody's making fun of me because I have my shoes on." One little boy was so proud of his new shoes (provided by the resource center). He showed them to everybody. They really feel proud of things like that. When they feel proud, then they do the best work. (teacher A, Griffith)

While the creation of family resource centers may make the connections between family life and school life more explicit, it is clear that these teachers have long embraced an ecological perspective of schooling and child development by recognizing the importance of what happens to students when they are dismissed from school and go home. The comments offered by school staff in this study suggest a widespread sense of both the challenge and constraint found in this interlocking relationship.

> It's my feeling that I can't teach a child that's been beaten. You can't just be concerned with the intellectual growth, the cognitive realm. You look at the whole child. If they are hungry, they are not going to learn. You can't teach the children until you get those problems resolved because they won't let you. The discipline, the behavior, they are crying out for somebody to help them. (teacher A, Mann)

> If they are worried about whether mother is home being beaten up by the boyfriend she brought home, they are not concentrating on what is happening. They may sit there in that seat and not move, but their mind is not focusing on what is going on in the room. Until you feel safe enough and secure enough that you can focus, you are not going to learn as much. (teacher B, Mann)

The observations recorded here suggest that the orientation toward direct and immediate problem solving facilitated through the family resource center pays dividends to families and schools alike. The impact of the family resource centers is measured in terms of both real numbers, such as the reduction of absentees noted by a principal, to the more anecdotal observation of a teacher whose student's medical needs were addressed with the help of a center coordinator: "He went from being a sad little boy to a big smile on his face." Success stories came readily from school officials and were punctuated with comments relating the turnaround of students and their families to the individual efforts of center coordinators. In Griffith County, for example, a boy who missed seventy-five days of school as a fourth grader prompted intense and immediate intervention from the center coordinator. With attendance a major problem facing schools, particularly in inner-city schools such as Horace Mann, many center coordinators spend considerable time responding to these cases. But rather than employ the punitive tactics of a truant officer, the resource centers attempt to reach the underlying conditions that may be triggering a spate of student absences. In this case, what did the family resource center do?

> Mark (Hoyt) took it as a personal project, which he does about any case you ask him to work on. He went to the home every morning and helped the mom to get the boy up. A whole lot of it was mom had to work. Lots of times she left him there to get up and get to school on his own. . . . Mark talked to mom about how to handle the situation, got her interested, and got the son more interested in school. (principal, Griffith)

After helping the mother get some counseling that she requested, Hoyt continued to visit the family periodically, offering support and encouragement. In his fifth grade, the boy missed only twelve days; as a sixth grader, he was admitted to the gifted and talented program.

The enthusiastic response to this level of problem solving, however, is tempered by teachers' perceptions of a deep and enduring instability in the family lives of students and by the set of issues that exceed the parameters of resource center interventions. As one teacher observed about the centers: "It's wonderful when we have a problem that seems made for this," such as the need for eyeglasses, immunizations, and clothing. For many teachers, the real problems relate to the values of parents toward schooling and the lowered expectations parents may have for themselves and their children. When looking ahead, teachers are less sanguine about the ability of center interventions to change behavior, attitudes, or values, as this teacher observed:

> I'm not sure that one lady sitting down in an office with a social worker can do that for a school like this where we have a magnitude

of problems that we have. It seems like maybe the task is too great. (teacher, Mann)

While the condition of family life often overwhelms and discourages teachers, the organization of family-school interactions at Griffith and Mann reflects and reinforces the social distance between parents and schools. Amidst these cleavages, family resource centers represent a potential organizational force for bridging the worlds of families and schools. The next section examines the irony of a resource center strategy that utilizes a disconnection from schools in order to establish connections with families.

DISCONNECTIONS

Patterns of family-school interactions are neither trivial nor distinct from the objectives of family resource centers and the larger goals of school improvement. Under conditions in which teachers do not regularly communicate with parents or center coordinators, the levels of trust and familiarity between families and schools implied under the Kentucky family resource center program may be difficult to reach.

The character and content of family-school interactions in schools with family resource centers reflect a pattern of conflict found in the accumulated research on relationships between teachers and parents (Lightfoot 1980, 1978; McPherson 1972; Waller 1932). Teachers in Kentucky noted that the boundaries between the private zone of family life and public responsibility of education are unclear and constantly shifting, giving rise to confusion on the part of both parents and teachers regarding the expectations of the other. Communication patterns between parents and teachers tend to exacerbate this ambiguity. Teachers' interactions with parents are typically short, irregular, and unsatisfying. Perhaps predictably, these relationships are associated with frustration and discomfort because interactions are often focused on problems (e.g., student misbehavior, learning difficulties). Other face-to-face interactions between parents and teachers are increasingly rare as many school districts in Kentucky move away from regularly scheduled parent-teacher conferences to an "as needed" arrangement. With the exception of some Kentucky teachers who noted an effort to make "good news" telephone calls to parents in the beginning of the year, these communications are reserved for a serious problem. When asked how much they knew about the parents of their students, teachers observed that their knowledge is gathered piecemeal, extracted from parent data cards (for employment information and addresses), from older siblings and other teachers, and from the students themselves. Face-to-face exchanges are extremely rare, with the exception of the open house event held in the fall. None of the teachers interviewed worked with parents on a classroom volunteer basis.

This uneasy alliance implied between parents and teachers is mediated by family resource centers, which disconnect from the school symbolically and physically in order to establish new and expanded channels of communication with families. As a transmitter for messages between home and school, coordinators focus on establishing family resource centers as *separate and apart* from schools. The irony, of course, rests with the fact that the centers were created to help link families with the social services that would enhance family functioning, with *schools as the linkage point* and nexus for intervention. What was missed in the design, however, was the nature of relations between families and schools in which interactions are rare and abbreviated. In the common context of schools as places where parents go only when there is a problem and, once there, feel uncomfortable or intimidated by the authority of school officials, the family resource centers work to balance a strategy of disassociation as a way of promoting deep and enduring connections with families. As Janice Spain, the coordinator in Louisville's Horace Mann Center, notes:

> I say that in all my speeches when I go out to talk to the parents: "We are not the truant officer. We are not the counselor. We are not the principal." That is the first line. I guess I'm apologizing.

The interest in recasting negative images of schools and school officials extends from role associations to organizational symbolism. The physical location of the center is a case in point. Center coordinators, principals, and teachers observe that a separate entrance from the school building or main office may diminish the discomfort and intimidation many parents associate with visits to school. A separate location also establishes a degree of confidentiality for parents who want to preserve the privacy of their interactions with center staff. As one social worker commented, parents who are coming to the center to seek help with clothing needs, utility bill assistance, or General Equivalency Diploma (GED) training may avoid the center if it means "having to go through the school to get to us." Currently on staff at the Mann Center in Louisville, she recalled the effect the location of her former center assignment had on establishing ties with parents:

> We were in a portable. One of the strong pushes that advisory coun-
> cil felt was that parents were still intimidated coming into a school
> building so they felt like if we were out and away and they didn't
> have to worry about the teachers seeing them or grabbing them and
> saying, "Your child has been acting up. . . . "

The center encourages parents to "drop-in" after they bring their kids
to school and provides free coffee and soft drinks to convey a more
comfortable, familiar, and home-like atmosphere. Some parents have
volunteered for school activities who have never before been involved
because, the social worker observed, "they are slowly getting used
to the idea that they can come into the school without it being a
problem."

The irony of establishing a center separate and apart from the
school building is found in the oppositional message it conveys to
school staff. The location that parents view as more open, friendly, and
accessible, teachers find remote and disconnected from their work life.
They rarely have time between classes to run to the portable across the
parking lot; there are few opportunities for the spontaneous hallway
meeting with the coordinator to discuss a student's family situation.
The trailer outside the school building translates—symbolically and
practically—to a set of activities and priorities *peripheral* to teachers'
realm of experience and expectation. As a consequence, the center
location underscores the separation of home and school by sending
contradictory messages of inclusion (to parents) and exclusion (to school
staff).

The irony of family resource centers severing ties symbolically or
physically from schools to establish linkages with families is matched
by the challenge of simultaneously maintaining relations with teachers and principals in order to facilitate a communication exchange
between families and schools. The role of the "go-between" represents
a critical edge against which school and center personnel measure the
potential impact of family resource centers.

TRANSMITTERS

The substantive and symbolic separation of family resource centers
from their host schools serves to establish a degree of neutrality and
legitimacy for the role that centers assume in providing a new medium of communication between families and schools. While the communication channel is established through the series of disconnecting

strategies, a complementary connective strategy—home visits—establishes the process that links families and schools *via the centers.* By
moving outside the traditional boundaries of written notices and telephone calls, home visits represent an expanded mode of communication and information sharing that is both more intensive and immediate
in negotiating the expectations and demands of teachers and parents.

At both center sites, teachers and principals reported wide and
extensive reliance on home visits for both information-gathering and
compliance purposes. Many teachers noted that they had tried unsuc-
cessfully to get parents to come to school to discuss issues and particular situations; a home visit from the center coordinator to discuss
matters and to provide transportation, particularly in rural Griffith
County, proved to be a successful strategy. For hard-to-reach families,
including those without telephone service, home visits represent the
only link between teachers and parents.

While the information exchanged with teachers and principals by
coordinators who make home visits provides a new medium of communication, this new network limits any direct access between families and schools. That is, to the degree that centers disconnect from
schools or are perceived to be separate from schools organizationally,
the exchange between families and schools is transmitted by an ancillary party. The home visits, and the centers more broadly speaking,
are construed by teachers and principals as expanding home-school
communications in the context of problem solving. The parameters of
communication and exchange are pegged to this specific need. To illustrate, when teachers were asked if the centers made any difference
in how well they knew parents or how often they saw parents, all the
teachers replied with a definitive no. Again, they acknowledged that
center staff were helpful in getting hard-to-reach parents to the school
for a conference, but, in many of those circumstances, the center coordinators negotiated the expectations for the teacher in his/her absence. Consider these observations: Has the family resource center
enabled teachers to get to know parents better?

> No, not really. . . . We get information back, but rarely do we have a
> three-way meeting, unless it's requested. If we need that, we go more
> to the principal or the counselor than we do the family resource
> center. (teacher, Mann)

> I don't think there has been any major move to link families and
> teachers. I think there has been a major move to link the children to

the resource center and the families to the resource centers, but as far as linking them to the teacher, no. That might be the missing link that needs to be to complete the circle. (coordinator, Mann)

To the degree that the family resource centers fail to fundamentally re-order the character and content of family-school interactions in terms of deeper interactions between parents and teachers, it may be interpreted as a missed opportunity to develop the partnerships crucial for student growth and success. A pattern of direct contact between families and schools provides the framework for a process that research has demonstrated increases understanding and promotes greater cooperation, commitment, and trust between parents and teachers (e.g., see Comer 1980; Epstein 1983; Henderson 1981). Within this environment, increased levels of parent involvement are likely to develop through which parents' attitudes are enhanced regarding the role they and the school play in the development of the child (Becher 1986; Gordon 1979; Keesling and Melaragno 1983; Rich and Jones 1977). Likewise, teachers benefit from this level of direct, face-to-face contact by gaining insights about their students and their home environment. Under the vocal and widespread call for greater parent involvement in schooling, the persistent social distance between parents and schools *with a family resource center* addresses one question (i.e., how do family resource centers impact family-school interactions?) while raising an opposite and potentially more troubling one. That is, besides the adaptive strategies characterized by disconnecting from host schools and establishing the transmitter-mediator role, how does social distance between families and schools impact the family resource center programs?

THE "MISSING LINK":
IMPLICATIONS FOR FAMILY RESOURCE CENTERS

The implications of the "missing link" are directly related to the conditions that threaten to undercut the central aims of family resource centers. That is, to the degree that distance and conflict characterize interactions between families and schools, centers face serious obstacles in strengthening family functioning and enhancing the growth and development of individuals in the ways the resource centers were designed to promote. For example, the coordinators at Griffith and Mann reported that the greatest disappointment in their second year of program operation was the response of parents to programs on parent education and literacy (two of the six core components) organized by the center and held at the school. These core activities are

designed to move beyond the centers' focus on *removing barriers* to an
emphasis on *promoting* the parenting and educational skills that contribute to student academic success. Repeated efforts aimed at bringing together a classroom full of parents to share ideas and interests,
however, have failed to enlist more than a half dozen participants at
any single event at either Griffith or Mann. The coordinators suggested that, despite efforts to make the activities celebratory and nonthreatening, parents who are generally unaccustomed to coming to
school (for any reason other than a serious problem), or are unfamiliar
with school staff, stay away. In sharp contrast, the participation rates
are the highest in the program categories related to basic and immediate needs: health screenings, clothing and food distribution, and
assistance with government aid programs—the elements related directly to the problem-solving imperatives underscored repeatedly by
teachers and principals. The lower participation rates for the centers'
parenting and literacy programs have prompted widespread concern
among coordinators regarding the perception of a narrowly defined
mission around crisis-oriented services. The resistance to this singular
focus raises questions connecting the centers' image to a stigma that
would further distance families from the school. Coordinators in this
study argued for a parallel track pointed toward promoting essential
skills and social relationships tied to student learning and educational
success. To be sure, a fundamental challenge for family resource centers may rest with moving from a function pegged to problem solving
and basic needs to one oriented around promoting family growth and
development—the central goal in the educational reform bill that established the centers. To the degree that this goal implies an educational partnership centered around the cognitive and emotional
development of children, and the mutual trust and understanding
between parents and teachers, the imperative to bridge the social distance between families and schools is, likewise, central.

The impact of family-school interactions on family resource center
programs includes the essential communication links that an integrated
social service program requires. Under this model, teachers assume
the central role for identifying and referring students and families for
assistance. Under conditions of strained and remote relationships with
families, and in the absence of regular face-to-face interactions that
promote trust and familiarity, teachers' specific knowledge of family
life is limited. As both teachers and center coordinators acknowledged,
even when teachers are informed (by their students) or recognize indicators of family need or distress, conditions have often reached a

crisis by the time a referral is made. Among teachers and coordinators, in fact, there is an impression that the centers are used by some as "dumping grounds" for the most serious and intractable problems teachers experience with students and their families. For family resource center coordinators, crisis-conflict management translates into time-consuming mediation and intervention for a limited number of families. Consequently, coordinators find that the goals of more widespread outreach to promote literacy and parenting skills are squeezed out by an imbalance of acute care referrals. As one coordinator observed: "Teachers need to understand that we are not just the lice control, or, if your student misses a couple of days, we are not just the absentee patrol. We do a lot more."

CONCLUSION

The ability of centers to "do a lot more" is necessarily constrained by the context in which they function. This chapter suggests that the level of influence may be greater in the direction of the effect of institutionalized patterns of family-school interactions on family resource centers than in the reverse. While it is far too early in the design and implementation of Kentucky's family resource center initiative to expect any fundamental alterations in the scripts that direct the actions of parents and teachers, these findings indicate the need to connect the dialogue on integrated social services to the impulses of reform in school-family-community networks. The images emerging from this early research document the interdependency of these parallel policies, while outlining the serious and negative implications of integrated services programs that ignore the social distance, conflict, and anonymity associated with family-school interactions. The interest here rests with making explicit the importance of home-school relationships to the central aims of improving the lives of students and their families embraced within a school-linked services model. The future and direction of these critical policy issues may turn on proposals that could be considered the antecedents to school-linked services, such as parent centers, teacher home visits, and student cohorts (Smrekar 1993), which fundamentally alter or enhance the character and content of relationships between families and schools.

This discussion highlights the impact of the family resource centers on addressing basic and fundamental family needs and on establishing expanded linkages between families and schools. While there are strong indications of the promising practice of establishing the *independence* of family resource centers, there is an equally compelling impression that efforts designed to enhance family functioning through a school-linked services model rest on promoting the critical *interdependence* between families and schools. By providing a new medium of communication between families and schools that is more intensive and immediate, family resource centers represent an important new challenge for demonstrating these linkages.

NOTES

1. The average grant award in 1992–93 was $71,500 (Cabinet for Human Resources, Commonwealth of Kentucky).

2. Most centers allocate a portion of their grant awards to fund additional part- or full-time staff, including a clerk/receptionist and/or a "family services specialist" (certified staff). In the first year of the program (1991–92), the Jefferson County Public School system "donated" the services of seventeen social workers (formerly attached to clusters of schools) to the individual centers funded in Louisville.

3. Data analysis focused primarily on four major areas: (1) the context of students' lives, including the nature of family, school, and community conditions; (2) the role of family resource centers in addressing issues of access to and coordination of social services; (3) the effect of family resource centers on the nature of family-school interactions; and (4) the impact of family resource centers on student/family functioning. Interview transcripts, observation notes, and document analyses were coded and summarized according to general descriptive categories generated by these concepts. Converging pieces of information from interview transcripts were cut up into small strips and arranged according to broad themes and categories, such as family needs, FRC role and utilization, FRC impact, and center-school interactions. Subcategories included topics such as home visits, communication patterns, and teachers' expectations. Pattern coding (Fetterman 1989; Miles and Huberman 1984; Yin 1989) was used to discover patterns among individuals and schools/centers. In addition, pattern coding was used to identify relations among individual centers and schools and the influence of various organizational and community conditions. Pieces of information from three sources—interviews, observations, and documents— were sifted and sorted for patterns of thought and behavior.

4. All names of schools and individuals used here are pseudonyms.

REFERENCES

Becher, R. (1986). Parent involvement: A review of research and principles of successful practice. In *Current topics in early childhood education*, ed. L. G. Katz, vol. 6, Norwood, N.J.: Ablex Publishing.

Boyd, W., and R. Crowson. (1993). Coordinated services for children: Designing arks for storms and seas unknown. *American Journal of Education* 101(2): 140–179.

Comer, J. (1980). *School power.* New York: University Press.

Cunningham, L. (1990). Reconstituting local government for well-being and education. In *Educational leadership and changing contexts of families, communities, and schools,* ed. B. Mitchell and L. L. Cunningham, Eighty-ninth Yearbook of the National Society for the Study of Education, Part 2, 135–154. Chicago: University of Chicago Press.

Epstein, J. (October 1983). *Effects on parents of teacher practices of parent involvement,* Report No. 346. Baltimore, Md.: Center for Social Organization of Schools, The Johns Hopkins University.

Fetterman, D. (1989). *Ethnography step by step.* Newbury Park, Calif.: Sage Publications.

Gordon, I. (1979). The effects of parent involvement in schooling. In *Partners: Parents and schools,* ed. R. Brandt. Alexandria, Va.: Association for Supervision and Curriculum Development.

Henderson, A., ed. (1981). *Parent participation-student achievement: The evidence grows.* Columbia, Md.: National Committee for Citizens in Education.

Keesling, J. W., and R. J. Melaragno. (1983). Parent participation in federal education programs. Findings from the federal programs survey phase of the study of parental involvement. In *Parent education and public policy,* ed. R. Haskins and D. Adams. Norwood, N.J.: Ablex Publishing.

Kirst, M. (1991). Improving children's services: Overcoming barriers, creating new opportunities. *Phi Delta Kappan* vol. 72, 615–618.

Lightfoot, S. L. (1978). *Worlds apart.* New York: Basic Books.

Lightfoot, S. L. (1980). Exploring family-school relationships: A prelude to curricular designs and strategies. In *A two-way street,* ed. R. Sinclair. Boston: Institute for Responsive Education.

McPherson, G. (1972). *Small town teacher.* Cambridge, Mass.: Harvard University Press.

Miles, M., and A. M. Huberman. (1984). *Qualitative data analysis.* Beverly Hills, Calif.: Sage Publications.

Smrekar, C. (1993). Rethinking family-school interactions: A prologue to linking schools and social services. *Education and Urban Society,* 25(2): 175–186.

Waller, W. (1932). *The sociology of teaching.* New York: Wiley.

Wilson, J. Q. (1989). *Bureaucracy: What government agencies do and why they do it.* New York: Basic Books.

Yin, R. (1989). *Case study research.* Newbury Park, Calif.: Sage Publications.

Chapter 2

Visible Differences and Unseen Commonalities: Viewing Students as the Connections Between Schools and Communities

H. Dickson Corbett
Bruce Wilson
Jaci Webb

Teachers working in an urban elementary school sadly shook their heads as they described the visible, often debilitating, problems their students faced growing up in the community surrounding the school:

> The kids come from very violent environments.

> Children see that the people with money are the drug dealers.

> The parents are so young; a lot of grandparents are raising the kids.

> Their only hope is to move away from all of this.

Worry creased the foreheads of parents and other community members when they depicted the observable ways in which the cultural

The preparation of this chapter was supported by funds from the U.S. Department of Education, Office of Educational Research and Improvement (OERI). The opinions expressed do not necessarily reflect the position of OERI, and no official endorsement should be inferred.

and political gaps between the teachers and the students manifested themselves within the school:

> Some teachers are very aloof to the children.

> Kids are left out because of their behavior.

> We get the teachers who do not want to be here.

> They get into their cars and they're gone.

Yet, with dogged insistence and optimism, parents and teachers alike asserted similar but unshared aspirations for the children who fell under their care:

> I want to see them become self-assured so that they have the confidence in doing the things they need to do. (Teacher)

> They need confidence in themselves; they are so quick to say "I can't." (Community member)

> They need to set a goal and to be able to achieve their goals. (Teacher)

> They need to be career-minded, to reach for it; it doesn't matter how high. (Community member)

The people making these statements—community members, parents, guardians, and teachers—were separated by differences as visible to them as the wrought iron fence that divided the schoolyard from the neighboring sidewalks. They saw their cultural, social, economic, and political dissimilarities and used these attributes as the building blocks for constructing adversarial relationships, with each feeling a need to compensate for the perceived detrimental situations in which the other placed children.

The basis for establishing meaningful community-school interactions in such a situation is hard to see, but we submit that unseen, but potentially binding, commonalities do exist. The commonalities revolve around what the adults would like to see happen with the children as a result of their schooling experiences. In the setting we have been studying for the last three years, there were parents and community members who had more in common with some of the faculty in this regard than the teachers had with each other. However, differences of opinion among teachers and similarities of opinion between some community members and teachers tended to be invisible— unseen because the opinions required words to bring them into focus and because the extended, productive, and direct dialogue about students that was needed to evoke these words rarely occurred.

The purpose of this chapter is to develop the argument that community-school relationships that ultimately serve the best interests of children are ones grounded in shared understandings about the kinds of people students should become. Initial efforts at generating increased community-school involvement, therefore, should attend to engendering the skills and opportunities that will facilitate airing these ideas. The strength of this "vision" will become the foundation for a richer and more supportive relationship that ultimately benefits everyone involved.

COMMUNITY INVOLVEMENT AND VISION-BUILDING

Community involvement has become an integral part of the national reform agenda, as evidenced by the Commission on Chapter 1's (1992, 10) plea in *Making Schools Work for Children in Poverty:*

> For the past decade, however, parent involvement through Chapter 1 has been muted. The Commission believes that it must be renewed with vigor, drawing on new knowledge about how best to encourage the involvement of parents in their children's education. There are many ways that schools can encourage parents to help their children. The new [Chapter 1] framework allows school discretion, yet encourages them to look beyond familiar but often superficial strategies such as asking parents to serve on advisory committees or sending them newsletters.

And the call for increased involvement and redefining schools' and communities' roles and relationships has broad-based support, as Michelle Fine (1993, 682) explains:

> Progressives and conservatives alike are appropriately distressed by a failing public sector, by broken promises of "professionalism" and empty dreams of reform 1980's style. Together, perhaps oddly, they are pressing parental involvement/empowerment in the vanguard of educational reform. Sometimes parents are being organized as advocates for their children, other times as teacher bashers, often as bureaucracy busters, more recently, as culture-carriers, increasingly as consumers.

Nevertheless, while many current reformers accept the assumption that parental involvement is good for students—and maybe even good for parents and guardians as well—tampering with existing relationships may accentuate the political and cultural barriers that bisect many urban school communities and, if not carefully handled, may exacerbate all too visible differences between professionals and parents. Fine (1991, 164) points to several such obstacles that can render increased community involvement meaningless:

> The image held by advocates and parents differs dramatically from what many schools and the U.S. Department of Education typically intend (Lightfoot 1978). Educational advocates, community representatives, and parents themselves seek school-family involvement that flows reciprocally (Henderson 1987). School policymakers and administrators, when addressing the school-family hyphen, more typically seek parents who will assist with homework, ensure positive motivation, and support schools in the home. Indeed, little was done to ensure that low-income parents and guardians at CHS [the school under study] were truly and powerfully engaged in the school-family dialogue. Opportunities to meet with these parents and guardians were exclusively available at school, rather than in the communities where students lived. Available child care, elderly care, transportation through dangerous neighborhoods in the evenings, or other means of ensuring parental access to school meetings were considered extravagant and unlikely to work.

Joyce Epstein (1990, 109) also speaks to the critical issue of institutional practices that can either invite disenfranchised communities into their schools or discourage them from approaching the schoolhouse doors:

> [Commonly] stated variables are not the most important measures for understanding parent involvement. At all grade levels, the evidence suggests that school policies and teacher practices and family practices are more important than race, parent education, family size, marital status, and even grade level in determining whether parents continue to be part of their children's education.

Embedded in these visible policies and practices are faculty and community beliefs about the neighborhood and the school which, in turn, can create an unending cycle of distrust and distance. Fine (1993,

682–683), pointing out the stifling environment for exchange that meaningless invitations to participate can create, makes this assessment:

> Parents enter the contested public sphere of public education typically with neither resources nor power. They are usually not welcomed, by schools, to the critical and serious work of rethinking educational structures and practices, and they typically represent a small percent of local taxpayers.

Even when cultural barriers are breached, political considerations may rise up to continue the separation. Seymour Sarason (1990, 29) explains:

> People rarely embrace a restriction or alteration in the scope of their accustomed powers. If reformers have steered clear of dealing with alternatives in patterns of power relationships, it is testimony both to a reluctance to change the system and an unwillingness to confront the conflicts such changes inevitably engender. The result has been that reformers rivet on problems they can deal with and gloss over problems they often regard as more important but too controversial.

Attempts to implement site-based management or to establish advisory groups that include parent and community representation likely evoke more questions than answers about the effective distribution of power and influence. It is left to individual schools, then, to figure out how to mesh various disenfranchised subgroups; how to educate people about the nature of schools, the work that is done there, and the process of participation in group decisionmaking; and how to accommodate shifting power relations and cultural diversity. Mindless efforts to include community members in formal decision making run the risk of becoming empty, rhetorical gestures, doing little to alter the role of parents in the school or the relationship of the school to the community.

Sorting out the power relationships is confounded when the implicit issues of race and class must be confronted explicitly—face to face. Not only are such issues controversial, beliefs about the cultural differences between and among faculty and community can be the most resistant barriers to successful learning operating in the school community. Such beliefs can lead to lower expectations, to a lack of respect, and to resistance on the part of both faculty and community members. That is, teachers may expect less from students from disadvantaged homes, they may have a disregard for the unfamiliar culture of students and parents, and they may resist efforts to bring them into sustained and meaningful contact with parents. Parents, on the other hand, may expect the worst from the institution of schooling, may believe teachers do not understand the realities of their lives or respect their values, and they, too, may resist efforts to involve them in a system that they feel has not served them well historically.

Unfortunately this situation may be self-perpetuating, since the greatest barrier may well be the lack of shared experiences that can lead to understanding. Without equal and substantive communication between groups, they may continue to see each other as stereotypes; and their limited knowledge of one another—coupled with their single-minded pursuit of the welfare of the children whose lives bind them together—will reinforce those stereotypes. The negative experiences, like those reflected in the comments that our study participants made about one another, are the more dramatic ones and therefore tend to become the episodal events that evolve into a "mythology" of schools and communities—which, of course, helps to pass on those stereotypes to subsequent generations of teachers, parents, and students.

Needless to say, the task of encouraging meaningful school-community involvement is daunting. What we would advocate is the inclusion of multiple voices in the discussion about what is in the best interests of children—with the consequence being an acknowledged and shared "vision" of how the school and community can nurture those interests. We agree with G. Wood (1992, 234):

> There is a great deal in the school reform literature today supporting the notion that schools with a clear mission statement will be more successful than those that are unclear about their tasks. What the schools in this book [Schools That Work] in particular have done is to elevate their mission statements to the level of a vision that everyone is beholden to. This vision is not limited to what kids learn about academics *in* school, but designed to encompass what sort of people they will be when they *leave* school.

After a description of our research activities, the remainder of this chapter will be devoted to (1) describing the visible differences that put a community and a school into an adversarial rather than a collaborative relationship, (2) identifying the different perspectives teachers and community members have concerning the sort of people students should become, and (3) explaining how these perspectives might become the basis for developing a more productive community-school relationship.

THE RESEARCH SETTING AND METHODS

Our discussion of parental involvement is based on a case study of the faculty, community, and students of Northeast Elementary School (a pseudonym). Northeast serves an economically and socially troubled neighborhood in the inner city of a large metropolitan area. Nearly 650 students from this neighborhood attend the school, 75 percent of whom come from African-American families and 25 percent of whom come from Hispanic families. The predominately female school faculty is roughly an equal mixture of African Americans, Hispanics, and Caucasians. None of the professional staff members is a resident of the school's attendance area. The few teachers who, at one time, did live in the neighborhood explain: "I grew up in the same environment and I managed to move out of it." However, almost all of the support staff are community members. In fact, the school is the largest employer in this neighborhood and is the only viable institution, other than the local churches, remaining in the area.

Our research began at the request of the principal and the faculty to gather information for, and from, them that would be helpful in the formulation of a school mission—an activity instigated by their participation in a Chapter 1 Schoolwide project. This effort allowed the school to spend targeted federal funds for the benefit of all children if the school adhered to certain planning and governance guidelines (e.g., developing a mission, and creating a broad-based school improvement council) and demonstrated student achievement gains. The staff members expressed discomfort about talking openly among themselves (much less with the community) about their aspirations for and concerns about the school and about urban education in general. They felt that speaking privately to a third party would result in "objective" feedback that might pave the way for larger groups to have substantive discussions at a later time. In the course of our interviews with the faculty, it became clear that they saw themselves as isolated—from the community, the school district, and from each other; the day-to-day, routine crises of an urban school simply precluded their seeing beyond their particular individual responsibilities. Thus, data gathering developed a second purpose: providing information that would help the school think better about how to connect with the world around it.

For this chapter on community-school connections, we draw mainly on qualitative data from a series of open-ended, semistructured interviews we conducted over a two-year period with all 44 faculty members and 24 support staff and community members. In initial interviews,

participants defined characteristics they wanted to see children develop in order to become successful people in the future and discussed the school's ability to encourage the development of those
attributes. Subsequent interviews focused more specifically on the
development of a coherent and commonly shared vision to guide the
school's efforts.

We examined the field notes taken during these interviews to locate (1) statements about the school, the community, and students and
(2) the meanings that interviewees attached to these statements (e.g.,
their responses to probes such as "what does that word mean to you?"
or "how does that situation/condition affect you as a teacher/commu-
nity member/parent?"). With respect to statements about the school
and the community, we took participants' initial comments and developed a slide show that combined the words with pictures of the setting that we, some teachers, and some community members had taken.
Reactions to the slide show contained additional insights into people's
interpretations of the nature and effects of the school and community
settings. These data inform the next section of the chapter on "visible
differences." We took the statements about children and categorized
them to see who offered similar characteristics of success and what
they meant by these terms. These data provide the grist for the "unseen commonalities" section.

It must be noted that the sample of community members was
biased. They were people who either had some official responsibilities
in the school (as teaching aides, maintenance staff, or crossing guards)
or were present almost every day for one reason or another (as parent
volunteers or to pick up their children or grandchildren). We talked to
16 of the former and eight of the latter. In a way, this makes the
teachers' lack of knowledge about possible commonalities with some
community members even more startling; they had counterexamples
to their collective wisdom about the community surrounding them
daily. Of course, the teachers perhaps regarded these people as insiders and did not take their views as reflective of any part of the larger
community. However, testimonies from one teacher and the community members that worked as classroom aides indicated that the aides
perceived that teachers did not particularly value their work or their
opinions. So, the community members did not feel like insiders. In
any event, the potential partnership that could have resulted from
uncovering commonalities with this possibly atypical but potentially
powerful group was unrealized. We anticipate extending our research
to other community members over time, as our acceptance in the setting by a broader range of people increases.

We also draw on the results of continuing classroom observations and an open-ended, semistructured survey designed to elicit student perceptions about their lives in school and at home. In addition, our involvement with the school has also allowed us to collect data during significant routine and special events, such as regular leadership team sessions, grade-level meetings, and parent assemblies and workshops.

VISIBLE DIFFERENCES

Teachers commuted into the neighborhood in the morning, saw the artifacts of urban decay, illegal drug dealing, and neglectful public services, and thought of what they must counter in teaching students; parents saw the limited presence of the educators in the community, felt their disdain for the local environment, and wondered how their children could possibly receive the caring and attention they deserved at school.

Such visible differences between the school and the community tended to put the two into an adversarial relationship, in the sense that each believed that the other placed children in situations that needed to be altered in order for the children to realize their potential. This is not to say that anyone in the setting deliberately tried to be antagonistic; indeed, everybody would have argued that they were simply doing their best to look out for the students' best interests.

These perspectives on the community and the school emerged in the course of interviews during which we asked people to talk about whether they felt that the school could accomplish what it should with students, what the obstacles to performing this task were, and what resources were available. The following two sections describe the overall, generalized themes that came out of these discussions.

Perspectives on the Community

Two vastly different views about the neighborhood emerged in the interviews. The teachers thought about only the negative images as they drove into the neighborhood each morning and exited it in the afternoon. And it was easy to see how that might happen; on first appearances that was exactly what most people, including us, saw. Most obvious were the dilapidated red brick and brownstone row homes, many of them either boarded up or gutted. What used to be magnificent architectural pieces had become isolated shells, with litter-filled and overgrown vacant lots replacing the homes that had burned or had been demolished. Graffitti and garbage grew as if from seeds, the natural progeny of urban detritus.

But those images only captured the starkly apparent and dramatic side of the story. Community members argued that people should look a little closer and appreciate the neighborhood from a more positive, albeit more subtle, side—and the photographs they supplied for the slide show mentioned above did just that. A more careful glance detected an occasional small park or garden that had replaced a vacant lot; a slight detour from a major street revealed an inviting and warm side street with homes having freshly painted facades and sparkling stoops; and a willingness to return to the area on special occasions found entire blocks closed to city traffic and people of all ages gathered to celebrate with their neighbors and loved ones.

The truth, of course, is that the two extremes were both there. So, whereas teachers proclaimed the area "a land of lots," the parents refrained "all of us don't live in crack houses." It was just a matter of through which lens they viewed the physical environs.

Of most importance, though, is that the visual images had analogues in the ways that the two groups viewed the day-to-day life of the children in the community. The teachers portrayed the neighborhood as chaotic. According to them, kids learned about life from their experiences on the street. They talked about kids who moved from home to home and who, on any given day, did not know where they would sleep that night. The only order was that imposed by violence and abusive behavior. Teachers painted a hopeless picture, one from which, if accurate, people would flee at the slightest opportunity:

> The height of deprivation is here. Drugs are rampant, going through generations. It is a tragedy here. . . . The family has broken down. There is no one stable link.

> Some kids have such problems at home. Consider what some of the kids come from. No one is taking the time to care for them. Their parents are in jail. I couldn't come to school with that on my mind.

Yet when we interviewed community members, they once again offered a contrasting portrait, one liberally sprinkled with examples of continuity missing from the teachers' composition. They spoke with pride about the school and the neighborhood as an extended family. Many of them had long-standing roots in the area; and, while they acknowledged the current problems attendant to many urban settings, historical remembrances tempered their harshness locally. For the students' part, they excitedly discussed block parties, having their grandparents just around the corner, and looking forward to going to the corner store after school for candy.

Perspectives on the School

Teachers' thoughts about what has to happen in school stem from their prevalent belief that the community's children come to school with deficits. These deficits were described as both material, "kids never see a book," and cultural, "they think this is the way life is." "You take them places," a teacher explained one day as an example, "and [kids say] 'I don't know where I am going'; they don't know what they're seeing!" The impact on children, as one teacher explained, is that "they'll always be behind, they'll never catch up." Another added, "they seem licked; for some kids, every day is a new day, a complete blank slate." Consequently, the school's role was to "make up" for that deficit, to provide lessons and experiences that parents and guardians could not. Thus, a teacher argued, "we have to expose them to life beyond their street, to what's outside their neighborhood." Or, as another teacher made the point, "I've heard some teachers say they [the students] are dumb; but [I believe] if they don't know it, it's because they haven't been exposed to it."

It is not surprising, then, that teachers looked inward for support in overcoming children's disadvantages. They described the school as "a haven from the outside, a safe haven," "an oasis," offering "food and a warm place in the winter" and "stability." In fact, teachers claimed that the predominant resource the school possessed was collegial support (mentioned by twenty-six of the thirty-six teachers who could identify positive resources available to them), as the following illustrate:

> The staff . . . they care and are supportive of other staff members. Why would you be here if you didn't care? Thank God I'm at Northeast. People speak out; they ask you for help.

> The faculty here is more uplifting, more motivated; people are really wanting to try to make a difference.

> Everybody is trying to work together.

In contrast, teachers often used adversarial terms in discussing their interactions with parents about school and students. For example, one teacher complained, "you call that parent about a problem with their child and the parent says, 'I'll beat your ass.' " Others stated:

Parents don't always back us up; there is a clash of standards.

Parents aren't on our side; they don't value education.

And when teachers did talk about parents taking an interest in their children's education, they felt that the interest was either misguided, "either the parents do the homework for the kids or don't make sure it's done," or superficial, "they don't participate in children's academics; they only come to school to get report cards." Overall, at least half of the teachers, when asked an open-ended question about obstacles in general, specifically identified parental attitudes toward education and conditions in the home that were unsuitable for learning (apart from the broader neighborhood situation) as the primary obstacles the school faced.

The disrespect and disregard that accompanied this portrayal was not lost on parents and guardians. They reported:

Some teachers talk down to the parents.

Some teachers may not care.

A lot of the good teachers are not here anymore. They don't want to participate anymore.

But more important, in the eyes of community members, was the impact of the lack of communication and understanding among the teachers about children. They were concerned that "kids are left out because of their behavior," believing that teachers often interpreted young children's inability to handle emotional problems at home as intentional disrespect, by both students and parents, of their authority. "Before you chew a parent out, find out what the problem is," cautioned one community person. Likewise, they feared that students' learning problems were too readily translated into lower estimations of the children's ultimate achievement potential, as revealed in instances where they heard teachers make comments like "this little boy can't learn." For community members, such statements helped explain why "by the third grade, [students] are turned off."

The community members who worked in the school, people for whom doors were open in both the school and the community, were kinder in their judgments about teachers' empathy. While they agreed that some parents were justified in feeling closed out, they also gave teachers credit for trying to reach the community with special events and parent workshops and for trying to educate their children: "The teachers basically take the time to help students." Still, they acknowledged that there needed to be a bridge in the school between the two groups. This situation created a special need for their services.

> The school needs to utilize part-time help more efficiently. We know the kids well. We should have more time to work with them one on one.

> This new teacher . . . it's really tough. I have to explain how things are. I'm used to a teacher knowing more about what they are doing.

> Employees like ourselves who are community workers in the school, we can relate to kids when teachers can't because we know them. It's a caring thing.

On the whole, however, teachers saw themselves as being the only adults striving to educate students on a daily basis and expected little assistance from outside the school walls. Parents read the visible signs of disdain for their capabilities and worried that this would translate into a less than suitable education for their children.

UNSEEN COMMONALITIES

We wondered whether the above perspectives would be reflected in the two groups' having totally different sets of expectations for students. If this were the case, then probably any seeds sown to instigate increased community-school involvement would land on inhospitable soil. On the other hand, we hear numerous parents, community members, and teachers speak of their intense desire "to do what is best for children." If these definitions of "what is best for children" were anywhere similar, then perhaps these common beliefs could serve as fertile ground for common action. To gather some insights into this issue, members of both groups were asked, "What characteristics would you like to see students develop in order to become productive citizens?," and "What do you mean by [each characteristic mentioned]?" We obtained usable responses to these questions—i.e., those that paired characteristics with their meanings for individuals—from 40 of the teachers and 24 community members.

Teachers' Perspectives

It would be incorrect to speak of "the teachers' perspective" because professionals' views of what they wanted to have happen with students as a result of schooling actually fell into three categories. One subset of this group talked about students in terms of what would make them successful in school; another subset described characteristics that would enable children to be successful in life in general; and a third bridged both of these perspectives. Interestingly, all three subgroups used the same descriptors: "self-controlled" or "disciplined," "respectful," "confident," "responsible," and "skilled." The differences resided in the meanings professionals attached to these words. The first subgroup saw the characteristics as being instrumental in making school run more smoothly, while the second seemed to emphasize the descriptors as being instrumental in the children's future outside of school. The third, of course, drew from both perspectives.

Success in school. Sixteen of the teachers used variations of the above five characteristics to describe what they wanted to see happen with their students. Underlying their discussions of what these terms meant was an emphasis on how students' acquiring them would affect daily life in schools.

For example, teachers mentioned *"self-controlled"* in the context of students' impulsive behavior. They wanted to see the students become "humanized" and "not so defensive" so that they would not act with their "fists first." Additional adjectives used in this light were "disciplined" and "self-disciplined." There was also a special usage of the words "reasoning ability" and "rational thinker." At first, it appeared to us that people were talking about higher-order or creative thinking in the traditional way; instead, what they meant was that students would "think before they act." Essentially, the bottom line was that, in developing self-control, students would not be so violent in their responses in school situations and would be more consistent in "following directions."

An immediately instrumental quality accompanied the use of the other four sets of characteristics as well. The term *"respectful"* had several beneficial components. "Respect for others" would translate—again—into less hostile interactions; "respect for others' property" would decrease the instances of stolen pencils, swiped candy, and soiled clothes; and "respect for adults" would increase the number of students who were willing to evidence better "manners" and act more "courteously."

With *"a better self-image"* and *"being confident,"* teachers wanted students to begin to "feel good about themselves." They perceived that this was a necessary step in getting the children to try harder to complete their work because they observed students giving up easily on difficult assignments and attributed this lack of persistence to students' low estimates of their ability. Our student interviews lent some credence to this argument because a significant theme running through their answers about why a particular subject was their favorite was that the subject came "easy" to them.

Teachers wanted students to become more *"responsible for their own actions"* or *"independent."* Primarily, this trait would lessen the need for teachers to continually direct students' actions. They wanted students who "don't have to be told what to do" and who would "work on their own." Part of responsibility also included being "prepared" for class.

Finally, in becoming *"skilled,"* students would demonstrate their knowledge of the "basics" and "academics" needed to pass successfully from one grade to the next and would become more adept in "communicating" with others. "Communicating" was discussed as both "speaking more clearly" and "listening better."

All in all, it seemed to us that this group of teachers saw these qualities as primarily furthering students' chances of succeeding behaviorally in school. Indeed, teachers themselves talked about these characteristics as prerequisites to the academic side of schooling: "Humanizing kids has to come before the [more] academic things," "Knowledge has to come after self-reliance," and "Gaining knowledge is negated by trying to discipline [students]." Of course, it would be grossly unfair to extrapolate this to mean that these teachers were unconcerned with students' futures. But they did tend to view the future as something that took a back seat to more pressing matters. As one teacher explained, "Once you get that together [manners, speaking clearly, and respect], then you can use what you learn here."

Success in life. The eighteen teachers that fell into this category similarly saw the five concepts as being instrumental, but, in this case, the benefits would accrue later in life. In fact, the most telling difference between the two perspectives was that this subgroup rarely, if ever, spoke of what would change in school as students became "self-controlled" (or "empowered"), "respectful," "self-confident," "responsible for their own actions," and "skilled." Instead, they concerned themselves with what would happen to the grown-up children when teachers were no longer around. Typical comments from members espousing this viewpoint were: "They won't have someone there all the time," "We won't be with them forever," and "When they go out in the real world, they can't fly off the handle." Rather than concentrating on what happens in school as being of primary importance, the teachers viewed schooling as almost subordinate to the pursuit of becoming adept at living in the "real world": "The school district focuses on things not as important as ['being happy' and becoming 'equipped to maintain yourself']."

Thus, the teachers defined *"self-control"* as "being empowered" and "gaining control over one's life." Having *respect for others* was seen as a step in becoming a "humanitarian" and/or "compassionate" person. While these teachers agreed with the others that high "self-esteem" could enable one to be *"confident* that you can succeed if you try hard," they stressed the importance of developing "a sense of hope" in life, of "knowing who you are," of being able to "retain one's ethnicity," and of being "happy" rather than completing assignments. Elaborations of having *"responsibility* for one's own actions" evoked descriptions of "goal-setting," "striving for the future," being "self-motivated to learn," "willing to learn for themselves," developing a "work ethic," and becoming "ambitious." And the *skills* these teachers emphasized ("knowing how to communicate" and "having a facility with numbers and words") were valued for their contribution to students' entry into "technical jobs" and having "life and survival skills."

Success in both. An outside observer might readily argue that teachers should focus on both success in school and in life. For whatever reasons, only six teachers did so in our interviews. These teachers bounced back and forth between the two perspectives, as one did in arguing eloquently for the need for students to become ready to take on "leadership roles" in the future and frustratedly wishing for students to "develop speed" in doing math problems. Similarly, another teacher claimed that it was most important for students to learn how "to know right from wrong with society" and decried students' inability to "be on time and ready" when class started.

Community Members' Perspectives

So, saying, as a good number of teachers claimed, that parents and teachers sometimes worked at cross purposes is already an oversimplified statement; as teachers attempted to put their views of what should happen with students into action, they probably worked with students in contradictory ways themselves (a hypothesis we have begun to explore with classroom observations). But where did community members' views of students fit into this picture? Did community members hold totally different aspirations for students? Did they tend to hold uniformly one of the perspectives teachers espoused? Or, did they replicate the same pattern as the teachers? Interestingly, the latter was the case, although proportionately more community members emphasized the "success in school" and "mixed" viewpoints than did the teachers.

Success in school. Still, the "success in school" arguments of 15 community people covered the same set of characteristics with similar meanings attached. Their *self-control* concerns flowed from seeing the "children acting wild" and being "defiant and disruptive" in the building. As one person commented, "Teachers spend half the day to quiet them [students] down." In the community's mind, this created the need for students to become more "disciplined" (a word that several people stringently emphasized), to become better at "following directions," and to "listen attentively to teachers." As was the case with the teachers, having self-control meant that students would exercise good "judgment" in how they responded to certain school situations.

Interacting with others in a *respectful* way, according to interviewees, would prevent children from "mouthing off," would help them get along with other kids, would engender "love in the classroom," and would discourage them from thinking that "it's in to bust on each other." The discussion also revolved around getting children to display appropriate "manners" at school, a term that covered everything from being "nice" to remembering to "flush the toilets."

Confidence was not directly mentioned as much by the "success in school" camp, except by two people: one who felt that to do well in school a student "had to feel good about their self," and another who believed "self-esteem" was destroyed by "all the little problems" some children have in school everyday.

Taking *responsibility* would help them to become more "prompt," "dependable," and able "to get work done on time"—a lot of which spoke to the need for better "work habits." Of course, "doing homework" was an oft-mentioned, visible component of being responsible.

The *academics* students would need to acquire included "basic fundamentals," "better reading [skills]," "math skills," and "study skills." No one mentioned the communication skills that the "success in school" teachers discussed.

Success in life. Only two community members represented the pure "success in life" perspective, expressing their ideas solely in terms of children's future prospects. The two did not refer to all five of the above terms in the interviews, but, in as compelling language as any of the teachers used, they shared their yearning to see students "have more *confidence* [because] you can't get no where without it," find "*a goal* to look forward to," and develop "*a love for learning* that is most important."

Success for both. Seven members of this group bridged the "success in school" and "success in life" perspectives, bouncing their ruminations back and forth between school and society. The school side included "a sense of fair play" in interactions with other students; "confidence in themselves" so they would not be "so quick to say I can't" when faced with new classroom tasks; "being on time and being where they are supposed to be" to show that they are "responsible for getting their education"; and "digging deeper into books" and "knowing where they are lacking in subject areas."

On the life side, these people discussed (1) being "kind and sympathetic" and having a "social awareness," (2) the fact that "grown people need to feel that they are vital," (3) being "career-minded," "willing to reach for it . . . it doesn't matter how high," and having "to get a goal and stick to it," and (4) having "curiosity," a "thirst for knowledge," and a desire "to continue to learn as analogues to *respectful, confident, responsible,* and *skilled.* The only one of the five qualities that these respondents ignored when discussing either school or society was *self-control.* Capturing the tie between the two perspectives, one person concluded, "If you do well in school [with respect to self-confidence], you will do well outside."

A DIRECTION FOR COMMUNITY-SCHOOL RELATIONSHIPS

Differences over the kinds of characteristics students should develop were more apparent within, rather than across, the two groups, insofar as both teachers and community members seemed to promote the success in school, success in life, and mixed perspectives. We do not believe that the three different perspectives were inherently antagonistic. Indeed, the similarities in language suggested that the real differences in meaning might be mostly ones of immediacy and expediency: the "success in school" viewpoint focused on the "here and now" and how students related to adults, while the "success in life" approach zeroed in on the "there and then" and how students would fare apart from adults.

This is the reverse of semantic problems where prople use different words to mean the same thing and resolve their differences with a shrug and "it's just a matter of semantics." At Northeast, people used the same words but attached different meanings to them. Such language similarity can pose a danger as well. Without paying careful attention to meaning, people might be too quick to agree at the vision-building stage and not realize the implications of their differences until they began to act. By this point, people might be too vested in following particular avenues to backtrack to the starting point and correct the misunderstandings.

So, as teachers embarked on their intended vision-building path, they would ultimately have to confront and resolve the differences within their group before any sort of action-guiding, meaningful statement could ensue. Given that the same issues would have to be addressed with the community before the vision could become salient for all adults who had a stake in the school, it would make sense that the conversation should be quickly extended to include this group.

Ideally, the product of the extensive dialogue about the school's vision would be the mixed perspective; that is, both the success in school and success in life positions would be acknowledged as valid and worthwhile *as long as* direct and strong connections could be made between what students were being asked to be like in school and what students should become as they grow up. In other words, the vision would illuminate the need for and the potential of aligning school-work and lifework.

But equally as important, perhaps, would be that, in the course of discussion, recognition would emerge of potential coalitions that could surmount the visible differences between the two groups. Vision-building activities, then, should be thought of as the means to unveil values held in common across groups and to assist the discovery of allies in advocating a better education for children. Of course, intense and rich discourse of the type we have in mind could solidify lines of opposition as well. But, stereotypes thrive in an environment of ungrounded assumptions, and their existence represents the greatest foe to concerted action.

Typically, school people "structure" parental involvement to "soften" the intensity of interactions and to avoid conflict. So, initially, the onus is on the school to facilitate this process by taking steps to increase the probability that extended dialogue will occur. Possibilities included:

• creating a welcoming environment for parents in the school, perhaps by designating a special room for parent/community activities,

• recognizing that participation is a two-way street and that the school should be more visible in the community,

• making the school the hub of social service agencies (one-stop shopping based on community need),

• arranging discussions about differing beliefs among and within groups,

• finding a "marriage counselor" to help groups resolve their differences,

• recognizing that these are "family problems" and that it is hard to have outsiders involved.

• using key parents to create bridges between the school and community groups.

• collaborating with other viable community institutions (e.g., local churches), and

• making more use of students' views as a natural bridge between adults' perspectives.

All of this will not be easy. The cultural and political barriers that we referred to earlier can still make the enactment of a vision difficult. The most needy communities and students are also often those that are the most cut off from helping to shape the definition of successful learning that should guide decisions about how the school can best serve them and how they can best serve the mission of the school. Caution should be taken, then, that parental involvement is not structured wholly at the discretion of the school—parents' definitions of appropriate and meaningful involvement should carry equal weight as relationships and roles are negotiated, especially if the parents are to support the vision at home. In developing a common vision of the type we recommend, Wood (1992, 237) advises:

> Further, in every case as many members of the school community as possible (if not all) are encouraged to share in the vision. This is clearly no easy task. But it is possible when we direct our attention

to what we want young people to *be* like when they leave school, rather than being preoccupied with what they will be able to *do* while they are in school. Here it is easier to find a common ground, based in democratic traditions, traditions that demand that as citizens and neighbors we pay close attention to the common good, be able to think carefully about and act on issues of public concern, and be tolerant of divergent or minority points of view. What these attributes of democratic citizenship mean for children of different ages and in various communities is best established by the local school community. But they do provide for any school a place to start in thinking through how to become a place that makes a mark on the lives of young people. The next step is to put them into practice.

In this situation, not only would teachers and administrators then have a responsibility to put those ideals into practice, but also the parent community would as well.

A useful way to think about the value of establishing collaborative links between parents and their childrens' schools is building "social capital." Social capital is the product of social and organizational relationships among people and is a resource for creating collective action (Coleman 1987; 1988). Such collective engagement among teachers and parents increases the payoff for students because the vision of the children's future becomes mutually reinforced and enabled both in school and at home (see Stone and Wehlage 1992).

A warning needs to be sounded as this call for mutual vision development and action builds. The school we discuss here is an elementary school. In a few years these parents and guardians and their students will move up in the feeder system to another school. LeCompte and Dworkin (1991, 210) critique change efforts that focus "on getting poor and minority students to become critical thinkers and to be aware and appreciative of their class and cultural heritage" because, if deeply embedded structural issues are not concomitantly affected, "they [the change efforts] can leave supposedly empowered students 'all dressed up, with no place to go.' " In an effort such as we propose, an empowered community of parents and students alike may have "no place to go" but to another school where they must fight the same battles of negotiation all over again in order to have a voice in their children's formal education.

Still, we would argue that the best hope is to go ahead and develop a vision anyway, one that ties the success in school and success in life perspectives together. As one community member explained, "Communication between a teacher and a parent can bring a teacher and child closer together." The kind of democratic participation in the education of children we envision goes far beyond helping with class parties, attending the annual school fundraisers, or even meeting teachers on Back-to-School night. In our opinion, strengthened by their "visible commonalities," parents and teachers would both become partners in creating the conditions for learning and colleagues in guiding children in their quests for productive lives. A parent eloquently summarized this argument by saying, "Kids learn better when parents and teachers are together."

REFERENCES

Coleman, J. (1987). Families and schools. *Educational Researcher* 16(6): 32–38.

Coleman, J. (1988). Social capital and the creation of human capital. *American Journal of Sociology* 94: 95–120.

Commission on Chapter 1. (1992). *Making schools work for children in poverty.* Washington, D.C.: American Association for Higher Education.

Epstein, J. (1990). School and family connections: Theory, research, and implications for integrating sociologies of education and family. In *Families in community settings: Interdisciplinary perspectives,* ed. D. G. Unger and M. B. Sussman. New York: Haworth Press.

Fine, M. (1991). *Framing dropouts: Notes on the politics of an urban public high school.* Albany, N.Y.: State University of New York Press.

Fine, M. (1993). [Ap]parent involvement: Reflections on parents, power, and urban public schools. *Teachers College Record* 94(4): 682–710.

Henderson, A. T., ed. (1987). *The evidence continues continues to grow: Parent involvement improves student achievement—an annotated bibliography.* Columbia, Md.: National Committee for Citizens in Education.

LeCompte, M. D., and A. G. Dworkin. (1991). *Giving up on school: Teacher burnout and student dropout.* Newbury Park, Calif.: Corwin Press.

Lightfoot, S. L. (1978). *Worlds apart: Relationships between families and schools.* New York: Basic Books.

Sarason, S. (1990). *The predictable failure of educational reform: Can we change course before it's too late?* San Francisco, Calif.: Jossey-Bass.

Stone, C., and G. Wehlage. (1992). *Community collaboration and the structuring of schools.* Madison, Wisc.: Center on Organization and Restructuring of Schools.

Wood, G. (1992). *Schools that work: America's most innovative public education programs.* New York: Plume.

Chapter 3

Conflict and Consensus: The Bitter and Sweet in a Community-School Coalition

Paul E. Heckman
W. Reed Scull
Sharon Conley

Connections among schools, families, and communities are receiving increasing attention in research literature (Bronfenbrenner 1979; Moll 1992) and are being viewed, particularly in urban communities, as important factors in educational reform (Sarason 1993). In addition, state and federal policy makers are encouraging efforts that connect schools and families with health and social service agencies (National Commission on Children 1991). The increase in connections and collaboration is argued to be essential for promoting the full academic and social development of children who are poor and of color (Shorr 1989).

In one Southwestern city, the value of connections between schools and parents/families/community is being explored through efforts of the Educational and Community Change (ECC) Project. The foundation-funded educational endeavor was designed collaboratively by university and school personnel for the purpose of studying and creating alternative structures for teaching, learning, and school governance (Heckman 1993). It began in one urban elementary school in 1990 and expanded to a second in 1992. Both schools are in a primarily Hispanic incorporated area within the boundaries of a larger city. About 55 percent of the families in this one-square-mile urban community live at or below the poverty level, and three-fourths of persons over the age of 18 do not possess a high school diploma or General Equivalency Diploma (GED). Within the project's two elementary schools, most students are predominately Spanish-speaking, possessing little or no English.

In the spring of 1991, efforts got under way to organize a community coalition to support the project's goals in education. The purpose of the coalition was to connect schools, families, health and social service agencies, and local governmental agencies (and where possible, create new configurations among these institutions) in a vital support system to promote the full development of the school children.

To provide an understanding of the ECC coalition's development and the competing influences in such a collaboration, this chapter initially examines the basic purpose of the ECC Project. In turn, the formation and development of the coalition are described. Finally, the paper illustrates the presence of both consensus and conflict in the coalition. Particular emphasis is placed on the eventual role of conflict in promoting greater cohesiveness among coalition members.

The word *coalition* has been defined as an "alliance or union of factions or parties" (Scott 1992, 288). However, it does not necessarily follow that consensus within coalitions is automatic. Indeed, observers suggest that conflict is prevalent within coalitions and may ultimately be necessary for the achievement of consensus (Bolman and Deal 1985; Lindblom 1968, 32).

PURPOSE OF THE EEC PROJECT

The project's broad goals are to create alternative educational practices, structures, and curricula, and, in doing this, it addresses the specific issue of why poor children of color who have a primary language and culture other than English do not often succeed in elementary and secondary schooling. Conditions that deter the success of these children are being studied, and alternative conditions are being tried. One premise of the project is that these children have different family and community advantages than students from middle- and upper-class, English-speaking families, and traditional schooling curricula, structures, and practices neither acknowledge nor address that issue.

From the project's inception, it has utilized the theory of John I. Goodlad (1979) and T. J. LaBelle (1982), which suggests that children exist and develop in an educational ecology that is composed of formal education (school), nonformal education (after-school organizations and activities, such as church, boys and girls clubs, etc.), and informal education (family/community life).

The project has advanced its work on the theory that, when continuity exists within the total educational ecology, children have a smoother road to educational achievement. For example, when language and knowledge in school are similar to—and build upon—what the children have learned in their nonformal after-school institutions and family educational systems, they can more easily acquire the theoretical and practical skills and knowledge offered by schools. Conversely, when knowledge and skills are developed in families and communities, there are fewer disparities among the nonformal, informal, and formal educational systems. When continuity exists and experiences are equally powerful in all aspects of the educational ecology, children are more likely to participate in—and benefit from—the larger society when they complete their formal educational experiences (Heckman 1993a).

Traditional schooling systems and practices have prevented or discouraged the development of powerful and continuous schoolwork by lack of consideration to children's nonformal and informal educational systems. As a result, many poor children of color often experience discontinuity in the work that they do in school. That is, the schoolwork does not build on what they know from their families and community, and traditional, academic science, mathematics, history, etc., appear unrelated and unnecessary to life in their "real world."

Efforts of teachers and administrators in the ECC Project's two schools are directed toward contextualizing school instruction. One of the first changes enacted after becoming involved in the project was combining classes of English-dominant and Spanish-dominant students, acknowledging the importance of knowing Spanish as well as English, and providing a link between the students' informal and formal education. In addition to many of the students becoming multilingual, an unexpected effect of this change was a decrease in hostility and behavior problems that had been developing between these Spanish-dominant and English-dominant students, nearly all of whom are Hispanic.

Teaching without traditional textbooks, work sheets, and processes of memorization and/or rote, much of the curriculum in each school is generated by projects and questions that originate with the students. Questions from students can launch entire projects within a classroom, with the students researching the answers, rather than being told the answers. Teachers are finding that students have a greater interest in school and learning when topics are explored that students "wonder about." Hands-on approaches are being used, and consideration is given to topics relevant to the students' nonformal and informal education, such as housing, food, health, money, and living things. Through these relevant issues, students are being taught to think and explore the way professionals perform their work, whether a writer or building contractor, scientist, landscaper, store clerk, government official, mathematician, etc.

Much of the first three years of the ECC Project was devoted to the teachers' exploring in dialogue their personal beliefs about traditional teaching practices, school structures, and curriculum. Time for the teachers to participate in dialogue sessions was made possible by the project's providing substitute teachers in the classrooms one day a week. It is through the dialogue sessions that research can be conducted on one premise of the project: Change in school structures, practices, and curricula must be conceived by and implemented by those who are most involved—teachers, school administrators, parents, and students. This process is known in the project as "indigenous invention" (Heckman and Peterman 1994). It does not preclude third-party involvement, but it denigrates the effectiveness of change efforts that are originated by legislation or edict and delivered to the schools for implementation.

CONCEPTS AND PRINCIPLES THAT SHAPED THE COALITION

The community coalition is an adjunct of the school project and a vital support system for the efforts going on in the schools. It is a major vehicle for influencing the nonformal and informal education of the students, and, primarily through parental involvement in the coalition as well as classrooms, teachers gain insight about the real world of the students. Much of their real world is heavily involved with problems and issues that confront the students' parents and the community as a whole: absence of health care and community safety, substandard housing, unemployment, and other social issues. These negative factors in the students' informal and nonformal education served as a backdrop to the eventual formation of the coalition, and there were several concepts and principles involved in its formation:

Indigenous Invention. Just as indigenous invention was a premise utilized in the process of school restructuring, it was carried over to coalition development. The ECC Project views indigenous invention to be as necessary in nonformal and informal education as it is in the schools. The assumption underlying the coalition's efforts is that teachers, parents, children, and other community members must be the inventors of their social worlds, and such invention can be accomplished in a purposeful manner (Berger and Luckmann 1967, c1966; Shils 1975, 7–8). Individuals can "challenge fate and social influences, to devise an answer to force, and to control passion, in order that human beings can produce intentional effects in this world" (Nyberg 1981, 21).

Macropolitical Ideas. Macropolitical ideas suggest that groups in the environment surrounding or outside the newly conceived organization would influence the degree to which the coalition would achieve its goals (Olson 1971, 132–167; Scott 1992, 116). S. B. Bacharach and B. L. Mundell (1993) found that various interest groups in the larger environment would impose their initiatives on organizations within that environment. Nevertheless, if the coalition was to become such a politically active group that would call on policy makers to attend to its interests (Petersen 1976), outside interest groups and individuals were needed. In addition to the influence those groups have in the distribution of material and human resources, resident members of the coalition stood to gain from them the knowledge and skills that relate to power. The project did not emphasize empowerment for the coalition but rather the understanding of power as "a quality of relations" (Nyberg 1981, 58). "Power is an aspect of the transaction-in-context; it is part of the action. It designates the expression of means or agency." Consequently, the project encourages coalition members to act cohesively in examining ways to change community structures and enhance their knowledge of effective procedures that can bring about change. When power is seen in this relational manner, it can be conceptualized as political power because coalitions of interest groups mobilize to enact change (Bacharach and Lawler 1980).

Micropolitical Ideas. Alliances among coalition members who live outside the project area and those who live inside the area developed at a gradual and steady pace. Such development reflects the micropolitics within the coalition. Also, minority interest groups within the coalition have developed shared meanings, agreed-upon plans, and taken actions together. However, the micropolitical concept implies that, over time, alliances among interest groups will change within the coalition and influence its success or failure (Scott 1992, 25). Mindful of that, there was emphasis on democracy within the coalition.

Democratic Process. The project tries to democratize power by encouraging every citizen in the community to make judgments about what aspects of the community are problematic and require efforts to change them (Dahl 1989; Dewey 1946; Lindblom 1990). In doing this, citizens are consenting or dissenting to the changes as they acquire adequate information that they comprehend well (Dahl 1989, 156). A democratic perspective of power is also encouraged as citizens together undertake cooperative efforts to develop and implement plans for addressing community issues (Olson 1971, 7). Information, understanding, and judgment constitute the ideal aims of education (Nyberg 1981, 90) and thus coincide with the purposes of the project.

Such mobilization of interests has a direct effect on what can be accomplished in the community and, subsequently, on what knowledge and skills can be encouraged in the total educational ecology. Some of the new learnings will consist of knowledge and skills related to what P. E. Petersen (1976, 44) has suggested that politically active groups, such as the coalition, can accomplish:

> (1) concentrate their energies on those issues having the greatest immediate impact on their interests; (2) develop new alliances as the issues and tactical situation changes; (3) migrate from one political faction to another as political leaders' positions on matters of group concern are modified; and (4) compromise their differences within a system tending toward equilibrium.

In effect, the influence and power of the coalition increase in direct proportion to the knowledge and skills used and acquired to influence and enact community changes.

EARLY FORMATION OF THE COALITION

Utilizing the organizing principles of Saul Alinsky (Boyte 1989) and a local Industrial Areas Foundation (IAF) group, the ECC Project hired a community coordinator with a master's degree in social work who began to meet with parents and other community members in their homes on a one-to-one basis. The coordinator sought to identify key community issues in addition to views of these individuals about schooling and education. Efforts were made to identify potential neighborhood leaders who might then organize their neighbors in various efforts to resolve problems in this community. Two such resident-leaders were added to the project staff. Also, house meetings among neighborhood people were encouraged so that residents could further examine their common interests and develop plans for addressing those interests.

When the project began, various interest groups within and outside the project area were working independently to address community issues and encourage changes. The project's one-on-one meetings with parents and other community residents and the house meetings became a means for identifying these agency directors and staff members who were working on related issues. Finding ways for these interest groups to work together to explicitly support improvement of these conditions in the community became an additional focus of the ECC Project. It was believed that creating a coalition of these groups would further the goal of connecting formal, nonformal, and informal educational systems.

Different interest groups have their own rationales and theories in support of whatever they advocate about school work, social issues, and relationships among schools, other educational institutions, and communities. Based on the belief that interest groups will determine and/or support what happens in schools and other parts of the educational ecology (Bacharach and Mundell 1993), the coalition identified and invited a variety of these groups to join in the project's community effort. These interested parties from inside and outside the local community included business persons, church officials, and administrators from the city school district, as well as parents, community residents, and members of leading civic groups.

The diversity of the groups invited to join was intentional for two reasons. First, it was believed that a broad base of support from many interested groups would be required to legitimate the alteration of existing educational ideas and practices and general community structures. Second, diversity would provide an opportunity for children and adults to acquire a broad array of knowledge and skills as they confronted and resolved community problems.

At that time, collaboration had become a major focus of many agencies and policy makers, who were seeking ways to improve the delivery of service (National Commission on Children 1991). To mention collaboration was to voice a code word that brought most human service agency people together. Several meetings of interested community agency people, including the school district personnel, were held; agreement was reached to form a coalition to support the project and improve the educational ecology.

Members of the coalition agreed to collaborate in promoting the reinvention of education in the project community, which included promoting alternative curricula, structures, and practices in the schools and developing the necessary knowledge and skills among neighborhood residents to act on their own behalf and have a political voice in addressing community problems. In a sense, there was consensus; various service groups and individuals from outside the community were willing to "come to the table" with parents and other community residents to address issues confronting this one poor community. At this stage, however, the coalition was more a group of outsiders than an association of concerned insiders.

DEVELOPMENT OF THE COALITION

In the three years since its inception, the coalition has developed bylaws, policies, and procedures, and membership has grown to more than 80 active participants, more of whom are from within the community than outside. A Governing Board has been elected and committees appointed to dedicate their efforts to four vital community concerns: education, housing, safety, and health and human services. Each committee communicates to the Governing Board before initiating activities, and, when broader sanctioning is required, actions are brought to the entire coalition for a vote.

Encompassed in the committee structures are the three educational institutions of school (formal education), after school (nonformal education), and family/community (informal education). First, with regards to formal education, schools constitute a significant resource in any community; indeed, in some communities they may be the only resource for bringing about change. The project began work in each of the schools by organizing weekly dialogue sessions among teachers, the principals, and the project staff, who served as facilitators. These meetings promoted examination of existing schooling activities and structures and implementation of alternative practices and structures. Such school inquiry was undertaken with the belief that because the school constituted an important community resource, redirecting that resource would build a foundation for the reconstruction of the total educational ecology. Meanwhile, the coalition's Education Committee focused attention on encouraging parents to question school practices and become more involved in school and classroom activities.

Second, in addressing the nonformal facet of the educational ecology, such as after-school club programs or daily organized activities, efforts were undertaken by the project staff and other coalition members to identify existing programs. The project's initial conception called for the school to link to existing after-school resources and then, after examination of these resources, to reconfigure them into new after-school activities connected to new school activities. Results of a survey, however, showed that few after-school programs existed in the project community: Only 80 of the 800-plus children in the two project schools could be accommodated in the existing after-school programs, some of which met only once a week. Therefore, instead of simply finding and linking existing nonformal programs to schools and families, it was necessary to develop new after-school and summer programs if all of the children were to have access. There was consensus among coalition members of the need for these programs, and the inadequacy of existing programs provided an opportunity for the children, teachers, parents, and other community members to work in a collaborative way. This effort included presenting a proposal and obtaining funds from the State for an after-school and summer program for children in the two schools. The program was developed and is supported by the project's coalition and the local YMCA.

Subsequently, inside members and outside members of the coalition utilized their areas of expertise in influencing local politicians to build a neighborhood youth center sooner than they had planned and to locate it next to one of the project schools. Inside members mobilized their neighbors to influence the local politicians, and outside members lobbied the city manager and heads of different city agencies to hear and act on the wishes of the community members.

Third, in the informal (family/community) facet of the ecology, the coalition introduced an adult education program, which includes GED preparation, English as a Second Language, and nutrition education; obtained a grant to map human and material resources in the community, and met with city council members and state legislators to raise awareness of community concerns. The coalition, by early 1994 was working with the city government in development of a comprehensive housing plan and the construction of 10 to 12 homes for first-time, low-income home buyers.

In some activities, children and adults worked collaboratively. For instance, children participated in a neighborhood clean-up program. Later, with the assistance of their parents and teachers, the schoolchildren made presentations to the city council and persuaded it to deed to the school district one city-owned lot, which is being developed into an urban wildlife habitat by the children and the Audubon Society.

In these examples, general consensus was evident among coalition members about the need for these programs and facilities. All continue to agree that they want to increase the knowledge and resourcefulness of community residents in a way that will enable them to bring about improvement in all educational, social, and lifestyle issues.

It must be acknowledged, however, that these successes often grew out of conflicting interests and ideas that existed when discussions began. Consensus is sweet; however, there is sometimes the bitter, when members have conflicting ideas on individual issues.

THE INEVITABLE PRESENCE OF CONFLICT

Organizational structural explanations for the analysis and development of a coalition usually overlook the inevitable conflicts of interests in a group and the process of creating consensus among members. However, conflict—like heat in making steel—can strengthen a coalition, contrary to the beliefs that conflict should be avoided and that too much conflict suggests a weakness and, therefore, an unhealthy and poorly developed coalition (Bellah, Madsen, Sullivan, Swidler, and Tipton 1991, 296; Reich 1988, 146; Scott 1992, 270; Shils 1975, 48).

Our argument in this chapter is that differing interests are identified through conflict and its articulation; and through the awareness of conflicting interests, vested interests are incapable of subtly directing coalition activities down unproductive or damaging paths (Shils 1975, 164). Within a coalition, special interest groups that otherwise would influence policies and actions in a community must rely on an explicit community process that includes articulation of ideas and concepts, thereby giving each of the members a somewhat equal voice. Finally, efforts to address conflicts—whether they are resolved or not—strengthens the coalition and the community (Shils 1975, 165) because all participants acquire new knowledge (Lindblom 1968, 115) in the process of articulation and argument. In this view, conflict becomes an opportunity for enhanced understanding rather than a threat to organizational existence (Conley, Cooper, and Robles 1991).

Within the ECC Project's coalition, conflict was evident in early interviews conducted with members who reside within the project area and members who live outside the area. While members share a common purpose—promoting the reinvention of education in the project schools and community—they have different views of who is best equipped or qualified to accomplish changes that will serve the schools and community.

One coalition member, who is a business leader residing outside the project community, viewed communications skills of insiders as a problem in dealing with policy makers, such as government officials:

> If you have not taken some steps to help them [residents within the coalition community] . . . to know how to talk to the politicians that

they're trying to get help from—or to the business people that they're trying to get help from—it can create a problem.

The sometime failure of residents to speak out was seen by this member as an obstacle, and, beyond that, he felt a need among residents for greater diplomacy in dealing with policy makers:

Once they [community residents] become comfortable talking, it can cause them to have a different kind of problem. Rather than get the help of the person that probably would like to help them, they create a barrier with that person where they don't want to help them or they are afraid to help, or they are afraid to even find out what they want.

Another outsider, a social-service provider, seemed to justify the reluctance of politicians to listen and respond to the voice of the insiders:

What can happen is that you can have citizens constantly on your back about everything and watching every move that you make and criticizing everything. . . . I've seen that happen before, so I understand that.

At the same time those views were expressed, the coalition, in general, was encouraging residents to take action toward change on their own behalf. Some interviewed insiders had gained enough confidence to feel they could accomplish their goals with or without the same communications skills or "know how" of members who resided outside the project community.

One resident member of the coalition commented:

When people believe that you can do something, you can do it easily, and it doesn't matter if it, if it takes time or whatever . . . I started to feel that because the people from coalition . . . they gave us a lot of support. They started to say, it doesn't matter if you [don't] speak any English, but have a voice. You can speak for your own self, you know, things like that.

The interviews, in general, revealed that coalition members from outside the community depicted members from inside the community as lacking, and needing assistance in developing, particular knowledge and skills.

On the other hand, coalition members who reside in the community see themselves as already learning and having knowledge and skills in changing their communities and relating to politicians. Their view suggests that, rather than adjusting to politicians' wishes, the politicians and other policy makers must accommodate the requests of local citizens.

In summarizing the interviews, some assumptions become apparent. Outsiders see the more important knowledge and skills needed to make changes as those that relate community people to those in power. They see importance in community members' being able to talk to politicians and business leaders in ways that those in power will hear messages that community members want them to hear. However, coalition members who reside in the community see the importance of a different set of knowledge and skills. They seek knowledge and skills to mobilize themselves and others to ask questions and gather information; they assume that it is the role of politicians to listen to their constituents.

These conflicting views between some insiders and some outsiders continue to be prevalent, as shown in the following example of establishing a wellness center. However, through articulation and argument, understanding and respect are being developed for opposing views and disparate knowledge and skills; it is a learning experience for community residents, as well as coalition members who reside outside the area. As outsiders articulate the messages and actions they believe necessary in dealing with policy makers, residents acquire new understanding of political processes. As insiders articulate their beliefs, hopes, and needs, outsiders gain knowledge and new insights about the community.

CONFLICT ON AN IMPORTANT ISSUE: THE WELLNESS CENTER

The following example focuses on how various competing views of coalition members manifested themselves in addressing a particular community issue. The selected issue pertains to health care and exemplifies an attempt by a well-meaning coalition member to bring a "wellness center" into the project community—a noble effort, but one fraught with conflict, depending upon the perspective of the members.

Addressing the issue is a legitimate concern for all project participants because there has always been a health-care inadequacy. To be more specific, community residents have to travel five miles to a county hospital or a community clinic. Few families have reliable transportation for such a trip, and the trip by bus requires a transfer to another route before arriving at the health-care clinic. Parents with little children find the trip exhausting; long waits for medical attention are the rule. For everyone, a trip for health care can take all day.

Consequently, in one-on-one interviews with members of the community and in coalition meetings, health care has emerged as one of the critical issues to be addressed. In acknowledging this issue as a critical problem, the coalition formed a Health and Human Service Committee to study ways to address the problem. Committee members met with the state director of health care and directors of local community health-care agencies; they visited several model programs in the city and in another nearby large city. A design for health-care delivery for the community was emerging, as well as the necessity to find money to enact these plans.

Just as progress was being realized, a member of the coalition who resides outside the community began gaining support for a countywide program that would bring a "wellness center" to the project community. This person, a well-respected member of the coalition and a community leader in the larger urban area surrounding the community, is a key player in the creation of wellness centers throughout the county. In that program, efforts are being directed to use both school district Chapter 1 funds and a local health maintenance organization's (HMO) resources to deliver health care to at least 18 pilot school sites in several school districts. The school district that oversees the project schools played a major role in the development of this plan; however, the project's coalition had no part in its development.

Ostensibly, each center would provide integrated services for poor families, including social services and health care. Persons involved in the development of the plan were leaders of various social service and governmental agencies and administrators of local health maintenance organizations. The HMO promised its services for at least a year, and other agencies agreed to work together at each site. Such an arrangement seemed like an answer to a perplexing problem. Although few, if any, persons from the neighborhoods or schools that were targeted for the program were in on the planning stages, the plan called each local community to create an Advisory Council, and, indeed, the coalition was to have representation on that council. However, according to the overall plan, these councils would serve only in an advisory capacity; the school district's Board of Trustees would govern the centers.

When several delegates of the school district presented the idea to the Health and Human Service Committee of the coalition, serious questions were raised about the offer. The wellness center representatives had stated that they knew what the community wanted and that the design of the center represented these wishes. When pressed about the source of that information, these individuals informed the committee that they had been in conversations with the principals of the two schools who had communicated the wants of the community.

Committee members then voiced their concern. Neither through the Health and Human Service Committee nor any other members of the coalition, had the community been asked to express its ideas about health care and other social service needs. This unexpected reaction offended the wellness center representatives, who could not understand why the community did not immediately accept the offer. At this point, a representative of the wellness center said that, since the community did not want the center, they would put it in another school community.

Subsequent negotiations then took place to clarify the community's issue with the proposed wellness center. Members of the coalition's Health and Human Service Committee appreciated the intent of the offer, however, they were concerned about who would develop the proposed plan and who would be in charge. They had their own ideas about particular health care and other social services.

In our view, the underlying conflict appeared to focus on whose knowledge and skills are being used and developed in the formation and enactment of the wellness center plan or any other plan to resolve a community issue. Those members of the coalition who live outside the community represent a view that will provide a different set of answers from those who live inside the community. These two views constitute two different interests, manifesting themselves from outside of the coalition (macropolitical) and inside of the coalition (micropolitical).

Certainly, the wellness center developers want to "serve" underserved people and areas; however, the proponents of the proposal appear to have developed their own knowledge and skills about health and other social service issues, what services and funds are available, and various ways that new services could be developed and funds provided in areas like the project community. A belief may also exist among the planners of the wellness center that the local community people do not have as much knowledge to understand issues related to the center as the center's developers. Moreover, doubts also may exist regarding the local community's capacities to govern the center once it is established, irrespective of who develops it. Such beliefs may be based in assumptions held by some of the founders of this nation about the tyranny of the majority (Kemmis 1990, 9–24).

The coalition's Health and Human Service Committee holds a different view. These members believe they have the capacity to understand the issues, to figure out alternatives, and to enact and govern any design that they and their colleagues create. Members want to take care of and serve themselves, a view that is critical to democratic governance (Dahl 1989, 52–79).

Consensus between the coalition and the wellness center group has emerged out of these conflicting views. Even though the wellness center proposal was not approved as developed and presented, agreements have now been negotiated. The coalition's Health and Human Services Committee and the outside group proposing the wellness center are developing a collaborative plan for what the center will do, how it will do it, and where. Shared responsibilities between the coalition and the wellness center planning group for further developing these agreements have also been worked out.

Finally, the coalition has recently made an agreement with the city and the wellness center group that the city will donate a vacant lot that is equidistant from each of the project schools. The school district will provide a portable classroom, and, at this stage, it appears that the coalition will run the developed wellness center.

HOW HAS CONFLICT STRENGTHENED THE COALITION?

Differences still exist among coalition members about various issues and will continue to exist at many junctures. These differences must be acknowledged, valued, and placed in a coalitional theoretical context. As Conley et al. (1991, 155–56) notes, "Conflict can serve as an opportunity for all constituents to recognize different interests [and to discern] sometimes subtle interests and influences embedded in organizational dynamics."

In acknowledging the differences and conflicts, we will be agreeing with Aaron Wildavsky (1987, 5), who suggested that "the quintessence of politics [is] the construction and reconstruction of our lives together." Such politics-in-action builds coalitions inside and outside of the coalition and positively affects what is going on now and will go on in the future in the educational ecology of the two ECC Project neighborhoods.

First, the conflicts reflect differences in wants, understandings of issues, and the preferred actions to be taken among the competing interests within and outside of the coalition. Coalition members have learned that such differences exist, that they can express their views about any or all issues, and that, through negotiations with each of the different interest groups, each group can retain a significant portion of what matters to it as a task is accomplished.

Second, each conflict situation has required coalition members to investigate the respective issue and work with others inside and outside of the coalition in figuring out ways to resolve the issue. These contacts provide the basis for the development of new knowledge and skills and relationships with a broader group of individuals who will serve as a network of interested parties in the work of the coalition. As new issues arise, the new knowledge and skills and relationships will be available in addressing and, perhaps, in resolving the new conflicts.

Finally, members are learning that they can make a difference in their own lives and the community when they work with others in the ways that the coalition is developing.

SUMMARY

In summarizing this chapter, the work of the ECC Project in the two elementary schools (the formal experience in the total educational ecology) is of primary importance. At the time of this writing—midterm of the project's fourth year—teachers continue to explore their beliefs and ideas about their former teaching practices, curricula, and school structures. More and more alternative teaching practices and structures are being tried. Emphasis is continually placed on contextual curricula.

The project is now focusing attention on student assessment. Convinced that standardized, norm-referenced testing does not portray a true picture of a student's knowledge or skills, project leaders are currently negotiating funding for the development of new student assessment measures. While there is reason for optimism, results of these assessment efforts will only be known in future years of the project.

In regard to the informal and nonformal educational experience, the theory of community/coalitional work and how it relates and promotes the educational development of children, as well as adults, continues to evolve. As we discussed earlier, education happens in an ecology of institutions in each community. The community coalition is one effort on behalf of the ECC Project's concept that the capability of children and adults is advanced in a total educational ecology. Conflict within this ecology is inevitable; however, with strong commitment to end results and through articulation and argument, conflict can promote the acquisition of knowledge and skills that can bring about change.

To this end, we summarize what has been learned thus far in the coalition's development as follows:

With regard to the macropolitics of the larger urban environment in which the project operates and in which the two project schools are embedded, the coalition has gained and exercised its power and gained influence in this larger political environment. This was evidenced when the wellness center representatives approached the coalition to gain its approval for placement and implementation of a center in the two project neighborhoods. To some degree, the coalition may be seen as "powerful" insofar as it was able to influence those in the broader community regarding the placement and delivery of social services in the school neighborhoods.

Such development also addresses the micropolitics within the coalition. Minority interest groups within the coalition have developed shared meanings, developed agreed-upon plans, and, in addition to the efforts to secure health care for the local neighborhoods, have taken other actions together in the community, such as efforts in the youth center and after-school programs.

What we have both to hope for and understand about the conflicting issues with regard to knowledge and skills in the coalition at this time is that differences will diminish. Hopefully, this will occur as more decisions and interactions occur among members of the coalition and as they take action together to change conditions in the community.

Because the project centers on what is happening in one community, the particular circumstances of this one community do not generalize to other communities. However, we believe as Robert K. Yin (1989) that our evolving grounded theory (Glaser and Strauss 1967) may be generalizable to—and may have implications for—related theories at work in other communities. The lesson learned so far is that the bitterness of conflict can educate and lead to sweet consensus when equal voice is allowed and all parties are committed to the same end result.

REFERENCES

Bacharach, S. B., and E. J. Lawler. (1980). *Power and politics in organizations.* San Francisco: Jossey-Bass.

Bacharach, S. B., and B. L. Mundell. (1993). Organizational politics in schools: Micro, macro, and logics of action. *Educational Administration Quarterly* 29(4): 423–452.

Bellah, R., R. Madsen, W. M. Sullivan, A. Swidler, and S. M. Tipton. (1991). *The good society*. New York: Alfred A. Knopf.

Berger, P. L., and T. Luckmann. (1967, c1966). *The social construction of reality: A treatise in the sociology of knowledge*. New York: Doubleday.

Bolman, L. G., and T. E. Deal. (1985). *Modern approach to understanding and managing organizations*. San Francisco: Jossey-Bass.

Boyte, H. C. (1989). *Commonwealth: A return to citizen politics*. New York: The Free Press.

Bronfenbrenner, U. (1979). *The ecology of human development: Experiments by nature and design*. Cambridge: Harvard University Press.

Conley, S., B. S. Cooper, and J. Robles. (1991). A coalitional view of site-based management: Implications for school administrators in collective bargaining environments. *Planning and Changing: Educational Leadership and Policy Journal* 22(3/4): 147–159.

Dahl, R. A. (1989). *Democracy and its critics*. New Haven: Yale University Press.

Dewey, J. (1946). *The public and its problems: An essay in political inquiry*. Chicago: Gateway Books.

Foster, W. P. (1980). The changing administrator: Developing managerial practice. *Educational Theory* 30(1): 11–23.

Glaser, B., and A. Strauss. (1967). *The discovery of grounded theory: Strategies for qualitative research*. Chicago: Aldine.

Goodlad, J. I. (1979). *What schools are for*. Bloomington, Ind.: Phi Delta Kappa Foundation.

Heckman, P. (1993). School restructuring in practice: Reckoning with the culture of school. *International Journal of School Reform* 2(3): 263–272.

Heckman, P. (1993a). Linking schools to the real world: Expanding notions of human capital development. *Journal of Thought* 28(1, 2): 83–94.

Heckman, P., and F. Peterman. (1994). Indigenous invention: New promise for school reform. Tucson, Ariz.: ECC Project.

Kemmis, D. (1990). *Community and the politics of place*. Norman, Okla.: University of Oklahoma Press.

LaBelle, T. J. (1982). Formal, nonformal, and informal education: A holistic perspective on lifelong learning. *International Review of Education* 28: 159–75.

Lindblom, C. (1968). *The policy making process*. New Haven: Yale University Press.

Lindbloom, C. (1990). *Inquiry and change: The troubled attempt to understand and shape society.* New Haven: Yale University Press.

Moll, L. (1992). Bilingual classroom studies and community analysis: Some recent trends. *Educational Researcher* 21(2): 20–24.

National Commission on Children. (1991). *Beyond rhetoric: A new American agenda for children and families.* Washington, D.C.: The Commission.

Nyberg, D. (1981). *Power over power.* Ithaca, N.Y.: Cornell University Press.

Olson, M. (1971). *The logic of collective action: Public goods and the theory of groups.* Cambridge: Harvard University Press.

Petersen, P. E. (1976). *School politics Chicago style.* Chicago: University of Chicago Press.

Reich, R., ed. (1988). *The power of public ideas.* Cambridge: Ballinger Publishing.

Sarason, S. B. (1993). *The case for change: Rethinking the preparation of educators.* San Francisco: Jossey-Bass.

Scott, W. R. (1992). *Organizations rational, natural, and open systems,* ed. 3. Englewood Cliffs, N.J.: Prentice-Hall.

Shils, E. (1975). *Center and periphery essays in macrosociology.* Chicago: University of Chicago Press.

Shorr, L. B. (1989). *Within our reach: Breaking the cycle of disadvantage.* New York: Anchor Books/Doubleday.

Wildavsky, A. (1987). Choosing preferences by constructing institutions: A cultural theory of preference formation. *American Political Science Review* 81(1): 3–21.

Yin, R. K. (1989). *Case study research design and methods,* rev. ed. Newbury Park, Calif.: Sage Publications.

Chapter 4

The Best of Both Worlds: Connecting Schools and Community Youth Organizations for All-Day, All-Year Learning

Shirley Brice Heath
Milbrey W. McLaughlin

This article considers ways that schools and community-based youth organizations (CBOs) could connect to build upon the strengths of each, respond explicitly to the realities of today's youth, and incorporate the attributes of the learning environments youth find most effective. The diverse and difficult needs of today's youth far exceed the ability of any single institution to meet them. Recognition of this fact has fueled policies that encourage or require such strategies as "integrated services," "interagency collaboration," "co-located or school-linked services," or "school-community partnerships."[1] As sensible as such proposals and policies appear on their face, they too often have had limited effectiveness. Frequently crafted by agencies or individuals unfamiliar with the realities of youth's everyday lives, such policies often reflect little attention to the strengths and weaknesses of the organizations brought together in mandated partnership.[2] Instead, they are more often driven by their anticipated effects on bureaucratic efficiencies than by the task at hand—helping youth develop as learners able to exist in their current worlds and to prepare for the work and social responsibilities of adulthood. Furthermore, while proposals for integrated services frequently put schools at the center with responsibilities for space, coordination, and oversight of health and social services, formal education institutions still "go it alone" in terms of being held exclusively responsible for providing the skills, expertise, and learning essential for youth to move to productive adulthood. Partnership with community organizations seldom extends to education.[3]

This article is based primarily on five years of field research in more than 60 successful youth organizations in three major urban communities. These findings are supplemented by interviews with students conducted in connection with a five-year comparative field study of secondary schools in eight metropolitan areas.[4] We argue here for serious and far-reaching rethinking of relationships among schools and other youth-based organizations in the community. We point out that, in the past decade, almost without being noticed by educators, CBOs with leaders committed to youth and their neighborhoods have been creating and maintaining institutions that are, on the one hand, highly educational, and, on the other, keenly oriented toward preparation for employment. We call on education administrators to consider what it might take to enlist and elicit the best of this world in collaboration with schools to forge all-day, all-year learning opportunities for youth. In particular, we point out the myriad ways in which CBOs provide numerous skills valued in both academic and employment institutions: oral and written language skills, experimentation with mathematical and scientific concepts, regular attendance with sustained commitment, and collaborative planning within a diverse group.

TALES OUT OF SCHOOL

Community-based organizations differ from schools in character and culture. Yet, where CBOs are successful in attracting and sustaining the interest of youth, their goals do not differ greatly from those of schools that center around learning and have respect for youth. Organizations that youth judge to be effective are "authentic" and supportive of their growth, development, and positive visions for a future. These successful CBOs provide a caring, personal setting where youth can count on the support of adults, where clear rules and concrete involvement in "real work" result in products that testify to youths' values as resources and to their abilities for acting as positive forces in their communities. Successful youth organizations provide links to the community and mainstream institutions, "authentic curricula" of the most fundamental kind—a learning, performing group in which it is safe to take risks, to stretch, and to learn new roles and ways of using oral and written language.

Illustration of these points comes from two brief case studies of CBOs of two very different types. The first, Liberty Theatre, is a grassroots drama organization in the heart of one of the most violent and crime-ridden neighborhoods of a midwestern city. Historically an African-American community, the area's high-rise projects are now home to an increasingly diverse group of residents. The second, Community Learning Centers (CLC), is an after-school educational enrichment program operating in a number of sites, both CBO- and school-based, in a western city made up of communities highly diverse both linguistically and culturally.

Case #1: Liberty: All for One

Located along a busy four-lane thoroughfare in the midst of massive 1950s housing projects, and squeezed in between a small insurance office and an abandoned small grocery, is the Liberty Theatre. Liberty provides a place for youth to go after school, on weekends, and during the summer; going to Liberty means taking an active role in the "job" of producing the best possible dramatic productions. Programs vary throughout the year. Illustrated here is a summer program funded through the mayor's office to enable Liberty to pay students between the ages of 14 and 18 minimum wage for six hours of work daily for six weeks, to produce plays that will be performed in the various parks and recreation programs of the city. When the students who meet low-income specifications set up by the funders come together, it is rare that any two will know each other. There is no audition, and acceptance into the program depends solely on whether or not their families' incomes are low enough for their youngsters to qualify for the mayor's program. Most of the group's members are highly marginal in school. Directors predict that at least half of these youth would drop out of school, if their time at Liberty did not give them the personal, literacy, and social studies skills that offer the extra boost that can keep them motivated to study and to stay out of trouble and away from the streets. Liberty also provides youth critical measures of self-esteem and personal confidence that enable them to keep going to school when everything they experience there is, as one young woman put it, "negative, negative, negative."

At Liberty, each of the three summer groups of 20–25 students, working under a separate director to produce a show, must bond and work rapidly to be able to "go on the road" with their performances within three weeks. There they will perform before squirming, active audiences of young children from across the city who attend the daycare programs of the parks and recreation facilities. Some of the youth in the theatre group, as well as in the parks programs they will visit, speak very little English, while others speak a variety of African-American vernacular dialects. As the players work together to produce their script for the play they will perform, they have to keep in mind their own language needs as well as those of their audience.

As one group, working under Tina, their director, struggles to develop their script and practice in the first three weeks, students talk often about how language, communication, and connections have to figure prominently in the show they will produce. During their brainstorming sessions of the first week, Tina makes audio recordings that she will spend part of the evening turning into dialogue segments the youth will perform the next day—revoicing their own words as they read the script and decide on the plot, movement, and dance that might accompany it. Each day portions get dropped, and, each night, new materials from that day's talk are added for the next day's script. By the end of the first week, the youth have shaped and reshaped their own words into an initial coherent piece they will try to pull together into a show with dance and music the next week.

In the first days of practice, Manuel, a Latino male with dark hair and eyes, sits quietly near Alonzo, who also speaks halting English. Manuel listens and indicates he knows what is going on by his broad smiles when the African-American males of the group pay any attention to him or when Sola, Tina's eight-month-old daughter, crawls off her blanket toward him. Onyx, a cheerful Latino/African-American young woman, wears her hair in cornrows and carries a huge smile for everyone. Especially friendly with all the girls, she shies away from the boys and pays close attention to Sola, playing with her whenever she can. Diego, a Latin male, is the tallest of the group, has a light mustache, and wears baggy pants and a cap with a marijuana leaf highlighted with gold metal trim on the side brim. He constantly performs, says he wants to be a professional actor, and has just declared a high school "major" in drama. When the company's work slackens, he suggests improvisation exercises, starts mocking African-American dance styles, or throws out joking insults to others of the group to stir up some action.

On a particularly hot day of the first week, when there is a lull in activities because members cannot decide how to represent all their cultures, Diego turns to Manuel and Alonzo and starts speaking rapid Spanish. Jonathan, the only African-American male in the group who comes anywhere close to matching Diego's size, starts joking about how "*Americans* speak English." Diego retorts with, "Well, *this* American speaks Spanish!" The two then begin to imitate what they regard as each other's dance steps and song styles, moving about the room playing alternatively bull and matador through their dances. The group steps back and laughs cautiously, while Tina watches quietly from the sidelines. Diego and Jonathan punctuate their singing with jibes about their favorite foods—insults thrown out in quick succession, with some from bystanders added. At one point, Tina claps her hands in the air sharply, compliments the two on their "show," and then asks the others how what they have just seen can fit into their full show. Answers fly back and forth, the idea accepted without question.

After several days, the script for the show they decide to title "All for One" emerges with an opening in which all members shout: "All for one!" Separate individuals strut in and out of other group members with "All for me," "No, all for me," or "No, all for one, and that one is me!" Shouts of "Me, myself, and I" fly back and forth across the group. The end of the shouting back and forth comes when one member shouts, "Hey if you want me to be for you, you better be for me, too." Later in the show, after contrapuntal lines along this theme, Diego and others replay their encounter that took place during practice, but with active incorporation of others such as Manuel and Alonzo.

Manuel: [in English] My, myself, I let me tell you why.

Alonzo: [in Spanish] I play baseball, basketball, and soccer—and I like to play them a lot.

Diego: [in Spanish] Yeah, you might like to play them but are you any good? [Both laugh as Alonzo moves over to stand beside Manuel]

Jonathan: Don't do that—

Diego: Do what?

Jonathan: Speak Spanish—

Diego: Porque?

Jonathan: I said don't—

Onyx: He just asked why?

Jonathan: Because I can't understand what he is saying.

Diego: You could try to learn Spanish.

Jonathan: Why? [looks thoughtfully at Diego, Manuel, and Alonzo and turns away] Awh, forget it!

Diego: [in Spanish] I don't know why this is such a big deal.

Jonathan: Oh, so you're talking about me now.

Onyx: No, he isn't, he just said he doesn't know why this is a problem.

Jonathan: It's a problem because this is America and we speak English.

Diego: Well, this *American* speaks Spanish.

They then look at each other and do mock battle that evolves into a dance, and they move off stage doing each other's steps. As they do so, the girls in the company move forward, doing a dance from Brazil that combines African and Latino elements. The boys move side stage and sway in rhythm as the girls perform.

The development of this scene came from much discussion of explorers and travelers about the world and what cultures have in common. At several points, they either got in the van to go to a nearby library or broke into groups to pore over materials that Tina had brought in for them. Once they decided on the dance from northern Brazil, Tina arranged for a teacher whose specialty was Brazilian dance to teach the group in both Spanish and English, with considerable discussion of the meanings of costuming and dance movements.

The name of this group, "All for One," emerged as the theme of their play and the impetus for the dances and songs they developed. In addition, this theme took them into research, as well as into discussions among themselves, of their various language backgrounds and attitudes toward communication and cultural preferences. Throughout their give and take of talk, they move back and forth between oral language, their own writings, and the written scripts that Tina produces from audiotape recordings she makes of their daily discussions. Tina asks them daily to write in their journals in response to specific trios of words, such as "me, myself, and I," or "lonely, alone, loneliness," that have come up in their discussions. They write also of places and people, of fear, of joy, of resistance, of help, of sustenance, etc.

Their daily writings contain ideas for the production and responses to the improvisation exercises they do during practice. In these exercises, two or three people sit before the rest of the group and are given several words chosen arbitrarily by the group. Those in the actors' seats must quickly create a dialogue and situation that makes use of those words for believable characters in settings that must be signalled by the dialogue. Work with words, as well as the physical revelations of emotions, fills their time during rehearsals.

The script thus gradually emerges for a forty-five minute show. Throughout script development, the group decides on areas of the play that need more research; and they go off to the library to collect material, or they watch documentary videos to build their visual images of the people and places they want to include in their play. Of their six weeks of summer work, the youths report what they see as the main features of what they learned about work and jobs.

> You gotta have patience with a lot of people. You gonna run into people who don't want to do this and don't want to do that, OK? You gotta learn to work around—learn to work with them.
>
> I think it's a social experience, working at Liberty. Cause we—everyone has a different personality, and we're trying to learn *together* how to work.
>
> Well, at this job, I never argued so much with people in my life!
>
> [the hardest thing is] understanding each other and, you know, getting along. Cause you got to first get along with a person before you work with him. You got to really get along. You can't start off with an attitude toward this person. Ain't going to get nowhere, so.

Of the writing and reading they do at Liberty, they say it is both easier than they had expected it to be and more powerful:

> It wasn't hard. No. Cause it—it came from something within. You know, she [Tina] asked us some questions about loneliness, about how we feel about things. And, you know, we just wrote! Everybody can write, right?

Manuel and Alonzo point out how important to acting that listening and imitating are, and how being at Liberty put them in the middle of a language-centered event. Alonzo adds: "I learning much English. . . . "

All the players point out that being at Liberty makes them proud and helps reshape some of their own habits. Jonathan says, of seeing his own words in Tina's script, "And when you looking on paper and you see your own words down and you not even knowing that they's down there, you know that make you feel good." He goes on to say that he now writes daily in a journal.

It is surprising and pleasing to Tina that these young players come away from the summer thinking a lot about learning and teaching, about who has taught them throughout their lives, and how they have learned. She and Liberty's executive director talk more about their dramatic productions as employment training than they have ever done in the past. The serious atmosphere of "this is work" runs through practice, rehearsals, and performances, as well as the daily routines of signing in and out, being docked in pay for tardiness and absence, and signing contracts. The youths, particularly males such as Diego and Jonathan, laughingly joke that Liberty sets them "free" from gangs on the street. Now they always have somewhere to go, something to do, and their busy schedule means they have good reasons why they "can't hang with trouble." Directors advise these youths on educational plans, hold mock employment interviews, and tutor them in interview and public speaking skills needed to sell themselves.

Tina remarks that because Liberty and other community organizations dedicated to projects with youths provide multiple ways of reaching the same goal, youths collect learning along the way from each and every kind of exposure—just in differing amounts. As she works with the youth, she expects consistent *focus* from them, a word she uses often to call individuals who seem off task back to work. She reminds them that daydreaming, losing focus, and not appearing interested "won't cut it on the job." At Liberty, the noise level is high, the pace rapid, the tasks multiple and simultaneous, with several groups working on different jobs throughout the room. Tina stresses the pressure that comes from knowing their work is their performance and that it will be "on stage," where they will be held accountable before their peers and outside evaluators. Both fear and a desire to "be good out there" drive their willingness to adhere to discipline and to stick to the hard work of drama in spite of their shaky relationships with school.

Case #2: Community Learning Centers: The Discovery of Knowing

Located in the grittiest section of the city, on a street peppered with prostitutes and drug addicts, WorkResource is a safe haven for adults and children alike. Although primarily Asian American, those attending the programs offered here come from many different countries and cultures, reflecting the diversity of the surrounding neighborhood. However, what all these people have in common is a low-income background and a shared struggle to support families and build careers; consequently, the promises that the nonprofit WorkResource holds forth—job placement or advancement as well as training in various skills—are highly attractive to the residents of this area.

In 1990, WorkResource decided to extend its services to youth in some way, and thus the nonprofit Community Learning Centers (CLC) was developed; it has since grown to serve four hundred children year-round at six sites throughout the city. Children, primarily third, fourth, and fifth graders, flock to CLC programs after school and on Saturday mornings to immerse themselves in the kinds of environments that extend the learning that school provides. However, CLC offers contexts that embrace a flow and set of interests akin to students' lives and with an eye to arming them with skills to benefit them beyond school into the workplace. The established objectives of CLC are to help children develop and strengthen skills in oral and written expression, achieve a level of competence with computer use, learn in fun and meaningful contexts that emphasize scientific and mathematic discovery and expanded awareness of their own and other cultures, and develop social skills and self-esteem.

Because of funding pressures springing from efforts to expand the program, in 1992, WorkResource hired an evaluator to assess how effectively the CLC program achieved these stated goals. Through observations, collections of writing samples, and interviews, the evaluator was able to see the kinds of learning that these classrooms nurtured. Multiple types of learning experiences wove in and out of the daily fabric of CLC, homes of the youths, and nearby resources, such as neighborhood family-owned groceries.

At CLC's principal site in WorkResource, children surge up the stairs and into the computer room, where all the activities of the one- and two-hour classes take place: typically, in sequence, class discussion and brainstorming, science experiments, and analytical and descriptive writing on the computer. Anywhere from fifteen to twenty-five children sprawl in chairs in front of the computers or wander the room, examining laid-out materials, trying to guess the focus of the day's experiment. Children's writings cover the walls, relating past experiments and outcomes. If children from a previous class are finishing up writing, incoming students excitedly look over their shoulders to read descriptions of activities on the screen. The children talk with one another animatedly. And the mixture of tongues is rich and various: Chinese, Spanish, Vietnamese ring in unison.

On a typical day, the teacher, Julie, calls the class to attention, and the children seat themselves as usual, each in front of a computer, and swivel their chairs around to face her. She begins by talking about crystals and asking the children if they can describe what crystals are. Some discussion follows, with the children calling out responses and

Julie prodding them to elaborate. Then she alerts them to the fact that many crystals exist in their own homes and asks them to guess their forms. After listening to their guesses, she then launches into a discussion of salt and Epsom salts and describes how they can be used as building blocks for the creation of larger crystals, which is the experiment they are to conduct this day.

The procedure for making crystals is listed on a board at the head of the class, and Julie goes over the instructions with the class, pointing out materials and encouraging the children to work together. The children pair up excitedly and allot tasks to each other, one setting up space on the floor, the other gathering materials. Throughout the experiment, the students good-naturedly vie with one another, comparing crystal size and formation. However, they also work collaboratively, exchanging helpful tips on the process with one another. One student asked another, "How did you do that?" inviting narrative and clarification from the other. Students look upon one another as valuable resources, roles that are further amplified by the teachers. Twenty minutes into the class, as the room is filled with the commotion and hubbub of eighteen students measuring cups of salt and water and recording quantities on charts, a student, Peter, comes in late. He comes over to Julie with a querying look, and she simply directs him to another student for explication and demonstration, calling out, "John, please explain to Peter what we're doing."

It is not unusual to see and hear a third grader instructing a fifth grader on the step-by-step process needed to conduct an experiment. Students even assist in translation; a Chinese-speaking student might explain instructions in Chinese to another Chinese-speaking student with limited English proficiency. Students become teachers and even experts as they orally exhibit and share understanding. In general, CLC classrooms are forums for the display and exchange of information and learning, and language is the bridge for such transactions. The genres of narration, clarification, and explication are essential elements of that language.

Students also do a lot of different kinds of reading throughout the classes, using multiple symbol systems to chart their course through the CLC curricula. They have to read and understand complicated sets of directions on the computer; they read one another's texts constantly, comparing their own work to others'. They read procedures from wall boards and, in some classes, learn how to decipher—as well as construct—graphs and charts that relate to science activities. Mathematics and science often interrelate. Math is a natural part of scientific experiments as children determine and plot the varying depths to plant different seeds in terrariums or the progressive heights from which they can drop an egg into a container without the egg breaking. Rulers are important tools for CLC students as they calculate various lengths and heights for experiments, and they become proficient with the language of measurement.

Science experiments by their very nature call for hypothetical and inferential kinds of thinking. CLC students consistently manifest these kinds of thinking as they posit what will occur in the course of an experiment. Teachers encourage children to practice such thinking by asking them "what if" questions. Students are compelled to make hypotheses and predictions and then to test them out empirically. For example, in one lesson on air pressure, the teacher asked children to make predictions by inquiring, "What do you think will happen to this ping pong ball when I turn on the hair dryer?" while holding the ball to the mouth of the blow dryer. Students conjectured and hypothesized excitedly and then watched as their predictions were borne out or refuted.

Children make inferences by means of the continual relation of activities to the real world. Ordinary household items become objects of unlimited promise: strings and nuts create pendulums; lemons, quarters, and nails act as batteries to power light bulbs. Such use of common materials also facilitates the children's re-creation of experiments at home, a possibility appealing to—and acted on by—many. Teachers also encourage this with suggested ideas. In one class, a student asks if a pendulum can "swing forever." The teacher suggests making one at home, starting the pendulum swinging at bedtime and then observing it upon waking in the morning. Home environments are viewed as opportunities for children to act as scientists, to make inquiries and test them out independently.

Across the sites, writing is viewed as the vehicle by which the students organize and present information learned or activities experienced. Teachers extend children's thinking and writing by asking questions encouraging elaboration or greater reflection. They occasionally suggest grammatical or punctuation corrections, but this is not emphasized in the CLC program. The fluidity and range of writing focus is of overriding importance, and students are encouraged to view writing as an experience free from rigorous correction and application to the standards of grammatical, punctuation, and spelling perfection that schools seem to expect. The idea is to free up writing from the fear of correction and censure. As class observations progressed, the evaluator noted the increasing fluidity and length of the students' writings. Children would typically print out at least a page of writing on the computer at the end of each class. These writings were then pasted into their own personal "books," the construction of which gave students a sense of accomplishment and pride. These books were consistently and enthusiastically shared with peers and teachers.

The benefits CLC students gain from the program extend beyond the easily measured ones of improvement in computer skills and reading and writing competency to include a whole range of language skills; in fact, a holistic language development takes place in the CLC classroom. Any assessment that is dictated by the standard school-devised methods of evaluation can only be inadequate to measure the full variety of language skills that are an integral part of the CLC curriculum and experience.

How do children view the CLC experience? In terms of the program's objectives, 88 percent noted on student evaluations that the program had made them a better writer. Many noted that it was "fun" to write in the CLC classes and that they wrote "a lot more." One child wrote, "Until I came here, I didn't know how to do a good report," and another remarked, "Here I write a lot better than I did in my school."

The majority of the children also cited increased knowledge in computer skills as a gained benefit and better understanding of science and the scientific process. Several students spoke of the ease and rapid pace of learning in the CLC classroom: "it was easy learning," "this program taught me how to think fast," "it taught me how to learn quickly."

According to these evaluations, 80 percent of the students attending CLC would elect to reenroll in the program, and 73 percent would recommend the program to their friends. The attendance figures also spoke of the children's high regard for CLC; although not mandatory, attendance averaged 85 percent across the sites. Children are drawn to return to CLC again and again by its nature of discovery and relevance to their own lives. Learning in this kind of setting is a (seeming) byproduct of activities that excite and engage children, inciting them to be active constructors of their own knowledge. CLC, like Liberty Theatre, is an organization where youngsters find respect, challenge, and activities that count as "real." At CLC, as in other effective youth organizations, young people are met and understood in terms of their local realities and life contexts.

THE BEST OF BOTH WORLDS

Tina and the Liberty Theatre players and the adults and children involved with CLC reiterate all the ways that community youth organizations provide not just or even MORE resources than schools. They provide DIFFERENT resources, resources of the type difficult for public schools to supply on a consistent or predictable basis. Schools, constrained by such factors as limited resources, collective bargaining agreements, accountability structures, commuting faculty, state curricula structures, and other instructional frameworks, as well as by insurance regulations, face real limits in terms of what their faculty can do and the kinds of learning environments they can create in the school arena.

From many perspectives, the youngsters fortunate enough to have found their way to Liberty and to CLC have the best of both worlds. Their CBOs work them hard, teach them much, and encourage them to stick to school and to build a belief that dedication will help move them along toward the job or work they all covet eventually. The environments they flock to in these CBOs foster the kinds of learning that will continue to benefit them as they seek to make their way through an increasingly complex society.

Youth across the nation report that they do not see their schools as offering them positive learning environments and sufficient support from their development.[5] Inner-city youth and others caught with many hours to fill without adult supervision and with few financial resources or opportunities, resent the negative attitudes, absence of positive expectations, and lack of respect they often encounter at school. Youth who come to school with limited skills in English, with little preparation or support for academic achievement conventionally conceived, say "there's no place for us" in school. Youth of all cultural and economic backgrounds say they feel "invisible" in school—that no one knows about them, cares about them, or supports them. School, as they experience it, generally is punitive and indifferent. Ironically, in society's premiere youth organization—school—young people too often experience disrespect and lack of personal support and recognition. "Nobody even tries to find out who we are." Both youths and their advocates complain as well that schools "aren't of the community. Come 2:30, they're outta there, the doors are locked," and so fail to provide youngsters the consistent, persistent support they need.

Youth advocates charge that schools are inattentive to the needs of today's youth and to their everyday realities. Contemporary youth often need jobs, not just to support the latest fad in adolescent apparel, but to support their families. Educators, community leaders assert, regularly misunderstand and underestimate the stress of youngsters' lives in terms of daily violence, financial and emotional insecurities, and difficult family circumstances. Youth agree: "they just don't listen to us; they just kick us out or fail us." Many of today's teachers, youth believe, "don't teach," or "don't teach in a way we can get."[6] Youth leaders concur with youth that the curriculum of most secondary schools appears irrelevant: "kids just don't see the payoff." Youth leaders also agree that young people from inner-city neighborhoods too often receive negative messages about themselves and their possible futures from school personnel—messages that drive youth from school and make the jobs of youth leaders such as Tina all the more difficult. "We spend at least an hour every afternoon making up for all the negative stuff kids hear about themselves in school," said the director of an after-school academic program. "All they hear all day is that they can't do it. We have to reassure them everyday that they can."

But schools have many resources critical to youths' productive learning and development. First and foremost, the vast majority of the adults who work in schools are there because of their commitment to young people and their education. Numerous teachers and administrators are not as unaware of the numerous needs of youth as many students believe them to be. Instead, bureaucratic and political pressures prevent their responding in the face of what teachers often see as "overwhelming" problems in the lives of young people outside of their school hours. The public schools of America house a veritable army of individuals dedicated to the well-being of youth, human resources that at present are overextended, undersupported, and often uninformed about the realities and cultures of the students who fill their classrooms. Many teachers, frustrated with the failure and apparent indifference of their students, elect on-the-job retirement and withhold the very energy and attention youths need. Many teachers say that they "just don't know what to do" to respond effectively to the difficult challenges and complex needs of contemporary students. Yesterday's training did not prepare them to work effectively with today's students. They have few experiences in their daily lives that enable them to understand inner-city life and the fears, responsibilities, and areas of special knowledge these students bring to school. Today's teachers teaching in urban schools have little direct contact with the families of their students, with their neighborhoods, or community traditions. Today's teachers "just don't know what to do" in large measure because they lack this information about who their students are—their values, language use, behavior patterns, or family circumstances.

Beyond these human resources, schools have material resources essential to learning and generally unavailable elsewhere. Schools house academic resources such as computers, laboratory equipment, audiovisual materials, and libraries that places like Liberty and CLC do not have. Schools have time and space dedicated to learning and youth—classrooms, gyms, auditoriums, playing fields. Schools have access to youth; schools are the social institution having the most routine and accepted contact with a community's youth. Schools have privileged and legitimate access to many of society's service institutions, such as social workers, health facilities, etc.

In nearly every American neighborhood exist community youth organizations such as Liberty Theatre and CLC that have the expertise, resources, and capacity to join with schools in promoting learning and development of young people. Most of these organizations have specific needs, some of which schools could help meet: library resources, personnel with expertise in specific subject areas, and gymnasium space and equipment. But few educators know much about CBOs, their activities and needs, and the ways they work with students in nonschool hours. Yet effective CBOs are powerful sites where just the kinds of learning and problem solving urged by school reformers take place: learning for understanding, higher-order thinking, transformational learning, for example. Arguments for more active student roles, collaborative learning opportunities, and the interactive construction of knowledge by youngsters working with a variety of sources for authentic audiences sound very much like the everyday practices of CBOs.[7]

Current policies and assumptions that confine responsibility for education to schools set aside the rich potential for learning during the time youth spend out of school. These hours, little considered by educators except for homework assignments, represent about 40 percent of the total time available to youth.[8] The hours before and after school represent a substantial block of time that can be put to constructive use by youth. For example, a Girls Inc. organization opens its doors at 6 a.m., offers breakfast and homework time for girls dropped off by their working mothers, buses the girls to school, picks them up after school, and offers afternoon educational, athletic, and artistic activities. Older girls help younger ones with their homework, plan dramatic performances for senior citizen centers, and prepare foods for a special party for their mothers. On Saturdays and Sunday afternoons, members of Girls Inc. go on outings together or visit the local children's hospitals or senior citizen centers with their performances or to read to children and elders.

Without such CBOs, many young people spend virtually all of their "free" time without companionship or supervision from responsible adults: "nowhere to go and nothin' to do." School occupies a relatively modest amount of a young person's time—6 or 7 hours a day, 180 days a year, and, in many cities, these hours are being whittled away minute-by-minute by budget cuts. In particular, arts programs are being cut, leaving youth without opportunities for the multiple communication skills and group work that drama and music, for example, offer. The arts share much in common with the activities of CBOs: opportunities to explore special interests and to put to use lessons or challenges presented in classes such as English or social studies. The arts, as well as athletics, offer possibilities to extend formal learning to nonformal settings and to work intensively for a shared goal with others whose backgrounds and interests may differ greatly from one's own.

Both schools and community-based youth organizations comprise institutions dedicated to the healthy development, accomplishment, and achievement of young people. Yet each generally operates in isolation, separated by policies that bundle "education" into school and by professional boundaries that distinguish between the educational role of the teacher, formally credentialed, and the recreational role of the coach, dramatics coach and director, or youth leader. These distinctions represent more than wasted resources and opportunities for youth; they fail to recognize the sizeable body of evidence that shows that young people learn, not only in school, but also in their neighborhood, in the experiences they have and the people they meet in their discretionary time.[9] Distinction between school and nonschool time as sites for learning overlooks consistent evidence that students, especially adolescents, do better in school if they can bring the enjoyment and engagement of their leisure time activities into the classroom.[10] Many inner-city youth experience their first socially valued success in their youth organization. The positive youth experience in CBOs translates into feelings of competence and confidence outside the organization, generalized self-esteem important especially to youth who are not academic superstars. The value of community-based voluntary programs, activities, and groups as a complement, or even alternative, to what schools provide emerges clearly in youths' descriptions of what they learn in CBOs and how it shapes their lives: "I really feel good about myself there." "I'm learning stuff for life." "Without [this organization], I'd be dead or in jail."

JOINING THE TWO WORLDS

We propose careful consideration of ways that formal and informal learning environments represented in schools and youth organizations could come together as seamless nonconflictual learning environments building on the strengths and resources of each. Youth need more and different supports for learning than either schools or CBOs can provide alone. Currently, conferences and professional organizations, as well as the professional staff, of the two groups never cross paths. While school reformers hold numerous conferences and planning sessions to discuss topics such as authentic learning and community-building in their institutions, youth leaders of effective CBOs accomplish these goals daily, often with little awareness that educational reformers now search for ways to implement means to these same ends (Heath and McLaughlin, 1994).

We present as one example of where such thinking might lead a youth-based approach to school-CBO connections that could enable learning all-day, all-year for youth—continuous involvement or "24-7" (24 hours a day, 7 days a week) as youngsters would term it. Our approach draws upon effective learning as we observed it in the more than sixty youth organizations such as Liberty Theatre, which we studied over a five-year period. The conclusions we draw from these diverse community youth groups lead us to rethink aspects of formal educational structures in such terms as:

Spaces and times of learning: As the center of a network of community institutions for youth, schools could become clearing houses for learning activities that would take place out of school as well as in school. These centers could become locations where youngsters place their individual learning portfolios and inventories of their participation in activities beyond the school, such as that with Liberty Theatre or CLC. Written reports, news clippings, script portions, and directors' recommendations could then "count" within the full repertoire of learning achievements of youngsters. Thus, life and learning out of school could be documented as supplementing and extending formal schooling. Since many activities of CBOs typically involve skills and attitudes that employers value (such as timeliness, communication and collaboration skills, and diligence), reports of students' participation in CBO activities could substantiate job readiness. For teenagers, such a clearing house could also be a career planning and placement center giving advice about both pursuing jobs and further education simultaneously—a goal most inner-city youth see as realistic for them.

Agents of learning and teaching: Teachers currently feel tied down to too many tasks, in addition to the teaching of their own content areas. If the staff of CBOs, such as Tina and the teachers of CLC, were to meet with school teachers at intervals throughout the year, they could jointly work toward achieving the learning activities and goals of particular students or groups of students. Many of the staff of CBOs either are or have been teachers; others are college graduates who work in youth organizations both because of their commitment to youth and the freedom that the flexible hours there allow for pursuit of their own arts or athletics interests. Tina is a writer and actress during the winter season; the summer work at Liberty allows her to write her own materials several hours a day and gain experience directing. During the winter, she takes part-time acting assignments and works on her own writing. She has many thoughts about teaching, drama coaching, and language development. Bringing her and others like her together with teachers of youth in schools would enable them together to extend and reinforce each other's efforts and goals.

Teachers, even those in tune and sympathetic with the pressures of growing up in urban America, also face real constraints in responding to the issues youth bring to school. "It's really awful," said a teacher worried about the abuse, lack of support, and difficult family situations endured by her students. "But it's so hard for me to spend the time with them I know they need. Five minutes, and I've got another class of 30 kids coming through the door." CBOs offer adults who can respond to these fears, insults, and personal hardships— feelings that preempt learning for many students. "You gotta have some place to put the anger, the negative," said a member of Liberty Theatre. "You gotta have some place to construct it into somethin' positive." CBOs can provide a place where youth can meet the needs that must be addressed before a student can take advantage of what school has to offer.

Content, methods, and materials of learning: Much of the learning within CBOs is performance based, demands that youngsters keep some written record of their individual progress, and requires following rules and listening to evaluations from outsiders who are strangers to the group and therefore are often frank, open, and thorough in their assessments. In addition, numerous informal requirements come up from day to day as the organization meets problems and youth are brought directly into discussion of the best ways to identify and solve these problems.

Contemporary theories of learning emphasize much that is already central to practice within CBOs. Those who have worked with these methods of teaching at CBOs can be helpful to teachers who may find it difficult to adjust to some of these practices. Within CBOs, writing is authentic, directed toward the achievement of group goals. Writing is used to learn, as well as to record research, and to draw in the feelings and ideas of individuals for later retrieval and work with other members of a group. Students learn to use sources and types of information from several different media, but not merely enough, since CBOs rarely match the research materials and library resources of schools. If students know that such material is necessary for their performance or for reading to elders or hospitalized children, they take up reading willingly and work to transform texts' shape and to integrate them into their own projected uses.

Promise and problems of partnership. The promise of joining the best of both worlds in the education of today's youth is apparent. CBOs provide communities of practice for much of what learning theorists currently advocate—performance-based assessment, collaborative learning, and long-term project-focused learning. If the deep division between schools and such organizations could be bridged for teachers and students, CBOs could become strong partners in the education of community youth. The advantages for youth of such partnerships are many. These partnerships would enable educators to view youth holistically, through knowledge of their neighborhoods, families, and friends, as well as their involvement in nonacademic activities. Only with such understanding can teachers build more effective instructional strategies that recognize students' strengths, interests, and needs. Together, schools and CBOs can create multiple opportunities for learning and enhance the diversity of experience available to young people. In partnership, schools and CBOs can better match teaching and learning styles and support and acknowledge the multiple intelligences of young people. CBOs present a way to address the gap that exists between the families of many nontraditional students and the school. Youth organizations can provide a bridge to mainstream institutions for both students and their parents; they can furnish schools with important knowledge about youth and their families. They can furnish families with information, access, and opportunities to play a positive role in youth's development.

In partnership, schools and CBOs can expand the numbers and types of adult role models available to youth and provide more diverse experience upon which youth can model possible selves and construct futures. CBOs are a valuable resource to schools seeking "parental" support and guidance. The caring adults found in youth organizations can play this role effectively. Indeed, it is the "imagined family" aspect of youth organizations that earns the commitment and loyalty of young people.

TRIALS OF COMING TOGETHER

Crafting and sustaining these partnerships, however, involves much rethinking of traditional relationships and effective response to factors that have frustrated past efforts of schools to gain partners.[11] The track record of such partnerships is not encouraging and the impediments many. Oddly enough, case studies of schools and of school programs that have worked effectively for student populations traditionally considered hardest to reach illustrate numerous features of CBOs. For example, one such study of a highly successful urban high school elective program termed "Program: Learning According to Needs" (PLAN) illustrates organizational and philosophical features that parellel those of effective CBOs (Abi-Nader 1990, 1991, 1992; cf. Heath and McLaughlin 1990). Yet teachers within this program labored to develop the scheme for their elective program with no awareness that a similar model existed in the after-school groups attended by many youth similar to those of their classes.

Just as schools often work with no knowledge of CBOs, so CBOs often feel the need to avoid partnering with schools in any way. Many individuals working in youth organizations find schools the "most difficult" partner among the many social agencies with which they have contact. It is not uncommon for directors of youth groups to report: "It is really tough working with schools. They want to be partners, but they also want to be in control. There are lots of things they just don't want to let go of. Principals, for example, see a pretty tight connection among teachers, students and parents. Everybody else, in their view, is outside of this. 'Our role is to educate,' they say. Well, a lot of us have a lot of trouble with this." CBO adults go on to point out that they believe that much of what they do with young people lies well within the realm of education—literacy, mathematics, social studies, building of positive attitudes, and stimulation of high standards and reliable performance.

Bureaucratic issues that individual schools often cannot overcome stand in the way of cooperation between CBOs and schools. For example, legal issues of confidentiality of student records and other information preclude sharing important information about youths' school experience with adults working with youth in the context of a community organization. But a more important obstacle lies in the different belief systems and sometimes divergent perspectives educators and CBO staff bring to questions of what today's youths need and ways to best meet those needs. Youth workers believe that many educators "are just looking at the narrow, cognitive side of [the youth]. They don't want to think about the links between recreation and learning environments."

Few effective channels of communication between schools and community organizations exist; both CBOs and schools are hampered by lack of knowledge about the activities, assets, and interests of the other institution. Schools particularly are isolated, and "have little idea of what's out there for kids, what's going on." Youths advise the "suits," representatives of public or private agencies concerned with youth issues, that "they've gotta get their hands dirty. They've gotta come on down and dwell in the projects . . . see and understand what young people are going through, the hardships." "They've gotta see what we see everyday." Educators also need firsthand knowledge of the neighborhood contexts in which their students grow up and move through. CBOs can provide important links for educators to the community and to the youth. Interprofessional training programs can provide opportunities for educators and staff of youth organizations to learn about each other's perspectives, belief systems, and expertise. Professional development time available to educators could well be spent in local youth organizations in conversation with staff about ways in which formal and nonformal curricula and activities could reinforce and extend each other. This time also could provide occasion for youth workers and young people to come to school and meet with teachers and administrators and share information about their activities and interests. For example, teen drama troupes such as Liberty Theatre provide compelling comment on youth's abilities and willingness to work hard when engaged in an activity—an opportunity for teachers and administrators to see youth they view as poor or indifferent students excelling at an activity freely chosen. Such occasions are useful starting points for developing understanding of today's students and the realities in which they move.

Breaking down the barriers that preclude youth from benefiting from the best of both worlds poses complex, difficult challenges to youth organizations and to schools. Where's the time? Where's the leadership? Where's the interest or support? Most importantly, where's the trust? First steps may well be small and frustrating as educators and youth workers strive to connect schools and CBOs around youths' learning. But the rationale for working hard to find and support those connections is evident in the inability of either institution to go it alone to meet the needs of today's urban youth and the promise of working together. A strong partnership between the schools and CBOs extends the learning environment to where young people are—or feel most comfortable being—and enables youth to learn all day, all year— not just 6 hours a day, 180 days a year.

NOTES

1. The David and Lucille Packard Foundation (Center for the Future of Children 1992) compiled a comprehensive report on school-linked services. Authors included in this volume explore the various strategies used to promote ties and collaboration between schools and social service agencies, as well as the pros and cons of placing schools at the center of services for children. See especially the essay by Robert Chaskin and Harold Richman, which challenges the taken-for-granted idea that school-linked services are a promising strategy to enhance resources for youth. Julia Koppich and Michael Kirst (1993) explored similar issues in their edited issue of *Education and Urban Society, Integrating Services for Children: Prospects and Pitfalls.* Robert Crowson and William Boyd (1993) examine related issues of school and community relationships and parental involvement in their children's experience with school and with other social service agencies.

2. See Juliet Langman and Milbrey W. McLaughlin (1993) for a descriptive analysis of the pros and cons of collaboration among youth agencies.

3. Innovative efforts to make "school like home," while often highly effective, also lay primary responsibility for change with school personnel. Analyses of such cases point out the need for a far broader frame of change than simply the reorganization of single local schools (see, for example, Martin 1992 and the proposal there for considering the nation as a "domestic realm").

4. The bulk of data used in this article comes from a research project funded by The Spencer Foundation and carried out between 1988 and 1993 by Shirley Brice Heath and Milbrey W. McLaughlin, with the assistance of Merita A. Irby and Juliet Langman. Melissa Groo, who contributed the portion of this article on Community Learning Centers, carried out the study of the organization she reports here. Research was done in major metropolitan areas in youth organizations that inner-city youth identified as effective. They were a diverse lot in terms of activities, affiliation, and organizational type. They

were, variously, nationally affiliated, church related, municipally supported, and independent. They were sports teams, club programs, scout troops, art projects, dance troupes, theater groups, or tutoring programs. They were located in community centers, church basements, their own building, or no particular place at all. We found no single focus, strategy, or organizational type associated with success. For each of our successes, we can point to an apparently identical activity that was "nowhere" in youth's assessment. What made the difference was the quality and character of the environment created for youth. Pseudonyms are used for each organization, and cities are not identified by name, since many of the organizations studied were unique, and their descriptions along with names of the urban areas would reveal their identities. See Heath and McLaughlin (1993, forthcoming) and McLaughlin, Irby, and Langman (1994) for extended description and analyses of the youth organizations we studied as part of this project. The second ethnographic study of students' experiences in secondary school settings was conducted under the auspices of the Center for Research on the Context of Secondary School Teaching at Stanford University, funded by a grant from the U.S. Department of Education, Office of Educational Research and Improvement (Grant # G0087C0235) awarded to Milbrey W. McLaughlin. (See McLaughlin and Talbert 1993; Phelan, Davidson, and Yu forthcoming; Phelan, Davidson, and Cao 1992, 1991). Quotations within this article from urban youth within schools about what happens for them there come from the interviews of these research projects.

5. Interview quotations used here are drawn from the ethnographic study of students' experiences in secondary school settings carried out by McLaughlin and Talbert.

6. See especially Davidson, Cao, and Phelan (1993) and McLaughlin and Talbert (1993) on the disjuncture between students' views of themselves as learners and teachers' perspectives about their students' interests, motivation, and behaviors. A consistent theme in our conversations with urban youth was their feeling that they wanted to learn and do well but found little receptivity or connection in school. Teachers, for their part, interpreted the attitudes and behaviors students described in terms of self-protection and pride as sullenness and lack of interest. Striking in our interviews with students and their teachers in urban high schools was how much they echoed each other's frustrations and aspirations. Both students and teachers wanted classrooms where learners were engaged actively, where effort was respected and supported. Both students and teachers were discouraged and cynical at the absence of these qualities in their classrooms. Phelan, Davidson, and Cao (1992) describe these apparently oppositional views of interests and experiences in secondary schools.

7. Howard Gardner (1991) elaborates the theory of multiple intelligences, the seven intelligences that underlie the different ways in which students

learn, perform, understand, and connect with information and experience. According to this theory about how people learn and represent knowledge, we are able to interact with and learn about the world through language, logical-mathematical analysis, spatial representation, musical thinking, and kinesthetic understanding. School, traditionally conceived and enacted, focuses primarily on only two of these intelligences, language and logical-mathematical analysis. Further, the educational practices evident in most classrooms assume that everyone learns in the same way and ignores other intelligences as paths of learning and understanding, as well as the different "profiles of intelligence" found in any classroom. As currently constituted, most schools and classrooms support the development of only a narrow aspect of any individual's intelligence and fail altogether to foster the intellectual development of students whose strengths are in other than linguistic or quantitative modes.

8. An examination of both the risks and opportunities of nonschool hours of youth was completed in 1992 by a commission of the Carnegie Corporation of New York (1992).

9. A number of researchers point to the importance of nonschool learning for adolescents' development and to their willingness to stay in school. (See, for example, Csikszentmihalyi and Larson (1984).

10. See, for example, Murtaugh (1988); Csikszentmihalyi and Larson (1984).

11. See the Julia Koppich and Michael Kirst (1993) volume for review of the pitfalls associated with various efforts to link schools with social service agencies or other institutions focused on serving youth and their families.

REFERENCES

Abi-Nader, J. (1990). "A house for my mother": Motivating Hispanic high school students. *Anthropology and Education Quarterly* 21(1): 41–58.

Abi-Nader, J. (1991). Creating a vision of the future: Strategies for motivating minority students. *Phi Delta Kappan* 72(7): 546–549.

Abi-Nader, J. (1992). Meeting the needs of multicultural classrooms: Family values and the motivation of minority students. In *Diversity and teaching: Teacher education yearbook,* ed. L. Odell and M. O'Hair. New York: Association of Teacher Education. pp. 212–227.

Center for the Future of Children. (Spring 1992). *School-linked services.* Vol. 2(1), *The future of children.* Los Altos, Calif.: The David and Lucille Packard Foundation.

Chaskin, R. J., and H. A. Richman. (Spring 1992). Concerns about school-linked services: Institution-based versus community-based models. In Center for the Future of Children *School-linked services.* Vol. 2(1), *The future of children.* Los Altos, Calif.: The David and Lucille Packard Foundation. pp. 107–118.

Crowson, R. L., and W. L. Boyd. (February 1993). Coordinated services for children: Designing arks for storms and seas unknown. *American Journal of Education* 101(2): 140–170.

Csikszentmihalyi, M., and R. Larson. (1984). *Being adolescent: Conflict and growth in the teenage years.* New York: Basic Books.

Davidson, A. L., H. T. Cao, and P. K. Phelan. (1993). The ebb and flow of ethnicity: Constructing identity in varied school settings. *Social Foundations* 7(1): 65–87.

Gardner, H. (1991). *The unschooled mind.* New York: Basic Books.

Heath, S. B., M. W. McLaughlin. (1994). Learning for anything everyday. *Journal of Curriculum Studies* 26(5), 471–489.

Koppich, J. E., and M. W. Kirst, eds. (February 1993). Integrating services for children. *Education and Urban Society* 25(2): 123–128.

Langman, J., and M. W. McLaughlin. (1993). Collaborate or go it alone? Tough decisions for youth policy. In *Identity and inner city youth: Beyond ethnicity and gender,* ed. S. B. Heath and M. W. McLaughlin, 147–175. New York: Teachers College Press.

McLaughlin, M. W., M. I. Irby, and J. Langman. (1994). *Urban sanctuaries: Inner-city youth and neighborhood organizations.* San Francisco: Jossey-Bass.

McLaughlin, M. W., and J. E. Talbert. (1993). How the world of students and teachers challenges policy coherence. In *Designing coherent educational policy: Improving the system,* ed. S. H. Furman. San Francisco: Jossey-Bass.

Martin, J. R. (1992). *The schoolhome: Rethinking schools for changing families.* Cambridge: Harvard University Press.

Murtaugh, M. (1988). Achievement outside the classroom: The role of nonacademic activities in the lives of high school students. *Anthropology and Education Quarterly* 19(4): 382–395.

Phelan, P. K., A. L. Davidson, and H. T. Cao. (1991). Students' multiple worlds: Negotiating the boundaries of family, peer, and school culture. *Anthropology and Education Quarterly* 22(3): 224–250.

Phelan, P. K., A. L. Davidson, and H. T. Cao. (1992). Speaking up: Students' perspectives on school. *Phi Delta Kappan* 73(9): 695–696, 698–704.

Phelan, P. K., A. L. Davidson, and H. C. Yu. (1994). *Students' voices: Navigating the borders of family, peer, and school cultures.* New York: Teachers College Press.

Chapter 5

Educating Homeless Children: One Experiment in Collaboration

Rebecca L. Newman
Lynn G. Beck

INTRODUCTION

The United States Department of Education estimates that there are 200,000 homeless children of school age, approximately one-third of whom are not in school. The National Coalition for the Homeless estimates that there are at least twice that number of children, and that one-half of them are regularly not in school (Wells 1990). Indeed, families with children constitute the fastest growing segment of the homeless population (Mihaly 1991). The federal Stewart B. McKinney Act, passed in 1987 and reauthorized in 1990, provides homeless children with certain educational rights, including the right to consideration of their parents' request that they continue to attend the school they were attending prior to becoming homeless. The act also requires states to have plans for the education of homeless children and youth and to remove the barriers to educational achievement that are faced by these children (First 1992; Gore 1990; Helm 1992; Wells 1990). Unfortunately, many schools and districts seem to be aware of neither the McKinney Act nor the state plans, and slow progress is being made towards implementation (First 1992: Helm 1992). Moreover, persons concerned about these children believe that there are many other barriers, unaddressed by the requirements of the McKinney Act, that make it difficult for the homeless to benefit from educational opportunities. Accordingly, a number of educators, social service providers, and others

are beginning to develop programs to overcome the barriers to educational success that they feel these students confront. Frequently, these
efforts require collaboration, on some level, among schools and various public and private agencies.

Beginning in January of 1993, we have engaged in an examination
of the educational needs of homeless children and their families and
of several efforts—requiring varying degrees of interagency collaboration—to address these needs. Four goals have both inspired and guided
us in this effort. First, we wanted to explore the experiences of homeless parents and, in our reports, to give voice to their struggles, successes, hopes, and fears regarding their children's education. Second,
we hoped to develop an in-depth understanding of efforts to provide
schooling for these children. In this regard, our concern was with
considering the day-to-day operations of programs, factors affecting
personnel working therein, and political and structural features supporting and inhibiting the work of individual organizations and the collaboration of several institutions. Third, we were concerned with assessing
the degree to which programs generated by these efforts addressed the
needs articulated by homeless persons, and, concomitantly, with assessing the quality of learning opportunities within those programs. Finally,
as a result of our data analysis, we hoped to identify implications and
applications of this research for educators who work with homeless
children and for policy makers and service agencies concerned with
building effective structures to serve this population.

In this chapter, we report the results of an investigation into Oak
Street School,[1] a school for homeless children involving an alliance
among a county department of education and two private organizations, in a California county where there are estimated to be 6,000
homeless[2] youngsters among its 60,000 children living in poverty
(Maharaj 1993). The background of this investigation is described in
the first section. We open with a brief review of the scholarship that
provides the theoretical underpinnings for our work.

Researchers have examined the educational problems of homeless
children from several perspectives. We briefly summarize the findings
of scholars addressing the problems of homeless students from three
such perspectives: (a) studies of the academic performance of homeless students; (b) studies identifying factors associated with
homelessness that are thought to contribute to the educational difficulties experienced by many homeless students; and (c) studies dealing with barriers to educational success that homeless children confront
within the school system itself. A related literature, on interagency

collaboration, examines actual and recommended strategies for meeting the educational and social needs of this population.

Following this brief literature review, we describe our methodology in this investigation. In the next section, we discuss findings, beginning with a brief description of some of the educational challenges encountered by the homeless families we met. Our attention then turns to Oak Street School, the program that was the focus of this investigation, one that involves cooperation among a county department of education, a private social service agency, and a church. In the fourth and final section, we reflect upon what can be learned from the Oak Street School collaboration that can guide scholars, practitioners, and policy makers in devising and implementing effective educational programs for homeless youngsters.

BACKGROUND OF THIS INVESTIGATION

Theoretical Framework

As noted above, two bodies of literature provided the conceptual underpinnings of this study. Scholarship on homelessness, and, specifically, on the educational experiences of homeless children, identified characteristic patterns in attendance and achievement of this population and suggested a number of links between educational policies and structures and successful and unsuccessful learning opportunities. This body of work also identified problems associated with homelessness that are believed to influence the effectiveness of educational and service efforts. It underscored, for us, the reality that any program or policy aimed at educating this population must be understood in light of the perceptions and experiences of those in a position to receive the services being offered. In a related vein, literature discussing the need for interagency collaboration in addressing the complex needs of homeless families and scholarship noting characteristics of effective and ineffective cooperative efforts guided data collection and analysis as we investigated one such program.

Literature on the educational experiences of the homeless. Scholarship on the educational experiences of homeless children has tended to fall into three categories. Some researchers have focused on the academic performance of these youngsters, while others have emphasized identifying conditions associated with homelessness that adversely affect learning. A third focus of inquiry has identified barriers to educational success that exist within the educational system itself.

Scholars within the first group, focusing on academic achievements, have analyzed the academic records of homeless children
(Rafferty 1991), tested homeless children (Bassuk and Gallagher 1990;
Shaffer and Caton 1984, reported in Rafferty 1991), or surveyed parents and/or teachers about the educational performance of homeless
children (Bassuk and Gallagher 1990; Hall and Maza 1990; Kozol 1988;
Maza and Hall 1988; Molnar 1988, reported in Molnar, Rath, and Klein
1990). These researchers and others considering their work, and, frequently, the body of related work on the educational problems of the
children of poverty, suggest that homeless children are at high risk for
educational failure. Homeless students are more frequently retained in
grade, more likely to be in special education, and more likely to be
performing below grade level than other poor children (Bassuk and
Gallagher 1990; Eddowes and Hranitz 1989; Gewirtzman and Fodor
1987; Hall and Maza 1990; Kozol 1988; Linehan 1992; Maza and Hall
1988; Molnar et al. 1990; Solarz 1991; Stronge 1992; Tower 1992; Van Ry
1992; Wells 1990).

The second focus of investigation has identified a host of non-
school-related barriers to the educational success of homeless children. These include serious medical and mental health problems, lack
of access to medical and mental health care, hazardous living conditions, inadequate nutrition, inadequate clothing, an exhausted or inadequate family support network, problems with domestic violence, lack
of childcare, problems associated with shelter living, and problems
with substance abuse (Bassuk and Gallagher 1990; Hall and Maza
1990; Maza and Hall 1988; Rafferty 1991; Rafferty and Shinn 1991;
Rivlin 1990; Robertson 1991a, 1991b; Shinn, Knickman, and Weitzman
1991; Solarz 1991; Sullivan and Damrosch 1987; Tower 1992; Van Ry
1992).

Research on school-related barriers to the education of homeless
children has found the educational system failing to address mobility-
related problems and programmatic barriers to the participation of
homeless students. Scholars have also documented problems of prejudicial treatment of such children. Homeless children repeatedly experience the problems associated with high mobility: changing schools
frequently can result in gaps in their knowledge and basic skills; they
may be placed incorrectly because records fail to catch up to them; it
is difficult to accomplish testing for special placement; time is lost
during moving and while adjusting to yet another new classroom and
curriculum; and so on. Many schools have no procedures for compen-
sating for these problems. Homeless children have also sometimes

experienced prejudicial behavior from peers or staff, and they are often unable to participate in extracurricular activities or to complete assignments due to lack of materials, space to study, and other needed support. They may also be found ineligible for programs in which they ought to be able to participate—such as free meals and Head Start—because of lack of records and failure of full communication between home and school (see, generally, Balfour 1991; Bullard 1993; Eddowes 1992; Eddowes and Hranitz 1989; First 1992; González 1990, 1991, 1992; Helm 1992; Johnson 1992; Korinek, Walther-Thomas, and Laycock 1992; Linehan 1992; Moyer 1990; Portner 1992; Powers and Jaklitsch 1992; Stronge 1992; Wells 1990).

Interagency collaboration addressing homelessness. The complexity of the problems linked to homelessness has inspired a growing literature on the importance of agencies working together to support and assist persons in this situation. Concomitantly, voices from many quarters have begun to argue that schools should—or could—serve as the hub of social service activity for children and their families (Crowson and Boyd 1993; Dryfoos 1991; Eddowes 1992; Eddowes and Hrantiz 1989; González 1990, 1991, 1992; Heath and McLaughlin 1987; Kagan 1989; Kirst 1991, 1993; Kirst and McLaughlin 1990; Linehan 1992; Schorr 1988, 1989; Wells 1990). Simultaneously, a corresponding body of literature on structuring, understanding, and evaluating interagency collaboration is developing (Crowson and Boyd 1993; Gray 1989; Guthrie and Guthrie 1991; Kirst 1991, 1993; Payzant 1992; Schorr 1988, 1989; Van de Ven and Walker 1984; Van de Ven, Walker, and Liston 1979). Even as researchers, policy makers, educators, and service providers in the public and private sector are stressing that agencies or schools—working in isolation—are unable to marshall the skills, resources, and personnel to address the complex circumstances created by poverty, many are warning that successfully mounting collaborative efforts is quite difficult.

THIS RESEARCH: SITE, SAMPLE, DATE COLLECTION, AND ANALYSIS

San Juan County,[3] located near Los Angeles, has a rapidly expanding number of individuals living in poverty. Numbered among these are an estimated 6,000 homeless children (Maharaj 1993). We selected this county as the site for our investigation because, in recent years, the county department of education, with the support of local government officials, has initiated two projects to address the educational needs of these youngsters. One of these involved a cooperative venture uniting the county, a nonsectarian, private social service agency, and a religious organization—a venture that has required policy changes, the allocation of funds and personnel, and alterations in the operation of all three institutions—in an effort to develop a school that could tailor its program to meet the educational needs of some of these children.

As we alluded to in the introductory section, we have conducted this research in three phases. In one phase, we focused on the experiences of homeless families, in an effort to understand the various factors affecting their interaction with the educational system. In a second, we concentrated on getting to know persons working with these families, attempting, among other things, to provide support so that children could have productive and successful educational experiences. In a third phase, we engaged in a case study within Oak Street School, a joint project of the county department of education, a local Neighborhood Club,[4] and a church.

In phases one and two, we conducted extensive, open-ended interviews with sixteen parents of homeless students and nineteen semistructured intensive interviews with the staffs of public and private social service organizations dealing with homeless persons, with shelter personnel, and with staffs of schools and districts with experience working with homeless students. We have also visited seven of the county's eighteen shelters for homeless families (or for women and children) and spent approximately two hours per visit observing the activities and interactions of parents, children, and shelter personnel. We have made repeated visits to and spent more than twenty hours in each of the only two shelters in the county that provide short-term, emergency housing for families. One of us (Newman) spent four to five hours per week over a two-month period, observing and participating at Oak Street School, the collaborative program that is the focus of this report. At this time we conducted formal interviews and engaged in informal conversations with a number of persons participating in this effort.

Interviews were tape-recorded and transcribed in two steps. The first step involved preparing field notes describing the person, site, and setting and a general summary of the interview, using the interviewer's notes and the tape. Material pertaining specifically to education was then transcribed and summarized, along with demographic data that situated the interview in a meaningful context. This material was coded and analyzed according to the method of constant comparative analysis pioneered by Barney G. Glaser and Anselm Strauss (1967) and further elucidated by others, including Leonard Schatzman and Strauss (1973), and John Lofland and Lyn H. Lofland (1984). Case study data were recorded in field notes and analyzed in a similar fashion, with the assistance of *Ethnograph,* a computer program for the analysis of text-based data. A third researcher—with extensive experience in qualitative research—reviewed our findings, provided helpful comments, raised some key questions, and, in general, confirmed that she shared our impressions of key ideas and issues.[5]

In this chapter, we concentrate upon the findings derived from the case study of Oak Street School. However, we have elected to briefly report on insights gained from our meetings with various homeless families in this county. We do this because these insights guided and grounded our analysis of the Oak Street collaboration, for, we reasoned, the success of this effort hinged, not only upon the ability of various agencies to work together, but also upon the degree to which this project was, in fact, meeting the "felt" needs of homeless families. In the sections that follow, we present our findings in the following order. We begin with a discussion of the educational challenges facing our homeless interviewees. This is followed by a section focusing on Oak Street School and on the manifestations and operations of the interagency collaboration that supports this institution. We then concentrate upon analyzing this effort and considering the way three agencies, working in concert, appear to be developing a program to meet successfully the educational needs of some homeless children.

AN OVERVIEW OF FINDINGS

Educational Challenges Facing Homeless Families in San Juan County

As we met parents residing with their children in shelters throughout San Juan County, we were struck by both the differences and similarities in their stories. Every person with whom we spoke had a unique story regarding the challenges she or he faced in attempting to see that their youngsters attended some sort of school and, further, that they benefited from that experience. As we reflected upon these stories, we were, however, struck by the fact that, despite the variety of their situations, these families did share certain concerns and fears. For example, we found that the lack of adequate clothing and child care discouraged many youngsters and school age homeless parents from attending school. Further, we discovered that physical and mental health problems tended to inhibit attendance and to prevent students from taking advantage of learning opportunities when they did, in fact, attend school. Problems with transporation posed a major educational barrier. Parents' lack of knowledge about options, and their unwillingness (usually born out of shame) to ask questions, inhibited positive schooling experiences for their children. Yet another problem arose from the living conditions within many of the shelters and motels. Even if children were in school, they were often unable to complete homework assignments because of the noise, crowded conditions, and lack of supplies in these settings. In the next section, we briefly discuss some of these, offering examples from our data that illustrate the perspective of homeless persons on their circumstances. As previously stated, we do so because our analysis of Oak Street School was influenced by our knowledge of the challenges and dilemmas facing the school's clients. We wanted to understand how interagency collaboration was working, but, more importantly, we wanted to know if, in fact, this effort was addressing the needs of homeless youngsters. In order to honestly assess Oak Street's effectiveness, we needed to understand the situations of those it attempts to serve.

Lack of adequate clothing and child care. Several of the mothers with whom we spoke worried about not being able to dress their children appropriately for school. Joy, hoping to enroll her children the week after our interview, asked if we knew of places in the area that could help with clothing. Lucinda's children had plenty of clothing—most of it in storage but accessible. However, at the time of our interview, she was completely penniless, with no immediate prospect of relief. She was worried about laundry money and was ashamed to send her children to school in dirty clothes. Irene reported that her children were embarrassed about their lack of appropriate clothes. "The only hard time is . . . this year, is that my kids were not able to get school clothes. That really, like, bummed them out."

In addition to noting that lack of clothing is a concern, almost everyone mentioned that the lack of affordable day care exacerbated the problems of homelessness. At times, this affected students' ability to attend school. One of the families we interviewed at an emergency shelter consisted of Tricia, a 33-year-old grandmother, her two daughters (15 and 18), and the two very young daughters of the 18-year old. They had been homeless for several months, bouncing from motel to shelter to motel. Despite this, both of the daughters were managing to get to school. Kendra, the young mother, was attending school from two to six every day—she was a senior and needed only a few credits to graduate. Most San Juan County school districts do not offer child care for the children of their students. Kendra's is one such district. She kept the babies in the morning, and her mother took over childcare at noon, which gave her the time to take the county's inconvenient and infrequent buses to school.

The day after our interview, however, Kendra would not be going. Her mother had an appointment with the housing authority for an interview for the "Once in a Lifetime Housing Assistance" program. The interview was at nine, but there was no telling when she would actually be called nor when she would finish nor whether it would be in time for her to take over the babies. Furthermore, there was the problem of how to accomplish getting the babies to her. The emergency shelter requires the families to be gone from 7:15 a.m. until 5:00 p.m., and both the shelter and the housing authority are miles from Kendra's school. So the family decided that Kendra and the babies would accompany Tricia to the Housing Authority office. That would provide a safe place for them to spend the morning, indoors, with access to restrooms and water fountains, and, if by chance things went well, Kendra might have time to take a bus from there to school.

Physical and mental health problems. Joy is a young Africa-American woman who is the mother of four children. Her three daughters— Tamara, Talika, and Isabol—were six, three, and one, respectively, at the time of our interview. Jerome, her son, was four years old. She was five months pregnant with a fifth child. None of Joy's children were in school, although it had been in session for over a month when we spoke to her. Tamara had begun attending kindergarten the previous year. However, for six months she had problems with her foot and was frequently unable to walk. The family visited a public clinic several times, but, on each occasion, the physician or nurse practitioner could find no reason for her pain. Eventually an X ray revealed that she had stepped on a sewing needle (Joy sometimes works as a seamstress) that had broken off in her foot. When this was removed, she was able to walk, but unfortunately, she missed so much school that she would have to start over. Joy feared that her daughter might be ashamed that she was "still" in kindergarten, since her younger brother, who would soon turn five, would also be enrolled. Joy, herself, reported that she had recently gotten food poisoning after eating at a soup kitchen, and all of the children had colds—as did many of the children whose families we interviewed.

Dionne, 36 and the mother of nine children, battles alcoholism and a major physical disability—she was born without part of one leg. Her husband is also an alcoholic, as were her parents, she says, who gave their children to an aunt when Dionne was three years old. Dionne gave her first five children to her sister, when she saw that she herself could not take care of them. The youngest four have been taken by the courts. In earlier episodes of homelessness, when the second set of children were still with her, they were often not attending school. Expressing a commitment to offering her children a stable life that includes education, Dionne was working on meeting the court's requirements for regaining custody. Regardless of the outcome of her efforts, we fear that she and her children will face many challenges. Years of emotional scarring in dysfunctional families have affected both parents and children and represent major hurdles that must be crossed if the children are to benefit academically and developmentally from their time in school.

Problems associated with extreme mobility. Many of the homeless parents whom we interviewed reported that their family was experiencing a prolonged period of instability and that they had a variety of school-related problems that were a function of frequent moves. Irene's family had left California and gone to Texas to seek work. They had found it, but then became unemployed again. Eventually, they moved back to California and moved in with relatives, but problems arose. They moved into an emergency shelter and then to a long-term shelter, where they were staying at the time of our interview. Irene and her husband were both working but neither had found a permanent, full-time job. Irene described this time in their lives:

> So we ended up moving, and then, you know, we're thrown back down off our feet. Then we get back up, we're doing real good. Something happens, we're thrown back down. Thing is, been, like, seems like, last five years we've been thrown down, brought back up, thrown down again!

Becky, newly arrived from Texas, had no car. She had been staying in motels and emergency shelters. Although school had been in session for three weeks when we spoke, she had not yet enrolled her children. She said "If I had a car, I would have enrolled 'em like that. [Snapping her fingers.] I would have just kept taking them, you know." Because she was not able to do this, she delayed enrolling her children. One of the boys had been in special education classes and speech classes in Texas, but she did not have his records with her. When she does enroll him, not only will he be behind because of his weeks or months out of school, but there may be further delays in placing him in these special programs.

Becky, at least, knew about her children's needs and the name of their last school in Texas. Another mother with whom we spoke reported that she had moved so many times in the previous year that she could not remember the name of her children's last school nor whether or not they had completed the year. Another mother, newly homeless, was driving her daughters to school, which was miles from the parks and emergency shelter where she had been staying. The day we met her, however, she had completely run out of money and gasoline. Having been middle class most of her life, she had literally *never* ridden public transportation and was so upset by the disasters that had befallen her that she could not even imagine learning how to use public buses to get her five- and seven-year-old daughters to school.

Problems linked to living conditions in shelters and motels. One of San Juan County's major emergency shelters features dormitory-style sleeping; the only nonsleeping room on the women and children's side of the facility is a tiny living room (which often serves as an additional bedroom) where the television is on until ten. Every tape of interviews done there features babies crying for the entire time the tape is running. A field note says, "Only a former kindergarten teacher and mother could do interviews here!" Three of the families we interviewed there had managed, thus far, to keep their children in school, and two of the mothers were also attending. When asked where she and her children studied, one said that, since they had to be away from the shelter between 7:00 a.m. and 5:00 p.m., she and her sons spent a lot of time at the public library. She added, though, that she was having difficulty getting her work done there because she had to find ways to keep her children quiet and occupied. She further noted that she was unable to obtain all of the books she needed to complete her assignments. Because shelter rules limited her family's stay to three weeks, she had not enrolled her boys in school and was trying to work with them herself at the library.

The life of families staying motels is equally unconducive to study. An entire family may stay in a single room. Most of their possessions are left with friends and family, abandoned, or stuffed into their cars. If the television is on, the baby is crying, or adults are talking or fighting, it is hard to concentrate on studies or get enough sleep. Most San Juan County slum motels, which cater to people on welfare and other desperately poor persons, are in areas where it is not safe for children to play or study outside. The motels, themselves, are dingy, unattractive places to stay—one mother told us she had turned down an emergency voucher for a private motel room (given out by a private social service agency) in favor of staying at a congregate shelter because it was cleaner and safer than the motel.

Shame and actual or anticipated discrimination. Underlying many of the problems mentioned above is an unwillingness on the part of the parents to admit their homelessness and to ask for help in solving education-related problems. Recently, two parents in Southern California, living with their family in a car, were arrested because their "pet rat" attacked and killed their infant son. Lucinda, aware of this story, feared she would be arrested, or that her children would be placed in foster care if officials discovered she was homeless. We assured her that *her* situation and that of the arrested parents were different. However, we could not promise her that she would not encounter discrimination. The reality that homeless persons are, at times, victims of prejudice and stereotyping was brought home to us as we listened to the story of Beth, the mother of three boys. She had gone to a school that was near the motel where she and her sons were staying, to see about enrolling her children. She reported:

> One day I was waiting in the office and I wanted to talk to someone, so I was just sitting on the chair. And I heard one of the ladies telling the other lady—oh, yeah, a little boy came in. And there was a lot of children that lived in the hotel [where she was staying] and then the lady said, "Oh, you have to wait over there, because . . . something about "the hotel children." And they would *call* them "the hotel children." To me it was very sad and discriminating.

When asked about her boys' experiences in that school, Beth said that she had left and never enrolled them. She concluded, in a resigned voice, "We weren't in the area very long, anyway."

One Collaborative Effort to Meet the Educational Needs of Homeless Families

Schooling the majority of San Juan County's homeless children. A number of homeless children in San Juan County do not attend school regularly. For example, a third or more of those staying in one emergency shelter in September of 1993 were not in school; there is no reason to think that the situation is any different at the county's other emergency shelter. The schedules of children living in cars, campgrounds, homeless encampments, and slum motels may be even more chaotic and less conducive to regular attendance than those of children staying at shelters.

The vast majority of homeless children who *do* attend school are in regular classrooms, including virtually all of those living in San Juan County's eighteen long-term family shelters (usual stay, sixty days). In many cases, their homeless status is not known to school staff, and no special provisions are made for them. Our evidence to date suggests that schools, in general, have not addressed the homelessness, nor offered inservice training for staff, nor considered whether new policies are needed to deal with this special population. Parents and shelter and school staffs have indicated that the degree to which homeless persons feel comfortable with and well-served by schools varies greatly and that positive experiences are usually due to a sensitive and concerned principal or teacher, not to policy nor established program.

San Juan County's special educational programs for homeless students. The San Juan County Department of Education operates two special educational programs for homeless children. One—called the Outreach program—provides a half-time teacher and aides who make weekly visits to children living temporarily in motels, campgrounds, parks, cars, and so on. The program, which began in December of 1989, has a mobile classroom, but staff also work out of their cars. The second program is Oak Street School, the focus of this chapter.

A case study of Oak Street School. In the case study of this investigation, we engaged in an in-depth examination of Oak Street School, which, as noted earlier, is a collaborative effort involving the San Juan County Department of Education, a local Neighborhood Club, and a church. Its express purpose is to provide educational services especially tailored to the needs of homeless youngsters facing the kinds of challenges we have just described.

Research questions. As we engaged in this study of Oak Street School, we were inspired and guided by several sets of questions. As we spoke with program developers and participants, we considered three related sets of questions. The first set concerns the policy environment of the Oak Street collaboration:

- What existing policies supported the development of the Oak Street School collaboration?

- What changes in policy were necessitated by the Oak Street School collaboration?

- What internal policies, if any, has the collaboration developed to support its efforts?

Another set of questions related to the organizational challenges encountered by persons involved in the implementation of the Oak Street program as the effort unfolded. We were interested in uncovering answers to the following:

- What successes and challenges are being encountered by persons involved in this collaborative effort?

- How are these challenges being addressed?

A third set of questions was linked to the fit between the Oak Street School program and the educational needs of homeless persons in San Juan County. In this regard, we asked:

- What aspects of the program at Oak Street School seem especially well- or ill-suited to address the academic needs of homeless students?

- What aspects of the program seem well- or ill-suited to address the nonacademic needs of this group of youngsters and their families?

Description of the Oak Street School Program

History. Founded in 1990, Oak Street School was initially the "brain child" of an administrator of the Neighborhood Club with a deep concern for the plight of the homeless.[6] She was aware the clubs in one or two other cities had been instrumental in the establishment of shelter schools and that the San Juan County Department of Education was already offering an itinerant outreach program to homeless students. She approached persons within the Department of Education about developing some sort of collaboration. Initially, these two organizations worked together to offer classes in the Neighborhood Club's gymnasium. When the church next door became aware of this effort it asked if it might be able to help, especially in the provision of classroom space and some resources.

Attendance and Scheduling. Students attending Oak Street School live in a relatively concentrated geographic area. Most are living in one of a number of slum motels. All are within reach of a van (operated by the Neighborhood Club), which picks them up for school every day. They attend school Monday through Thursday, from 9 a.m. to 11:30 a.m., and spend Friday mornings at the Neighborhood Club. They are given breakfast and lunch on all of those days as well. Students attending may be in grades kindergarten (K) to eight, and there is a capacity of eighteen students. During the two months when we visited the school regularly, it was almost always at capacity. During this time, nine children left the program, seven entered, and eight were there for the entire period. On the other hand, during the previous five months there had been virtually no turnover, and there were some students who had been in the program for over a year. Because the age range is so wide and the attendance so varied, students were not assigned to grade-level classes. They generally worked independently, assisted on a one-to-one or small-group basis by the two professional staff members and the volunteers.

The role of the Neighborhood Club. The Neighborhood Club provides transportation, breakfast, and lunch for Oak Street students. Neighborhood Club staff and volunteers arrange for the food supplies and do the cooking, serving, and cleaning up. They also supervise the children during mealtimes and provide a program of activities on Friday mornings. The club also recruits many of the volunteers who serve as tutors in the school. When the school began, classes were held in the Neighborhood Club gym. The club originally hoped that it would be able to run its part of the program on an entirely volunteer basis. This proved to be impossible, and two Neighborhood Club staff members were devoting approximately 50 percent of their time to the Oak Street School effort at the time of our study. They were the Director and Assistant Director of Children's Programs and were also responsible for the club's fee-based after-school-care program. In the afternoon, they were assisted by several paid child-care workers and van drivers who worked with children from both programs. In the mornings, they had only themselves and the volunteer cooks, usually one a day. At the time of our study (early spring 1993), both were quite new on the job, having been there only since September 1992 and January 1993, respectively. The director and her assistant were responsible for the Friday morning activity program, for supervising the children at mealtimes, and for seeing that there was food and that it was prepared. The volunteer cooks usually devoted one or two full mornings a week to the program. They arrived in time to have breakfast ready at 8:30 to 8:45 a.m., and lunch at 11:30, and then stayed to clean up. The club also has a custodian who helps to care for the facility.

The role of the church. When the church next door became aware of the Oak Street program, it offered the use of rooms in its large classroom building. The church provides the rooms without charge, handles the custodial services for the facility, and provides a variety of other supports. It is also the source of some of the volunteers. The school uses its television and VCR, and a church outreach purchases program supplies. During the period when we were observing and participating, this committee asked the teachers and Neighborhood Club staff for a "wish list" and purchased the requested items at once. One of us was there the day a chart easel arrived. As the teacher assembled it, she noted that she had requested it only a couple of days earlier, and she indicated that the church typically responded quickly to expressions of need on the part of the school's staff.

The role of the County Department of Education. The San Juan County Department of Education provides a half-time teacher and a half-time instructional aide for the school. Because the students involved in the program are classified as independent study students, the salaries of the teacher and aide are not a function of average daily attendance (ADA), California's usual device for determining school funding, in the same way that regular teachers' salaries are. Rather, they are paid on the basis of the "work accomplished" independent study model used by some other programs, such as home-study and independent-study-type continuation high schools. There is no established amount of time that independent study students must attend class; they must only be making reasonable progress. The Department was already using this funding arrangement in the Outreach program, and it allowed them to establish a school day shorter than the usual day. Students attend class only four mornings a week, for a total of 10 hours for the week. This allows the staff, employed only half time, the extra time needed for such tasks as planning for such a diverse group of students, making home visits, and organizing additional assistance needed by the families.

The school's teaching staff has experienced many changes. When the program first started and was operating in the Neighborhood Club gym, several staff members were sometimes there at one time—occasionally, as many as two teachers and three aides, all struggling to work in one big room, with a wildly diverse group of children, some with very spotty educational histories. As the program stabilized and the classrooms in the church became available, they moved to the current model—one teacher, one aide, and a varying number of volunteers. We have been there when there were as many as six volunteers, and as few as two.

The teacher who was there during the two months when we were observing and participating in the program had just begun teaching there. Her experience was as a special education and resource teacher, so she was used to small groups and individuals working on many different levels. The aide had been with Oak Street ever since the program began. She is a college graduate, with course work in education, although she does not have a teaching credential. She also worked in the itinerant teacher Outreach program. Since many students came to Oak Street after a period of involvement with the Outreach program, she had known some of them, and their families, for a year or more.

The role of the volunteers. The volunteers are a highly skilled group. Many are retired or former teachers. They are recruited in a variety of ways. Some come in through a county volunteer center. Others have responded to a mention in a local newspaper column of the "neighbor helping neighbor" variety. Some call and volunteer after a story about the program runs in the paper. Others hear about it from friends. One, a former teacher and nursery school director, learned about the program from a classmate in an art class at a local junior college. Most spend a morning or two a week at Oak Street, although one, a recent college graduate trying to decide on a career in teaching, was coming every day when we were there. Some concentrate on a special task, such as teaching music or using a phonics program on a one-to-one basis, others perform a variety of tasks.

The academic program. The students usually meet in three classrooms, grouped primarily by age. Most work is individualized, although some small-group instruction also occurs. The program concentrates on reading and mathematics and is, for nearly all students, heavily remedial.

The Oak Street School students. When we asked one Oak Street teacher what the students were like, she responded by saying that they were just like any other students. Some could be in GATE (California's Gifted and Talented Education program); others probably belonged in special education. Another teacher was less generous, telling one of us that "the ability to write a simple sentence is not common." Our own conclusion, based on observation and on working with the students as both a tutor and an instructor, is that there were probably more students working below grade level than above but that some were very bright, indeed. First grader Alejandro, looking at a playdough recipe written and illustrated on a large chart, observed that each person was going to get to put in two spoons of cream of tartar. (There were four students, and the recipe called for eight teaspoons.) Fifth grader Chris wondered how old Maya Angelou was—they had been given only her birth date. When invited to come to the board and figure it out, he immediately inquired whether or not she had had her birthday yet this year, knowing that the response would affect the answer he was calculating. Other children, doing less well academically, exhibited high levels of what Howard Gardner has called "interpersonal" intelligence (Blythe and Gardner 1990). On the other hand, many of the children were struggling with basic reading and math skills, and the ability to write a simple *paragraph* did seem to be rare. Most students had been in and out of many schools. Many had been out of schools altogether, been "found" and enrolled by the Outreach program, and then come to Oak Street as places became available.

We did not see any behavior at Oak Street that we have not observed in regular classrooms. Children occasionally fidgeted, played with their clothes, and chewed gum; one or two even "fell" over in chairs or crawled under the tables. Our current sense is that there was relatively more such behavior than in typical well-run classrooms, which is not surprising; these children were living chaotic lives. However, each behavior was also less disruptive than in normal classrooms of thirty-five students, because the groups were so small and the adult-student ratio so high. This meant that the adults could generally ignore the behavior and either distract the child or just let the behavior fade, which made for a much less confrontational relationship with students than these students might have elicited in other settings.

Policy Issues in Developing This Collaborative Effort to Educate Homeless Children

Existing policies supporting the development of the Oak Street School collaboration. Several preexisting policies and practices of the participating organizations in the Oak Street School collaboration facilitated the development of the collaboration. These included a history of cooperation between Neighborhood Clubs and public schools and certain aspects of California's educational law and educational delivery system. It is necessary to know something about how education is funded and governed in California in order to understand the importance of these preexisting policies and practices.

California's public schools are essentially funded by the state, although local school districts, with locally elected boards, establish and operate the schools. Districts receive monies (around $5,000 annually per child), allocated according to the district's average daily attendance (ADA). If some other entity is given the right to establish a public school within a school district's boundaries, and to collect the ADA for children who attend, the local district loses money. Legislation and policy drastically limit the ability of other entities to establish such schools and collect ADA.

Most counties have several schools districts—there are twenty-seven in San Juan County. However, some unique classes of students may need schooling that individual districts are unable to provide—for example, youngsters in trouble with the law or chronic truants and runaways. The state's education code therefore provides that county departments of education may operate special "county community schools" for such students. ADA for participating students goes to their district of origin; the county department of education then bills the districts for each student involved, and the ADA is transferred to the county department of education's account (Erikson 1993). This practice provided a model for establishing a school for homeless students.

In California, as elsewhere, many Neighborhood Clubs and similar organizations provide after-school care for children attending public schools. These programs are usually fee-based, although scholarships and sliding scale tuitions may be available. Children are picked up from school by these organizations, and there is some limited interaction betweeen the schools and the programs. Schools sometimes refer parents needing child care to the programs; the schools and the organizations usually feel positively about each other. This cordial familiarity was helpful when the discussions that led to the establishment of Oak Street began, since one of the first hurdles was obtaining permission to operate a "competing" public school from the local district in which the school was to be located.

Fortunately—and amazingly—this district also had a policy and program history that facilitated development of the Oak Street collaboration. Some years earlier, the district child welfare and attendance office had become concerned about children whose homeless families were camping in a county park within the district. The district began an energetic outreach program to these families and eventually provided bus service to children living there. Several employees in the chilc welfare and attendance office also became active in private efforts to supply food, clothing, blankets, and other necessities and treats—such as Christmas presents—to these families.

There were, then, a variety of state and local organizational practices and policies in existence that facilitated development of the Oak Street collaboration.

Changes in policy necessitated by the Oak Street collaboration. When the collaboration among the San Juan County Department of Education, the Neighborhood Club, and the church began, very few policies and practices were in place in any participating organization to guide or support such a collaborative endeavor. Both of the noneducational agencies had been involved in some projects that required that they work together with other institutions, but neither had developed formal governance structures nor guidelines for resource allocation for shared activities. Instead, the persons involved in such efforts simply developed operational strategies as various projects unfolded. Worthy of note is that neither the Neighborhood Club nor the church had policies in place *prohibiting* collaborative endeavors.

Establishing the school required immense cooperation from the school district in which Oak Street is located and led to a change in the state's education code, which required the cooperation of all districts and state legislators in the county. As previously explained, funding for schools is distributed to local districts by the state, according to formulas based upon average daily attendance (ADA). State law allowed districts to reimburse county departments of education for the cost of educating certain classes of students in "county community schools" (Oak Street's classification). However, students in such schools "belong" to their home districts; the ADA goes to the districts, and they, in turn, reimburse the county department of education.

This presented great difficulty when San Juan County's Department of Education began its Outreach program for homeless students in 1989—many of the students were not registered in *any* county district or were moving constantly from one district to another. An informal agreement evolved in which all students served in the program were "registered" in a single urban district (whether or not they had ever lived or attended there); the ADA went to that district and then was collected by the County Department. Even so, the funding process was what one official described as "a nightmare," and the County Department of Education began an effort to simplify the system.

After enlisting the support of the county's school districts, and with the assistance of a local homelessness advocacy group, the County Department of Education appealed to a local legislator with a long history of support for education and the interests of the homeless. She was asked to help develop and carry legislation that would simplify the transfer of monies. What emerged was a law allowing county departments of education to establish "county community schools" to serve the homeless *and* providing that ADA for such students be paid directly to the County Department of Education, which would be considered the "district of residence" for these children. The fact that this process had already begun, as planning for Oak Street began, greatly reduced the collaborators' concerns about legal and financial barriers to establishing the school.

Staff of the agencies involved told an interesting story in regard to the passage of this legislation. When this representative first introduced this bill, a number of other policy makers assumed that it was motivated by a desire on the part of San Juan County citizens to segregate the homeless in a separate school. According to all involved, this idea had not entered their minds; they were simply trying to broaden the options for these youngsters. They noted, however, that it took "quite a bit of scrambling," with officials from various agencies across the county and advocates for the homeless lobbying for passage of the bill, before the skeptics were willing to support it.[7]

Policies the collaboration has developed to support its efforts. Within the Oak Street collaboration, little has been done, thus far, to establish formal policy. As we note in the next section, crises or immediate needs tend to be the forces that inspire decisions; these decisions, then, become the unofficial policies and standard operating procedures of the collaboration. Participants in this effort indicate that this ad hoc approach has both merits and weaknesses. They endorse the idea that procedures, rules, and guidelines need to be flexible but bemoan the reality that, sometimes, crises occur because no policy is in place to prevent them. In that regard, officials from the Neighborhood Club and the County Department of Education are working to develop greater coordination and tighter planning.

The Unfolding of Interagency Collaboration in the Oak Street Effort

Successes and challenges encountered in this collaborative effort. In the collaborative venture resulting in Oak Street School, there have been some genuine successes. The greatest, perhaps, is the reality that a county department of education, a relatively small, private, social service agency, and a church have managed to put together and operate such a program at all. Students seem very comfortable there— students who might have had difficulty in larger, more regimented classes. Because the program had been operating for less than three years at the time of which we write, and the pace had been hectic, no staff person had yet had time to examine records and get some sense of how the children's attendance and performance compare to local norms, but such an effort may well reveal that these students attend more regularly and/or achieve at greater rates than do others similarly situated but attending regular public school classes. Certainly, teachers, aides, and volunteers at Oak Street believe that this is the case.

Some real problems, however, have arisen in the unfolding of this effort. For example, the planning process for implementation was brief and inadequate; goals were not articulated, and no standards by which to measure success were established. Two crises illustrate the incompleteness of the planning process. The first nearly ended the program before it began. The Department of Education had promised to provide transportation for the students. At the last minute, because of budgetary constraints, it was unable to do so. Rather than give up the idea of the program, the Neighborhood Club took responsibility for transportation and then quickly had to raise the funds to allow them to do so. Although this problem was resolved, representatives of the Neighborhood Club felt some frustration over being forced to scramble at the last minute.

The second illustration of incomplete planning concerns the use of the volunteers; two difficulties involving volunteers might have been avoided if more complete planning had been done. The first problem arose because the Neighborhood Club staff members had imagined that they would be able to use volunteers to handle cooking and student supervision before, during, and after meals and for the Friday morning enrichment program. When we were spending time there, using volunteer cooks had been reasonably successful, but primarily so because of the dedication of two women who each often worked two or three mornings a week. Not surprisingly, it proved impossible for the cooks to supervise the students at mealtimes, and a reliable supply of volunteers for this purpose, and for the Friday morning program, never materialized. The Neighborhood Club ended up hiring additional staff. We found ourselves wondering if better communication and planning among all three agencies could not have circumvented this problem. Certainly, educators who are used to overseeing groups of children for extended periods of time and on a daily basis are well acquainted with the personnel needs created by efforts to feed, supervise, and teach a group of eighteen active youngsters. On the other hand, funding for extensive planning was never available, and a functioning program, providing real service, nevertheless emerged—and in a very short time, at that.

Another problem with volunteers, which is related to lack of communication and planning, arose in the course of this collaborative effort. At Oak Street, as of early 1993, there had not been enough discussion of who was responsible for what, and no organization had taken responsibility for training volunteers. Those individuals did not receive any formal orientation to the program, nor was there time set aside to explain the curriculum. Volunteers spoke of their frustration over this, and some raised serious questions about the program. One, who had come for the first time on a day when the aide who worked with the younger children had a "sub" wondered aloud to us about the fact that "the volunteers have more education than the teachers." Believing that some volunteers were not being used effectively, another volunteer, herself a credentialed teacher, observed that "all this help" might better be used in overcrowded, regular public school classrooms.

A related concern is redundancy of program efforts. Persons familiar with the problems and pitfalls of collaborative efforts have suggested that it is vital that participating agencies be intimately acquainted with the programs, policies, and services of the other participants (Crowson and Boyd 1993; Guthrie and Guthrie 1991; Payzant 1992). At Oak Street, planning and communication have focused primarily upon the immediate needs of the program, and personnel from the participating agencies have not had the time to become acquainted with each other's resources. For example, people at the Neighborhood

Club, sensing a need, were talking about starting a jobs program for parents. They had not done any formal needs assessment, their analysis of the parents' position was somewhat limited, and they did not seem to be aware that the County Department of Education, local districts, and community colleges already have programs that might be very relevant. Indeed, we saw several areas where there is considerable overlap with other available programs, including some in regular public schools.

Efforts to address the challenges of cooperative work. Most efforts to cope with the challenges of interagency efforts at Oak Street School have evolved in reaction to problems as the program has developed, as illustrated by the stories we have told about the transportation crisis and the need to hire staff to supervise Oak Street children when they were at the Neighborhood Club. This second problem was not solved, however, simply by hiring someone to care for the Oak Street children. They were being supervised by volunteers and, later, by a paid coordinator, while the children in the club's fee-based after-school-care program were overseen by different staff. Inevitably, there were conflicts over space, supplies, rules, and so on. This was eventually resolved by a turnover in staff and the club's decision to put its new after-school program staff in charge of the Oak Street children, as well. Had the planning process not been primarily reactive, this conflict might have been anticipated and defused in advance.

Interestingly, perhaps the collaboration has not learned as much from this incident as they might have. Two sets of rules for the children's behavior were in effect when we were studying the program intensively—one in the classrooms, under the teaching staff, and another at the Neighborhood Club, where children were supervised by Neighborhood Club staff. Neither organization was even aware of this, until one of us asked a Neighborhood Club staffer about it; she then asked us to get her a copy of the classroom rules. There is also great lack of clarity about supervision of the children at transitional times; for example, there is no standard policy about what should happen if the children arrive for lunch and no Neighborhood Club staffer is on hand. This situation arose on three different occasions when we were observing at the school: one time, the teacher asked one of us to stay (we did); one time the teacher stayed until a Neighborhood Club staffer arrived; and one time the children were simply left under the supervision of the volunteer cook—who was not in the room and could not see the children from the kitchen. Such problems are normal; the difficulty is finding the resources for the planning and communication needed to deal with them.

There is also the possibility that there is a limit to the ability of the Neighborhood Club to come up with financial backing in response to future crises. One thoughtful observer told us:

> I do see a lot of social service agencies get carried away. They try to take on too many things, and nothing gets done very well. A goal, even before you expand a program, whether it be monetary concerns or not, is that they're doing a really good job in what they're doing.

Worthy of note is the fact that we did not find resistance to the notions of better communication and planning and a clearer delineation of responsibility. Indeed, Oak Street program staff are reflecting on some of these matters themselves. For example, the educator who oversees the program is concerned about the issue of program quality and articulation with regular classrooms and has made some curricular and staffing changes in the 1993–1994 school year. In turn, the chief administrator of the Neighborhood Club is looking for funding to do volunteer training, and all of the staff members to whom we spoke of these matters reflected thoughtfully upon them during our conversations.

The "Fit" Between Oak Street's Program and the Needs of Homeless Children

Academic needs. After her first visit to the program, one of us wrote in an observer's comment in her field notes: "My goodness! They had thirteen children and eight adults, all of whom are probably college graduates and most of whom seem to have been teachers, and the best they can do is provide individualized support for doing workbooks?" This comment reflects our greatest concern about the match between Oak Street's programs and the academic needs of its homeless students. Many of the students seemed to be entering the school already behind their nonhomeless peers and, ironically, may be receiving less in terms of content than—and are definitely spending less time in school than—their more privileged counterparts. Whether this situation can be remedied is not clear.

As previously explained, the children are in class only ten hours per week, and the curriculum is essentially limited to reading and math. Occasional science or social studies lessons occur, but there is certainly no coherent curriculum in these areas, nor in the arts—

although music is taught once a week by a wonderful volunteer. There is also no physical education. Indeed, they do not even have recess. For children who spend the rest of the day crowded into rooms in motels located in places where it may be dangerous to play outside, this seems unfortunate.

We suspected initially that the workbook-focused nature of the program might be partially a function of underuse of the volunteers, and still think so, but this problem is not easily resolved. Perhaps training for the volunteers would be helpful, but there is evidence to suggest that many volunteers prefer the somewhat limited nature of their involvement. As educators who have worked with paraprofessionals know, it is easy to simply tell an aide or a volunteer to "help Diego with page seven in his math workbook"; little explanation is required, and the next volunteer can easily take up where the previous one left off. If, however, students are working on individually designed tasks using literature and math manipulatives, for example, each successive person who works with a student will need an orientation, daily written records will need to be kept to track progress and prescribe new activities, and so on. All of this takes time and energy—outside the classroom.

The limited time for academics is also not a problem that is easily addressed. Although both the County Department of Education and the Neighborhood Club would like to expand to a full-day program, with the current funding scheme, this would require the addition of sixteen more pupils—to generate funds for a full-time teacher and aide. The pupil:teacher ratio would then be the same as in any other classroom—in a class which covers nine grade levels. In addition, if pupils attended full time, staff would have no "extra" time to devote to home visits, to meeting social service needs, to individualizing curriculum, and so on.

Moreover, the student population can have a very high turnover, which may mean that a very highly structured but individualized approach involving workbooks may be the most realistic option. As for the concentration on reading and math, that may be precisely what is needed. Perhaps these children, most of whom are far behind their peers academically and have had inconsistent and sporadic school experiences, will benefit more from ten hours a week of individual and small group tutoring in reading and math than from a longer day and a more diverse curriculum in a regular classroom. We, however, contend that it would be good for there to be more individual diagnosis and prescription than we observed, that it should be possible to diversify the curriculum to some extent—for example, using content-area materials and themes in reading and math instruction—and that Oak Street needs to consider establishing guidelines for how long students stay in the program before being transitioned to regular classes. There has also been frequent turnover in the teaching staff—there has been a new teaching arrangement every year, so far, which has complicated curriculum development and program continuity.

It is important to note that the program's administrator (in the county office) is concerned about these same issues and has made major changes for the 1993–1994 school year—stabilizing the teaching force and introducing an improved curriculum that has been successful with home-schooling students in the county. There are also plans for doing more diagnosis of individual students and for more attention to transferring students to regular full-day programs if their academic and other needs can be met there.

It should also be said that there is no question that parents and students respond positively to the program *as it stands*. One family we met had gone to great lengths to stay in the area *just* so their children could continue to attend Oak Street. The children, both bright, had made great improvements, not only in academics, but also in behavior and ability to stay on task, both the teaching staff and Neighborhood Club staff told us—an assessment obviously shared by the parents.

Nonacademic needs. Oak Street School is certainly a "homeless-friendly" place. All of the adults working with the children are interested and welcoming. Discrimination is not an issue. Other students do not present a problem, either, for everyone is in the same situation. The three agencies involved make every effort to overcome nonacademic barriers that might inhibit the children's learning. School supplies are provided, and students are usually given donated backpacks to keep them in. Homework for primary students goes home in zip-lock plastic bags, along with the crayons, paper, pencils, scissors, and other supplies that are needed. Transportation, a challenge for many homeless families, is provided. The personal connection between Oak Street families and the drivers of the Neighborhood Club vans, plus the ability of the drivers to "follow" students if they move within a reasonable distance, probably enhances the attendance of these pupils.

The meals provided by the Neighborhood Club would also be available in regular schools, but the breakfasts at the Neighborhood Club—which feature such items as hot French toast, pancakes, and scrambled eggs—are better than the cold breakfasts typically served in public schools. The volume of food available is greater than in public school meals, as well—a real issue for older children, who often find school meals too skimpy. On the other hand, fresh fruit and vegetables rarely seemed to be on the menu. Most food comes from local food pantries, which stock only staples, and the menus are a function of the availability of food and the planning of volunteer cooks.

When the program began, it offered access to medical care, but the community services agency which provided this care lost its grant and the program ended. There are no mental health or dental services, either, but the close relationship between the adults and the children makes it somewhat more likely that families will ask for help when it is needed, and the staff is quick to try to find resources when they become aware of a need. Additionally, the Neighborhood Club and church provide donated clothing, Christmas presents, and holiday celebrations. The school and the children are also frequently recipients of gifts and services from businesses and the community at large.

CONCLUSION

As we engaged in this investigation, we found ourselves seeking to relate the answers we were finding to specific questions about Oak Street School to an additional, more general question:

• What can we learn from the Oak Street collaboration that can guide scholars, practitioners, and policy makers in developing and implementing effective educational programs for homeless youngsters?

Reflecting on findings, we discovered that both the successes and challenges encountered by those involved in this effort held valuable lessons. To the extent that Oak Street has been successful, it can be said that the collaborative aspect of the undertaking has, in many ways, been responsible. Concomitantly, the problems we have seen suggest insufficiencies in the collaborative process that could have been addressed earlier; doing so, we feel, would have strengthened the program.

Success as a Function of the Collaborative Aspects of This Effort

Oak Street School could not exist without the collaboration of the participating agencies. The very fact of Oak Street School's existence bears witness to a genuine concern for the homeless, to a willingness to consider nontraditional approaches to serving this population, and to persistence in seeking ways to implement alternative educational strategies in San Juan County, California. These attitudes, in our view, are contributors to the success, thus far, of the collaboration. Also important are the many ways persons involved in the effort have sought to be responsive to the multiple needs of the youngsters they serve. The fact that door-to-door transportation is provided; the reality that, at Oak Street, there is no stigma attached to homelessness; and the provision of nutritious meals, take-home supplies, clothing, and the like all indicate that persons involved in this collaboration are sensitive to the complexity of the circumstances facing their clients.

It seems to us that both the energy fueling the cooperative undertaking and the ability of Oak Street's workers to provide a range of services grow out of the fact that this is a multiagency effort. The Neighborhood Club is able to draw upon their fund-raising and organizing experience in the community to fund services that the County Department of Education cannot—such as the transportation and the Friday morning enrichment activities. Neither they nor the church have complicated bureaucracies and rules and purchasing departments. If Oak Street needs a chart rack, the church can have it there two days later. If neither the county nor local districts can transport the children, the Neighborhood Club can find a way. The church has committees that are used to providing financial support and materials to worthy causes—and, of course, an unused classroom building and custodial services to go with it. Southern California is currently experiencing a classroom shortage, and many schools already have regular classes meeting in such places as school libraries; it is doubtful that a local school district could have provided Oak Street with a "home." The County Department of Education already had experience in working with homeless children, the political clout to work for enabling legislation, and the connections to local districts required to get the necessary permission to operate a "competing" public school program. It is unlikely that the Neighborhood Club, the original initiator of the effort, could have managed all this—nor, of course, could they have supplied teachers, materials, and curricula as easily as the County Department of Education could.

Difficulties That are a Function of Insufficiencies in the Collaborative Process

The challenges that Oak Street has encountered are also related to the ways in which this particular collaborative process has unfolded. Problems with needs assessment and the establishment of goals;

communication, governance, and stewardship; finance; and the lack of planned formative and summative evaluation are related to both the problems that they discussed with us and the concerns that we, ourselves, have about the program.

Needs assessment and the establishment of goals. Grace Pung, Larry F. Guthrie, and Robert Guthrie (1991) suggest that collaborative attempts to provide integrated services for children, such as Oak Street's, begin with a thorough needs assessment and a survey of available resources. Would-be collaborators can then determine whether or not they have something to offer, and whether there will still be needs unmet. The Guthries (1991), Robert Crowson and William Boyd (1993), and Thomas Payzant (1992) all emphasize the need for wide community participation in this effort, and for sufficient time for the process; Michael Kirst and Milbrey McLaughlin (1990) would like to see students, themselves, involved. In the case of Oak Street, this process occurred in a very truncated manner.

The San Juan County Department of Education had done some research into the problems of homeless children prior to establishing their original outreach program, and experience garnered in that program indicated that there was a population of children in slum motels that could be a source of students. However, no formal effort was made to learn why these children (some of whom had been living in the same motel and attending Oak Street for more than a year by the time we were there) were not attending regular school, when others, living in the same motels were doing so.

No serious efforts were made to learn whether other agencies could be enlisted to provide some of the services Oak Street children needed—such as medical care, for example, which Oak Street, itself, was eventually unable to provide. The collaborators do not always use each other's expertise, either. For example, the County Department of Education surely has consultants familiar with the Department of Agriculture's surplus foods program. The Neighborhood Club staff doing food shopping was unaware of this program, until one of us mentioned it, but it is widely used by public schools.

The collaborators also had only the most general sort of goals for the program. As it unfolded, this became a problem. If a new need, such as the need for mental health services, arises, ad hoc decision making about whether the collaboration should try to meet it is the norm—there are no guidelines. In addition, without formal goals, it has been hard for the participants to define success and to consider whether the effort they are expending is worthwhile.

Communication, governance, and stewardship. Scholars examining the process of interagency collaboration advocate that plans for collaborative efforts specify means for sharing information and for day-to-day communication (Crowson and Boyd 1993; Guthrie and Guthrie 1991; Kirst and McLaughlin 1990; Payzant 1992). Participants in the collaboration need to know about each other's resources, policies, and procedures and need to keep each other informed of their actions in regard to the collaboration. At Oak Street, we found the Neighborhood Club considering offering job training to parents that might better have been provided by the County Department of Education's Regional Opportunities Program (ROP)—of which they were unaware. They had never discussed this idea with the County Department of Education, probably because it is hard to find time for vital short-range planning, let alone for discussion of long-range proposals such as this one. We found that neither the Neighborhood Club nor the school's staff were aware that they had established two separate codes of behavior for the children.

No strong system was in place for even the most ordinary communication—for example, a volunteer log book with room for comments existed but was not regularly used, and no similar communication path for staff existed at all. Volunteers giving many hours of service that were vital to the collaboration's success sometimes harbored serious reservations about the program—which no one was aware of or addressing. For example, a volunteer who devoted two mornings a week to the program asked one of us what we thought about how little time the children spent at school. Did we not think they should have *extra* time, rather than less? If this makes her increasingly uncomfortable, she may become a less enthusiastic volunteer—but there is no formal way for her to surface this valid concern.

Governance procedures are equally vague. Barbara Gray (1989) argues that collaborative efforts to solve problems are difficult when the collaborative partners have unequal power. Crowson and Boyd (1993) speak of the need for someone—or some agency—to have "stewardship" of collaborations—there has to be someplace where "the buck stops." However, they note, this is not easily arranged; if one individual or agency is "in charge," in some sense, of a collaborative effort, they are likely to have line authority in only their own organization.

How will they exercise needed supervision of the employees of other agencies? (Public schools are familiar with this problem; principals, for example, may have unclear authority over auxiliary personnel such as Chapter One staff, who are paid by categorical monies, or those paid by county offices of education, as speech teachers, for example, often are.) Oak Street avoids confrontation over these matters; there are no power struggles, but perhaps this is primarily because *no* one agency or person truly *has* stewardship or tries to exercise power; *no* one agency or person is responsible for seeing that the goals of the program are met and commitments are kept. Indeed, the goals are mostly implicit, and commitments are not strongly articulated. This does not mean that agencies and individuals are *not* deeply committed, only that the goals and commitments are general and imprecise, and cannot readily guide policy.

Finance. In a thoughtful article on financing school-linked services, in *Education and Urban Society,* Michael Kirst (1993) suggests that the best procedure is not to seek new sources of funding for services for children and families. Schools will never have the funds to hire nurses, doctors, dentists, social workers, and psychologists in sufficient numbers, he says. Rather, "schools must use existing financing sources for programs in health, social services, juvenile justice and so on, . . . [diverting] these funding and program streams and aiming them at one location at or near the school" (167). Seeing the Neighborhood Club struggling to finance meals, transportation, supervision, and limited social services for these children, we had to wonder if these should be the resources they brought to the collaboration—and how long they could bear these burdens. In a related vein, Crowson and Boyd (1993) observe that the provision of consolidated services for children is not necessarily less expensive than providing fragmented services, although, hopefully, it may be more effective and equitable. Indeed, initially, collaboration may be *more* expensive than noncollaboration, because time is needed to plan, to do cross training of agency personnel, and so on. At Oak Street, such efforts have not been made; they are needed, but none of the partners has the money to finance this extra planning and training time.

These observations about financing collaboration might also be made about financing innovative educational services, and Oak Street is a case in point. The special educational environment Oak Street hopes to provide—low teacher:pupil ratios, individualized programs, the social and emotional support needed to foster an environment where learning *can* occur—do not come cheap. Indeed, the only way Oak Street has been able to provide such an environment is by way of two major compromises: they have seriously shortened the school day and narrowed the curriculum. It may well be argued that these compromises are worth it—that attendance is better and academic improvement greater than it would have been had these children continued trying to attend regular public schools. Unfortunately, due to lack of necessary time and funding, the collaboration has not yet been able to test the truth of these assertions.

Lack of formative and summative evaluation. Scholars and practitioners investigating current efforts to provide comprehensive services to school children and their families—whether via collaborative efforts or not—emphasize the need for evaluation of these undertakings (Crowson and Boyd 1993; Guthrie and Guthrie 1991; Payzant 1992). They also note that the outcomes of such efforts can be extremely difficult to measure, since they may occur over long periods of time. We may not know the impact of interventions for very young children at risk for educational failure until we compare those children with controls when both groups are in their early twenties, for example. In the case of homeless children, the very difficulties that cause some of their educational problems—high mobility, lack of records, confounding socioeconomic variables—make it *extremely* difficult to do such evaluations. Simply examining attendance records for children who move several times a year for several years may be impossible—they are likely to have partial cumulative folders in half a dozen districts. Identifying a group of "controls" for comparison purposes—highly mobile homeless children who do *not* attend programs such as Oak Street, for example—is not only difficult, but following *their* progress would present similar problems. Thus, standard evaluation procedures would be difficult to implement.

This being said, it is still important to make the attempt, and, thus far, the Oak Street collaboration has not been able to do so. Again, this is partially an issue of funding. The teaching staff in the program has no time for such work, nor does the paid staff of the Neighborhood Club—not that they could get access to academic records anyway. There is also the issue of what is most important—service to children who are clearly in need, or evaluations advocated by legislators and university scholars. A case in point is a recent recommendation to Congress made by the federal office charged with implementing the educational provisions of the Stewart B. McKinney Homeless Assistance

Act. This office had been directed to do a feasibility study that would devise a plan for counting the number of homeless school-aged children in each state. The feasibility study found that such a survey would cost $1 million. Program directors recommended to Congress that the study not be done; the money, they felt, could better be spent on the children (F. Vinson, personal communication, 3 February 1994). Oak Street staff can make a similar argument.

Nevertheless, careful analysis of data on the educational needs and progress of Oak Street's youngsters could improve the curricular and pedagogical dimensions of this program and, in turn, educational outcomes for the children it serves. This could have an impact far beyond the twenty to forty children this program can serve in a year; the costs involved in doing such an evaluation should be considered in light of this larger purpose.

As we have seen, San Juan County is believed to have as many as 6,000 homeless children. The vast majority of these will never get to come to Oak Street School, nor is it likely that 150 to 200 other Oak Street Schools will be developed to serve them. These youngsters will continue to attend public schools—often several in a single year. It should also be noted that the very existence of Oak Street may have lulled the community at large into believing that "homeless children are being taken care of in our county." The school is regularly featured in newspaper stories, and many organizations and individuals have contributed generously to the program. Community groups have extensively refurbished one of the Neighborhood Club vans, sponsored Christmas shopping sprees for the youngsters, and donated clothing, gifts, and so on. Local persons whom we meet in other contexts, learning of our interest in homeless children, frequently tell us "Oh, there's a wonderful school you should visit"; further discussion often elicits an indication that they believe "all" homeless children are being taken care of there. This is, of course, not Oak Street's fault but illustrates the complexities of developing public policy, trying social innovations, and sustaining community concern and support.

Oak Street cannot, of course, hope to "take care of" all San Juan County's homeless children, but Oak Street *could* serve as a laboratory for devising, testing, and validating materials and approaches to be used with homeless—and other very mobile—students. The County Department of Education, which operates the school, is in a perfect position to disseminate this information to all schools within the county. The county could offer in-service workshops and materials and, possibly, assume responsibility for such support services as maintaining the records of highly mobile students, doing instant assessments when such students arrive at a new school, handling placement paperwork, and so on. It is clear that none of this can be done without some additional source of funding, but, if it were done, a successful Oak Street could do far more than it is presently able to do—which is to assist a small group of homeless students. With careful collection of data, and critical scrutiny and adjustment of programs and practices, Oak Street could become a "lighthouse" school, illuminating a path towards improved educational outcomes and enhanced life chances for many of the county's neediest students.

NOTES

1. Oak Street is a pseudonym.

2. The term *homeless* is variously defined. In this instance, the compilers of the statistic have used a "broad" definition, similar to the definition used in the federal McKinney Homeless Assistance Act: A homeless person is "one who (a) lacks a fixed, regular, and adequate nighttime residence or (b) lives in a shelter, an institution (other than a prison or other institutionalized facility), or a place not designed for or ordinarily used as a sleeping accommodation for human beings" (Stronge 1992). This includes persons living temporarily in campgrounds, cars, motels, garages, and parks, as well as those in shelters and on the streets.

3. San Juan County is a pseudonym for the Southern California county where we conducted this investigation. Similarly, organizational and interviewee names have been changed.

4. We have chosen to call the organization involved a Neighborhood Club, a name which we have made up.

5. We are deeply grateful to our colleague, Patricia McDonough, Assistant Professor of Education in the Graduate School of Education and Information Studies at the University of California, Los Angeles, for this assistance.

6. She is currently employed as the director of one of the county's largest shelters.

7. We were not surprised to hear of this suspicion, given the very conservative reputation of San Juan County, but feel sure, ourselves, that those persons involved in the founding of Oak Street had no such motives and note that many local homeless parents and advocates for the homeless supported the founding of the school enthusiastically and continue to support it now.

REFERENCES

Balfour, R. (January 1991). Teaching the homeless. *Thrust for Educational Leadership*, 30–32.

Bassuk, E. L., and E. M. Gallagher. (1990). The impact of homelessness on children. *Child and Youth Services* 14(1): 19–33.

Blythe, T., and H. Gardner. (1990). A school for all intelligences. *Educational Leadership* 47(7): 33–37.

Bullard, S. (1993). Where the heart is. *Teaching Tolerance* 2(2): 19–25.

Crowson, R. L., and W. L. Boyd. (1993). Coordinated services for children: Designing arks for storms and seas unknown. *American Journal of Education* 101(2): 140–179.

Dryfoos, J. G. (1991). School-based social and health services for at-risk students. *Urban Education* 26(1): 118–137.

Eddowes, E. A. (1992). Children and homelessness: Early childhood and elementary education. In *Educating homeless children and adolescents: Evaluating policy and practice,* ed. J. H. Stronge, 99–114. Newbury Park, Calif.: Sage Publications.

Eddowes, E. A., and J. R. Hranitz. (1989). Educating children of the homeless. *Childhood Education* 65(4): 197–200.

Erikson, J. T., and Associates. (1993). *California laws relating to minors.* Gardena, Calif.: Law Distributors/Harcourt Brace Jovanovich Legal and Professional Publications.

First, P. F. (1992). The reality: The status of education for homeless children and youth. In *Educating homeless children and adolescents: Evaluating policy and practice,* ed. J. H. Stronge, 79–95. Newbury Park, Calif.: Sage Publications.

Gewirtzman, R., and I. Fodor. (1987). The homeless child at school: From welfare hotel to classroom. *Child Welfare* 66(3): 237–245.

Glaser, B. G., and A. L. Strauss. (1967). *The discovery of grounded theory: Strategies for qualitative research.* Chicago: Aldine.

González, M. L. (1990). School + home = A program for educating homeless students. *Phi Delta Kappan* 71(10): 785–787.

González, M. L. (1991). School-community partnerships and the homeless. *Educational Leadership* 49(1): 23–24.

González, M. L. (1992). Educational climate for the homeless: Cultivating the family and school relationship. In *Educating homeless children and adolescents: Evaluating policy and practice,* ed. J. H. Stronge, 194–211. Newbury Park, Calif.: Sage Publications.

Gore, A. (1990). Public policy and the homeless. *American Psychologist* 45(8): 960–962.

Gray, B. (1989). *Collaborating: Finding common ground for multiparty problems.* San Francisco: Jossey-Bass.

Guthrie, G. P., and L. F. Guthrie. (1991). Streamlining interagency collaboration for youth at risk. *Educational Leadership* 49(1): 17–22.

Hall, J. A., and P. L. Maza. (1990). No fixed address: The effects of homelessness on families and children. *Child and Youth Services* 14(1): 35–47.

Heath, S. B., and M. W. McLaughlin. (1987). A child resource policy: Moving beyond dependence on school and family. *Phi Delta Kappan* 68(8): 576–580.

Helm, V. M. (1992). The legal context: From access to success in education for homeless children and youth. In *Educating homeless children and adolescents: Evaluating policy and practice,* ed. J. H. Stronge, 26–41. Newbury Park, Calif.: Sage Publications.

Johnson, J. F. (1992). Educational support services for homeless children and youth. In *Educating homeless children and adolescents: Evaluating policy and practice,* ed. J. H. Stronge, 153–176. Newbury Park, Calif.: Sage Publications.

Kagan, S. L. (1989). Early care and education: Beyond the schoolhouse doors. *Phi Delta Kappan* 71(2): 107–112.

Kirst, M. W. (1991). Improving children's services: Overcoming barriers, creating new opportunities. *Phi Delta Kappan* 72(8): 615–618.

Kirst, M. W. (1993). Financing school-linked services. *Education and Urban Society* 25(2): 166–174.

Kirst, M. W., and M. W. McLaughlin. (1990). Rethinking policy for children: Implications for educational administration. In *Educational leadership and changing contexts of families, communities, and schools,* ed. B. Mitchell and L. L. Cunningham, 69–90 (89th yearbook, part 2, National Society for the Study of Education. Chicago: University of Chicago Press.

Korinek, L., C. Walther-Thomas, and V. K. Laycock. (1992). Educating special needs homeless children and youth. In *Educating homeless children and adolescents: Evaluating policy and practice,* ed. J. H. Stronge, 133–152. Newbury Park, Calif.: Sage Publications.

Kozol, J. (1988). *Rachel and her children: Homeless families in America.* New York: Fawcett Columbine.

Linehan, M. F. (1992). Children who are homeless: Educational strategies for school personnel. *Phi Delta Kappan* 74(1): 61–66.

Lofland, J., and L. H. Lofland. (1984). *Analyzing social settings: A guide to qualitative observation and analysis*, ed. 2. Belmont, Calif.: Wadsworth.

Maharaj, D. (May 14, 1993). Plight of children worsens. *Los Angeles Times* A1, A26–27.

Maza, P. L., and J. A. Hall. (1988). *Homeless children and their families: A preliminary study.* Washington, D.C.: Child Welfare League of America.

Mihaly, L. (1991). Beyond the numbers: Homeless families with children. In *Homeless children and youth: A new American dilemma*, ed. J. H. Kryder-Coe, L. M. Salamon, and J. M. Molnar, 11–32. New Brunswick, N.J.: Transaction.

Molnar, J. M., W. R. Rath, and T. P. Klein. (1990). Constantly compromised: The impact of homelessness on children. *Journal of Social Issues* 46(4): 109–124.

Moyer, K. (1990). Schools for the homeless. *Education Digest* 55(6): 48–50.

Payzant, T. W. (1992). New beginnings in San Diego: Developing a strategy for interagency collaboration. *Phi Delta Kappan* 74(2): 139–146.

Portner, J. (December 9, 1992). Schooling the homeless: Few programs address the daunting challenge. *Education Week* 12(14): 1, 14–15.

Powers, J. L., and B. Jaklitsch. (1992). Adolescence and homelessness: The unique challenge for secondary education. In *Educating homeless children and adolescents: Evaluating policy and practice*, ed. J. H. Stronge, 115–132. Newbury Park, Calif.: Sage Publications.

Rafferty, Y. (1991). Developmental and educational consequences of homelessness on children and youth. In *Homeless children and youth: A new American dilemma*, ed. J. H. Kryder-Coe, L. M. Salamon, and J. M. Molnar, 105–139. New Brunswick, N.J.: Transaction.

Rafferty, Y., and M. Shinn. (1991). The impact of homelessness on children. *American Psychologist* 46(11): 1170–1179.

Rivlin, L. G. (1990). Home and homelessness in the lives of children. *Child and Youth Services* 14(1): 5–17.

Robertson, M. J. (1991a). Homeless women with children: The role of alcohol and other drug abuse. *American Psychologist* 46(11): 1198–1204.

Robertson, M. J. (1991b). Homeless youth: An overview of recent literature. In *Homeless children and youth: A new American dilemma*, ed. J. H. Kryder-Coe, L. M. Salamon, and J. M. Molnar, 33–68. New Brunswick, N.J.: Transaction.

Schatzman, L., and A. L. Strauss. (1973). *Field research: Strategies for a natural sociology.* Englewood Cliffs, N.J.: Prentice-Hall.

Schorr, L. B. (1988). *Within our reach: Breaking the cycle of disadvantage.* New York: Anchor Books.

Schorr, L. B. (1989). Early intervention to reduce intergenerational disadvantage: The new policy context. *Teachers College Record* 90(3): 363–374.

Shinn, M., J. R. Knickman, and B. C. Weitzman. (1991). Social relationships and vulnerability to becoming homeless among poor families. *American Psychologist* 46(11): 1180–1187.

Solarz, A. (1992). To be young and homeless: Implications of homelessness for children. In *Homelessness: A national perspective,* ed. M. J. Robertson and M. Greenblatt, 275–286. New York: Plenum.

Stronge, J. H. (1992). The background: History and problems of schooling for the homeless. In *Educating homeless children and adolescents: Evaluating policy and practice,* ed. J. H. Stronge, 3–25. Newbury Park, Calif.: Sage Publications.

Sullivan, P. A., and S. P. Damrosch. (1987). Homeless women and children. In *The homeless in contemporary society,* ed. R. D. Bingham, R. E. Green, and S. B. White, 82–98. Newbury Park, Calif.: Sage Publications.

Tower, C. C. (1992). The psychosocial context: Supporting education for homeless children and youth. In *Educating homeless children and adolescents: Evaluating policy and practice,* ed. J. H. Stronge, 42–61. Newbury Park, Calif.: Sage Publications.

Van de Ven, A. H., and G. Walker. (1984). The dynamics of interorganizational coordination. *Administrative Science Quarterly* 29: 598–621.

Van de Ven, A. H., G. Walker, and J. Liston. (1979). Coordination patterns within an interorganizational network. *Human Relations* 32(1): 19–36.

Van Ry, M. (1992). The context of family: Implications for educating homeless children. In *Educating homeless children and adolescents: Evaluating policy and practice,* ed. J. H. Stronge, 62–78. Newbury Park, Calif.: Sage Publications.

Wells, A. S. (1990). Educating homeless children. *Education Digest* 55(8): 30–32.

II

Organizational and Management Issues Surrounding Coordination

Chapter 6

Structures and Strategies: Toward an Understanding of Alternative Models for Coordinated Children's Services

Robert L. Crowson
William Lowe Boyd

INTRODUCTION

The soaring number of American children living in poverty has triggered a surge of efforts to improve the coordination of services for children. With the breakdown of traditional family structures, the multiple needs of children and families, particularly in poverty areas, are unprecedented. Sadly, our fragmented service-delivery system in urban America far from meets these multiple needs adequately. Many believe that human services institutions in urban environments (e.g., health, education, family social services) can be much more effective if restructured toward a complementary and coordinated system of children and family assistance.

This problem is much easier to frame than are the structures and strategies for its solution. There is no "one best way" to restructure human services institutions toward coordination. Although practical

The research reported here was supported in part by the Office of Educational Research and Improvement (OERI) of the U.S. Department of Education through a grant to the National Center on Education in the Inner Cities at Temple University. The opinions expressed do not necessarily reflect the position of the supporting agencies and no official endorsement should be inferred.

savvy about "what works" and "what doesn't" is growing, a great deal remains to be learned about the design and implementation of successful collaborative ventures (Behrman 1992, 7; Crowson and Boyd 1993). Toward that end, this paper compares and analyzes features of the models represented in five coordinated services efforts located, respectively, in Chicago, Houston, Los Angeles, Minneapolis, and Charlotte, North Carolina.

The variety of contemporary coordinated ventures is impressive. Efforts to date have ranged from state-level social service coordination, to state encouragement of local coordination, to citywide and countywide initiatives, to neighborhood and school-site experimentation. Although schools have been involved in most of these projects, relatively little agreement exists about the best models for service coordination.

For example, there is some disagreement over whether it is more effective for service coordination to be "school-based," or based outside the school but closely "linked" to schooling, or "community-based" and not directly linked to schooling (Behrman 1992). A school-based approach benefits from the school's position as a dominant neighborhood institution but can suffer from excessive control by schools. A school-linked approach can more effectively balance school and nonschool contributions but may still be too heavily "institutions" oriented. A community-based model can incorporate a wider diversity of resources and facilities (e.g., churches, community organizations, clubs) but may lose a bit of focus and "sharpness" in its dispersion of stakeholders (see Chaskin and Richman 1992). In addition to questions of "base," approaches to service coordination so far have ranged widely in the scope of services provided, in the client populations targeted, in the sources of funding, and in the very nature of the collaborative relationship (e.g., informal and voluntary, formal and "contracted," etc.).

Despite the diversity of approaches to service coordination thus far, many common administrative problems and issues have been faced in much of the current experimentation. The commonalities in administrative issues are such that a number of quite useful handbooks and guidelines for services integration have now been developed. While respecting the diversity of approaches, these handbooks offer valuable suggestions to nearly all projects in such problem areas as the sharing of confidential information, locating funding sources, developing "trust" between agencies, designing an evaluation system, and involving the community (see, for example, Bruner 1991; Melaville with Blank 1991; Blank and Melaville with Asayesh 1993).

The handbooks reflect an accumulating craft knowledge on how to effectively implement service coordination. They build upon a solid growth in the understanding drawn from parallel experiences across the diversity of efforts—experiences drawn from such "lighthouse" experiments as New Beginnings in San Diego, the Cities in Schools projects in more than a dozen states, the Walbridge Caring Communities effort in St. Louis, and the New Futures interventions in four of our nation's cities.

What the handbooks and guidelines and experiential evidence to date do not adequately provide are insights into "deep structure" issues in cooperating institutions that may need to be addressed in successful services integration. Such issues are often recognized, however. Indeed, it is not uncommon to find in the available handbooks such observations as: (a) "child and family-serving institutions" must "fundamentally change the way they think, behave, and use their resources"; (b) training should help participants to " 'unlearn' the attitudes and behaviors common in highly bureaucratic, agency-centered, and problem-oriented institutions"; and (c) "the culture inside all institutions and agencies represented on the collaborative must change" (Blank, Melaville, and Asayesh 1993).

Thus, despite the knowledge gained from experience, we still need to know more about the complex and difficult matter of bringing separate public sector institutions toward successful collaboration. Talk of "fundamentally changing" the ways in which institutions behave and changing institutional "cultures" recognizes that deeply imbedded qualities of organizations tend to come into play in service-coordination experimentation. Among these deep structures are the separate reward and personnel systems, environmental relationships, operating procedures and "conventions," and resource-management systems that uniquely characterize each institution's "lifespace." Difficult enough to fathom as separate institutions, the structures of institutions in processes of coordination can become exceedingly abstruse.

Building upon our earlier review of the literature on the coordination of children's services (Crowson and Boyd 1993), this paper focuses on a comparison and analysis of the models represented in five cases of children's services experimentation. Our analysis is informed also by some recent theorizing on the topic of institutional collaboration (see, particularly, Gray 1991; Gray and Wood 1991; Wood and Gray 1991). Our major goal here is to identify and highlight some central questions to be asked, and some alternative administrative models to be explained, in institutional collaboration.

One sense of comparative "models" can be gleaned from analyses of differing programmatic goals and program "outcomes" in service coordination (see Wang, Haertel, and Walberg 1992). Some common programmatic foci to date have been parent education/participation and school-readiness interventions, teen pregnancy and teen parenting collaboration, dropout prevention, substance abuse prevention, and the more generic linkage of an array of services to children and families (e.g., educational, medical, mental health, welfare, employment, legal). In an examination of outcomes among a sample of fifty-five initiatives that they arranged by program type, M. C. Wang, G. Haertel, and H. J. Walberg (1992) report some early (although varied) evidence of success—but they also report that the evidence is insufficient to know just how well "collaboration" is contributing to these outcomes.

Alternatively, our inquiry begins to address the models question from a combined process and institutional "structures" orientation. A first important issue our discussion and analysis raises is, *just how much coordination among services is necessary and desirable?* The literature on coordinated services tends to be ambivalent on this issue. For example, while distinguishing between cooperation and collaboration, Hord (1986, 22) says that both are "valued models, but each serves a unique purpose and yields a different return." But she then muddies the water by saying that "collaboration is highly recommended as the most appropriate mode for interorganizational relationships" (26).

The five projects we examine here vary in the degree to which they approach the rational ideal of full coordination and collaboration, but all nevertheless have achieved some quite impressive accomplishments. The fact is that any kind of cooperation is probably an improvement over a total (or almost complete) lack of coordination. And, indeed, all five of the projects examined here have moved well beyond the stage of simple cooperation, and all five deserve accolades for their achievements.

The idea of alternative models for coordinated ventures has been advanced, not only by Shirley M. Hord (1986), but also by B. A. Intriligator (1992), who suggests that interagency interactions can be usefully examined along a continuum of cooperation to coordination to collaboration. In cooperation, the independence of individual agencies may be little affected, changes in institutional policy and structure are minimal, and "turf" is not a serious issue. Under collaboration (at the other end of the continuum), however, there will be a loss of institutional autonomy, *interagency* policymaking in place of agency independence, and a need to go beyond turf toward consensus and well-established trust. Experience thus far nationally suggests that, rather than either cooperative, coordinative, or collaborative, some efforts have tended simply to be "co-located." However, even in colocation, difficult issues can arise over shared facilities usage, managerial control, resource allocation, professions protection, and information flow.

Another way of comparing coordinated services, we have suggested (Boyd and Crowson 1992), is according to their differing styles of administrative implementation. Projects are frequently initiated as *strategic* interventions—pragmatically and iteratively moving toward a goal of coordination and problem solving as the project unfolds. An alternative model is a strategy of *systemic* reform, where key institutional constraints (e.g., conflicting reward systems, differing norms and conventions, professional training differences) are identified early and incorporated into strategically preplanned reform implementation.

A more comprehensive comparison of theoretical models for organizational collaboration has been offered by B. Gray and D. J. Wood (1991). They warn that there is yet relatively little theory that adequately addresses interorganizational behavior and relationships. Nevertheless, in a companion piece of work, Wood and Gray (1991) suggest a means whereby the array of theoretical perspectives can provide at least the beginnings of a general theory of collaboration. Key variables they identified are: (a) the role of the convener in collaboration, (b) the impact of environmental complexity and control upon collaboration, and (c) the impact of both individual and collective self-interests upon collaboration (Wood and Gray 1991).

In the pages to follow, we draw on much of this early work as a rough conceptual guide for an examination of a few selected efforts in children's services coordination. Brief profiles of children's services projects ("cases") in five cities are presented below—followed by a deeper, comparative discussion of the projects from the perspective of institutional analyses.

THE CASES

The profiles presented below are based upon information collected through site visits, interviews with project participants, descriptive and evaluative project reports, and presentations and discussions concerning the five projects at an invitational conference on "School-Community Connections" held in October 1992. The five projects are:

The Minneapolis Youth Trust; The "Nation of Tomorrow" Partnership in Chicago; Houston's "School of the Future" initiative; the "Family Service Center" Project in East Los Angeles; and "A Child's Place" in Charlotte, North Carolina.

While these five projects cannot fully represent the current diversity and creativity in coordinated services experimentation, they do provide an instructive range of initiatives. Because these projects are still in various stages of development, they do not necessarily represent unequivocal models of success in service coordination. Still, each one represents a significant advance over fragmented, traditional approaches to children's services. We begin our profiles with the Minneapolis Youth Trust, a citywide, macrolevel model, and then turn to profiles of four programs focused on specific schools.

The Minneapolis Youth Trust

The Youth Trust is a citywide collaborative organization involving Minneapolis employers, schools, and a number of youth-serving agencies. Formed in 1989, with leadership from the Mayor's Office, the Trust is focused heavily upon building the work readiness and employability of young people in Minneapolis. It describes its major goal as helping to prepare "all youth growing up in Minneapolis with the skills and experiences needed to become productive workers and successful adults." (Scannapieco 1992, p. 3)

The Youth Trust is a partnership of member organizations (primarily Minneapolis-area business and nonprofit employers) who are asked to contribute annually to the support of the Trust, to develop jobs for youth, and to contribute volunteers (primarily mentors) from the ranks of their employees. In 1990–91, some 189 employers were contributing members of the Trust. Additional resources are provided by the McKnight Foundation.

The Trust is an umbrella organization, with three divisions of activity. The *Buddy System* is a first activity-recruiting adult volunteers from the member organizations to work with children and youth as friends, mentors, or tutors. A second division of the Trust is the *Job Connection,* an effort by members to help youth develop work values, career options, and successful work experiences. Employers provide internships and summer jobs, and work generally to develop the employability of Minneapolis youth. The third division of the Trust is *School Partners,* a set of school partnerships joining a business or nonprofit member of the Trust and a Minneapolis public school in a relationship individually designed to match Trust-member resources to school needs. (Johnson 1992)

The Nation of Tomorrow, Chicago, Illinois

The Nation of Tomorrow Project is a five-year (1989–1994) partnership between the University of Illinois, the W. K. Kellogg Foundation, four African-American and Hispanic communities in Chicago, and a target public elementary school in each community. The name is derived from a statement eighty years ago by President Theodore Roosevelt: "When you take care of children, you are taking care of the nation of tomorrow."

With the University as initiator and convener, the Project attempts to link academia, four public schools, parents, and various community agencies in a set of collaborative working relationships. School-based, in a set of Chicago elementary schools characterized by concentrations of poverty and racial isolation, the project seeks to improve children's learning and development as well as to change relationships and connections among key urban institutions.

The Nation of Tomorrow targets four primary elements in children's lives: the family, the school, community child care and youth opportunities, and community health-care agencies. The Project contains three major program components. The first of these, *Family Ties,* focuses on parent education and involvement in the education of their children at school. Its activities are intended to involve parents, social service providers, clergy, teachers, and other community leaders in developing parent education programs that will be taught by parents in each community. Parent involvement and institutional linkages are facilitated by teams of Family Advocates who are persons hired from each community.

A second component of the project is *Partners in Health.* This component seeks to promote the health of children and youth using a grassroots, community-based approach to assist parents in understanding and taking greater responsibility for the primary health care of their children. The third project component, *School Enhancement Activities,* is designed to assist teachers and administrators in each school with their own professional learning and development. (Crowson, Smylie, and Hare 1992; Smylie, Crowson, and Hare 1992).

Houston's School of the Future

With support from the Hogg Foundation for Mental Health, three of Houston's public schools inaugurated the "School of the Future" project in the Spring of 1990. The schools are a middle school serving grades 6 through 8 and two K through 6 elementary schools. Similar projects were inaugurated simultaneously in Austin, Dallas, and San Antonio. The Houston schools serve concentrations of minority students (largely Hispanic) and serve communities experiencing critical center-city problems of school dropout, teen pregnancy, substance abuse, inadequate health care, family poverty, and unmet family needs.

The overall objective of the Project is to enrich and enhance the lives of children in each of the school-communities—through an integration of health and human services, an involvement of parents and teachers in the work of the school, an involvement of both public and private organizations in the project as partners, and the development of a strong commitment to the project among school staff members.

By 1992–93, the School of the Future project was in its third year—with a long list of activities underway to involve parents more fully in the schools, to provide family counseling, to enrich the academic and extracurricular offerings of the schools, to affect family functioning and student health-related problems, to address alcohol and drug abuse issues, and to coalesce neighborhood organizations around children/families and their needs. (Arvey and Tijerina 1992)

The Family Service Center, East Los Angeles

The Murchison Street School, an elementary school in East Los Angeles, is the site of a newly developing "Family Service Center." The K through 6 school is among the lowest-achieving schools in Los Angeles. It serves a deep-poverty neighborhood of the city, and is more than 95 percent Hispanic in student enrollment.

The project has been initiated by school staff in partnership with the California State University at Los Angeles. Still in the early stages of implementation in late 1992, the Family Service Center started by opening a parent center within the Murchison School. The intent of this effort was to welcome parents, provide parenting workshops, channel parents into school involvement, and offer a "resources/referral" facility to families vis-à-vis services information. A second element of the project, much at the initial development stage in late 1992, is the implementation of a multiservice center at the school site—bringing an array of city, county, and community agencies into cooperative alignment with the project.

Staff members in the Center are assigned by their "home" agencies and work with clients on a referral basis. Case managers are employed by the Center to assess family-assistance needs, provide direct services when appropriate, refer families for assistance to appropriate agencies, follow up on referrals, monitor outcomes, and assist with transportation needs. (Bilovsky and Zetlin 1992; Zetlin and Bilovsky 1992)

A Child's Place, Charlotte, North Carolina

Located in downtown Charlotte, A Child's Place provides education and a range of social services for homeless children and their families. The facility opened in the Fall of 1989 in a downtown church, moving in 1992 to space in a nearby public elementary school. The client families and children tend to live in shelters or motels for the homeless in the downtown area.

The highly transient students at A Child's Place remain an average of just eighteen days. While enrolled, the students are provided with medical, dental and eye exams and other needed health services. Clothing is provided, as well as a "pack" of school and personal-hygiene supplies. The center also assists in family resettlement and provides parent and child support/counseling.

The staff of the center includes a coordinator, a teacher, an aide, and a social worker (with the designation "family advocate"). The center is supported by the Charlotte Public Schools, by corporate donors, and by the contributions of private social service agencies. Public social service agencies are not involved. (Mickelson, Yon, and Carlton-LaNey 1992)

The cases briefly profiled above represent two projects in which a local university is a key partner, one citywide project initiated with leadership from the Mayor's Office, one project with very little outside funding, and one project with much direct, initiatory involvement on the part of a private foundation. All of the projects involve the public school system, but with varying degrees of scope and intensity. The Minneapolis effort is citywide, with member-organization partnerships distributed among an array of city schools. The Chicago, Houston, and Los Angeles efforts are focused upon just one or at most four school sites. The Charlotte program began in a church and is now only incidentally lodged in a school.

The projects also differ somewhat in the degree to which the traditional educational roles and activities of schools are affected by collaboration. The Minneapolis partnerships tend to be "add-ons," with few demands upon educators to change roles or perspectives. The Chicago and Houston projects appear to seek a somewhat more extensive blending of the children's service mission into the instructional behavior of the school. The Los Angeles effort likewise seeks a change in school mission but through the less intensive procedure of offering educators increased referral options for selectively identified children and families in need. And, the Charlotte program is as yet unclear as to whether it is a social service program first and educational second, or vice versa.

These comparative elements in the profiled cases are summarized in Table 6.1. It should be noted that, in all five instances, there is the combination of at least one "outside" organization (often in the role of

TABLE 6.1.
Case-Comparative Structures of Collaboration

	Convening Organization	Institutional Focus	Extensiveness of Planned Collaboration
Mineapolis Youth Trust	Mayor's Office	Selected schools, citywide	Added services for participating schools
Nation of Tomorrow (Chicago)	Area University	Four inner-city schools	Simultaneous emphasis on children's services and school/instructional improvement
School of the Future (Houston)	Foundation/School District Partnership	Three central-city schools	Integration of health-human services into the school mission
Family Service Center (East Los Angeles)	Area University/School Partnership	A central-city school	Services at the school site for children and families, plus goal of improved student achievement
A Childs Place (Charlotte)	Private Social Service Providers	A school-based center for a special clientele	Unresolved conflict in mission between social services and education

convener as well as project participant) and there is some expected impact upon the institutional behavior of a school or schools. In its simplest form the expected impact upon the school may be an expansion of the noninstructional array of services to children and families; in a more complex form, the expected impact may be a change in the school's sense of mission and in the school's linkage between classroom instruction and this changed mission. It would be important to ask in any inquiry into service coordination just what is the nature of the expected impact upon the school as an institution and, alternatively, just what is the expected impact upon any other, cooperating institution(s).

FROM CASE COMPARISON TO INSTITUTIONAL ANALYSIS

The Idealized Process of Collaboration

It is no accident that imprecise and confused terminology is found in the service-coordination literature to date. With little attention to key differences in meaning, projects are interchangeably and variously labeled as efforts toward services coordination, integration, or collaboration. As far back as 1986, however, Shirley Hord suggested that there are significant differences in attributes and relationships between coordinative and collaborative arrangements. Much conflict can arise, she concluded, from the simple fact that the individuals involved in a project may be unclear as to *which* model (coordination or collaboration) is the central expectation (Hord 1986: 25).

Table 6.2 summarizes some distinctions Hord (1986, 24–25) made between the two models. In brief, she suggested that cooperative relationships tend to be much influenced by one organization (X), with less than fully comparable involvement and coequality (resources, communications, leadership, etc.) on the part of another organization (Y). Collaborative relationships, on the other hand, involve a fully shared service and shared resources, expertise, communications, and control. The "product" under collaboration is not a service either X or Y would have provided alone.

Hord's (1986) comparison of cooperation and collaboration helps to clarify the confusion that continues today in establishing the structures of projects through an identifying terminology. Few of the children's services experiments across the nation, including the five profiled above, are clearly at the cooperative or the collaborative end of the continuum. They are all somewhere in between.

TABLE 6.2.

Distinctions Between Organizational Cooperation and Collaboration*

Cooperation Model	Collaboration Model
Convening or Beginning Processes	
1. Organization X approaches organization Y for help, tolerance, and cooperation in completing a task. Minimal contribution of resources is expected from Y. X completes the task and develops a "product," but as an outgrowth of the cooperation of Y.	1. Organizations X and Y agree on and join forces to plan/execute a shared product or service. Organizations agree on goals and on projected results or outcomes.
Institutional Focus/ Ownership	
2. X provides resources and expertise; Y provides access and setting. X often arranges funds and may pay Y for contributions.	2. Both organizations contribute staff, resources, and capabilities. Mutual funding is obtained.
3. Control continues to be lodged separately in each organization; leadership from one of the organizations is characteristic.	3. Shared, mutual control develops; dispersed or delegated leadership is characteristic.
Process Requirement/ Characteristics	
4. X determines nature of communication, conveys information to Y, and responds to requests from Y.	4. Communication interactions and roles are established; channels and "levels" of communication are clarified.
5. X undertakes the bulk of the project's activity with permission from Y.	5. Both organizations spend time and energy. Expertise/action is contributed by each side. A combined staff comes into being; trade-offs are arranged.
Product	
6. An "Us/them" process mode develops.	6. A "We" process mode develops.
7. A product or service is essentially produced by X, but Y may be able to use it and may benefit from the work of X.	7. A shared product or service emerges, one not possible if X and Y had approached the tasks as separate agents.

*Adapted from Shirley M. Hord (February 1986), A Synthesis of Research on Organizational Collaboration. *Educational Leadership* 43(5): 24–25 (Figure 1).

In many of the projects to date there is outside funding and an outside convener (e.g., a university). The projects typically introduce additional, noneducational services to schools and neighborhoods, with the intent of *inducing* many of the processes and characteristics of collaboration that Hord (1986) identified. The projects tend to go beyond the overinvolvement of organization X and minimal involvement of organization Y that is identified by Hord (1986) as cooperation. However, the projects also do not reach the shared sense of mission, mutuality, "product," communications, and expertise that Hord (1986) identified with collaboration.

The borderline existence of most children's services projects thus far (somewhere between cooperation and collaboration) suggests that key questions for further inquiry might be: Just where does a project sit procedurally on a continuum of cooperation to collaboration? and what evidence is there over time of movement either toward or away from collaboration? Many projects may show uneven progress and some continuing struggles among the various elements toward collaboration (e.g., improved communications linkages but little sense of mutual control). It may be out of a careful documentation of these struggles and the various compromises that surround them that much added administrative understanding can evolve.

Towards an Understanding of Institutional Structures in Collaboration

To summarize briefly, the state of the art in children's services collaboration has typically not progressed to an idealized point where participating organizations in projects share completely in the delivery of services, agree fully on goals and outcomes, contribute resources equally, share control and leadership, communicate and interact smoothly, and operate as "we" rather than "us/them."

Rather, it is far more likely thus far that projects will be struggling with problems in blending other services into the institutional dominion of the school, in reaching a shared sense of mission and shared leadership/control in collaborative ventures, and in building effective communicative linkages between the project's array of service providers (Crowson and Boyd 1993).

On the other hand, the extant literature also suggests that many efforts in children's services collaboration may have successfully pushed beyond the minimal, "coordination" stage as defined by Hord (1986). Organizations X and Y in most experiments are both providing resources and leadership. New staff roles are to be found; struggles toward an effective compromise in control and communications issues are typical; and there is at least the sense in most projects that a shared product is a worthy objective—a product that goes well beyond the narrowly 3-R's role of the local school.

The beyond-cooperation but not-quite-collaboration status of most experimentation to date is well recognized in the handbook and guidelines literature (see particularly, Bruner 1991; Melaville with Blank 1991; Blank, Melaville, and Asayesh 1993). Nevertheless, it is our sense that, while a thorough understanding of struggling-toward-collaboration *processes* is vitally important, it is also vital to understand, as thoroughly as possible, the complexities of *institutional structure* that come into play in collaborative ventures.

Thus, the remainder of this paper works toward a better understanding of the interorganizational domains of collaboration. The focus is upon the following key aspects of institutions under collaboration: (1) the convening process (the beginnings of a shared goal structure); (2) institutional interests and reward systems; (3) institutional "conventions"; and, (4) institutional environments.

These four aspects of institutional collaboration, of course, do not capture the totality of the many organizational behaviors that are critically affected by collaboration. Our analysis tends to take a "structures" approach, following the theorizing of a "new institutionalism" school of organizational analysts (particularly March and Olsen 1984, 1989; Powell and DiMaggio 1991; and Wilson 1989). From a social-psychological perspective, we are neglecting (at present) some important issues for collaboration in professional socialization, administrative leadership group dynamics, and bargaining/negotiating. These are recognizably important, as indicated in our own earlier review of the coordinated services literature (Crowson and Boyd 1993).

For heuristic reasons, as in our treatment of coordination-to-collaboration as a potential continuum, we suggest that each of our four institutional structures can be usefully conceived in similar "continuum" terms. This notion is summarized in Table 6.3—where, quite simply, the suggestion is that institutions moving effectively toward children's services collaboration will begin to give evidence of passing well beyond some "preconditions" in the convening process and will give some evidence of shared institutional interests, environmental adaptations, and institutional conventions. Each of the institutional structures is discussed briefly below, with data from the case studies, and with some key research questions.

TABLE 6.3.

Institutional Continua Towards Children's Services Collaboration

1. *Institutional Goals*
   From Separate Goals ⟶ to Shared Institutional Goals

2. *Institutional Interests*
   From Institutionally Separate Interests ⟶ to Shared Collaborative Interests

3. *Institutional Environments*
   From Institutionally Separate Adaptation ⟶ to a Shared Environmentalization

4. *Institutional Conventions*
   From Institutionally Separate Conventions ⟶ to Shared Collaborative Conventions

1. Institutions and the Convening (Goal Structuring) Process. Wood and Gray (1991) suggest that any of a number of institutional "preconditions" are necessary for collaboration to occur. These may range from a developing sense of shared resource dependence to a sense of increased efficiency or cost reduction through collaboration, to a reconceptualization of the "central problem" facing a domain of organizations that motivates collaboration (Wood and Gray 1991).

There has been some attention to a goal of increased efficiency in discussions of coordinating children's services, particularly with regard to initiatives at the state level. But there is little evidence to date of greater efficiency or cost reduction as a realistic outcome (see Useem 1991).

Similarly, there is little evidence thus far of children's services collaboration that grows out of a sense of resource dependency—that is, where institutions competing for the same resources attempt to share their mutual stake in that base. Indeed, much of the children's services experimentation to date has involved add-ons of extra resources (e.g., from foundations, universities, or corporations) rather than efforts toward a direct sharing of a common base. This has had the side effect of placing much of the press toward collaboration within a not-very-powerful framework of short-lived, add-on funding.

By far the most common of the preconditions in the literature on coordinated children's services has been a growing reconceptualization of the central problem of educating an urban population. In earlier work (Crowson and Boyd 1993), this was summarized as: (1) a renewed sense of the ecological interdependencies among schools, families, and neighborhoods; (2) a recognition that effective investments in education require complementary investments in children's health, nutrition, family stability, housing, and the social capital of the community; and, (3) a renewed sense of the vital child-development role of the school in blending academics into the social, moral, and emotional development of children.

Although there is seldom evidence of lengthy discussion among project participants, there are indications of such conceptualizations of the problem in four of the five projects profiled earlier:

> The Minneapolis Youth Trust offers its partnerships as "a long-term commitment to the human resource development of Minneapolis youth" (Scannapieco 1992, 2).
>
> Houston's School of the Future recognizes that "family, neighborhood, school, and community service resources "must come together

as a working system if they are to be responsive and effective in addressing the challenges for optimal development" of children (Arvey and Tijerina 1992, 7).

Chicago's Nation of Tomorrow talks about "enhancing the capacities of and functional relationships among multiple institutions with which children interact from early childhood through at least early adolescence" (Smylie, Crowson, and Hare 1992).

The Murchison Family Service Center (East Los Angeles) discusses "an integrated client-centered approach for dealing with the multiple problems of inner city students" (Bilovsky and Zetlin 1992).

Despite these statements of a central problem behind their collaboration, there is some evidence that many projects find it difficult to build from the precondition of a reconceptualized problem into the sharing (of goals or missions) that characterizes a convening process. Evidence of such a process, Wood and Gray (1991) claim, is to be found when participants actively orient their discussions, decisions, and actions around the problem domain that brought them together in the first place.

In a project pursuing a public schools and business partnership toward "the human resource development of Minneapolis youth," for example, some early-in-the-project feedback from the business side of the partnership (Johnson 1992) was that:

> "The teachers are very hard to stay in touch with. They have short work hours and are usually in the class. They don't have voice mail, which would make our interaction a whole lot easier! For now, we will begin using FAX machines more" (3).
>
> "I am not convinced that partnerships are the way to go. They seem to be a last minute effort to save our education system—like an emergency room. The problem is very deep. We are willing to take part, but we have to ask ourselves, 'Why are we doing it?'" (8).

Similarly, in Chicago's Nation of Tomorrow project a convener's goal of strengthening relationships among "multiple institutions" that serve children encountered some of the following difficulties (Levin 1992):

> A number of respondents feel that there is a conflict between expectations of The Nation of Tomorrow as a project to support the ongoing activities of the school, versus a project which has its own set of activities.
>
> Participants spoke of a continuing program of school personnel expecting Nation of Tomorrow staff members to function within the

traditional school employee model, with far more supervision and less freedom to come and go as they please.

The [school] administration does not understand the role of family advocates. They generally see them as social workers, as people to come in when there's a crisis. They don't see them as a proactive person, a person who prevents.

In sum, our theorizing suggests that a key task in moving institutional structures toward collaboration involves success in negotiating a convening process—a process that may involve some preconditions (particularly the sense of a shared central problem), then some progress toward shared goals in addressing the problem. Among the many questions to be asked in further inquiry into the convening process in children's services projects are: (1) To what extent do project participants across cooperating institutions share a sense of the "common problem?" (2) To what degree is there evidence, over time in ongoing projects, of progress toward an across-instituitons sharing of goal or mission? And, (3) what are some identifiable characteristics of projects that have moved well along a continuum toward a shared sense of goal (e.g., lengthy planning time, explicit written agreements, strong, goal-oriented leadership)?

2. *Institutional Interests.* In a classically simple and insightful statement, Edward Banfield (1970) once observed that most political issues arise out of the maintenance and enhancement needs of large formal organizations. In the case of public schooling, such needs can revolve around key institutional interests in protecting jobs, budgets, programs, facilities, turf, and enrollments.

Each of the institutional members of a collaborative will bring to the partnership a set of its own interests—interests rooted in its own reward system. It is principally for this reason that some theorists are wary of school-*based* children's services programs, favoring school-*linked* efforts instead (Behrman 1992). The argument is that the reward system of the school system will tend to dominate in a school-based endeavor. For the same reason, Michael Kirst (1991) stresses the importance of "glue money" if separate agencies are to be attracted toward partnered services to the same children. The challenges in finding a bit of glue are evident in the research literature, which now contains numerable examples of institutional reward systems pulling partners in exactly the opposite direction from the complementary impact upon children that has been intended (see Crowson and Boyd 1993).

Institutional interests and the underlying reward system often can be a central part of the hidden curriculum of a project, not easily unearthed except through careful, on-site observation. Examples can be drawn from some fieldwork accompanying Chicago's Nation of Tomorrow project—reported by Robert Crowson, Mark Smylie, and Victoria Hare (1992), Smylie, Crowson, and Hare (1992), and by R. Levin (1991, 1992).

First, this experiment has wrestled mightily with a structure for project governance that seems to fail to fit adequately into the school's system of rewards for administrative control. An array of new personnel and school-linked roles has been added by the experiment to each project school—from family advocates to family health-care experts, to community-services personnel, to improve-the-schools consultants. Each school site has received the services of a project coordinator, as a tie-it-all-together specialist.

Not adequately considered, however, has been an institutional reward system that places full responsibility for anything gone wrong at the school site upon the shoulders of the building principal. The building principal has traditionally been rewarded for remaining fully in control of his or her school—an incentive of even greater saliency under a reform law in Chicago that places the principal's tenure in the hands of each Local School Council.

Consequently, principals have felt constrained in the Chicago experiment to reach strenuously toward added control of a school site that (under its children's services experimentation) is facing new dimensions of program complexity and ambiguity. Some early-in-the-project feedback has been that:

> It isn't clear that the schools have each become completely reconciled to all the new actors—to all the new things going on. There may be a sense to some of the principals of activities out of control, balanced against their sense of much greater responsibility for it all (Crowson, Smylie, and Hare 1992, 11).

Or, as one principal puts it:

> I really feel like I'm running two schools. I've got the entire school to run and then this project over here on the side that I'm trying to move . . . I'm taking my time from what I could be doing in the school to do it (Smylie, Crowson, and Hare 1992, 23).

Second, the Chicago experiment has yet to resolve some key issues in a blending of the institutional interests of its major partners. The University of Illinois, as a key partner, has tended to bring persons to the experiment (faculty and staff members) with extremely flexible time schedules, with research and scholarship interests, with a change-the-schools philosophy, with respect for work-life autonomy, and a general preference for nondirective and nonhierarchical styles of intervention.

By contrast, the school partners have tended to bring to the experiment severe resource needs, inflexible schedules and time limitations, a teacher-and-pupil classroom orientation, and an administrator-directive style of management. It has been in the interest of the project schools, furthermore, to access the experiment's (foundation-provided) resources as an add-on to the continuing work of the school; but it has been in the interest of the university to try to use the experiment's resources as a bit of school-change leverage.

The strains between interests are reflected in some feedback from project participants. One site coordinator observed that:

> Most school people have never worked independently like we are supposed to do. They [the principals] want someone to watch over our every move. They want us to report to someone as if we are in the military (Levin 1992).

A family advocate (a person in an outreach-to-the-community role) noted:

> The project has been absorbed by the school. We are becoming more and more school personnel. We are extra bodies (Smylie, Crowson, and Hare 1992, 20).

Similarly, a university faculty member concluded:

> There's a continuing problem of school personnel expecting Nation of Tomorrow staff members to function within the traditional school employee model, with far more supervision and less freedom to come and go as they please (Levin 1992).

In sum, each institution in a collaborative will be full of its own self-interests. These will be rooted in institutional reward systems—systems that can be significantly challenged by the process of collaborating and by encounters with the reward systems of partnering organizations. While it would be highly unlikely to expect cooperating institutions to change their own reward structures fundamentally, movements toward successful institutional collaboration should show progress toward some shared interests and rewards—sufficient to override the pulling of separate institutional interests. Among the key questions to be asked are: (1) What identifiably separate institutional interests and reward structures can be noted in a project among the active institutional "players?" (2) To what degree can evidence be found, over time, of some common interests in and rewards for collaboration in a project? And, (3) what are the observable effects upon a collaborative project of any clashing interests between a home organization and its collaborating unit(s)?

3. *Environmental Control.* In discussing the development of the "School of the Future" effort in a Houston middle school, Arvey and Tijerina (1992) note that a "negative community image" of the school was one of the "primary concerns" of project staff. Community memories of a particularly violent incident some five years earlier were still being reflected in parental decisions to send their children to magnet and private schools rather than to this neighborhood institution. It was hoped that this negative image could now be changed. Additionally, the project developers hoped to address some perceived deficits in community resources in the neighborhoods served by all three of the project schools—particularly the lack of organized activities for children and of places for children to play, as well as the lack of readily accessible medical clinics or other health care providers in the neighborhoods.

A somewhat different relationship with the community is behind the effort to provide a "Family Service Center" at the Murchison Street School in East Los Angeles. Here, one of the central goals is to link the resources of the school more effectively with an array of fragmented services in the community—particularly health, mental health, social welfare, and juvenile justice.

Each of these projects is consistent with philosophies of children's services coordination, which stress the importance of school outreach as investments in the "social capital" of their neighborhoods (Coleman 1988a, 1988b) and/or as recognition of the necessary developmental linkage between education and a range of other, complementary social services.

In short, under children's services coordination both schools and other-services agencies are hard pressed to become newly "environmentalized" (Trist 1977). Despite a history of other-services provision (e.g., school lunches, medical and dental inspections, guidance) with solid roots in the turn-of-the-century era of Progressive reform, public schools have not been regarded as overly open institutions. Indeed, Tyack (1992, 25) argues that school systems have been adept over time at transforming such other-services innovations into "smoothly running parts of the *pedagogical* machinery (emphasis added.)"

Trist (1977) and, more recently, Gray (1991) observe that institutions acting independently but sharing a common field (e.g., providing similar or overlapping services, sharing a clientele, drawing upon the same resource base) can add considerably to the turbulence of one another's environments. Such turbulence can lead to an added recognition of institutional interdependence, but it also can lead to much higher levels of both shared and individual uncertainty (Trist 1977).

The sense here is that, as the public schools join forces with other social service providers in a given community, these cooperating institutions are brought together into a renewed engagement between organizational structures and the external environment. Consequently, they may be raising considerably their levels of institutional turbulence and uncertainty.

A public school that confines itself to the 3 R's, and follows old dictates of "closedness" to parent/community involvement, inhabits an environmental niche all its own. But a public school that shares space with the parks department, operates an on-site community health clinic, sends social workers out into the neighborhood, opens its doors to parents and volunteers, offers after-school tutoring and recreation, and liaises with the local library—finds itself in an environment of much finer complexity. Not only school rules and regulations now define its professional life space but health, recreation, social work, and library rules must henceforth be considered as well. Not only a politics of schooling now characterizes its activities but a politics of other professions and a politics of the neighborhood now become defining characteristics of the school's institutional persona.

The effective accommodation of the new environmentalization of partnering institutions under service coordination remains a central issue. *First,* there is evidence, per Tyack's (1992) historical observation, that projects to date have encountered a tendency by educators to institutionalize service coordination under education's pedagogical persona.

For example, in a study of British experimentation, Johnson et al. (1980, 1) report that after nearly two decades of a British amalgamation of children's welfare, health, and education services: "Long standing issues such as the ways that teachers, education welfare officers, social workers, and other supporting services worked together were unresolved." Furthermore, teachers in the British experiment—accustomed to thinking of children in classroom lots and to a sense of boundary among school, home, and other-service agencies—had great difficulty in reconceptualizing their roles in more "pastoral" or caregiving terms and in valuing the work of other-service professionals as highly as their own (Johnson et al. 1980, 95–97).

The most clearcut example from field records of a struggle over the educational institutional of a children's services endeavor comes from the work of Mickelson, Yon, and Carlton-LaNey (1992) in describing "A Child's Place." The authors note that the initial director was a director was a professional educator who:

> was a stern disciplinarian who believed that her role as teacher was part of her "ministry," that it was God's will that she teach these homeless children. She also believed that the children needed to be taught that there were consequences for their actions because "the reason they were homeless was that their parents had never learned that lesson" (Mickelson, Yon, and LaNey 1992, 17).

A replacement director saw the role in more coordinating services terms, but the result was a loss of attention and an estrangement from the program's pedagogical players. Conclude Mickelson, Yon, and Carlton-LaNey (1992, 19): "The tension between the social service staff and the educational staff continues":

Similarly, in an examination of the "Nation of Tomorrow" project in Chicago, Smylie, Crowson, and Hare (1992a, 13–14) observe that:

> project participants have observed that a number of the "school people" have had difficulty "getting their heads around" the project's philosophy, and have had difficulty reconceptualizing the work of the school in terms that go beyond classroom instruction within the school's "four walls." As an example, there were reportedly some strains in the health services component of the project when added nursing resources were interpreted by school personnel as new (but traditional) school-nurse resources. The newly added nurse-professionals themselves, however, saw their responsibilities as proactively "bringing the community in" as part of a "community model" of school nursing.

Second, there is often some evidence of an unresolved placement of the risk of environmental relations "gone problematic" in the back-and-forth negotiations among the key institutional partners in children's services coordination. In our first example above, drawn from Tyack (1992), the suggestion was that institutions—often schools—can try to redirect environmental turbulence and bring it under control within their own orbit. Here, the suggestion is that new conflict-ridden domains of environmental turbulence can be raised.

In the literature, perhaps no aspect of collaboration illustrates this second condition quite as well as the issue of confidentiality of information. There are real and important considerations in the sharing and pooling of information about children and families among service providers. For good reason, confidentiality restrictions are well rooted in constitutional guarantees of personal privacy and in statutory provisions, as well as in the ethical standards of the differing professions. This exists, despite equally good reasons why shared information is needed for continuity in children's service delivery and a more efficient and effective use of child-assistance resources (see Behrman 1992; Kahne and Kelley 1991; Joining Forces 1992).

Family consent agreements and release forms, plus careful guidelines on security of access and the data limits to be allowed in automated information systems are among the proposed solutions. Nevertheless, the more critical "deep-structure" issues between cooperating institutions go beyond release forms to environmental turbulence issues of a feared loss of turf control, a distrust of other professionals' use of "our" information, and sets of ethical and legal concerns (including fears of lawsuits) when information leaves any of a number of traditionally tightly closed systems. Indeed, information on their clients constitutes the most significant of property rights held by each of the professions (see Demsetz 1967).

In sum, children's services collaboration raises additional environmental issues for each of its institutional partners. There is a tendency for one or more partners to attempt to institutionalize the resulting environmental turbulence within its ongoing structures (e.g., to pedagogize service coordination). There also can be a tendency for environmental turbulence to lead to, and reflect, a loss of environmental control among the partnering institutions—with conflicts which may or may not be resolved in a newly shared environmentalization. Among the key questions to be asked in further inquiry are: (1) What evidence of environmental tensions, or turbulence, is to be found in ongoing children's service coordination projects? And, (2) what evidence can be found of efforts to incorporate environmental issues into ongoing institutional structures versus creating newly shared structures of collaborative environmental control?

4. *Institutional Conventions.* Institutions serve an extremely important function for those who work within them—the function of imposing elements of order upon what might otherwise be an extremely ambiguous and (in the terminology of March and Olson [1984, 743]) "potentially inchoate world." An institution's special "order" is to be found in its unique history, its allocations of time, the management of its external environment, its normative structures, its special demographic characteristics, and its symbolic behavior—for example, its ceremonies, stories, rituals (March and Olsen 1984).

It would not be inconceivable for each of the partners in a children's services cooperative to bring to the partnership a near-fundamental difference in institutional order. Compare, for example, some of the conventions of health-care institutions (especially hospitals) with those of public schools. Increasingly, visitors in hospitals are recognized as a valuable element in the healing process. Although there are often sign-in procedures and visiting hours, these rules frequently are loosely observed. Close family visitors are increasingly permitted to stay overnight; and quasinursing roles for them are often permitted. By contrast, the public schools are surely a bit more welcoming than years ago, and some (often tutorial) roles are now granted frequent visitors; but the visitor in education is still not typically regarded as integral to the learning process—and the "Visitors Report to the Office" sign is taken seriously. Similarly, we note that, in health care, there is frequently much more procedure, ritual, rule-following, and care taken at the intake end of service provision than at the service-leaving or release end. In public education, clients are not released; rather, their completion of program at the outtake end is specially celebrated, often with close friends and relatives joining in an often large-scale assembly.

Key differences such as these, in the workaday drama of public-service institutions, are also found between public schools and institutions for criminal justice, public housing, parks and recreation, child protection, and family assistance (see Lipsky 1980). Again, the differences are a central part of the separate order of each institution.

There has been some recognition in the children's services literature (particularly by Gardner 1992, and by Kahne and Kelley 1991) that the tensions emanating from the comparative institutional conventions of cooperating organizations can be of serious concern.

Nevertheless, relatively little in-depth investigation has occurred into the problems of (and issues in) bridging these potentially noncompatible institutional structures—even when, in many cases, a change in convention is central to the very philosophy of service coordination.

For example, one of the central tenets of coordinated services is that the timing of services to families is currently far from optimal. Earlier interventions might prevent later consequences. Nevertheless, the system of queuing that in many service arenas now tends to wait for crises to develop before special services are provided loses the value of prevention (Melaville and Blank 1991). Interestingly, in response, schools in inner-city environments have increasingly lengthened the school day, year, and often the week. Many are now open both earlier and later in the day, on into the summer, and some on into the Saturday portion of the weekend. The age of school-going also has been extended downward into the child-care years. These alterations accompany a new stress upon the child-development role of the school.

Despite the press toward school-based and school-linked coordination, the timing of needed services for children and families generally conforms poorly to education schedules. Late nights, weekends, and hot summers are often times of greatest need. Services provided at these times often do have a crisis origin, but out of crisis may also come a receptivity to prevention. The timing of a child-development and a prevention orientation is a far cry from the timing of a services orientation that must be there as events unfold, that must respond quickly and comprehensively to needs, that must be as effectively reactive as proactive.

Some meaningful differences in "convention" between participating institutions can be seen in the projects under review for this report. Excerpts from interviews with both business and educator participants in the Minneapolis Youth Trust, for example, give a flavor of the barriers to cooperation in educator versus business lifeways (Johnson 1992):

> Getting the partnership off the ground was harder than expected. There were communication barriers along with different work styles, values, and objectives. They don't always match between the two groups. Even the two calendars are so different (3).
>
> We've had a hard time setting meetings. The partnership involves a lot of busy people. Currently, we don't have regular meetings (3).
>
> Teachers are overwhelmed. Meetings are back to back with classes and teachers often come in "frazzled," not ready to switch gears (4).

Businesses lack the awareness about what is meaningful in the lives of children at different ages. This is a barrier to planning activities (6).

Teachers are not used to running meetings efficiently, keeping on task (6).

Houston's "School of the Future" project has placed a very heavy emphasis upon the involvement of parents as one key group of project partners. Excerpts from a report by Arvey and Tijerina (1992) indicate that differences in convention between school and community also can be important barriers:

One incident that really brought home the differences in the expectations of planners and the experience of the people affected was the first partnership luncheon. Our parent representative, a woman actively involved for the past five years in her children's school and a perceived leader among parents, had never before attended a "luncheon" (26).

[P]arents had no indication of what was expected. There were strong cultural norms that made it difficult for a woman to feel comfortable in a leadership role outside the home. The very language—organization, procedures, goals, objectives, priorities, planning, motions, and consensus—was not within the language or experience of these parents. Even when schools provided babysitters and stipends for child care or transportation, women did not participate (25).

In summary, daily life in every institution has a special rhythm. The rhythms of an institution's behavior are reflected in its use of time, in the queuing or time-processing of its clients, and in the time constraints that develop around the activities of its inhabitants. Institutional rhythms are also reflected in the various conventions that together help to establish each institution's sense of order—including such elements as: what institutions separately celebrate, what they consider vital to getting a job done (e.g., efficient, on-task meetings versus time alone to plan and prepare), what special language is used to describe the work of the institution, and what expectations of behavior/performance surround those who serve and are served by the institution.

Institutional conventions can be so fully integrated into work lives that they seem fully natural. Thus, it may not be readily apparent that use of the word *luncheon* can be a barrier to school-community relations or that the not-so-efficient and only-vaguely-on-task meetings of educators can be frustrating to partnering business people. Among the key questions that emerge in this arena of institutional-structure concerns are: (1) What identifiably separate institutional "conventions" of possible importance to collaboration can be noted among the partners in ongoing service-coordination projects? (2) Is there evidence in the ongoing projects of separate institutional conventions that are in some degree of conflict with collaboration? And, (3) to what extent is there evidence of a coming together of differences in institutional conventions under collaboration?

CONCLUSION

Table 6.4 succinctly summarizes the theoretical framework we suggest as a guide to further inquiry. Every experiment in children's services coordination can be examined first as a point along a *process* continuum, from little-to-no integration of services to a collaborative ideal in the integration of services. Few experiments to date have failed to achieve some progress toward collaboration, but few have progressed very far toward the ideal. The determinants and characteristics of progress on the process dimension of collaboration are still underexplored terrain but so also is the question of the extent to which, and the circumstances under which, full collaboration is desirable or necessary.

Second, each of the experiments in children's services coordination can be examined as an exercise in the impact of institutional *structures* upon the administrative effort. While many institutional characteristics may be of importance to such an analysis, our review suggests four as key: Goal structures, institutional interests, environmental controls, and institutional conventions. Significantly, these are among the elements described by Seymour Sarason (1990) as the most "intractable" of organizational characteristics in school reform. Every venture in children's services coordination is likely to struggle informatively (and often creatively) with issues important for our knowledge base in moving from some institutionally *distinct* structures toward institutionally *shared* structures.

We note that key questions of shared probleming, finding common interests, resolving environmental tensions, and a coming together of conventions may be central to successful services integration. By no means, however, do we suggest that a degree of success in the integration of services is the final criterion by which to measure final accomplishment in collaborative ventures. To be sure, the end product should eventually be improved health, welfare, educational improvement, and life's chances for children and youth.

TABLE 6.4.
Structures and Strategies: Toward an Analysis of Administrative Issues and Alternatives in Children's Services Collaboration

The Process Dimension

	Separate Institutional Service Provision	Institutionally Collaborative Service Provision
Goal Structures	Minimal agreement on nature of the problem	Shared sense of problem and shared goals
Institutional Interests	Institutionally self-interested	Common institutional interests and merged reward structures
Environmental Controls	Independent environmental accommodations	Interdependent environmental accommodations
Institutional Conventions	Identifiably distinct conventions	Blended or shared institutional conventions

The Institutional Structures Dimension

Nevertheless, as the evaluation of a number of projects to date has indicated, such hard evidence of goal attainment is not readily at hand. Indeed, it is our claim in this chapter that a much more thorough attention to the deep structures of institutional collaboration may quite possibly be a necessary precondition to impact-upon-the-client measures of success. As Seymour Sarason (1993, 36) has framed it: One of the key "tricks" in any effort to engender change "is how to develop some kind of forum to prevent you from unduly underestimating complexity." One framework for those who would consider such a forum is offered here.

REFERENCES

Arvey, H. H., and A. Tijerina. (1992). The school of the future: Implementation issues in a school/community connection. Paper presented at an Invitational Conference on School/Community Connections: Exploring Issues for Research and Practice, 23–24 October. Washington, D.C.: National Center on Education in the Inner Cities.

Banfield, E. C. (1970). *The unheavenly city.* Boston: Little, Brown.

Behrman, R. E., ed. (Spring 1992). School-linked services. In *The future of children,* 2(1), Center for the Future of Children, Los Altos, Calif., pp. 4–5.

Bilovsky, R., and A. Zetlin. (1992). CSLA-Murchison School Partnership Family Service Center. Unpublished project description. Los Angeles: School of Education, California State University at Los Angeles.

Blank, M. J., A. I. Melaville, and G. Asayesh. (April 1993). *Together we can: A guide to crafting community-based family-centered strategies for integrating education and human services.* Washington, D.C.: Department of Education, Office of Educational Research and Improvement (OERI).

Boyd, W. L., and R. L. Crowson. (1992). Integration of services for children: A political economy of institutions perspective. Paper presented at an Invitational Conference on School/Community Connections, 23–24 October. Washington, D.C.: National Center on Education in the Inner Cities.

Bruner, C. (April 1991). Thinking collaboratively: Ten questions and answers to help policy makers improve children's services. Washington, D.C.: Education and Human Services Consortium.

Chaskin, R. J., and H. A. Richman. (Spring 1992). Concerns about school-linked services: Institution-based versus community-based models. In *The future of children,* ed. R. E. Behrman, 2(1), Center for the Future of Children, Los Altos, Calif. 107–117.

Coleman, J. S. (1988a). Social capital in the creation of human capital. *American Journal of Sociology* 94 (supple): S95–S120.

Coleman, J. S. (1988b). Statement before the Select Education Subcommittee of the Education and Labor Committee of the House of Representatives, April. Washington, D.C.

Crowson, R. L., and W. L. Boyd. (February 1993). Coordinated services for children: Designing arks for storms and seas unknown. *American Journal of Education* 101(2): 140–179.

Crowson, R. L., M. A. Smylie, and V. C. Hare. (April 1992). Administrative issues in coordinated children's services: A Chicago case study. Paper presented at the annual meeting of the American Educational Research Association (AERA), San Francisco.

Demsetz, H. (1967). Towards a theory of property rights. *American Economic Review* 57: 347–359.

Gardner, S. L. (Spring 1992). Key issues in developing school-linked integrated services. In *The future of children,* ed. R. E. Behrman. 2(1), 85–94.

Gray, B. (1991). *Collaborating: Finding common ground for multiparty problems.* San Francisco: Jossey-Bass.

Gray, B., and D. J. Wood. (1991). Collaborative alliances: Moving from practice to theory. Paper prepared for a special issue on Collaborative Alliances: Moving from Practice to Theory, *Journal of Applied Behavioral Science,* vol. 27, Numbers 1 and 2.

Hord, S. M. (February 1986). A synthesis of research on organizational collaboration. *Educational Leadership* 43(5): 22–26.

Intriligator, B. A. (1992). Designing Effective Inter-organizational Networks. Paper presented at the annual meeting of the University Council for Educational Administration (UCEA), 31 October, Minneapolis, Minn.

Joining Forces. (January 1992). Confidentiality and collaboration: Information sharing in interagency efforts. Denver, Colo.: Education Commission of the States.

Johnson, D., et al. (1980). *Secondary schools and the welfare network.* London: George Allen and Unwin.

Johnson, M. (October 1992). Emerging themes from interviews with twenty Minneapolis school-business partnerships, winter and spring. Minneapolis, Minn.: Minneapolis Youth Trust.

Kahne, J., and C. Kelley (October 1991). Assessing the coordination of children's services: An organizational approach. Unpublished paper. Stanford University School of Education.

Kirst, M. W. (April 1991). Improving children's services: Overcoming Barriers, Creating new opportunities. *Phi Delta Kappan* 72(8): 615–618.

Levin, R. (1991). University and elementary school faculty interview summary, Nation of Tomorrow Project. Unpublished report. Center for Urban Education Research and Development, College of Education, University of Illinois at Chicago.

Levin, R. (1992). Interviews with project participants, the Nation of Tomorrow Project. Unpublished Report. Center for Urban Education Research and Development, College of Education, University of Illinois at Chicago.

Lipsky, M. (1980). *Street-level bureaucracy: Dilemmas of the individual in public services.* New York: Russell Sage Foundation.

March, J. G., and J. P. Olsen. (1984). The new institutionalism: Organizational factors in political life. *American Political Science Review* 78(3): 734–749.

March, J. G., and J. P. Olsen. (1989). *Rediscovering institutions: The organizational basis of politics.* New York: The Free Press.

Melaville, A. I., with M. J. Blank. (January 1991). *What it takes: Structuring interagency partnerships to connect children and families with comprehensive services.* Washington, D.C.: Education and Human Services Consortium.

Mickelson, R. A., M. Yon, and I. Carlton-LaNey. (1992). Slipping through the cracks: The education of homeless children. Paper presented at an Invitational Conference on School/Community Connections, 23–24 October. Washington, D.C.: National Center on Education in the Inner Cities.

Powell, W. W., and P. J. DiMaggio, eds. (1991). *The new institutionalism in organizational analysis.* Chicago: University of Chicago Press.

Sarason, S. B. (1990). *The predictable failure of educational reform.* San Francisco: Jossey-Bass.

Sarason, S. B. (1993). *The case for change.* San Francisco: Jossey-Bass.

Scannapieco, M. (1992). Project 3.3, school-community programs, Minneapolis Youth Trust. A field report to the National Center for Education in the Inner Cities. Philadelphia: Temple University, College of Education.

Smylie, M. A., R. L. Crowson, and V. C. Hare. (October 1992). The principal and school-level administration of coordinated children's services. Paper presented at the annual meeting of the University Council for Educational Administration (UCEA), Minneapolis, Minn.

Trist, E. (1977). Collaboration in work settings: A personal perspective. *The Journal of Applied Behavioral Science* 13(3): 268–278.

Tyack, D. (Spring 1992). Health and social services in public schools: Historical perspectives. In *The Future of Children,* Center for the Study of Children, Los Altos, Calif. ed. R. E. Behrman, 2(1), 19–31.

Useem, E. L. (April 1991). What a difference a recession makes: The rise and fall of integrated services for at-risk youth in Massachusetts. Paper presented at the annual meeting of the American Educational Research Association (AERA), Chicago.

Wang, M. C., G. Haertel, and H. J. Walberg. (1992). The effectiveness of collaborative school-linked services. Paper presented at an Invitational Conference on School/Community Connections, 23–24 October. Washington, D.C.: National Center on Education in the Inner Cities.

Wilson, J. Q. (1989). *Bureaucracy: What government agencies do and why they do it.* New York: Basic Books.

Wood, D. J., and B. Gray. (July 1991). Toward a comprehensive theory of collaboration. *Journal of Applied Behavioral Science* 27(2): 95–114.

Zetlin, A., and R. Bilovsky. (1992). "Integrated Services Center Links School, Family, and Community." *The CEIC Review* (Sept.): 6–7.

Chapter 7

The Principal and Community-School Connections in Chicago's Radical Reform

Mark A. Smylie
Robert L. Crowson
Victoria Chou
Rebekah A. Levin

In 1989, Chicago's public schools began the nation's "most radical" experiment in school district decentralization. Each of the city's nearly six hundred schools acquired its own governing board in the form of an elected Local School Council (LSC). Six of each council's eleven members are parents and community representatives. Armed with the power to hire and fire their building principals, these councils also acquired significant, previously centralized controls over school-site budgets, curricula, and school-improvement planning (Hess Jr. 1991).

Just one year later, in 1990, with decentralization well underway, four of Chicago's inner-city elementary schools entered additionally into a foundation-funded experiment in coordinated children's services. This five-year project joined the four schools with the University of Illinois in collaborative efforts toward parent-and-community outreach, youth and health services, and school improvement.

The purpose of this paper is to examine the community-school connections implications of these initiatives. Specifically, we identify some instructive issues, problems, and lessons concerning school-site administration that emerge from this unique combination of efforts to promote organizational change in urban education. We begin with a brief discussion of pressures from decentralization to bring the community in to schools. We turn to a discussion of pressures associated with coordinated children's services to take schools out to the community. We then present our case of a coordinated children's services project in Chicago's decentralizing public school system. We discuss in some depth our observations of how principals shape a complicated and often contradictory array of community-school connections associated with this reform-within-a-reform.

DECENTRALIZATION: BRINGING THE COMMUNITY "IN" TO THE SCHOOL

An observational study of Chicago principals in the late 1970s, long before decentralization, found them engaged in a complex process of buffering their schools from the external environment (Morris, Crowson, Porter-Gehrie, and Hurwitz 1984). Principals sought actively to "harness" the unpredictability of the surrounding community, protect their schools and even "the larger organization" from community pressures, and socialize parents and the community into "reasonable" expectations of the local school.

Most principals were also found to be actively engaged in assisting individual parents and pupils with special needs, finding ways to spark greater parent interest and participation in the school, and probing their communities for resources (including the key resource of pupil enrollment and attendance). Such efforts toward a bit of outreach could be politically subtle and even tricky for principals. Parent involvement was generally not allowed beyond established buffers. Even then, active parents might be used creatively by principals inside the school as informants to report parents' perspectives on what's "really going-on" in the building (Morris et al. 1984).

Some early findings from research about the recent decentralization of the Chicago schools suggest some change. From the buffering of years past, Bruce McPherson and Robert Crowson (1992, 16–17) observe that now,

> [T]he community is less dangerous to educators than it once was. The LSC [Local School Council] is merely a representation of the community that has moved inside the school. The community used to be held at arm's length by most Chicago principals. That is the way the central office wanted it. Aspects of it occasionally were manipulated by astute principals, with or without permission, but a we-they mentality predominated in ghetto, working class, and

gentrified school communities. The doors were locked, and the sign on the front one said, "Report to the Office." But no longer, say these principals. The community and not the bureaucracy is the source of employment and hence allegiance. The community now is a potential source of support rather than a constant locale of trouble and conflict.

By no means can it be claimed that the community has become an accepted partner in school-site governance in all of Chicago's public schools. There is great variability (see Bryk, Easton, Kerbow, Rollow, and Sebring 1993). Some Chicago principals have learned strategies common to many school district superintendents—how to handpick their councils and how to control the policy-decision agendas that come to their councils. Other principals still fear council intrusion into the "real work" of the school. They attempt to maintain the old barriers, particularly with regard to a legislatively-mandated aspect of the reform process—joint school-community formulation and implementation of a school-improvement plan (SIP). Some plans have been the product of teacher, council, and administrator cooperation. Other plans have been administrator devised and then handed down to school and community. Nevertheless, even if old ways die hard for many Chicago administrators, there can be little doubt of the conclusion lodged in a simple quote from the *Chicago Sun-Times:* "School reform has opened up the can. It brought the community in" (Vander Weele and O'Donnell 1991, 14).

COORDINATED CHILDREN'S SERVICES: TAKING THE SCHOOL "OUT" TO THE COMMUNITY

Bringing the community in to the school is one matter. Taking the schools out to the community is quite another. An increasingly popular notion in urban education is that neighborhood schools should actively reach out to their communities with an array of coordinated services for families and children (Crowson and Boyd 1993). This notion has historic roots in the turn-of-the-century "Gary Plan" of Willard Wirt, the Mott Foundation's community-schooling initiatives of the 1940s and 1950s, and some of the "Great Society" experiments of the 1960s (Tyack 1992).

The new interest in improved outreach is also much associated with James Coleman's (1987, 1988) emphasis upon the need to strengthen "social capital" available to children in poverty. Coleman's insight is buttressed significantly by societal indicators of child abuse, delinquency, health, income support, and housing quality that show, together, the negative effects of declining access to support services for large numbers of children and youth (see Hodgkinson 1989, 1991; Kirst 1989, 1991; Littell and Wynn 1989). In addition, there is a renewed appreciation in education of: (a) the *ecological* interdependencies between schools and other social services (e.g., health, housing, recreation); (b) the importance of *complementary investments* in children's development and lives; and (c) the value of *developmental linkages* between the overall care and the successful education of children (Crowson and Boyd 1993).

Consistent with these perspectives, several coordinated children's service initiatives have recently developed across the nation. Among these "lighthouse" experiments that are charting new waters are "New Beginnings" in San Diego, "Walbridge Caring Communities" in St. Louis, various schools across the country in the Comer School Development Program, "Success for All" interventions in Baltimore and other cities, and "New Futures" projects supported by the Annie E. Casey Foundation (see Payzant 1992; Blank, Melaville, and Asayesh 1993; Dolan 1992; Melaville 1991; Wehlage, Smith, and Lipman 1992). Most outreach and services-coordination experiments, including the lighthouse efforts above, are by no means fully implemented or solidly in place. They are very much in the throes of what have been discovered to be some common "deep structure" problems. Common implementation difficulties have been found in: (a) cross-agency blending of professionals who have been trained distinctly and separately, (b) loosening of turf boundaries between service providers, (c) barriers to meaningful communication among partners to coordination, (d) removal of the "red tape" and procedural constraints to cooperation, and (e) leadership development in collaborative situations where there is little recourse to direct authority (Crowson and Boyd 1993).

Each of the experiments in children's services coordination takes place in its own, special milieu of city politics, environmental forces, and institutional histories. In some theorizing on the topic of collaboration, Gray and Wood (1991) point out that differing configurations of institutional partners and their environments can constitute separate domains of collaboration, each of which requires its own levels of special understanding. In this regard, Chicago's "reform-within-a-reform" offers insights into the difficulties in children's services coordination that may be unique, and only applicable, to the special school-reform context of Chicago. Nevertheless, Gary Wehlage (in Crowson and Boyd 1993) has noted that service-coordination experimentation in urban schools is quite likely to be just one part of a diverse menu of school restructuring (e.g., teacher work redesign, consumer choice, and decentralization). Such initiatives can easily collide head-on with one another, particularly at the building level, if they are not carefully thought through.

THE CHICAGO CASE: THE NATION OF TOMORROW

In fall 1990, the University of Illinois, in a project joining both of its campuses, inaugurated a coordinated children's services partnership with four low-income communities in Chicago. These communities include Austin, Englewood, West Town, and Pilsen. One public kindergarten through eighth grade elementary school was chosen to serve as the focal institution for service coordination in each community. Primary funding for the five-year project is from the W. K. Kellogg Foundation and the University of Illinois. The administrative home for the project is the Center for Urban Education Research and Development on the University's Chicago campus.[1]

The project, entitled "The Nation of Tomorrow," espouses an "ecological view of children's learning and development" (Nucci and Smylie 1991, 83). The project's title is derived from a statement made eighty years ago by President Theodore Roosevelt: "When you take care of children, you are taking care of the nation of tomorrow." The aim of this project is to enhance the capacities of and functional relationships among multiple institutions with which children interact from early childhood through at least early adolescence. Because it is impossible to involve all institutions with which children interact, the project targets four primary types of institutions in children's lives: (1) the family; (2) the school; (3) community child care and youth programs; and (4) community primary health-care agencies.

The Nation of Tomorrow contains three major program components that together constitute a collaborative institutional approach to serving children and families. University faculty from education, social work, cooperative extension, nursing, and kinesiology are among those involved in different program components. A first component, called "Family Ties," focuses on parent education and involvement in the education of their children at school. Its activities involve parents, social service providers, clergy, teachers, and other community leaders in developing parent education programs that are taught by parents in each community. This component links more effectively families with schools and schools with existing child care programs, after-school youth programs, and other social service agencies in the community.

Parent involvement and institutional linkages are facilitated by teams of Family Advocates who are hired from each community. While based in the project's elementary schools, these Family Advocates work in the communities to help families determine their needs for child care and youth programs and select community services that best meet their needs. They also work to promote stronger relationships between the schools and community service organizations.

A second component of the project is Partners in Health.[2] This component promotes the health of children and youth using a grassroots community-based approach to help parents understand and take greater responsibility for the primary health care of their children. It helps parents learn more about the health-care services available to their communities, how to gain access to them, and how to make them work in the best interests of their children. This component is conducted primarily through the project's elementary schools by full-time school nurses whose responsibilities are to coordinate and work with teams of Family Advocates (from the Family Ties component of the project) and Child Advocates, who, like the Family Advocates, are hired from the community. Each team works in its community to assess health needs of children and youth, link families and primary health-care providers, and help improve health education programs in the school.

The third project component, School Enhancement Activities, assists teachers in each school with their own professional learning and curricular and instructional program development. This component is based on collaborative models of staff development and school improvement. It proceeds from the premise that organizational problems in the school must be addressed before significant improvements can be made at the classroom level. This component seeks greater collaboration among teachers and school administrators in professional development and school improvement activities.

The project is administered by a university-based director and staff. University faculty members and staff are coordinators of the three program components. The project is overseen by an Operations Board that consists of university, community, and school representatives. The principals from the four project schools are designated school representatives. In addition, each community is served by a full-time site director who works out of the school and serves as a liaison between the university and the community and among community institutions (including the school) involved in the project.

SOURCES AND METHODS OF ANALYSIS

The data on which we base our observations come from several related sources. One source of data consists of accounts of three of the authors who are participant observers in the Nation of Tomorrow Project. These accounts include regularly recorded field notes documenting project activity, as well as periodic reflective and analytical progress reports to project administration. A second source consists of formal interviews of and regular informal interactions with other project participants, notably university faculty and staff working in the School Enhancement Activities component of the project. These interviews were conducted in the spring of 1991 and 1992, the second and third year of the Nation of Tomorrow project. They sought to elicit insight into administrative issues in service coordination in the schools and communities but also at the university.

Data were also drawn from archival records of project activity. These records, particularly interim and annual progress reports, contain data from formal interviews of principals and teachers that are conducted annually as part of the project's ongoing evaluation. This evaluation is being conducted by one of the authors of this paper.

Data from these multiple sources were analyzed using a constant comparative method of content analysis (Glaser 1978; Glaser and Strauss 1967). Emergent themes and patterns in the data were identified and reconciled across sources. It should be mentioned that the schools, principals, and other key personnel in this fairly well-publicized project are easily identified. Therefore our findings and supporting evidence are often pitched at a necessary level of generality. The findings we report suggest themes that we detect *across* the project's schools. These themes vary by building, however, we refrain from discussing such site-by-site variations to protect the confidentiality of those involved.

It should also be noted that our analysis discusses an experiment, and the larger Chicago reform in which it is embedded, that is still very much in process. The Nation of Tomorrow continues with funding through August 1994. Our observations are obviously mid-stream, with caveats aplenty regarding the long-term salience of issues or the means whereby those issues may be resolved.

A THEORETICAL NOTE

A "power-to-the-community" reform of decentralized school-site governance and a services-coordination "restructuring" of attitudes toward clients challenge in tandem some of the most basic *conventions* that drive schools. Institutional conventions, note James March and Johan Olsen (1984), help provide an extremely important function for those persons who work within an organization—imposing elements of order upon what might otherwise be an extremely ambiguous and a "potentially inchoate world" (743). An institution's special "order" is often found in that which derives from its unique history, its allocations of time, the management of its external environment, its normative structures, its special demographic characteristics, and its symbolic behavior (e.g., ceremonies, stories, rituals) (March and Olsen 1984, 1989).

Mention has already been made of the buffering functions of Chicago principals in the days before decentralization, functions that are still well represented symbolically in the "Visitors Report to the Office" signs on school doors and, once in the office, the chest-high counters that separate visitors from staff. Similarly, in service coordination, existing school conventions provide few built-in mechanisms for collaboration. Schools are not usually structured with even the simplest of organizational linkages upon which service coordination depends. Indeed, fragmentation and role specialization, rather than interdependency, are traditionally the workaday reality of schools. Robert Crowson and William Boyd (1993, 160) observe:

> Typically, guidance counselors advise students in near-isolation from teachers, troublesome pupils are sent from the classroom to the school office, certain pupils are pulled from the classroom for specialist help in reading or speech therapy, the extracurriculum (from football to chess club) exists as a separate program for which teachers receive added pay, and professional specialists, from nurses to librarians, are allocated their own turf in the school where their independent control is honored.

It is within the framework of the school's many separate and separating conventions that building principals seek to provide the glue necessary to hold a school together. Amid a typical lack of interdependency, principals have been found to spend a good bit of each day seeking to insure, or at least negotiate, within-school cooperation. For example, they juggle time schedules, fill gaps in work activities (e.g., covering for an absent teacher), closely monitor the school at busy moments (e.g., recess, lunch, dismissal), acquire and distribute supplies and equipment, settle personal disputes and other flare-ups, encourage a meeting of reporting deadlines, and ask for help or extra effort from the staff (e.g., for another committee assignment, an added pupil or two, etc.) (Morris et al. 1984). These activities help principals feel "in control" of organizations that are notoriously loosely coupled, heavily fragmented, and role specialized. To be, or feel, in control is important, for principals bear the risk of things gone wrong anywhere in the school organization. They are typically charged as stewards with the consideration of individuals' rights, maintenance of morale and energy levels, and encouragement of productive effort. They are responsible for foul-ups, events gone awry, and unresolved conflicts.

Principals must also interact with and satisfy the demands of a diverse and numerous group of stakeholders inside and outside their school communities. These stakeholders include but are not limited to teachers and teacher unions, students, parents, community leaders, and district office personnel. Stakeholder relationships are the very foundation of principal evaluation and accountability (Henry, Dickey, and Areson 1991). Yet different stakeholders do not necessarily share similar interests, goals, or organizational identities with principals or with one another. They may hold different expectations and make competing demands on principals that cannot all be met (Swidler 1979).

Many principals try to strike a balance, to satisfice. They attempt to minimize risk, avoid trouble, and achieve acceptable levels of outcomes to keep everyone happy. House and Lapan (cited in Fullan 1991, 145) summarize the problem this way:

> The principal has no set of priorities except to keep small problems from becoming big ones. His [sic] is a continuous task of crisis management. He responds to emergencies daily. He is always on call. All problems are seen as important. This global response to any and all concerns means he never has the time, energy, or inclination to develop or carry out a set of premeditated plans of his own. Containment of all problems is his theme. The principal cannot be a change agent or leader under these conditions.

Joseph Shedd and Samuel Bacharach (1991) note that "stable sets of arrangements" (i.e., conventions) typically evolve anew to keep peace. These arrangements often include tried-and-true administrative devices, such as avoidance, insulation, problem separation, rule and role redefinition, and ambiguity. These devices do not lend themselves well to innovation generally or service coordination particularly.

In sum, the press for organizational stability in principals' work may be challenged on several fronts by the introduction of decentralization and service coordination in schools. Although principals ordinarily play a sentinel's role in guarding the school door against potential disruptions from outside, service-coordination and decentralization initiatives attempt to open new doors and create greater community access to schools. They also introduce new actors, roles, expectations, and values into the school organization. These new roles, expectations, and values may conflict or compete for priority with one another and with existing roles, expectations, and values.

Principals' efforts to gain and maintain within-school cooperation are complicated significantly not only by the introduction of new actors but also by the absence of structural and social linkages, a lack of precedent for work role interdependence, plus concomitant confusion and ambiguity. These challenges may constrain principals' efforts to manage and control their schools. And while challenges to cooperation, order, and stability increase, so do the risks for principals as they face new and varied expectations for accountability (Smylie and Crowson 1993). In the next section, we examine our Chicago case of coordinated children's services to explore some ways in which principals respond to the press toward new institutional conventions while simultaneously paying obeisance to conventions of old.

THE PRINCIPAL AND COMMUNITY—SCHOOL CONNECTIONS

The following vignette illustrates a central dilemma posed by service coordination and decentralization. This dilemma puts principals in the difficult position of reconciling pressures to open schools, as well as to take school-based services out to the community with pressures upon them to maintain institutional control and stability. The vignette shows the potential loss of principals' control when services are extended to the community. At the same time, it illustrates principals' conservative responses to this risk. The "pulling in" behavior illustrated here has also been identified in other studies of principals' responses to decentralization of school governance (see Bryk et al. 1993; McPherson and Crowson 1994; Smylie and Crowson 1993). Finally, this vignette shows a fundamental difficulty faced by service providers, who must be client oriented to do their work with children, families, and community institutions effectively but also must attend to the risks of outreach and to the conservative tendencies of principals and other school professionals (see Lipsky 1980).

As noted earlier, a central component of the Nation of Tomorrow project is the employment of community residents who serve the project as Family Advocates. The Family Advocates use the project schools as bases to reach out to parents and families, bring services to the needs that surface, engage in parent education, encourage parent involvement, and bring leadership in the community (e.g., clergy, other-service providers, community leaders) together around the needs of families and children. The public schools have a record of somewhat similar outreach in the employment of professional social workers (usually in itinerant, one-day-a-week-per-school roles). However, the Family Advocates supply a much more intensive (but nonprofessional), closer-to-the-community representation of this activity. Furthermore, it will be remembered that the Family Advocates work within a larger school-governance context where another set of parent and community representatives comprise the majority of each school's Local School Council.

It did not take long for the Advocates and then for other project staff to discover that the Family Advocate role brought access to much extremely personal and privileged information about neighborhood families and their children. Such information, whether withheld or shared, could be powerful politically in the school and community. Moreover, such information collected by (or available to) persons who share the authority of the school now represents a decided risk to the school. A blow-up, the foundations of which an Advocate may know about while the principal remains uninformed, provides a decided threat to the principal's "I'm-in-control-here" legitimacy with the school's governing body.

The project's principals stipulated that the data, the information uncovered by Family Advocates in the course of their activities, must be shared with them. The principal, they argued, bears the burden of ultimate responsibility, and this burden requires access. The Family Advocates responded that much of the information is highly confidential, and parents will only participate in the project if assured confidentiality. The information should remain fully within the domain of the Family Ties component of the project, they contended.

In a showdown on the issue, project administrators ruled that, indeed, the responsibility borne by principals warrants their access to the Family Advocate data. Project participants observed, consequently, that the Family Advocates are now collecting little information and sharing less. Principals are busily trying to find out what has been held back. The relations between principals and the project's from-the-community employees have been damaged.

As this vignette shows, the addition of service coordination and increased numbers of parent, community, and professional personnel in the schools adds exponentially to the complexities and ambiguities of principaling. The principals in this case have responded in generally cautious, strategic, and conserving ways.[3]

First, principals, in varying degrees, compartmentalized and isolated the project from routine school functions. Second, they engaged in entrepreneurial behavior, treating the project as a reservoir of resources for their schools. Finally, principals evoked a wide range of control mechanisms to influence project implementation. Each of these responses aimed at satisficing, at striking an acceptable compromise among the demands of the coordinated services project, the goals and demands of the school, and key stakeholder groups in the school community. Each seemed aimed at reducing complexities and ambiguities introduced by the project (and school reform) and maintaining internal order to meet immediate school needs and achieve existing school goals.

Compartmentalization

While decentralization in Chicago "opened the can and let the community in," most of Chicago's principals, including the four in our case, have struggled hard to maintain separation between reform policy and everyday school administration (see McPherson and Crowson 1992, 1994). Principals are expected, even more so now, to run their schools successfully. To talk therefore of a new emphasis upon "functional relationships with multiple institutions" is to talk of the possibility of a fundamental breakdown in running the school. For now other actors, other institutional players, have a voice. Far better to continue to compartmentalize.

It was discovered early on in the Nation of Tomorrow project that the principals understood this dilemma intuitively. Despite their initial endorsements of the project, the principals held varying conceptions of its aims, its approaches to service coordination and change, and their responsibilities to promote project implementation. These conceptions were not necessarily consistent with those of the project. Project staff observed the difficulties of principals (and many teachers for that matter) "getting their heads around" the project's philosophy of service coordination, collaboration, and empowerment. They also observed difficulty in the principals' ability to conceptualize the work of their schools in terms that went beyond traditional instructional activities within the four walls of the building.

Accordingly, the principals tended to view the project as an add-on rather than as an endeavor vital to their schools' missions. They perceived the project as a pool of resources that could supplement ongoing school activities; achieve existing school goals; satisfy expectations and demands of teachers, parents, and community leaders; and ensure their own accountability to the school community. The principals did not view the project as one that necessarily posed different goals for their schools or that called for significant changes in school-level work roles, relationships, or activities.

Operating from these starting points, the principals tended to treat the project as a separate entity, a useful but not integral or necessary addition to their schools. They considered it secondary to the primary goals and activities of the school. The principals held the project at a distance, close enough to take advantage of its resources but far enough away that it did not impact significantly on the daily life of their schools. They seemed to see clearly that desirable separation of reform from administration would be endangered if the school reached out and extended services too far *into* the policy arena of the community.

Entrepreneurial Strategies

While the principals adopted an ancillary and compartmentalized view of the project, they nonetheless perceived it as a valuable commodity. Each used a variety of strategies to capture project resources for their schools and communities. The principals adroitly turned project-level administrative meetings into forums to lobby for fair shares of monetary and personnel resources. They learned to circumvent project leadership and what they perceived to be cumbersome, unresponsive administrative protocols within the project and the administering university to obtain desired resources. For example, several principals bypassed project Site Directors and Program Component Coordinators to contact and recruit directly individual university faculty to work with teachers in their schools. Others sought to build coalitions with college-level administrators to influence project administrators' decisions concerning resource distribution.

Once acquired, it was not unusual for the principals to redirect resources from purposes acknowledged to be important to the project as a whole to purposes more consistent with existing school goals and ongoing activities. Nowhere is such redirection more apparent than in principals' attempts to redefine project staff members' roles and absorb their activities into their schools. These actions appear keyed to meeting immediate, pressing needs of the school and, of course, fit conventions regarding what people who work in schools are supposed to do. For example, when the project's nurses were first assigned to their schools, most were asked by principals to provide traditional health-care services and perform related administrative duties (e.g., serve sick students, conduct vision and hearing examinations, check immunization records) in addition to the community liaison and health education roles they were supposed to perform in the project. The nurses complained, for they saw themselves professionally as community- and family-health nurses, not school nurses. Nevertheless, as time passed, the traditional activities assigned to the nurses by the principals began to supplant and preclude the innovative.

Similarly, principals began to redefine the Family Advocates' roles. Several brought these project staff members into their schools to solve immediate problems or crisis situations concerning individual students and parents. By refocusing their activities inside the school, the principals' actions compromised Family Advocates' abilities to perform their institutional liaison and family development roles in the communities. They reduced the threat of project personnel out loose and uncontrolled in the community.

Avoiding crises is one of the most important managerial conventions in school-site management. Proactive activity out in the neighborhoods and among parents offers the danger of creating or fostering crises. Furthermore, an entrepreneurialism that brings more resources, particularly personnel, into the ongoing and familiar-to-all work of the school is a solid indicator of successful principaling that is easily understood as progress by the principal's employers, the Local School Council.

Control Mechanisms

As we noted earlier, this coordinated services project created new expectations for schools and introduced new actors into the buildings. It led to increased organizational demands, ambiguities, potential loss of control, and, indeed, greater responsibilities for principals, all at a critical time of citywide reform in school-site governance. Not all the project's schools accommodated these changes well. As one project staff member observed:

> It isn't clear that the schools have each become completely reconciled to all the new actors, to all the new things going on. There may be a sense to some of the principals of activities out-of-control, balanced against their sense of much greater responsibility for it all.

In order to confront new demands and ambiguities, the principals sought to exert greater control over various aspects of the project inside and outside their schools. They did so to balance stability and control within their buildings with satisfactory levels of outreach and community participation. In city schools, maintaining control is one of the strongest of institutional conventions. The principal is directly at risk when control is lost, and control is easily lost as activities, services, and outreach efforts multiply.

The principals in this case employed several different types of control strategies. They established communication and reporting systems to stay informed of project activities. They also began to micromanage project activities in their schools. The principals took on the role of gatekeeper to regulate project personnel access and activity in the buildings. Finally, they worked in different ways to influence the agendas of project activities and monitor and influence the work of project staff.

For the most part, the principals acted consciously and strategically. Their aim may have been self-protection from the individual risks posed by the scope and ambiguities of the project. At the same time, the principals may have sought a more conservative and stable course for the implementation of this service-coordination project to keep their schools on a more even keel in an already uncertain and pressure-filled context of school decentralization. Our data do not allow us to disentangle these objectives. We suspect, however, that individual and institutional interests in this case are compatible and reinforcing and that the principals were trying to achieve some combination of the two. In the sections that follow, we describe how the different types of control strategies were used.

Communication and reporting systems. From the beginning, each of the principals insisted on being kept informed of project decisions and activities within their schools and communities. The lengths to which these administrators would go to enforce this value are illustrated well in the earlier vignette regarding the confidential information available to Family Advocates.

The primary and central source of most of the project-related information was the Site Director. Several principals worked informally with their Site Directors, expecting to be informed of all planned activities and problems that might occur. Others established more formal procedures, such as weekly meetings and reporting forms. Expectations placed on the Site Directors for keeping their principals informed were considerable. Failure to provide accurate information in a timely manner was one of the primary sources of strain between the principals and the Site Directors. The hierarchical conventions began to shape the coordinative relationships and functions of the Site Directors.

Micromanagement. As the project evolved and as growing numbers of persons became engaged in school-based community outreach, principals became increasingly involved in the daily operations of project management within their schools. For some, this involvement extended to keeping track of building use, meeting schedules, teacher attendance in staff development activities, and the comings and goings of university faculty, Site Directors, and Family and Child Advocates. As discussed below, it also extended to a more direct role in monitoring and supervising project personnel assigned to their schools.

This increased level of involvement came at considerable cost. Several principals have expressed frustration with what one termed the TNT (The Nation of Tomorrow) Burden. While also attesting to compartmentalizing the project, one principal claimed, "I feel like I'm running two different schools." Despite the additional burden, this form of micromanagement helped principals regain some control over an ambitious and ambiguous enterprise. Indeed, on the positive side, according to some project participants, greater principal involvement even led to increased morale and coherence in project implementation.

Gatekeeping. In similar risk-acknowledging actions, the principals placed themselves at the pinnacle of school-level decision making. They became the final arbiters of activities that would take place in their schools and how those activities would be conducted. In fact, very little of this project has been initiated inside the schools without principals' knowledge and consent.

Interestingly, this gatekeeping function has not been characteristic of the principals' own employers, the Local School Councils. The LSCs have been little involved in the development of policy and setting directions for the Nation of Tomorrow project. To be sure, some principals have taken care to verbalize linkages between the project and the school's Improvement Plan, which *is* LSC approved. However, in the main, the evidence suggests that principals see the project as an add-on and as an activity to be compartmentalized from the governance and oversight that might be exerted by the Council.

Several examples illustrate the principals' gatekeeping influence, and illustrate as well a gatekeeping function that speaks to the principals' *own* political agendas rather than their Councils'. In one example, a principal who had initially expressed interest in establishing a School Enhancement Activity, proposed by a university faculty member, blocked its implementation because of tensions between that principal's school and another school outside the project that the university faculty member wished to include in the activity. In a second example, a principal stymied implementation of a curricular initiative jointly planned by school and university faculty. A teacher recalled:

> The school administration gave verbal encouragement to our group, but s/he did not follow through or hear the ideas that were generated.

Not all gatekeeping functioned to shut out activity unwanted by the principals. The principals embraced and advocated initiatives that they perceived to be in the interests of their schools. In a final example, a principal invited and publicly advocated an initiative to develop plans to restructure the school day and create more time for teacher collaborative planning and staff development activities. Indeed, this principal sought out and obtained funds to compensate teachers for developing these plans during the summer.

As principals located school-level project decisions in their offices, they also employed a number of mechanisms to control the pace and outcomes of project decision making and activities within their schools. In several instances, principals delayed the inauguration of activities that they were ambivalent about or objected to by being inaccessible to teachers or project staff when decisions had to be made. They also delayed project activity by taking matters under advisement for extended periods of time. As one university faculty member observed of a school:

> Everything is channeled through the principal's office. Opportune moments and momentum are lost when the principal is unavailable or delays decisions in order to "study" the matter.

Another strategy that has influenced the pace of decisions and activities is the designation of assistant principals as liaisons between project staff and the principal. Another university faculty member observed:

> I have much more regular contact with the assistant principal. Yet there are many areas where [s/he] can't make a decision without consulting the principal. There's delay that slows everything down.

On matters of mutual interest and concern, the principals expedited decision making and implementation of project activity in their schools. They granted project personnel direct access, called planning sessions, and urged progress. While expecting to be kept informed throughout, they divested implementation decisions to project personnel to increase the pace of valued activity.

Influencing work agendas. One of the strongest and most lasting conventions still to be found in even the most restructured school districts is that the principal is the central, work-defining authority of the school (see Bryk et al. 1993; Malen and Ogawa 1988; McPherson and Crowson 1994). In several instances, principals in this case sought to influence the substantive agendas of project activities, agendas that according to the project principles were to be jointly constructed by participants. Several university faculty members noted that much of what they did in the schools was dictated by principals who wanted to see particular things happen. One university faculty member recalled the successful attempts of a principal to enlarge the focus of a School Enhancement Activity to incorporate specific issues of the principal's concern and an initiative that the principal wanted to see adopted by the faculty at large. While these matters were important to the principal and to the achievement of schoolwide goals, they went well beyond what participating teachers and the university faculty member wished to do.

Principals also influenced work agendas by sanctioning participation in project activities. When activities were consistent with principals' interests and concerns for the school, they were more likely to support their initiation and teacher participation. In an extreme example, one of the principals explained how [s/he] attempted to use the project to influence the school's curriculum:

> I demanded of the teachers this year that they take full advantage of [the university faculty member's] input. I've requested, no demanded, that they write a curriculum. That one School Enhancement Activity went debunk mainly because the lack of sharing of information and the actual implementation of what they received in an intellectual capacity, from professional to professional. I'm demanding that they write a curriculum and align that curriculum with the goals and objectives of the State, using [the university faculty member's] information and things that they discuss. What I want to see is a hard copy of their thoughts and the best practices we could possibly use.

Generally, when the principals supported project activities, teacher and university participants felt encouraged, and the activities were more likely to succeed. Several university faculty members pointed to the cooperation of principals in helping start specific staff development and curriculum development activities. On the other hand, when principals discouraged participation, efforts to initiate project activities did not get very far. With respect to some suggested staff development and school improvement activities, teachers reported indifference on the part of their principals toward participation. Over time, this indifference engendered ambivalence among teacher participants who began to believe that without their principal's support nothing significant would come from their work. A small number of teachers from one school described hostility directed at them for their participation in a particular School Enhancement Activity. These teachers were frustrated by what they perceived were the principal's efforts to undermine their attempts to bring about change in the school. This frustration led some teachers to withdraw, leading eventually to cessation of the activity.

Supervising project personnel. A final means by which principals sought to exert influence is through monitoring, supervision, and accountability of project personnel assigned to their schools. Most project staff who work in the schools over time reported less freedom to come and go as they pleased. Some reported more frequent meetings with the principals and less independence in their work. Others told of the establishment of elaborate reporting systems so that principals could keep better track of project activities inside and outside the school. According to these staff members, increased monitoring and supervision tied them to the school and compromised their ability to form effective community linkages.

At the center of the press for accountability is the Site Director. Interestingly, compartmentalization of the project also gave principals a chance to place blame for anything gone wrong on the heads of the *project's* key site-based leaders rather than accept responsibility as the *school's* key leader. As the project progressed, the role and the work of the Site Directors came under increased scrutiny. During the third year of the project, when the Site Directors' positions were being assessed, the principals attempted to gain more control over these persons' work. The principals contended that because of their positions as "person[s] at the top of the pyramid" in their schools, it should be they, rather than the Project Director or Program Component Coordinators, to whom Site Directors are first accountable. The principals sought to redefine the Site Directors' roles, increasing the time they spend working in schools and broadening their supervisory responsibilities over all project personnel assigned to their schools. The net effects of these changes were to increase principals' control over the Site Directors and increase the Site Directors' accountability to the principals. At the same time these changes served to reduce principals' own responsibility for project success.

CONCLUSION

Our Chicago case finds four schools engaged in a reform-within-in-a-reform that involves a "bringing-in" of the community to school governance and improvement activities and simultaneously a "reaching-out" of child and family services to the community. While the coordinated services initiative and the decentralization of schools in Chicago are still very much in progress, we draw two general conclusions at this time.

First, both the larger Chicago reform and the four-school initiative in children's services coordination are still at an early-days stage of implementation. There may be much impact yet to come from both initiatives, particularly from Chicago's decentralized structure of school-site governance. Nevertheless, there is some evidence of change and adaptation in the four project schools. Persons who live in the communities are employed as advocates for children and families. Although struggling with tensions between in-school conventions and out-in-the-community service provision, the project schools are learning a new outreach role. There are new opportunities for teachers' professional learning and development. There are new services and resources available to children and their families. And, there is increased interaction among each school, parents, and other institutions in the four-project communities.

Our *second,* and larger, conclusion is that the *persistence* of organizational forms and processes, most of which are *not* conducive to community-school connections, comprises a yet little-understood barrier to service coordination reform. Shedd and Bacharach (1991, 191) address this issue clearly, noting that many structures and behaviors in school administration operate together as "a relatively stable set of arrangements for making ad hoc adjustments to competing pressures." The competing pressures in our Chicago case are clear and involve a citywide reform to let communities *in* to school-site governance and an experimental project designed to take schools as service providers and coordinators *out* to their communities. There are pressures involving efforts to enhance professional development in the schools while the school staff and administration are simultaneously adjusting to decentralized decision making and increased involvement of parents, community members, and teachers in school governance. There are also pressures from introducing a parallel set of project administrators, the Site Directors, into schools that were at the same time trying to accommodate a reform that placed the building principal's very employment in the hands of a parent and community representative majority on the Local School Council.

Focusing primarily upon the building principal, our analysis uncovered a tendency for tried-and-true conventions of school administration to grow in saliency under the competing pressures of community-relations reforms. Indeed, because the pressures of our case were not symmetrical, our ability to observe the fall-back conventions that principals used was much enhanced. When complexity, ambiguity, and risk reign, that which is persistent and seemingly dependable in administration looms large.

Thus, an outreach initiative producing much new but potentially risky information about families succumbed to the convention that the principal is properly in charge. Loosely-coupled schools succeeded in compartmentalizing reforms meant to encourage collaboration. Staff members and services designed for outreach, for advocacy, were pressured by schools to refocus upon in-school rather than out-of-school activities. Under the twin instabilities of decentralized governance and services-outreach reform, we find paradoxically that close control and micromanagement of what is going on *in*side the the school become paramount.

At the heart of a growing body of literature labeled "the new institutionalism" is an inquiry into the complexities of persistence above change (e.g., March and Olsen 1989; Powell and DiMaggio 1991). Of key interest are questions about how the order of an organization is maintained through its symbolic systems, routines, classifications, habits or conventions, rules, environmental interactions, and disciplinary processes. How do these forces come into play to maintain order and minimize uncertainty when an organization is newly faced with conflict, contradiction, and ambiguity? And, what is the impact of the principal who marshalls the forces of order and stability that are simultaneously necessary for institutional adaptation and preservation of ongoing institutional integrity?

It would be easy to interpret the organizational stability efforts of principals generally, and in this Chicago case specifically, in negative terms, as a power issue or an administrative control issue. It might be far more instructive to examine closely principals' behavior as an important window into the very difficult struggles to maintain institutional order and stability when faced with the press of external change.

Of course, as we acknowledged in our discussion of control strategies, individual control and institutional stability are not necessarily competing interests. They may be interdependent and mutually reinforcing. A principal's control and power may be preserved and even enhanced through institutional order. Indeed, as new accountability systems evolve in decentralizing school systems (see Smylie and Crowson 1993), principals may find that maintaining institutional order and stability in the face of disruptions posed by fairly radical reforms is evidence to some stakeholders of individual leadership and competence. Yet, it also seems that as individual control interests and institutional stability grow to reinforce one another, not much gets changed, and the substantial benefits that may accrue to children from deep structure changes in schools called for in community-school connections reforms go denied.

NOTES

1. For a more detailed description of the Nation of Tomorrow project, see Nucci and Smylie (1991). See also, Crowson, Smylie, and Hare (1992) and Smylie, Crowson, and Hare (1992).

2. The Partners in Health component was not initiated at the outset of the project because of budget limitations. It began in 1992 with resources from the University of Illinois and the Robert Wood Johnson Foundation.

3. An added difficulty is encountered, of course, when there is principal turnover during the course of the project. Indeed, one of the schools experienced three different principals during the project's first twenty-two months.

REFERENCES

Blank, M. J., A. I. Melaville, and G. Asayesh. (1993). *Together we can: A guide to crafting community-based family-centered strategies for integrating education and human services.* Washington, D.C.: Department of Education, Office of Educational Research and Improvement.

Bryk, A. S., J. W. Easton, D. Kerbow, S. G. Rollow, and P. A. Sebring. (1993). *A view from the elementary schools: The state of reform in Chicago.* Chicago: Consortium for Chicago School Research, University of Chicago.

Coleman, J. S. (1987). Families and schools. *Educational Researcher* 16(6): 32–38.

Coleman, J. S. (1988). Social capital in the creation of human capital. *American Journal of Sociology* 94: 95–120.

Crowson, R. L., and W. L. Boyd. (1993). Coordinated services for children: Designing arks for storms and seas unknown. *American Journal of Education* 101: 140–179.

Crowson, R. L., M. A. Smylie, and V. C. Hare. (1992). *Administrative issues in coordinated children's services: A Chicago case study.* Paper presented at the annual meeting of the American Educational Research Association, San Francisco.

Dolan, L. J. (1992). *An evaluation of social service integration within six elementary schools in Baltimore.* Washington, D.C.: National Center on Education in the Inner Cities.

Fullan, M. (1991). *The new meaning of educational change,* ed. 2. New York: Teachers College Press.

Glaser, B. G. (1978). *Theoretical sensitivity: Advances in the methodology of grounded theory.* Mill Valley, Calif.: Sociology Press.

Glaser, B. G.. and A. L. Strauss. (1967). *The discovery of grounded theory.* Chicago: Aldine.

Gray, B., and D. J. Wood. (1991). Collaborative alliances: Moving from practice to theory. *Journal of Applied Behavioral Science* 27: 3–22.

Henry, G. T., K. C. Dickey, and J. C. Areson. (1991). Stakeholder participation in educational performance monitoring systems. *Educational Evaluation and Policy Analysis* 12: 177–188.

Hess, G. A., Jr. (1991). *School restructuring, Chicago style.* Newbury Park, Calif.: Corwin Press.

Hodgkinson, H. L. (1991). Reform versus reality. *Phi Delta Kappan* 73: 9–16.

Hodgkinson, H. L. (1989). *The same client: The demographics of education and service delivery systems.* Washington, D.C.: Institute for Educational Leadership, Center for Demographic Policy.

Kirst, M. W., ed. (1989). *The conditions of children in California.* Berkeley: University of California, Policy Analysis for California Education, University of California.

Kirst, M. W. (1991). Improving children's services: Overcoming barriers, creating new opportunities. *Phi Delta Kappan* 72: 615–618.

Lipsky, M. (1980). *Street-level bureaucracy.* New York: Russell Sage Foundation.

Littell, J., and J. Wynn. (1989). *The availability and use of community resources for young adolescents in an inner-city and a suburban community.* Chicago: University of Chicago, Chapin Hall Center for Children.

Malen, B., and R. T. Ogawa. (1988). Professional-patron influence on site-based governance councils: A confounding case study. *Educational Evaluation and Policy Analysis* 10: 251–270.

March, J. G., and J. P. Olsen. (1984). The new institutionalism: Organizational factors in political life. *American Political Science Review* 78: 734–749.

March, J. G., and J. P. Olsen. (1989). *Rediscovering institutions: The organizational basis of politics.* New York: The Free Press.

McPherson, R. B., and R. L. Crowson. (1992). *Creating schools that "work" under Chicago reform: The adaptations of building principals.* Paper presented at the annual conference of the University Council for Educational Administration, Minneapolis, Minn.

McPherson, R. B., and R. L. Crowson. (1994). The principal as mini-superintendent under Chicago school reform. In *Reshaping the principalship: Insights from transformational reform efforts,* ed. J. Murphy and K. S. Louis. Newbury Park, Calif.: Corwin Press.

Melaville, A. I. (1991). *What it takes: Structuring interagency partnerships to connect children and families with comprehensive services.* Washington, D.C.: Education and Human Services Consortium.

Morris, V. C., R. L. Crowson, C. Porter-Gehrie, and E. Hurwitz, Jr. (1984). *Principals in action: The reality of managing schools.* Columbus, Ohio: Charles E. Merrill.

Nucci, L. P., and M. A. Smylie. (1991). University-community partnerships: Addressing problems of children and youth through institutional collaboration. *Metropolitan Universities* 2(1): 83–91.

Payzant, T. W. (1992). New Beginnings in San Diego: Developing a strategy for interagency collaboration. *Phi Delta Kappan* 74: 139–146.

Powell, W. W., and P. J. DiMaggio, eds. (1991). *The new institutionalism in organizational analysis.* Chicago: University of Chicago Press.

Shedd, J. B., and S. B. Bacharach. (1991). *Tangled hierarchies: Teachers as professionals and the management of schools.* San Francisco: Jossey-Bass.

Smylie, M. A., and R. L. Crowson. (1993). Principal assessment under restructured governance. *Peabody Journal of Education* 68(2): 64–84.

Smylie, M. A., R. L. Crowson, and V. C. Hare. (1992). *The principal and school-level administration of coordinated children's services.* Paper presented at the annual meeting of the University Council for Educational Administration, Minneapolis, Minn.

Swidler, A. (1979). *Organizations without authority: Dilemmas of social control in free schools.* Cambridge: Harvard University Press.

Tyack, D. (1992). Health and social services in public schools: Historical perspectives. In *The future of children,* ed. R. E. Behrman, 2(1), 19–31.

Vander Weele, M., and M. O'Donnell. (14 April 1991). Schools in ruins. *Chicago Sun-Times,* pp. 12–14.

Wehlage, G., G. Smith, and P. Lipman. (1992). Restructuring urban schools: The New Futures Experience. *American Educational Research Journal* 29: 55–96.

Chapter 8

Schools as Intergovernmental Partners: Administrator Perceptions of Expanded Programming for Children

Carolyn Herrington

Educational administrators are increasingly becoming partners with other local providers in the delivery of intergovernmental programming. No longer able to remain within a "splendid isolation" from other local governments, schools are becoming partners in a wide variety of programmatic responses to the declining conditions of children and the increased fiscal stress of all human services institutions. Intergovernmental programs are defined as policies and programs that develop within the interstices of existing local governmental structures. Intergovernmental administrators are officials who develop policy for or manage programs that are jointly sponsored by the government by which they are employed and by one or more other governments. The entities involved may include local general and special purpose governments, as well as federal, state, and substate regional governments that deliver services directly. It also includes nonprofit and for-profit organizations that deliver publicly subsidized services. It usually involves the sharing of personnel, facilities, and equipment.

Research within the field of educational administration has focused primarily on documenting the growing needs of children, the inefficiencies and dysfunctions of the current child service delivery systems, and advancing arguments for why schools must join with other human services agencies in addressing these needs (e.g., Kirst 1991). Early evaluations of some initial demonstration projects have documented the enormity of the enterprise and the resistance displayed by social institutions, particularly schools, to working collaboratively (Center for the Study of Social Policy 1991), and there are beginning to appear writings whose perspective is more critical (Crowson and Boyd 1993; Herrington and Lazar 1994). Little has appeared within the educational administration literature investigating the managerial and leadership issues raised for educational administrators by these new programmatic linkages. The article provides an analysis of the pressures being placed on schools to become more active in intergovernmental programming, reviews the research on barriers to effective intergovernmental programming, and explores the challenges these new programs pose to educational administrators as determined by in-depth interviews with a small sample of school principals and district superintendents.

CHANGING LANDSCAPE OF LOCAL GOVERNMENT AND SCHOOLS

A Century of Separation

Around the turn of this century, public schools became separated from other local governments. Propelled by both urban educational reform movements and attempts to professionalize school administration, school systems became increasingly separate and then isolated from the municipal and county governments that served the same area and children. The governmental reforms of the early part of this century emanated from an attempt to free schools from partisan politics and political corruption. School boards, school administrators, and the school systems strove for and attained a "unique function" image that, in general, accorded school people higher status and higher salaries than other municipal offices and officials (Cremin 1988). School districts became special purpose governments with their own taxing authority, own rule-making authority, and separate election cycles. However, this separation isolated education from other human services impacting children. As school district boundaries became independent of other local governments, their jurisdictional lines often bore no relation to other admininstrative or political divisions. Politically, the isolation was reinforced by the nonpartisan character of most school district races (Wirt and Kirst 1992). When pressure to meet the needs of children forced schools to take on noninstructional functions, schools usually preferred to set up parallel service systems under their aegis. Schools often acquired exemptions from licensure or certification requirements in other professional areas allowing teachers to carry out the new responsibilities or creating separate professional programs under the control of colleges of education and state departments of education, such as school psychologists, school nurses, and school counselors (Herrington and Lazar 1994).

Increasingly, however, this separate status and the isolation of school districts from other local governments is being questioned. The percentage of children living in poverty, living in homes headed by mothers only, lacking medical insurance, entering the juvenile justice system, engaging in high-risk behaviors, such as too early sexual activity, unprotected intercourse, substance abuse, and street violence and living in substandard residences rose throughout the eighties (Children's Defense Fund 1989; Hodgkinson 1989). Furthermore, other community infrastructures that supported healthy child development in the past are weakening. Roles previously assumed by extended families, neighborhoods, and religious institutions are being left by default to the public sector (National Commission on Children 1991). As society has become more complex, community life more secular and individuals more mobile, neighborhoods have become less vital and neighbors more isolated. As a result, city, county, and other local governments are under increased pressure to strengthen their services on behalf of children and their families and are turning to schools as potential partners.

Pressures for Collaboration

Because schools represent the largest publicly subsidized program for children, they are a critical part of any comprehensive approach to improving the condition of children. For virtually all communities, the most extensive infrastructure of facilities, personnel, data, and expertise on children resides in the public school system. A recent study sorting out all governmental funds for children within the federalist system calculates total *federal* outlays for children at approximately $59.5 billion, while total *state and local* expenditures for public elementary and secondary schools, $90.0 and $80.0 billion respectively, exceed that figure by a factor of three. Even if indirect federal support is included (i.e., tax expenditures), another $98.1 billion, federal support still falls short of state and local outlays. (See Table 8.1). To capture this large set of resources, federal and state governments and private foundations are encouraging or requiring schools to become partners in intergovernmental programming for children.

TABLE 8.1.
Estimated Public Expenditures on Children
Fiscal Year 1989
(in billions)

FEDERAL	
Direct Expenditure	
Income Support	$20.74
Nutrition	13.49
Social Services	4.43
Education	9.09
Training	2.26
Health	5.11
Housing	4.37
Subtotal	59.49
Tax Expenditures	38.64
TOTAL ALL FEDERAL	98.13
STATE AND LOCAL	
State elementary & secondary education	89.99
Local elementary & secondary education	80.03
State and local AFDC	6.07
State foster care	.99
State Medicaid	3.20
TOTAL STATE AND LOCAL	$180.28

*Source: J. Juffras and E. Steuerle. Public Expenditures on Children, Fiscal Year 1989. Paper presented to the National Commission on Children, November 1990, Airlie, Virginia.

Federal Program and Policy Initiatives. The federal Education for All Handicapped Children Act of 1975 laid the groundwork for closer cooperation between health and educational providers through the requirement that school districts provide educational services to all students no matter how severely handicapped, thus encouraging information sharing and joint planning between schools and other health and human service providers. The federal stimulus for closer coordination increased dramatically with the 1988 amendments to the Act, in particular, Part B focusing on three- and four-year olds and Part H focusing on infants and toddlers. The federal government challenged states to develop local interagency coordination and service delivery structures for early intervention services. While there is considerable diversity in how states have chosen to structure approaches to Parts B and H, many have required local governments, school districts, and community-based organizations to engage in coordinated planning, data collection, and service sorting (Herrington 1989). The most recent set of amendments to the federal government welfare programs, the 1988 Family Support Act and especially the Job Opportunities and Basic Skills (JOBS) training program requires that programs look at family needs broadly while addressing employability issues. Education, training, child care, and medical components must be addressed, as well as case management services (National Center for Children in Poverty 1992). Further linkages with the education system have been proposed by states as they implement JOBS, including requiring welfare recipients to guarantee the attendance of teenage children in high school, under threat of loosing eligibility, as Wisconsin has done. Finally, the first of the national goals in education is proving a stimulus to interagency coordination as states and local districts develop strategies to assure that all children start school ready to learn (Goals 2000 Community Exchange 1993).

State Comprehensive Educational Reform Initiatives. Many state education reform initiatives emphasize redesign and restructuring of the entire delivery system, and a critical element is often comprehensive approaches, through school linkages, to health and social services needed by children. The Kentucky Education Reform Act includes provision for school-based Family Resource and Youth Services Centers to be administered by the school or a consortium of schools (David 1993). Advisory councils, in addition to including school personnel, parents, and community representatives, are to include staff of the public and private services used by the centers for referrals. As part of the 1991 education reform legislation in Florida, schools and districts will be required to develop collaborative agreements with agencies within the community, such as the state health and human services agency, other governmental agencies, public libraries, and medical practitioners (Florida Department of Education 1993).

Philanthropic Community. A striking consensus exists among major child-oriented foundations about the potential inherent in comprehensive, community-based approaches to children and families with multiple problems. Guided in no small part by the influential work of Lisbeth Schorr and Daniel Schorr (1988) and Michael Kirst (1991), philanthropic interests, including the Annie E. Casey Foundation, the Pew Memorial Trusts, and the Robert Wood Johnson Foundation, have placed their considerable clout and funds behind such integrated-services approaches. Key to their concept of what is necessary to achieve a critical mass of leverage over the current service delivery systems is the horizontal integration of policy, planning, and service delivery at the local level (Center for the Study of Social Policy 1991; Liederman et al. 1991).

INTERGOVERNMENTAL PROGRAMMING AND SCHOOLS

Growth in Intergovernmental Programming

As a result of these external pressures, school systems are becoming a part of the local intergovernmental context. Intergovernmental activity at the local level has been increasing since the 1960s. The increase was stimulated by the large number of federal programs inaugurated in the late sixties, imposing regulatory and implementation responsibilities on local governments and was followed in the '70s and again in the '80s with attempts to redefine the relations among federal, state, and local governments through deregulatory and block-granting approaches. The net result has been dramatic growth in the amount of activity among federal, state, and local governments, and the creation of a highly complex set of intergovernmental relations at the local level. According to Robert Agranoff (1986, 3),

> The growth in public systems has created hundreds of new relationships between the federal government and the states, between the federal government and local governments, between the states and local governments, between local governments, and between governments and the private sector. The dynamics of these interactions tend to involve the transfer of money through categorical grants and, in some cases, over more flexible block grants. Intergovernmental fiscal transfers and program designs have altered formal theories of American federalism, which stress the independence and divided functions of each level, to an intergovernmental relations where the cutting

edge lies in the relationships between levels of government as those actors share in the performance of expanding functions. Thus, intergovernmental relations has emerged as the result of a complex and interdependent system, involving an increase in governmental units, in the number and variety of public officials, in the intensity and regularity of contacts among these officials, in the importance of these officials' attitudes and actions, and in the preoccupation with financial policy issues.

Table 8.2, modified from Agranoff (1986) to emphasize child-oriented examples, displays the diversity of local service provision within the intergovernmental context, and illustrates the range of purpose and authority of agencies that deliver publicly subsidized services at the local level.

TABLE 8.2.
Local Providers of Governmental Services

1. Local general purpose governments, e.g., cities, and counties.
2. Special purpose local governments, e.g., school districts, mental health districts, transportation districts, special education districts, children services, vocational education districts.
3. Federal programs, e.g., Social Security Administration offices and Veterans Administration offices.
4. State programs, e.g., substate units of state public assistance, rehabilitation, employment security, mental health, and other agencies.
5. Regional units of state departments where substate functions are combined, e.g., regional units of state human services departments.
6. Special purpose regional agencies.
7. Nonprofit community and voluntary agencies, e.g., YMCA, family service associations, Salvation Army, Catholic charities, mental health associations.
8. Proprietary agencies, e.g., home health-care agencies and sheltered homes.

Modified from Robert Agranoff. (1986). *Intergovernmental Management.* Albany, N.Y.: State University of New York Press.

Schools and Intergovernmental Programming

Schools have not been a major player in these new sets of intergovernmental relations until recently. However, they are being pulled in as
children's issues become a major priority for general purpose local
governments. According to the National League of Cities and the
National Association of Counties, children's issues is one of the fastest
growing areas of concern to local governments. A 1988–89 survey of
350 American cities undertaken by the National League of Cities (Born
1989) indicated that local governments are highly involved with children and family issues, the intensity of involvement is significant, and
the level of involvement is predicted to increase sharply. Fifty-four
percent of cities reported involvement in early childhood education,
60 percent in dropout prevention, and 44 percent in school counseling.
The intensity of involvement is remarkable, too. Significant percentages of cities reported major involvement in areas such as substance
abuse prevention for children, job training and placement for youth,
delinquency prevention, recreation activities, and preschool child care,
all areas involving some level of coordination with schools. And finally,
significant numbers of cities anticipate increased involvement in the
near future in virtually all of the areas.

Pressures to collaborate identified above are already having a significant impact on schools. A recent study documented that interagency
activities are already encoded in school laws in many states statutes
(Policy Center Network 1990). The study based on seven states representing 41 percent of the school administrators in the country found
a significant level of statutorily mandated responsibilities for school
principals in the area of children and youth policies. For examples,
principals were charged with responsibilities in the area of child abuse
in almost all of the sampled states, for child health in almost three-
fourths of the sampled states, and for interagency coordination in a
little less than half of the states sampled (Herrington and Schuh 1989).
(See Table 8.3).

Obstacles Posed by Intergovernmental Programming

There is a growing body of research on intergovernmental programming in the human services. On the whole, it is cautionary documenting obstacles that impede successful pursuit of shared program
outcomes. It underscores the fragile nature of the alliances, the jurisdictional disputes that confound effective and accountable administra-

TABLE 8.3.
Statutorily Mandated Responsibilities for Child and Youth Services
by Policy Area and by State

Policy Area	States						
	CA	FL	IL	OH	SC	TX	UT
Child Abuse	X	X	X	X		X	X
Missing Child				X		X	
Confidentiality Privacy Rights		X	X	X			
Due Process	X	X		X	X	X	
Safety	X	X		X	X		X
Child Health			X	X	X	X	X
Interagency Coordination			X	X	X		
Parent-Related		X	X	X	X	X	
Day Care				X			

Modified from C. Herrington and J. Schuh (1989). Cross-State Analysis of
Children and Youth Policy. Tallahassee, Fla.: Center for Policy Studies in
Education.

tion, and the lack of political consensus behind shared administrative
arrangements and program objectives. In particular, it identifies the
most significant technical, professional, and political barriers to successful programming resulting from the shared jurisdictional nature of
the program. At the technical level, confounding issues centered around
the mechanics of shared personnel, facilities, and equipment. At the
professional level, the obstacles were determination of the scope of the
programming, the roles of the different participants, and differing
organizational and professional cultures. At the political level, stabilizing support of the senior political and administrative leadership and
managing community reaction were most commonly mentioned
(Agranoff 1986; Agranoff 1982; Wright 1978). The intergovernmental
research echoes many of the discussion and findings of research bearing on integration of services for children.[1] Intergovernmental programming is distinguished from the more general area of integrated
service programming in that it is restricted to the sharing of facilities,
personnel, and equipment under the control of one government with

another. Governmental (or governmentally subsidized) programs tend
to be more organizationally stable and fiscally secure than private and
voluntary human service agencies.

INTERVIEW METHODOLOGY

A sample of school-building administrators and school superintendents
within the state of Florida involved in intergovernmental programming
were interviewed about their experiences administering intergovernmental programming. The interviews lasted from twenty to sixty minutes, were conducted between November 1993 and February 1994 over
the telephone. Follow-up interviews were conducted as necessary. The
interviews were exploratory in design permitting the interviews to
direct the interview in directions they believed important to the
established topic of intergovernmental program administration and leadership. Because the focus of this article was on issues of educational
administration and leadership, data were collected only from line
administrators, i.e., building principals and district superintendents (or
associate superintendents) for instruction. Administrators with staff
responsibilities for intergovernmental programming, such as district
health coordinators or assistant principals for student services, were not
included in the interviews. For the purpose of interviewing, intergovernmental programming was operationally defined as a program that
included placement on a school campus of personnel, facilities, or equipment under the primary control of an agency other than the school
board.[2]

TECHNICAL, PROFESSIONAL, AND POLITICAL ISSUES FOR PRINCIPALS

The most frequent programming in the sample was in the areas of law
enforcement and health. The most common program was the assignment of an officer from the sheriff's department or city police to a
campus. Every school interviewed had a school resource officer. Second in frequency were health services. The most common health
professional found on campus were nurses who were employees of
the county public health unit. Other health professionals included
physicians, dentists, psychologists, and mental health counselors. The
next group of programs mentioned most often, but a distant third,
were social workers, including family counselors and in-take counselors. Parenting programs were fourth. Most of the programs consisted
of one full-time person who was on the payroll of another agency,
though there were a number of modifications of this basic arrangement. Most schools had at least two different programs; some had as

many as five. Utilization of facilities and other resources was less common than shared personnel. Usually the school provided the equipment and facilities needed.

Twelve building-level principals were selected for interviews. They had all been recommended by senior state or district administrators as having distinguished themselves by their administration and leadership in running intergovernmental programs in their schools. The programs represented a mix of federal, state, district, foundation, and private sector-sponsored programs and a mix of programming in the areas of health, law enforcement, social support, and family counseling. All the schools served large percentages of students coming from at-risk environments and included a mix of elementary, middle, and secondary schools. The interviews sought to elicit information about technical issues that arose in operating the program, particularly in the areas of personnel, resources, facilities, and regulation. The principals were questioned about their professional attitudes regarding the programming, the nature and degree of their direct involvement, and their assessment of how the programming would evolve in the future. Finally, they were questioned about political issues that arose within the community.

The responses from the principals interviewed did not support the cautionary notes sounded in much of the intergovernmental literature about the jurisdictional obstacles posed by intergovernmental programming. On the whole, the principals did not report technical problems arising from sharing or joint ownership of facilities, equipment, and personnel. They did not report conflict resulting from different professional or organizational cultures. They did not report problems with generating or maintaining acceptance of the nontraditional programming by political leaders, community residents, or parents.

Technical Issues

No respondent described major technical or administrative problems as a result of different agency personnel on their campus, shared facilities, or shared equipment or as a result of the provisions of interagency agreements. After starting up and ironing out of wrinkles, the programs, according to all the principals, were self-sufficient and required the principals' direct attention only on an exceptional basis. Not a single principal reported any implementation or operational difficulties of any significance.

Two problem areas were remarked upon by some principals, but only upon probing, and the principals insisted these were minor issues.

About one-third of the principals acknowledged initial problems re-sulting from a lack of understanding of the school climate or a lack of sensitivity to children by personnel from other agencies. An example was a physician (a retired surgeon) who was considered to be gruff at times toward students. Another example was a police officer hand-cuffing, spread-eagling, and arresting a teenager in the classroom. Protocols were subsequently put in place to restrict professional be-havior that was deemed inappropriate in school settings. The only other area of concern, mentioned by three principals, was scheduling. Employees were sometimes required to observe the working hours of the other agency. In one high school, this meant the public health nurse stayed in the office until 5:00 p.m., which created a security risk because, at times, she was the only person in the building. The other agency was unwilling to modify the schedule because the employee needed to be available by phone or to attend meetings at times at which the agency scheduled them. Scheduling of leave also emerged in interviews as an issue, particularly in regards to summer employ-ment. However, all these issues were deemed minor by the principals.

Professional Issues

On the whole, the presence of these programs, personnel, and facilities on the campus did not pose new professional challenges, at least ac-cording to the principals, nor require an inordinate amount of their direct attention. When asked their professional assessment of the value of the new programming for their schools, every principal without exception was unequivocally enthusiastic. Indeed, virtually everyone of them said they could no longer imagine the school without the program. The degree to which these programs had become a part of the organizational life of the institution was noted by the principals' expressed frustration if any of the personnel were not available five days a week. Principals in schools where the nurses, police officers, family counselors, or pediatricians were shared with other campuses complained stridently about gaps in access, even though hardly any of these personnel had been present at all as few as four years ago.

When asked if the new programming was challenging their pro-fessional knowledge base or required additional skills or competen-cies, the principals responded in the negative. Most principals did report, however, that their appreciation of the large number of chil-dren living in very trying circumstances increased as a result of hav-ing the different professionals on campus. For example, school administrators and teachers were more likely to know if a girl was pregnant or if a student was HIV-positive or if the family was going through a crisis. These same conditions may have existed in the past, but personnel at the school were less likely to know about it. Attention directed by a public health nurse to a hurt elbow might result in more revelations about other problems the student might be having.

Principals were asked if conflicts had surfaced between the teaching staff in the schools and the personnel from other local governmental agencies. No principal reported any problems at all. To the contrary, they reported that the new personnel were warmly received by the teaching staff because it relieved them of situations the teachers believed themselves unprepared or unable to handle. Principals also stated that, to their knowledge, teachers did not see themselves in competition for facilities, space, equipment, resources, or status with the new staff. It is clear from the interviews with the principals that the other agencies' nonschool employees were expected to conform to the norms of the schooling culture. Usually the services the employees could perform were more limited in the school setting than what they were allowed to do via their own professional regulations; at the same time, most were asked to extend their activities in areas peculiar to schools, notably class instruction. For example, public health nurses were restricted from services that they were entitled to perform by virtue of being a registered nurse. The same nurse, on duty at the county public health unit, would not be under similar restrictions. Likewise, the school resource officers were curtailed in the functions they could perform in the school setting. For example, they might be prevented from making arrests on campus. On the other hand, all were asked to be active in the classroom providing direct instruction in their areas of expertise. County public health nurses were called upon to teach segments of courses that dealt with human biology or at-risk behaviors. Sometimes the nurse was authorized to talk more frankly about AIDS or homosexuality, for example, than teachers. Police officers were invited into the classroom to discuss issues such as bike safety and conflict resolution.

Though all the principals were extremely enthusiastic about the new programs, few were closely involved with the new personnel or services. When asked their degree of involvement, only one said it was extensive, most said small. Similarly, only one of the principals said the impetus for the program originated at the school level. The others reported that the ideas had been developed by district staff, and they were informed that they had been selected for participation.

Only two of the school principals said they were personally involved in the writing of the proposals.

The principals' knowledge of programming details was often surprisingly thin. Many of the principals, when asked who was paying the salaries of some of the interagency program staff, were unable to answer. A not uncommon response was, "I think he is paid half-time by the county public health unit and half-time by the school district, but I am not sure." During the interviews a number of the principals revealed considerable confusion on their part about student confidentiality rights, particularly concerning pregnancies and HIV status. Most of the principals had an assistant principal to whom the program personnel reported, and the principal's direct involvement consisted primarily of initial welcoming and orientation. After that a principal was pulled into operational matters only on an exceptional basis. If principals became involved at the district level concerning the program, it was almost always with the district program coordinators, not the principal's line supervisor.

There was some indication that, with time, principals became more active in finding opportunities to integrate instructional and noninstructional programming. For example, one principal having obtained child care facilities adjacent to the campus was now trying to work out a program whereby students who worked in the child care facility could take parenting classes at the facility and receive high school credit. Another principal who jointly administered an after-school recreational program with the parks and recreation department was now trying to also offer a nontraditional performance-based high school degree program at the recreational facility for students who were at risk of dropping out of the traditional high school program.

All the principals were asked if their schools would be considered school-based management (SBM) schools. No pattern of principal involvement in the new program areas could be related to the schools' designation as SBM.

A number of principals noted that none of the new programming had included any additional administrative support, so their workload was increased. When asked if they thought preservice training was needed in this area, most principals believed that more knowledge about the conditions of children should be included in preservice curricula for administrators, but only one believed that there were unique management or administrative skills that needed attention in the preservice curriculum. Virtually all principals hoped to increase the amount of programming they had in these areas in the future, though, at the same time, they predicted that the coordination of the additional programs and personnel would be an additional burden for them.

Political Issues

No one believed that public support within the community suffered as a result of hosting these programs on campus. None had had even minor public relations problems. Most believed that community support was strong. All the principals reported that they had begun the new programming with extensive public education, sending information home with the students and seeing that pieces covering the new program were reported in the local newspaper, and believed that continually keeping the community informed was critical. One principal said that, though his school program did not provide contraceptives, there were times when community members thought it did. However, the misunderstandings had never resulted in any serious public relations problem. There was only one school in the sample that provided prescriptions on campus to obtain contraceptives. That principal, like the others, reported no adverse public reaction. (This school was in an extremely poor, largely migrant agricultural community.) Many of the principals were actively seeking funding for expansion of these programs. For example, a high school that had a physician half a day a week was seeking funds to expand the number of hours the physician was on campus. The most common new program areas being pursued were parenting classes and child care or nurseries. Seeking Medicaid-eligibility for their school in the future was mentioned by two principals.

TECHNICAL, PROFESSIONAL, AND POLITICAL ISSUES
FOR SUPERINTENDENTS

Five superintendents (or, in two cases, associate superintendents) were interviewed. They were selected to provide a mix of district size, community composition, and intensity of intergovernmental programming. The sampled districts included one of the ten largest urban school systems in the country. The other four districts ranged in enrollment size from 14,000 to 38,000 students. Two would be considered socially conservative with large rural populations. Two others would also be considered fiscally conservative by virtue of large senior citizen populations. Under ten percent of the households in the two districts have children of school age. Three of the districts, the large urban district and the two rural districts, would be considered front runners in the area of intergovernmental programming and have received national recognition for innovative approaches. The superintendent interviews also were organized by technical, professional, and political issues. However, the superintendents were asked, in particular, to describe the larger organizational and political challenges posed by this new area of programming.

Intergovernmental Programming

Superintendents were asked to describe the nature and scope of intergovernmental programming in their districts. Their responses underscored the variety of programmatic relationships: sponsors included local, state, and federal governments, nonprofit agencies such as foundations and community-based voluntary social health services and agencies, and for-profit organizations such as hospitals. Interviews with the superintendents revealed the precarious nature of the many financial arrangements. All were time-limited, experimental, pilot, or demonstration projects. The most stable programs were state categorical programs, but even these were subject to annual competitive grants. None of the districts to date had folded the operating expenses of these projects into their general operating budgets. The financial arrangements were complex, stitched together from multiple sources, ad hoc, and unstable. Tapping into more permanent funding streams in the future, such as Medicaid or general state aid formulae, were under consideration.

Superintendent interviews reiterated the basic findings from the principal interviews: though problems of a technical nature did arise in the operating of the programs, particularly in the areas of facilities, none was significant enough to disrupt or impede the implementation of the new programming. Similarly, superintendents did not report any substantial challenges to the professional or organizational cultures of schools as a result of the new programming. Finally, superintendents reported no significant political problems associated with implementation or planning in new areas. In regard to future programming in this area, superintendents (as did principals) predicted considerable expansion in both the number of services and the type of services. Superintendents differed from principals in one important area, however. Superintendents predicted an increase in political concern and community resistance as the numbers of programs grow and the types of services expand.

Technical Issues

Superintendents did not report that the operationalization of these programs posed any significant or unique technical challenges. The most common complaint was the lack of available facilities or the lack of appropriate facilities, particularly ones that might provide privacy for physical examinations or counseling. However, almost all of these problems had been worked through and serviceable accommodations found.

All the superintendents were currently planning for program expansion over the next few years. The superintendents predicted considerable growth in the types of intergovernmental programming. Projects in advanced stages of planning included substations of police stations; branches of public libraries; child care facilities, adult literacy classes, food stamp offices, child protection team offices, family counseling, and mental health counseling. Superintendents stressed that these areas of expansion differed considerably by neighborhood and that it was important that programming respond to the needs of the community being served. In all districts the current programming was restricted to high-risk communities and to only a few of them. None of the districts had a districtwide program.

Professional Issues

Superintendents did not report that the presence of noneducational personnel in the schools was upsetting the organizational culture or challenging professional norms of educators. Despite repeated probing, no significant issues surfaced.

The superintendents all served in various capacities on task forces and planning groups involved in intergovernmental planning and coordination on behalf of children. These groups usually also involved social services directors, sheriff departments, health care community, parks and recreation departments, and the schools. One superintendent mentioned at times it was difficult to convince other representatives that schools were serious about working collaboratively with other agencies and were committed to long-term involvement and cooperation.

Interviewees did not substantiate a need for additional professional training in these areas. Two superindendents did mention that, for some principals, attitudinal problems arose. According to these superintendents, a minority of principals continued to state that noneducational services were not part of their job and that they were concerned they were not trained to handle these types of programs. Interestingly, as noted above, none of the principals currently running expanded services programming believed additional training was necessary.

Political Issues

The superintendents on the whole agreed with the principals that to date there had been no substantial political or public relations problems. This is significant because of the wide variety of districts represented by the five superintendents. The large urban district was experimenting with very innovative programming. It had received considerable federal funds in a one-time federal appropriation, which allowed completely new facilities to be built that could be designed to house radically different programmatic arrangements. Another district was a very conservative, relatively poor, sparsely populated rural community in northwest Florida, a part of the southern Bible Belt. This district had one of the first full-service school projects in the state and was in the advanced stages of development of a comprehensive computerized management information system to be jointly utilized by the school system and the health and human services department. Its efforts in this area have attracted national attention. A third district was the target of criticism by religious fundamentalists in the community over outcome-based education. However, though one of their schools had a health clinic on campus with a part-time physician and was planning for a permanent facility for the clinic, no community opposition to this programming had surfaced. In none of the five districts had the intergovernmental programming attracted opposition, and in only one had it prompted even questioning by the community. In this district, the superintendent reported that concerns had been expressed by a few members of the district regarding whether the schools were duplicating services that were being offered elsewhere in the community and thus wasting resources. However, this issue had been raised in only a minor fashion by a senior citizen tax watch organization.

The superintendents' perspectives differed from the principals considerably in one area: four of the five superintendents predicted greater political and public relations problems in the future. The issues were seen to be in three areas: the extent of the services, the nature of the services, and the constituencies receiving the services. All the superintendents predicted that services would increase significantly. In fact, it went beyond prediction. All were currently engaged in negotiations for expanded services in the very short term. As the number of services and programs increased, greater problems were forecasted in the areas of facilities and coordination. The sheer magnitude of increased programming was predicted to involve a scrambling for facilities and resources. Facilities, in particular, were seen as a major problem, as the districts were expecting overall student enrollment growth over the remaining years of the decade. Coordination was also seen to be a growing problem as the programs matured from pilot or project status, and efforts are made to institutionalize expanded services in large numbers of schools. For example, one superintendent was currently making plans to have a full-time nurse in every school. The current pilot project was financed with a special grant from the health and human services department and involved only two schools. The superintendent was carving out resources from the regular operating budget of the district to provide every school with a full-time nurse because the project schools had so clearly demonstrated the need. At the trial stage, schools that were ready for the new programming could be selected. However, as the project went from trial status to full-scale implementation and all schools were expected to participate, it meant that schools that may not be ready would be required to make the necessary adjustments.

Another superintendent mentioned political problems they were hoping to be able to avoid in the future. The district's commitment to program expansion in the area of full-service schools would require more facilities. However, the district was preparing a substantial request to the legislature for more facilities' appropriations based on classroom overcrowding. The district administrator was concerned that, if the state thought they were designating school space for noninstructional purposes, it might undercut the position that they needed extra funds for classrooms. Their decision to try to house most of the new extrainstructional programs in portables was driven as much by political considerations as programmatic requirements.

Superintendents predicted that the nature of the services would diversify over the next few years. The two most common services to date were public health school services and school resource officers, both of which were proving noncontroversial. Greater problems were anticipated in the areas of other health services, particularly services regarding adolescent health issues and in the area of family services. It was anticipated that community reaction to family services, in particular, might be negative. One reason cited was that, as services for families at the school site increase—such as mental health counseling, welfare and food stamp application services, and adult literacy—parents might be uncomfortable with the types of adults coming onto the school grounds while the children are at school. On the other hand, another superintendent argued that embedding some of the children's services within a family-centered approach would diffuse criticism that schools were appropriating the role of parents.

Finally, it was suggested that there might be some sorting out in community reaction along class lines. One superintendent predicted that middle-class parents might become more critical of services from which lower-class children primarily benefit, particularly if the services were seen to be drawing resources away from the academic program. Another superintendent noted that one group of major beneficiaries of the new programs was illegal immigrants and that this might produce a backlash. Another superintendent feared a stratification between community members who had children and those who did not. There was concern that citizens who did not have children might not fully appreciate how children's lives were changing. This was further complicated by class distinctions. The elderly were, on the whole, more affluent than the families with school-aged children.

However, the superintendent in the rural, conservative community that was further along in this area of programming than any other stated the opposite. He believed, based on his five years of working with full-service school approaches, that community support would grow in the future. He stated that, even in a conservative community such as his, the appreciation for the problems children and society in general were facing was growing daily, and the community members were changing their opinions about the role of schools virtually overnight.

DISCUSSION OF FINDINGS AND IMPLICATIONS FOR POLICY AND RESEARCH

There is no question that, as long as the condition of many children and families in the United States remains so worrisome and the fiscal stress experienced by human services institutions so severe, schools will be under pressure from other governments to become partners in programmatic responses to the declining status of children. The first half of this article defined intergovernmental programming, identified the pressures currently being exerted on school systems to join with other local governments, and noted the central role of schools and their infrastructure of personnel, facilities, and resources in local governmental strategies to improve child outcomes. The second half of the article provided data from interviews with school administrators on the nature of services currently on campuses and issues of shared governmental programming. Findings from the interviews suggest that intergovernmental programming is being introduced at schools without significant negative organizational reactions, implementation difficulties, or community resistance.

These data suggest that the cautionary notes expressed by many researchers and child advocates on the obstacles posed by school systems and school personnel to coordination on behalf of children must be explored more fully. Further research is needed to determine the degree to which the nature of the services, the professional identification of the service providers, and the extent of interaction with traditional schooling operations may impact organizational receptiveness.

The interviews suggest that some of the features of the programs sampled might be responsible for the absence of significant jurisdictional and organizational problems. This view is buttressed by research that has shown that, historically, schools have demonstrated remarkable adaptability to additional duties, functions, and responsibilities as long as fundamental accommodations are not challenged. (See Crowson and Boyd [1993] for discussion of the research on schools as political entities and implications for coordinated services for children.) From this perspective, one could argue that it is the parallel, but not integrated, nature of the programming that accounts for the lack of implementation or organizational problems in the schools in this sample. The professional culture and norms, the standard operating procedures, and the behaviors of the new members to the school community may be tolerated as long as none challenges the existing accommodations negotiated among the core school personnel, i.e., the instructional staff and the school leadership.

The opportunity to hand-off noninstructional problems to the personnel from the other agencies was the primary value of this programming to teachers, according to the principals. Every principal interviewed reported that the teaching staff was delighted to be able to drop what were seen as noninstructional problems in the lap of another responsible agent who presumably had the role, authority, and expertise to deal with them. Likewise, the principals stated that these programs did not require significant monitoring on their part. The two most common programs in the schools sampled—public health and law enforcement—may be particularly amenable to inclusions within schools precisely because they are quite distinct from education.

There is little overlap in services and professional competency between these two areas and education. Furthermore, both professions are housed in stable, governmental organizations (county public health units and police or sheriff departments) that are strongly supported by the public and maintain secure organizational niches. This provides them with some measure of resistance from undue challenges to their areas of expertise and professional norms if challenged by educators.

This line of analysis suggests that parallel versus integrated programming may avoid some jurisdictional problems encountered in more tightly coupled programming. The disadvantage of this approach would be the lack of synergies that many advocates of integrated programming hope for, particularly in serving children who come from materially and social impoverished backgrounds. James Comer (1984) and Willis Hawley (1990) both argue along developmental lines for integrated approaches that can treat an individual child's and family's problems in a holistic manner. While perhaps greater outcomes for children would be achieved through more integrated approaches, given the dire warnings issued by so many researchers on the pitfalls of integrated services, a more politically pragmatic if programmatically compromised approach as suggested here may be a viable policy option for some children in some communities.

Further research is needed to calculate the relative benefits of smooth implementation and organizational accommodations versus more robust but problematic integrative approaches. Research is needed to distinguish among mixes of services required by different communities and the relative toleration by educators for different professions and for different degrees of penetration of noneducational programming on school sites.

One further observation needs to be made. If the relatively smooth accommodation to date of the intergovernmental programming within schools is due to the clear professional boundaries among the different players, future programming as predicted by the superintendents interviewed may prove more challenging. Principals' acceptance of further programming may be tested if it continues to be unaccompanied by any additional administrative support. Teacher acceptance may be tested as programs expand into areas that bleed into areas of instruction, such as family counseling and mental health. Finally, community and political acceptance may be tested as programming moves beyond public health and law enforcement. Both of these programs are well established and not subject to reoccurring debates over their value to society or their legitimacy. The same is not true for social work, child care, welfare benefits, and family counseling. Opportunities for disputes among professionals and within the community may increase if schools become ever more intimate partners with other local governments as they work to serve the needs of today's children.

NOTES

1. As summed up by Crowson and Boyd (1993, 152), integrated services approaches face problems of "the indeterminacies of added funding from outside the school system; the problems of space, facilities management, and differing personnel and salary policies; the necessary negotiation of new roles and relationships between educators and other client-service personnel; the need to nurture effective leadership and a necessity for careful planning; the challenge of professional preparation programs and professional procedures with little by way of a natural 'glue' between them; and the tough issues of communication, confidentiality, and information retrieval that are present in any interagency or 'networking' initiative."

2. The interviews have a number of limitations that must be recognized prior to any assessment of the findings' import. One, the sample of principals (12) and superintendents (5) is small. The value of the interviews lies not in their generalizability but in the degree to which initial responses could be more fully explored through follow-up questions. Second, all of the principals and three of the five superintendents ran programs judged successful by independent observers. Thus, one could argue, by virtue of the selection criteria, the sample is biased towards successful programming arrangements, and the sample may not be representative of similar programs in other sites. However, given the strong degree of agreement among the interviewees on critical questions, the interviews are still revealing. Three, the interviews did not include staff directly responsible for program delivery. Interviews with the public health nurses, the police officers, or the in-take counselors stationed in schools may have revealed a different perspective on organizational acceptance and programmatic accommodations. It is possible that line administrators might be unaware of significant obstacles. However, on the other hand, one would expect that, if significant problems were being experienced by the direct service providers, there would be at least some knowledge of the problems by the line administrators and that under persistent probing by the interviewer at least some suggestion of problems would be acknowledged. This did not prove to be the case. Persistent probing failed to reveal admissions of any but minor problems.

REFERENCES

Agranoff, R. J. (1982). Meeting the challenges and changes in human services administration: Devolution, deregulation, reduction and privatization. *Journal of Health and Human Resources Administration* 4(2): 384–85.

Agranoff, R. J. (1986). *Intergovernmental management.* Albany, N.Y.: State University of New York Press.

Born, C. E. (1989). *Our future and our only hope: A survey of city halls regarding children and families.* Washington, D.C.: National League of Cities.

Center for the Study of Social Policy. (1991). *The new futures initiative: A mid point review.* Washington, D.C.: The Center.

Children's Defense Fund. (1989). *A vision for America's future, an agenda for the 1990s: A children's defense budget.* Washington, D.C.: Children's Defense Fund.

Comer, J. P. (May 1984). Home-school relationships as they affect the academic success of children. *Education and Urban Society* 16(2): 323–37.

Cremin, L. A. (1988). *American education: The metropolitan experience: 1876–1980.* New York: Harper & Row.

Crowson, R. L. and W. L. Boyd. (February 1993). Coordinated services for children: Designing arks for storms and seas unknown. *American Journal of Education* 101(2): 140–179.

David, J. L. (1993). *Redesigning an education system: Early observations from Kentucky.* Washington, D.C.: National Governor's Association.

Florida Department of Education. (1993). *Blueprint 2000: Transition system.* Tallahassee, Fla.: Author.

Goals 2000 Community Exchange. (1993). *Community update,* 5 August. Washington, D.C.: U.S. Department of Education.

Hawley, W. D. (1990). Missing pieces of the educational reform agenda: Or, why the first and second waves may miss the boat. In *Education Reform: Making Sense of it All,* ed. S. B. Bacharach. Boston: Allyn & Bacon.

Herrington, C. D. (1989). Infants and toddlers early intervention program. *Politics of Education Bulletin* 16(1): 5–7.

Herrington, C. D. (October 1990). *Public policy and children: An intergovernmental analysis.* Paper presented at the meeting of the Association of Public Policy and Management, San Francisco, Calif.

Herrington, C. D. and I. Lazar. (March 1994). *Family services in the schoolhouse: Pitfalls and possibilities.* Paper presented at the meeting of the American Educational Finance Association, Nashville, Tenn.

Herrington, C. D. and J. Schuh. (1989). *Cross-state analysis of children and youth policy.* Tallahassee, Fla.: Center for Policy Studies in Education.

Hodgkinson, H. H. (1989). *The same client: The demographics of education and service delivery systems.* Washington, D.C.: Institute for Educational Leadership.

Juffras, J., and E. Steuerle. (November 1989). *Public expenditures on children, fiscal year 1989.* Paper presented at the meeting of the National Commission on Children, Airlie, Va.

Kirst, M. W. (1991). Improving children's services: Overcoming barriers, creating new opportunities. *Phi Delta Kappan* 72: 615–618.

Leiderman, S., E. C. Reveal, A. Rosewater, S. A. Stephens, and W. C. Wolf. (1991). *The children's initiative: Making systems work.* A design document for the Pew Charitable Trusts. Philadelphia, Pa.: Center for Assessment & Policy Development.

National Center for Children in Poverty. (Fall 1992). Integrating services integration: A story unfolding. *News and Issues.* New York: The Center.

National Commission on Children. (1991). *Beyond rhetoric: A new American agenda for children and families.* Washington, D.C.: The Commission.

Policy Center Network. (1990). *State policy and the school principal.* Denver: Education Commission of the States.

Schorr, L. B. and D. Schorr. (1988). *Within our reach: Breaking the cycle of disadvantage.* New York: Anchor Books/Doubleday.

Wirt, F. M., and M. W. Kirst. (1992). *Schools in conflict: The politics of education.* Berkeley, Calif.: McCutchan.

Wright, D. (1978). *Understanding intergovernmental relations.* North Scituate, Mass.: Duxbury.

Chapter 9

Institutional Effects of Strategic Efforts at Community Enrichment

Hanne B. Mawhinney

Throughout North America, efforts to foster collaboration among schools, communities, and social service agencies are underway, and "experimentation has been growing at a pace that makes the tracking of developments difficult" (Crowson and Boyd 1993a, 148). The literature describing new school-community linkages is rich with experiential evidence (see Smrekar 1993), much of it underlining the diversity of the approaches to service coordination. These first-generation examinations have provided useful documentation of problems and potential responses to overcoming issues in collaboration (Behrman 1992; Bruner 1991). However, recommended responses, such as enhancing communication and developing trust among partners, ensuring that funding is provided, and involving the community, have typically not resolved deeper organizational issues. Collaboration, is after all, a form of organization, one that may change the established procedures, the constituent rules, and the cultural elements that define schools as they are conventionally structured. Yet, for the most part, current research has not undertaken the kind of organizational analysis that explains the effects of the challenges created by collaborative initiatives to the institutionalized patterns within organizations.

With a few notable exceptions, current research has not examined the process of collaboration as one of many forms of social coordination reflected in a core conception of organization: the "process of institutionalization" (Jepperson 1991, 150). These exceptional efforts have begun to provide theoretical direction for understanding the

223

complex processes involved when schools engage in collaborations with other organizations in their communities. Robert Crowson and William Boyd (1993b), for example, have begun a systematic, theoretically framed study of collaboration drawing from new institutional theories of social organization. The assumption of their approach is that more integration of services for children is better and that an end state of collaboration, although difficult to achieve, is the ideal. Crowson and Boyd suggest that "every experiment in children's services coordination can be examined first as a point along a continuum, from little-to-no integration of services to a collaborative ideal in the integration of services" (41). Although this line of reasoning provides some criteria with which to assess the degree of collaboration of projects, it is not without problems. Conceiving of collaboration as an ideal state characterized by common institutional goals, interests, rewards, and conventions leads inevitably to the conclusion that some permanent "collaborative" structure is possible, a conclusion fraught with practical and theoretical problems. Crowson and Boyd observe, for example,

> few experiments to date have failed to achieve some progress toward collaboration, but few have progressed very far toward the "ideal." The determinants and characteristics of progress on the process dimension of collaboration are still under-explored terrain. (41)

On the basis of this approach, Crowson and Boyd conclude that most documented initiatives reflect a "beyond-cooperation but not-quite-collaboration status" (1993b, 21). They argue that while a "thorough understanding of struggling-toward-collaboration processes is vitally important, it is also vital to understand, as thoroughly as possible, the complexities of institutional structure that come into play in collaborative ventures" (21). This is especially important because, rather than reflecting systemic reform efforts where "key institutional constraints (e.g., conflicting reward systems, differing norms and conventions, professional training differences) are identified early and incorporated into strategically preplanned reform-implementation, "most collaborative efforts involve "strategic interventions pragmatically moving toward a goal of coordination and problemsolving as the project unfolds" (6).

PURPOSE

We need to learn more about the strategic actions of single organizations, such as schools, that are engaged in collaborative initiatives that may change their institutional practices and organizational forms. Research on current initiatives has identified institutional effects that appear to influence the collaborative processes that evolve, yet these effects have only begun to be analyzed. Much more must be done in order to understand impetuses for strategic efforts at collaboration by schools and the extent to which these efforts result in changes in their organizational structure, through conceptual lenses that will inform both policy and practice of collaboration. Current thinking in the new institutionalism in organizational analysis outlined by Walter Powell and Paul DiMaggio (1991), and others, offers insights that can help to frame the direction for productive research on strategic collaborative initiatives. The purpose of this chapter is to lay out a path for an institutional analysis of strategic interventions for collaboration.

THEORETICAL FRAMEWORK FOR ANALYSIS

This chapter is informed by recent theorizing on structures and strategies for collaboration by Crowson and Boyd (1993a, 1993b) and by the theoretical insights of the new institutionalism found in recent work by organizational theorists (Jepperson 1991; Powell 1991; Powell and DiMaggio 1991; Scott 1991). In order to respond to the problematic dimensions of current collaborations identified by Crowson and Boyd (1993b) and outlined in the following section of the chapter, a conceptual framework was developed from the theoretical concepts proposed by new institutional theorists. Three hypotheses formed an initial framework for analysis of strategic choice and organizational change (Powell 1991; Scott 1991). These hypotheses were refined through an iterative process of analysis of the strategic efforts to promote the community collaborative effort to enhance the life chances of students observed in an ethnographic study in one Canadian high school. The critical ethnography (Grant & Fine 1992) undertaken in the study, and described in the discussion of the theoretical basis of the methodology that follows, drew from the perspective of school leaders in the collaborative initiative. The intent of this chapter is to describe an institutional framework for analysis of their strategic efforts at collaboration that extends existing theoretical conceptions of school-community relations.

A NEW INSTITUTIONALISM IN ORGANIZATIONAL ANALYSIS

In recent years, a renewed interest in the study of institutions has resulted in new insights about the nature of social processes in organizations. These insights share "a common conviction that institutional arrangements and social processes matter" (DiMaggio and Powell 1991, 3). In this theoretical frame, an "institution represents a social order or pattern that has attained a certain state or property; institutionalization denotes the process of such attainment" (Jepperson 1991, 144). The notion of order or pattern reflects the standardized interactions or routines that are chronically reproduced in organizations. In the sociological tradition, therefore, the new institutionalism recognizes that the "constant and repetitive quality of much organized life is explicable not simply by reference to individual, maximizing actors but rather by a view that locates the persistence of practices in both their taken-for-granted quality and their reproduction in structures that are to some extent self-sustaining" (DiMaggio and Powell 1991, 9).

Research on the involvement of schools in collaborative initiatives has documented their resistance to change and the persistence of their organizational structures and patterns. Guidelines for overcoming the forces of institutional reproduction in schools are being put forward. Crowson and Boyd (1993b) for example, argue that a key task in "moving institutional structures toward collaboration involves success in negotiating a 'convening process' a process that may involve some preconditions (particularly the sense of a shared central problem), then some progress toward shared goals in addressing the problem" (25). In their view, this requires overcoming the limitations on collaboration imposed by the effects of institutional interests, that emphasize "protecting jobs, budgets, programs, facilities, 'turf,' and enrollments" (26). Children's services organizations involved in a collaborative will each be influenced by their own self-interest rooted in their institutional reward systems. These reward systems may be "significantly challenged by the process of collaborating and by encounters with the reward systems of partnering organizations" (29).

These findings emphasize the persistence and reproduction of institutional patterns in schools in the face of pressure to collaborate and to change structural arrangements. At the same time, many researchers have found that schools do engage in numerous collaborative initiatives. Despite the constraints imposed by institutional patterns, some schools do change structural elements to facilitate collaboration, and these changes are at least partially institutionalized into daily practices. Crowson and Boyd (1993b) point out, however, that the strategic choices involved in collaborations and the extent to which the organizational changes they generate are institutionalized are not well understood. In the discussion that follows, neoinstitutional theories provide guidance to an analysis of the dimensions of the collaborative initiatives evolving at Beachwood Collegiate Institute, the site of the theoretical ethnography reported in this chapter.

STRATEGIC CHOICE AND ORGANIZATIONAL CHANGE

Neoinstitutional theorists provide some direction for understanding various patterns of institutional change. For example, Powell (1991, 197) explains that organizational change arising under the powerful constraints of institutional persistence is both "costly and difficult." Powell proposes that

> Change, when it does occur is "likely to be episodic, highlighted by a brief period of crisis or critical intervention, and followed by longer periods of stability" or development dependent upon positive feedback from incremental adjustments.

For our purposes, the above quotation will serve as Hypothesis 1. Implied is that institutional practices vary in the rate and extent of their diffusion. Powell (1991) notes that "institutionalization is always a matter of degree, in pat because it is a history dependent process" (195). Institutionalization is also conditioned by the complexity and thus the heterogeneity of institutional environments. Recent neoinstitutional theorizing recognizes that institutional environments are complex, often creating conflicting demands on organizations. Complex resource environments establish the requirement that organizations respond strategically to external demands (Powell 1991, 195). Neoinstitutional thinking suggests that organizations may accommodate conflicting institutional demands in different ways. They may compromise with or resist external pressures, play one source of legitimacy and support off against another, or comply with some expectations while challenging others" (195). The interorganizational relations evident in children's service collaborations create a differentiated and competitive institutional environment that forces organizations like schools to exercise strategic choice (Scott 1991, 170). Crowson and Boyd (1993b) conclude that coordinated services projects are "frequently initiated as strategic interventions" (6).

Richard Scott (1991, 170) suggests that choices available to organizations vary from fairly simple decisions concerning organizational processes to significant selections of the type of institutional environment with which to connect. School leaders may identify the programmatic focus for collaboration. Depending on the decision, the school will be engaged with quite different institutional environments, varying in regulatory pressures, funding arrangements, and many other important aspects. It is possible, therefore, for organizational actors to deliberately, and strategically, choose structural models. Neo-institutional researchers have observed that organizational decision makers adopt institutional designs and model their own structures on patterns they believe to be more "modern, appropriate, or rational" (178). A proposition, which we shall refer to as Hypothesis 2, follows from Scott's analysis:

> Structural changes acquired or adopted through the strategic choice of an organizational decision maker will be less superficial than imposed or induced structural changes.

Structural changes can also be incorporated by less conscious decision processes. School leaders may not necessarily consciously decide to add collaborative components to their administrative structures in order to deal more effectively with the kind of differentiated environment they currently operate within. Scott (1991) describes the institutional process of organizations incorporating environmental structures as occurring when organizational structure evolves over time through an adaptive, unplanned, historical process. A proposition, which we will refer to as Hypothesis 3, for the incorporation of environmental structure follows:

> Institutional change may occur via a broad array of adaptive processes occurring over a period of time and ranging from co-optation of the representatives of relevant environmental elements to the evolution of specialized boundary roles to deal with strategic contingencies.

The three propositions just outlined lay out a direction for an analysis of the strategic responses of the staff of Beachwood Collegiate to exogenous shocks and internal pressures created by the changing conditions of youth in their school. A key question in such an institutional analysis is:

• In what way and to what degree do the staff of schools like Beachwood collegiate alter their practices and create the opportunity for new collaborative organizational arrangements in response to exogenous shocks and internal pressures?

The three propositions suggest that an analysis responding to this question should consider: the pattern of institutional change, the extent to which structural change is generated through strategic decisions by educational leaders, and the various adaptive processes that evolve as initiators deal with the strategic contingencies arising in collaborations. These three themes form the orienting frame in the analysis that follows.

THEORETICAL BASIS OF THE METHODOLOGY

Powell (1991) argues that "to explain how social actors and the patterns of action they engage in are institutionally anchored, we need both detailed ethnographic studies that reveal how institutional practices become legitimated and large-scale, longitudinal studies that explore the staying power of institutional arrangements" (201). This chapter reports on an ethnographic study of the issues perceived by collaboration initiators in a high school located in a suburb of Toronto that is part of a three-year larger scale study by the researcher of collaborative initiatives evolving in several high schools in different Ontario province communities. Consistent with the basic assumptions of new institutional theories, the study reported here was grounded in an interpretive orientation to inquiry that adopts a holistic conception of social relations. Institutionalism, as "a theoretical strategy that features institutional theories and seeks to develop and apply them" can be distinguished from other lines of sociological theory by its "phenomenological conception of causal units and processes" (Jepperson 1991, 153). The "high constructiveness" of institutionalism denotes that "the social objects under investigation are thought to be complex social products, reflecting context-specific rules and interactions" (153). Institutionalism is also distinguished by its focus the higher levels of social organization. This structural dimension emphasizes the unmediated effects of "a nested system of social programs," which includes multiple orders of organization (154).

This chapter draws from an ongoing study of interagency collaboration in Ontario (Mawhinney 1993). Data for this qualitative, "policy-relevant ethnography" were gathered through analyses of documents, memos, and records and through in-depth interviews (Grant and Fine 1992, 420–422). Three initiators of a high school collaborative were interviewed during two rounds of on-site visits separated by six months. To ensure confidentiality they, their school, and others associated with the project were given pseudonyms.[1] Each respondent's specialized knowledge of the project required that the two sets of tape recorded, in-depth interviews, lasting from one and one half to three hours, be conducted using nonstandardized questions.

The researcher also gained conceptual understanding of school-community relations by analyzing documents provided by the respondents. They included copies of correspondence, reports, memos to collaborative partners, school newsletters, school calendars, school goals/objectives, proposals, and research reports. Ethnographic field notes were also taken recording "high inference interpretive" observations of the school, and its community (LeCompte and Preissle 1993, 228). As "building blocks of analysis, interpretation, and theory building," these "high inference descriptors" were derived from the researcher's developing conceptual framework (228).

The ethnography reported in this chapter departs from classical ethnography in that detailed descriptions of the organization and its routine activities are not given. Traditionally, the purpose of ethnographic fieldwork has been on painstaking depictions, an emphasis which has led to the "claim that some ethnography was atheoretical, in that it refrained from making claims that could be generalized beyond a narrow range of settings to more general sociological principles" (Grant and Fine 1992, 420). Recent reinvigoration of sociological theory has led to proposals for a more "systematically theoretically grounded" approach to ethnography (240). This chapter responds by presenting "a focused, theoretical ethnography" in which material extraneous to the problematic issues of the collaborative initiative studied have been eliminated. In this approach, conceptual issues raised in theoretical analyses of institutional change are brought into the chapter to help construct an understanding of this complex social process. Linda Grant and Gary Alan Fine describe this approach as one of using "ethnography as theory" (419). Consistent with the theoretical orientation to ethnography adopted, in what follows ethnographic data are used to generate further understanding of the institutional dimensions of strategic interventions to promote collaboration.

STRATEGIZING COLLABORATION AT BEACHWOOD COLLEGIATE

Beachwood Collegiate has, in the past year, come to be viewed as a model for addressing the needs of youth through collaboration with agencies and community groups. It did not come to this status as the result of systemic change by its school board, the Frankburn School District, or as the result of policy direction from the Ontario Ministry of Education, or through the effort of any of the agencies in the children's service sector in which it is embedded. Instead, collaboration was the result of a strategic response of school staff to the stresses on the institutionalized routines and procedures of the school created by an increasing number of youth experiencing severe difficulties. Jeff Rogers, the vice principal of Beachwood, explains that the school's working class community has felt the impact of the closure of a large car parts manufacturing plant in recent years. The current recession, combined with the impact of industrial restructuring in southern Ontario has left many families in the school's community under economic duress. In addition, the community has become increasingly transient as economic migrants from the Atlantic provinces move into the cheaper accommodation the community offers. They join immigrants from Eastern Europe, the Middle East, and the Caribbean.

The school has seen the impact of these social, economic, and demographic changes on the students. Rogers agrees that the school is facing a more turbulent environment as a result of these changes. These changes and others have contributed to the increase in the numbers of youth with very serious problems during the past few years. Beth Francis, a special education teacher in the school, observes that

> the neighborhood supports a lot of drug dealers, a lot of prostitution, there is a lot out there for the kids to be exposed to. A lot of kids come from welfare homes which probably are second or third generation welfare families who know the system and the expectation that when [the young] turns 16 they quit school and go on welfare.

These changes began to impact directly on the school in the early 1990s, and by 1991 teachers were noticing more students with very serious problems in their classes. The current collaborative initiatives began as the result of a strategic meeting of school needs with the opportunity for response to that need created by Beth Francis who joined the staff of the school in September 1991. Beth's extensive experience in running a withdrawal program in another school district brought a new resource to Beachwood: a different perspective on how interventions for youth with special needs could be delivered than was found in the Frankburn School District. In the district Francis had come from, special education was a booming business. High schools in that district had separate special education departments for serving the needs of all exceptionalities. In that district, the conventional practice was to institutionalize school-based special education services as separate departments with their own budgets. In contrast, in the Frankburn School District special education is provided through a few consultants and is not given institutional status in the organizational structure of the school. Moreover, the convention of the board is only to support assistance for students with specific learning disabilities through the communications classes that Francis was hired to teach. In order to receive assistance, these students must be identified and designated as exceptional through the legal identification and review process established in legislation by the government of Ontario. Behavioral exceptionalities are not conventionally identified in this board as requiring special support.

In Beachwood's case the institutional conventions of the school board were not conducive to meeting the needs of the growing number of students who exhibited the kind of behavioral problems identified in the large-scale, longitudinal *Ontario Child Health Study* (1987) as an outcome of the serious problem of child poverty among families receiving social assistance and among the working poor. Beth Francis's experiences in running a behavioral withdrawal class became a resource for the guidance department of the school and especially by Jeff Roger, who joined the staff of Beachwood as a first time vice principal at the same time that Francis was hired.

Operating within the institutional constraints established by the board meant that the students that Rogers began to bring to Francis initially received only short-term assistance. Rogers comments: "we weren't so much interested in a withdrawal approach; we felt that behavioral withdrawal was out of focus" with the norms of the school. What the school did want, according to Rogers was to "find some way of helping the kids and at the same time helping the staff who had some of those kids in their classes who were very disruptive or very withdrawn or just not as academically capable." Within months of her tenure at the school, Francis recalls: "I had this huge population of kids who didn't fit any category. They were just kids who otherwise would have fallen through the cracks, and we were trying to keep them going as best as we could." The situation, in her view, arose because of the convention in the board that was to use behavioral consultants to provide guidance for classroom teachers on some possible modifications they could use. Francis believes that this practice creates "a huge gap in servicing."

Francis' strategic response to these conditions initiated a path that eventually led to the collaborative initiatives currently underway in the school. In January 1992, confronted with a group of students whose needs did not fit into the institutionalized practices of the board, Francis wrote a proposal for Jack Brown, Beachwood's principal, to establish a program "targeted at the kids who normally would have just dropped out," kids that school guidance counselors and administrators felt were not benefiting from normal programming. Consistent with the school's preference for no full withdrawal, the students came as they needed to receive extra help. Another element in determining the path toward collaboration at this point in the evolution of the process was Francis's proposal to include a collaborative "school team referral process" in the program. The strategic choice by the principal and the staff to formalize the high-risk referral team process further defined the path toward collaboration. Francis observes: "the problem is that, if you have a school team, and you refer kids, and you identify them, and they are in need of assistance, then you have to have the program to put them into." Through this adaptive process the school staff began to address the strategic contingencies of meeting the needs of their students by initiating some structural changes.

By the end of Beth Francis's first year at Beachwood, an initial referral process had been established, and she had provided extra assistance to this new category of special student. Jeff Rogers, as a new vice principal, had been put in charge of handling the administrative issues that arose. In June of the first year, because of the success of the program, Rogers, Francis, and members of the guidance department developed a more formal proposal to take to the staff to continue the program for a second year. Staff support was, and continues to be, required because of the institutional constraints imposed by the school board's failure to fund special education programs directly. Rogers notes that because of these funding constraints the teacher required to staff the program has come out of regular staffing, with teachers picking up extra students. The willingness of the teachers to continue support for a second year enhanced its legitimacy.

Structural changes in school and classroom practices for dealing with high-risk students, although not permanent, did signal the beginning of the institutionalization of these practices. The development of the high-risk referral program resulted from both strategic and adaptive responses by the school. Beginning in the second year, the members of the team met every second week to review referrals. Jeff Rogers recalls that the team learned as it developed the referral process:

> Initially we looked at every possible helping mechanism we could use within the framework of the educational system, which meant all the things that we offer here in this building and the services that the board offers us.

Several changes were incorporated, which, in his view, "broke with the traditional pattern of student-teacher interaction." Teachers, school administrators, and support staff were provided with forms that asked for the reason for the referral, targeting academic, behavior, testing, and personal aspects of the student's behavior. Among the behaviors targeted were those associated with youth risk: poor attendance, tendency to be a loner, apathy, peer group problems, conflict, disruptive behavior. Providing a time-out kind of program as the result of some of the teacher referrals for disruptive behavior generated considerable support from the faculty.

These structural changes took on a collaborative dimension during the second year of the program. Beth Francis comments:

> In the second year, I realized that, for a lot of these kids, what we could offer as a school was just not enough. In many cases there were already a lot of outside players. Many of the kids belong in or are in the care of the Children's Aid Society; so they have social workers, and they have counselors for that agency. A lot of my girls live in the group homes, so they have primary care workers.

Beth Francis concluded that, if the program was to have a game plan, it would have to include "all the various others that were going to be important in the student's life." Her strategic response was to develop a network of contacts with the agencies that she felt were involved with her students. She comments: "I started to make phone calls and asked if they would like to come in and be part of an educational plan." Initially, other agencies did not understand why they should be involved. Their institutional conventions defined their role in ways that they believed were inconsistent with the work of the school. Francis describes her initial contacts with child care workers:

> They really didn't understand why I would want them to be involved, but I reminded them that "the kids are under your care; decisions made on their behalf go through your workers, and we would like you to be part of that so that you understand the ramifications of what we are trying to do in school."

During the second year, Francis gradually established a network of contacts with community agencies, a process of community outreach she describes as time and energy consuming:

> I have spent thousands of hours over the past three years just mak-
> ing phone calls and saying: I am new to the area, what does your
> service do? What do you offer? and just getting a list of people
> that I have made contact with that can come in. I can call and make
> an appointment whether it's for counseling around sexual abuse or
> whatever.

By January 1993, Francis's strategic efforts had begun to have an impact on the school. The staff members were supportive, and new organizational practices had at least begun to be institutionalized. Neoinstitutional theorists would suggest that institutionalization may be a function of the positive feedback that adaptive responses and strategic efforts generate. Powell (1991) refers to this phenomenon as a "path dependent process" in which strategic choices can become "magnified by positive feedback" (193). The success was also influenced by Francis's entrepreneurial strategies and the acceptance of her specialized boundary role to deal with the strategic contingencies in addressing the needs of at-risk youth by Rogers and the school staff. In this process, the path created by the school's adaptive responses to external and internal pressures developed a collaborative thrust.

This collaborative tendency was given additional legitimacy when Beth Francis was informed of a pilot project promoting community enrichment to enhance the life changes of adolescents in which the board had agreed to participate. The project, which involves a university team monitoring three different high school collaborative initiatives, was promoted, although not funded, by the Provincial Ministry of Education. Its senior evaluator is widely known for his research on, and advocacy for, at-risk youth. Although the school's decision to become involved in the pilot project did not provide additional funds, it was certainly influenced by the status involvement in the project provided to the key participants and the legitimacy that was accorded the school. Francis's work with the high-risk referral program continued; however, Jeff Rogers took over the role of school representative for the initiative and was given the opportunity to gain status as a new administrator associated with a successful collaborative initiative through his involvement in public presentations on the pilot program.

Neoinstitutional theory suggests that involvement in the pilot program had the effect of giving the school's efforts a name and focus that were legitimated by the established norms and authorities in the educational sector (Scott and Meyer 1991). Schools, operating as they do in strong institutional environments, find this kind of legitimation particularly useful in giving credence to their work arrangements and procedures. This explains why, soon after the school's proposal to be part of the pilot project was accepted, the referral team began to focus on extending into the community to identify resources for the high-risk program. Midway through the second year of the program, Jeff Rogers began to compile a data base of community contacts. He comments that the referral team sat down and asked "who are the agencies in the community that we each deal with on a regular basis?" Team members like Beth Francis, have their own contacts; however, the problem from Rogers' perspective is that these contacts are often transferred from one office to another so schools are constantly forced "to reestablish contact through somebody else." By the end of the second year of the program, the team had compiled a priority list for initiating the collaboration with agencies. Rogers recalls that "we didn't want too big a piece initially, and so we came up with about ten agencies that we felt in this specific community we would deal with on a regular basis." In June, these groups were invited to an inaugural meeting to begin to discuss establishing "some solid and creative communication channels." Rogers chaired the meeting and describes his apprehension "that it is when you have all these different agencies with their own ax to grind that you will get all this political stuff" and his elation when he found that the agencies were more than amenable: "I felt like a genius when I walked [out of the meeting because] the agencies indicated that it was about time we started doing something like this."

The affirmation of the legitimacy of this approach by members of the community gave impetus to the institutionalization of the collaborative arrangement within the broader organizational structure of the school. The high-risk referral program gained additional resources. However, as was the case when it had been initiated the previous year, having resources meant that a program was required. Francis's program did provide short-term withdrawal for severe cases; however, the broader, and in some cases more preventative, mandates of a number of agencies required that a less defined home be found to accommodate the community enrichment offered by the agencies. In September, the school therefore decided to provide a separate room and a schedule for agencies who committed to being available at that location for a period of time. Care was taken to design a schedule that fit both ends of the day and the school's cycle in order to maximize student involvement and minimize negative impact on programming.

Students named the project CLUE: Community Link Up Education, and designed colorful brochures outlining the five initial collaborating agencies, the services they provide, and details regarding
scheduling and availability. By November 1993, these agencies had
been on site long enough to have an impact on the school's operations.
The guidance counselor, Jean Brown, describes the spillover benefits
of the involvement of the agencies in the regular school program:

> We use the services of agencies like the "stay in school" program all
> the time. We have transferred some of the services of the women's
> outreach into our grade nine program. They focus on things like
> what is a positive relationship? I think that high-risk kids will ben-
> efit, and kids who may be on the fringe may benefit also; I know that
> there will be educational transference and delivery to larger numbers
> of students.

REFLECTIONS ON INSTITUTIONAL PERSISTENCE AND CHANGE

What has been described here is a partial institutionalization of the
three programs that have developed from the initial strategic initiatives Beth Francis took. Threats of incomplete or partial institutionalization of these collaborative processes are real. In the case of Francis's
community-supported high-risk withdrawal program, there is the
continual risk that it will not be sustained by the faculty. Funding cuts
to school boards because of Ontario's continuing recession mean that
schools will be required to reduce staff. Francis's program operates
only through the willingness of other staff to carry extra students.
Both Francis and Jeff Rogers recognize the danger this poses to any
further institutionalization of the program. For Rogers, charged with
protecting the viability of the organization, this means that he has an
added incentive to support community enrichment of the school. Rogers
strategizes from this perspective:

> I separate the CLUE program, which involves outside agencies, from
> the resource program. They work well together because one comple-
> ments the other. CLUE is for the whole school, but the resource pro-
> gram for particularly high-risk students can be supplemented by the
> CLUE program for certain things. But the truth of the matter is that
> I don't have to give up the CLUE program if, because of staffing cuts,
> I have to give up the resource program. What may happen is that, if
> we have to give up the resource program because of budgetary cuts,
> we may have to crank up even harder the community involvement

to take the place of the program. I hope we don't because the high-risk withdrawal program is desperately needed in a high school setting.

Francis recognizes the precarious status of the resource withdrawal program, noting that support is a constant battle especially when services have to be cut:

> We only have this many staff to meet the needs of these kids, so what gets cut and what stays? I am always on the edge because resource is not part of any department. The board agrees with what we do but does not sanction it with funding.

Change in the structuring of funding would be required for the resource program to become fully institutionalized. Although she recognizes that CLUE offers complementary services, she does not necessarily see CLUE and her resource withdrawal program as competitive. In her view, CLUE enhances the possibility of continued support for her program.

> The more the CLUE program develops apart from the resource program and they work independently in the school, the more it becomes part of the school, and there is less likelihood that somebody will say, in a numbers crunch, we bump all of you out.

Francis is, however, also an astute strategist in institutionalizing her resource withdrawal program. She has expanded her own network of community connections, enriching the resource withdrawal in entrepreneurial ways that go well beyond the involvement of agencies in CLUE. She describes the extraordinary means to which she has gone to gain support from the community: "I canvassed service clubs telling them we have no money, and the Rotary Club adopted us this past summer as their stay-in-school initiative . . . and then what we did was we wrote a ton of letters over the summer to all kinds of businesses in the neighborhood and said: Is there any way you can help us?

Francis's efforts to enrich her withdrawal program with community involvement provide a counterweight to the precarious support that she has in the formal organization. Neoinstitutional theorists would ague that the legitimacy of the program will only be enhanced to the extent that the support she gains is acknowledged by the school and the community. Schools operate in environments that give tremendous value to legitimation of the plausibility of the work arrangements and procedures. The kind of community enrichment that Francis is promoting is, however, not uncontested. Her community outreach symbolizes an advocacy approach to at-risk youth that goes well beyond the traditional definition of education's role. For Francis, when the school has tried everything but the resource room and it hasn't succeeded, then "Let's wipe the slate clean, take care of all his or her courses and try something different." She opposes, in principle, the practice of passing students on to an alternative school because their programs do not have good success rates. Francis views community enrichment as a means of achieving some improved success.

Her view is, however, not shared by others in the school. School counselor Jean Brown argues from a very different set of assumptions when she says that

> there are those kids in resource that we have not served and we never will. The danger I see is that if we try to do more than we're capable of doing we will miss those kids that might be in the middle. We're not a social agency; we're a school.

These differing views of what constitute appropriate conventions and roles underline that program goals may be contested within an organization. The success of an attempt at institutional change "depends not simply on the resources controlled by its proponents, but on the nature of power and the institutionally specific rules by which resources are produced, allocated, and controlled." (Friedland and Alford 1991, 254). Francis was able to draw on her expertise and experience in initially gaining support for the withdrawal and high-risk referral programs. Her strategic efforts encouraged school staff to establish a collaborative thrust to its efforts. Without the power of secure funding, she must, however, seek other sources of support. Reaching out and gaining support and acceptance from the school's community is a strategic attempt to institutionalize the organizational change represented by the program.

The preceding analysis underlies the force of institutional persistence and reproduction. Powell (1991, 194) illustrates this process by noting that organizational actors like Rogers, Francis, and Brown "construct around themselves an environment that constrains their ability to change further in later years." The power of institutional conventions defining the established norms of the education sector is evident in the taken-for-grantedness of the board's approach to supporting special education. There is also evidence in this case confirming findings of current research on collaboration, that schools often institutionalize within their existing structures the environmental turbulence created by collaborative engagements. Rogers ensured that CLUE operates within the institutional conventions of the school, and he will likely continue to make certain that the program continues within these parameters. Researchers observe that schools often "pedagogize service-coordination" rather than create new shared structures with other agencies (Crowson and Boyd 1993b, 36). Jean Brown, Beachwood's guidance counselor, speaks with delight at the transference of the services of the agencies into the school's operating framework. This is a taken-for-granted assumption that she shares with Rogers. Although Francis's approach is a much more flexible community enrichment outreach, she also institutionalizes the services offered by agencies and other organizations within the constraints imposed by the organizational structure of the school.

Neoinstitutional theorists conclude that belief systems, rather than organizational structures, account for the orderliness and coherence of schools (Scott 1991). Research has shown that institutional beliefs, rules, and roles become "coded into the structure of educational organizations" in powerful ways (180). This ethnography has documented the power of institutional beliefs, but it has also shown that they may be contested in a school's internal and external environments. Meyer, Scott, and Deal (1981, 159–160) argue that "agreements on the nature of the school system and the norms governing it are worked out at quite general collective levels, . . . from participating in the same institutional environment, from sharing the same educational culture." Institutional change such as is required of a school engaged in collaboration will be constrained to the extent that this process is not accepted as a legitimate organizational goal for education at the collective level. Beth Francis's struggles to institutionalize her version of community enrichment illustrates that general, collective support for this kind of collaboration may be required, but it is not sufficient to support organizational change.

CONCLUSIONS AND IMPLICATIONS FOR FURTHER RESEARCH

Implicit in current concerns over how to move schools toward engagement with their communities is the presence of an often unspecified model of collaboration as the ideal. Current research on linkages among children's services has documented constraining and successful policies and practices on the basis of that ideal. A pervasive conclusion is that movement toward collaboration has been slow, if there has been any movement at all (Smylie and Crowson 1993). In short, collaborative initiatives tend not to become so fully integrated that they are absorbed into the institutional conventions of collaborating organizations. Instead institutional change is partial and contested. The ethnography reported in this chapter confirms that institutionalization of collaborations is often dependent upon positive feedback from incremental adjustments. It confirms the proposition that the institutional change required to produce collaboration occurs through a broad array of adaptive processes. The ethnography also suggests that the structural changes required to produce collaborative initiatives in schools may be generated through strategic decisions by educational leaders such as Rogers and Francis but that those decisions are constrained by the institutional environment in which schools are embedded.

There are a number of directions for further research on collaboration that extend the institutional path of analysis laid out in this chapter. A key task of this theoretical research agenda is to explain variation in the strength of institutional rules that constrain collaborative efforts. We need to know why some institutional arrangements support these efforts. The link between policies and practices should be examined to understand incomplete institutionalization of collaborative efforts. Research should examine how "policies may be introduced but not reproduced, or practices may take a firm hold for a short period, only to quickly wane when their source of normative support erodes" (Powell 1991, 199). We need to understand if, and how, policies promoting collaboration that carry neither sanctions nor rewards are able to influence changes in organizational practices.

NOTES

1. Quotes attributed to Jeff Rogers, Jean Brown, and Beth Francis are taken from transcripts of tape-recorded interviews conducted in June 1993 and in December 1993.

REFERENCES

Behrman, R. E. (1992). Introduction: School-linked services. *The Future of Children*, 2(1):4–18.

Bruner, C. (1991). *Thinking collaboratively: Ten questions and answers to help policy makers improve children's services*. Washington, D.C.: Education and Human Services Consortium.

Children First: Report of the advisory committee on children's services. (November 1990). Toronto: Queen's Printer for Ontario.

Crowson, R. L. (1992). *School-community relations, under reform.* Berkeley: McCutchan.

Crowson, R. L., and W. L. Boyd. (1993a). Coordinated services for children: Designing arks for storms and seas unknown. *American Journal of Education* 101(2): 140–179.

Crowson, R. L., and W. L. Boyd (1993b). *Structures and strategies: Toward an understanding of alternative models for coordinated children's services.* Paper presented at the Annual Meeting of the American Educational Research Association, Atlanta, Georgia.

DiMaggio, P. J., and W. W. Powell. (1991). Introduction. In *The new institutionalism in organizational analysis,* ed. W. W. Powell and P. J. DiMaggio, 1–38. Chicago: University of Chicago Press.

Friedland, R., & R. R. Alford. (1991). Bringing society back in: Symbols, practices, and institutional contradictions. In *The new institutionalism in organizational analysis,* ed. W. W. Powell and P. J. DiMaggio, 232–263. Chicago: University of Chicago Press.

Grant L., and A. Fine. (1992). Sociology unleashed: Creative directions in classical ethnography. In *The handbook of qualitative research in education,* ed. M. D. LeCompte, W. L. Millroy, and J. Preissle, 406–446. San Diego: Academic Press.

Jepperson, R. L. (1991). Institutions, institutional effects, and institutionalism. In *The new institutionalism in organizational analysis,* ed. W. W. Powell and P. J. DiMaggio, 143–159. Chicago: University of Chicago Press.

Le Compte, M. D., and J. Preissle. (1993) *Ethnography and qualitative design in educational research,* ed. 2. San Diego: Academic Press.

Mawhinney, H. B. (1993). Discovering shared values: Ecological models to support collaboration. In *The politics of linking schools and social services,* ed. L. Adler and S. Gardner, London: Falmer Press.

Meyer, J. W., W. R. Scott, and T. E. Deal. (1981). Institutional and technical sources of organizational structure. In *Organization and the human services,* ed. H. D. Stein, 151–178. Philadelphia: Temple University Press.

Ontario Child Health Study: Children at Risk. (1987). Toronto: Queen's Printer for Ontario.

Powell, W. W. (1991). Expanding the scope of institutional analysis. In *The new institutionalism in organizational analysis,* ed. W. W. Powell and P. J. DiMaggio, 183–203. Chicago: University of Chicago Press.

Powell, W. W., and P. J. DiMaggio. (1991). *The new institutionalism in organizational analysis.* Chicago: University of Chicago Press.

Scott, R. W. (1991). Unpacking institutional arguments. In *The new institutionalism in organizational analysis,* ed. W. W. Powell and P. J. DiMaggio, 164–182. Chicago: University of Chicago Press.

Scott, R. W., and J. W. Meyer. (1991). The organization of societal sectors. In *The new institutionalism in organizational analysis,* ed. W. W. Powell and P. J. DiMaggio, 108–140. Chicago: University of Chicago Press.

Smrekar, C. (1993). Rethinking family-school interactions: A prologue to linking schools and social services. *Education and Urban Society* 25(2): 175–186.

Smylie, M. A. and R. L. Crowson. (1993). *Developing the institutional infrastructure for children's service coordination: A Chicago experiment.* Paper presented at the Convention of the University Council for Educational Administration, Houston, Texas.

Chapter 10

School-Business-University Collaboratives: The Economics of Organizational Choice

Patrick F. Galvin

INTRODUCTION

Educational partnerships can be defined as any arrangement (among a remarkable variety) in which business, community, and university representatives pool resources and expertise with public schools in a common effort to improve the quality of education. During the last few decades, there has been a growing belief that the traditional bureaucratic, hierarchical, and authoritarian structures are not well-suited for governing schools during these turbulent and changing times (Kirst 1993; Davis 1986). The emerging model of governance can, by comparison, be described as collaborative, nonhierarchical, responsive, and organic (Sirotnik and Goodlad 1988; Neal 1988, Sarason 1979). So pervasive is the belief in the potential of these newer organizational structures as a means of efficiently promoting public educational reform that one can reasonably ask why more educational services have not been produced and delivered through collaborative arrangements. More relevant to the purpose of this paper, however, is the question of how such collaborative arrangements will evolve to establish themselves within the institutional environment in which educational services are produced and distributed to students.

In this paper, concepts derived from the line of inquiry described by Barney and Ouchi (1986) as "organizational economics" are used to examine this question. This framework is particularly appropriate to the study of partnerships because, as Jensen and Meckling (1986) indicate, whenever cooperative alliances are formed, problems of agency (organizational economics) are present. The paper presents a case study in which these conceptual tools are applied directly to the analysis of a partnership whose growth has put it in competition with existing organizational structures for service dollars, students, political capital, and other scarce resources. In doing so, the paper will help clarify both the potential problems partnerships face as they evolve and the utility of the organizational economics framework in understanding these issues.

BACKGROUND

Public education has always involved partnership arrangements with universities and businesses (see Sirotnik and Goodlad 1988 or Gross 1988 for a historical perspective). There is a very important difference between the partnerships of the past and the vision of partnerships in the future, however. In the past, the activities of partnerships have supplemented and supported a highly centralized and bureaucratized school organization. In the future, partnerships are envisioned as having a considerably expanded role that fundamentally changes the nature of school governance; the shift being from one that is centralized and hierarchically structured to one that is decentralized, horizontally structured, and inclusive of families, business, universities, and social service agencies. In such a view, educational partnerships would not just supplement the activities of schooling but would be fundamentally involved with the governance, production, and delivery of educational services.

There are many reasons for this changed view of how educational organizations should be structured and governed, not the least of which are changes in the scope of responsibilities assigned to schools. Effective education, according to William Bennett (1993), John Hoyle (1993), and others requires that children arrive at school ready to learn. Problems such as teen pregnancy, child abuse, malnutrition, and poverty, not only put children at risk of failing in school, but they also compromise the effectiveness of current investments in education. Martin Blank and Atelia Melaville (1993), writing in conjunction with the U. S. Department of Education, argue that there exists an increasing recognition that "the institutions and agencies whose mission is to nurture and strengthen children and families must collaborate . . . no single institution has the resources or capacity to do the job alone" (vii). According to these advocates of partnerships, without the collaborative efforts of families, businesses, and other social organizations, these significant problems will continue to undermine the effective delivery of public educational services.

The vision of partnerships working at the core of educational organizations, actively involved in the production and delivery of educational services, is predicated on the assumption that partnerships are able to operate more effectively and efficiently than existing organizational arrangements. But to say that educational partnerships hold such comparative value, or even to cite cases where such effectiveness has occurred, is quite different from assuming that these advantages are manifestations of a paradigmatic shift in the governance of schools. (See Sirotnik and Goodlad 1988 for a reference to this language.) To effectively alter the structure of school governance, educational partnerships will have to do more than elaborate on underdeveloped service niches such as teen-pregnancy programs; educational partnerships will have to evolve as a primary structure by which schooling is organized and produced. When Michael Kirst (1993), William Bennett (1993), Michael Walsh (1993), Theodore Gross (1988), and others describe the evolution of partnerships as a change necessary to improve public education, they are calling for the institutionalization of partnerships. These proponents are suggesting that the successful long-term impact of partnerships depends upon their becoming more than random and opportunistic arrangements. If partnerships are to effectively impact the organization of schools, they must establish themselves as reliable actors within the environment. In other words, references to partnerships as representing a "paradigmatic shift" are really calls for the institutionalization of partnerships as a governance structure by which schools operate.

THE PROBLEM

The premise that educational partnerships can emerge as a primary means (but not an exclusive means) for producing and delivering educational services is based on the assumption that such arrangements are a better way of doing business. Certainly this is the message of academics, educators, and business people who argue that the problems society confront cannot be solved by schools working in isolation. But if one recognizes the potential of educational partnerships to do what public schools are currently unable to do, it does not necessarily follow that they will be able to maintain such a comparative advantage as they expand from relatively small scale operations to larger organizational efforts. This question is fundamental to understanding the future potential of educational partnerships.

This question of scale and efficiency is not addressed in the literature on educational partnerships, although the implicit assumption is that the economies of scale and collaborative specializations gained through partnerships will maintain a comparative advantage over existing organizational efforts. But such an assumption requires at least two basic conditions. First, that the organizational environment in which partnerships operate remains constant even as the partnership innovation expands to assume a larger and more significant role. Such an assumption runs contrary to a large body of organizational theory which suggests that a prime directive of all organizations is survival (Scott 1992; Thompson 1967; Lawrence and Lorsch 1967). If the production and governance structures of partnerships remain at the margins, public school administrators may not see them as a threat to their viability; but as partnerships grow and begin to capture resources (students, teachers, dollars, attention, etc.) that otherwise would go to public schools, administrators may feel threatened and respond by seeking ways of controlling or assimilating the services of partnerships into their own structure. In other words, as long as educational partnerships do not compete with the core activities of public schools, there will be relatively little competition for factors of production such as teachers, scheduling time, students, materials, classroom, and public dollars. However, the vision for educational partnerships is that they will evolve to assume a central role in the governance of public education. As partnerships evolve, public school organizations are likely to respond in ways that will undermine the current comparative value partnerships enjoy.

The second assumption underlying the premise regarding the relative advantage of educational partnerships over public schools (even as they evolve within the institutional environment) rests on the belief that the internal costs of operating partnerships will remain constant. If the viability of educational partnerships is at all related to the cost of organizing them, then the question of how expansion and institutionalization will effect the cost of governing collaboratives is fundamental to predictions about their future. If the cost of governance increases significantly with expansion, then the marginal benefits of collaboration may not be sufficient to outweigh the marginal costs of increased governance requirements. Thus the question with regard to the viability of partnership organizations is whether they can survive their own success: whether partnerships can maintain efficient operation of their service and governance as they evolve from simple to complex organizations.

As a framework for examining this question, a theory of agency is outlined in the following section. Central to this theoretical model is the role of markets and the concepts of information costs, bounded rationality, and opportunism. These concepts are introduced as a framework for understanding the likely consequences of expanding educational partnerships within a market environment. After discussing this theoretical framework, a case study is introduced illustrating many of the theoretical ideas described. Generalizations from a single case study cannot be made, so the paper concludes with a speculative discussion of the case study's theoretical implications.

THE THEORETICAL FRAMEWORK

The literature describing educational partnerships largely reflects a policy framework in which the merits of partnerships are analyzed in terms of legislation and practice. Absent from this literature is a sound theoretical framework by which the organization and behavior of partnerships can be described. The lack of a cohesive theory of organizational partnerships/cooperatives has been noted by several authors in various fields: Richard Hall (1991) in the field of organizational theory; David Billis (1993) in the field of public welfare agencies; Dennis Young (1988) in the field of nonprofit organization; and, Jones and Maloy (1988), specifically, in the field of school partnership.

There is some recent evidence that this void is being filled. David Hammack and Young (1993), for example, have just published an edited volume that examines the role of the nonprofit organization in a market economy. One of the premises of the book is that the traditional distinctions between profit/nonprofit and private/public sector organizations is rapidly disappearing. Their work calls for an increasing recognition of the markets in which voluntary organizations operate. Voluntary organizations, Hammack and Young note, are not able to tax the public to support their existence. As is the case with for-profit organizations, they must maintain their viability by raising revenues to cover costs. Unlike public bureaucracies that monopolize a single service (e.g., public schools), voluntary organizations must compete within the marketplace for their market share.

Educational partnerships are not so different or unique in character that one should ignore the implications of the message provided by Hammack and Young. Businesses and universities respond to a great number of requests for support. Continued support for educational partnerships will require evidence that current investments of time, dollars, and expertise are wisely spent. Hammack and Young note that it is not surprising as investments in partnerships increase, that consumers want information about the quality of services provided, evidence of fiscal accountability, and plans for the future. The provision of such information is not costless. While the importance of information has long been recognized in the study of organizations, the influence of costs associated with obtaining this information, as it effects market exchanges and organizational structure, has only recently been examined (Williamson 1975). Agency theory examines the problem of how organizational arrangements are structured to reduce these costs (Jensen and Meckling 1986). Such a perspective offers important insights on the behavior of collaboratives in general and more specifically educational partnerships.

Organizational Economics Defined

Barney and Ouchi (1986) and William Hesterly, Julia Liebeskind, and Todd Zenger (1990) describe organizational economics as a line of inquiry that borrows from microeconomic theory, organizational theory, and organizational behavior. To describe organizational economics as a line of inquiry is to distinguish it specifically from a theoretical framework in and of itself. Hesterly, Liebeskind, and Zenger (1990) suggest that organizational economics is better understood as a way of thinking about organizations and organizational behavior. To recognize Hesterly's point helps clarify why one reads about agency theory, transaction cost theory, and evolutionary theory, all under the rubric of organizational economics.

The conceptual underpinnings of the inquiry associated with organizational economics is attributed to Ronald Coase's (1937) observation that markets and firms are simply alternative ways of organizing economic exchanges. The argument rests on the recognition that few, if any, markets meet the stringent criteria for perfect competition so frequently invoked for the sake of neoclassical and microeconomic studies: scenarios in which consumers are believed to have complete information about products, where there is supposedly homogeneity of products, and where there exists large numbers of traders. In a perfectly competitive market, exchanges between sellers and providers would be fair by definition, but, in reality, sellers often have information about the quality of services and goods that is not available to buyers until after the exchange. These information asymmetries make consumers vulnerable to the opportunistic exploitation of sellers.

When consumers do not have full knowledge of products, or when consumers are not able to easily substitute alternative services or products (or they are not able to find alternative suppliers), then they must content with the possibility that the market price system does not properly reflect the true value of a service or product. There are numerous ways to protect oneself from such exploitation, including collecting information about the product, writing short or long term market contracts, or developing more complex organizational arrangements. According to Coase, the specific governance structure of any exchange is largely a matter of comparative advantage, at least over the long run. This perspective assumes that market structures are efficient and that the emergence of firms (vertical integration of exchanges) reflects market efficiencies rather than market failures.

Organizational economics offers important insights into the structure and organization of markets and, indeed, offers an explanation as to why there exists such a diversity of organizational and contractual solutions to the problems of market exchanges (Barney and Ouchi 1986). Applying such a framework to public schools suggests that there may be market constraints and exchange efficiencies that help explain the structure of schools. This is to say that the public education organizations may reflect equilibrium efficiencies that are not commonly acknowledged; for example, the lock-step pay scale for teachers can be understood as a means by which the complex contracting issues associated with assessing and rewarding of teacher merit are resolved efficiently. As the role and function of educational partnerships expands, they will undoubtedly face similar problems. The argument that follows from the above theoretical framework is that, as partnerships grow, they are likely to confront the same imperative to reduce agency costs and, hence, may arrive at contractual and organizational solutions similar to those used by public schools. Assuming market efficiencies, the problem of resolving costly contractual issues (both within an organization and between organizations) is described as the "agency problem."

Agency Theory: Capital Markets, Ownership, Information Costs, and Monitoring

The term *capital markets* refers to the issue of how organizations acquire resources. There exists a considerable literature in organizational theory that examines the impact of the resource environment on the behavior of organizations (Pfeffer and Salancik 1978; Selznick 1966;

March and Simon 1958), and the concern agency theory brings to the question can be viewed as a continuation of that theoretical line. A key difference between the two theoretical perspectives, however, is that agency theorists work with assumptions about the efficient characteristics of markets. Thus, to characterize the difference between the perspectives, many organizational theorists use models of organizational power and market domination that ignore the influence of competitive markets to explain organizational behavior and structure, while agency theorists draw attention to issues of ownership, information, and monitoring as a framework that explicitly recognizes the efficiency characteristics of the market. Agency theory assumes the viability of markets even while acknowledging the problems associated with the costs of information, writing contracts, bounded rationality, the problems of small numbers of trading partners, and the potential for opportunistic behavior (Barney and Ouchi 1986).

Jensen and Meckling (1986) described the issue of ownership as fundamental to understanding agency response to issues of costs and organization. Where ownership is clear, which is to say that the individuals who invest in the agency are those who bear the risks and rewards, there is little reason to think that decisions will not be in the best interests of the agency. By contrast, assuming that individuals are self interested, where managers do not own an agency and hence do not bear the full cost of their decisions, decisions may conflict with the best interests of the agency. This is to say that the decisions of individuals may be self-satisfying and not in the best interests of the true owners. Where individuals are not monitored or otherwise constrained by the owners, they may, for example, structure an organization in ways that reduce their own work load even if the decision compromises the potential earnings of the organization as a whole. Owners concerned about reducing these costs are forced to hire agents who gather information and monitor the behavior of these managers.

If, as neoclassical economics assumptions dictate, information were perfect and actors were perfectly rational, then there would be no costs associated with monitoring potential cheaters. However, not only is it difficult and expensive to get information about decisions of actors within an organization, but it is also difficult and expensive to process the information into a rational policy that best supports the interests of an agency. Further, there are costs associated with monitoring individuals once assessments of individuals are made and policies to limit their behavior are in place. The assessment of teacher performance and the problems of implementing merit pay programs is a good example of the issues identified. In a market where there was perfect and complete information, the costs associated with gathering the necessary information to judge teachers would be negligible, and, hence, since information would be complete and instantaneous, there would be no need to monitor the exchange. Such frictionless exchanges are fundamental to the underlying assumptions of neoclassical economic theories. Not so for organizational economics, and hence the basic question underlying agency theory is one of how firms economize on the cost of gathering information and monitoring exchange agreements (whether within the firm or between firms).

Information costs have an important role in agency theory: driven by an interest in efficiency, agency theorists argue, owners will seek organizational and contracting solutions as ways of reducing these costs. Labor union contracts, short-term or long-term exchange contracts, and various organizational structures are all solutions to the agency problem (whether organizational or contractual in nature). These are the arrangements by which owners are able to control and limit the problem of agency costs. It is in this context that Jensen and Meckling describe organizations as a "legal fiction which serves as a nexus for a set of contracting relationships among individuals" (1986, 219). These contracts are the essence of the firm not only with employees but with suppliers, customers, and creditors. Oliver Williamson (1975) draws similar conclusions about the nature of organizations, arguing that the problems agencies must resolve trading between firms are exactly those that must be resolved with exchanges within the firm. With this introduction to the basic concepts of agency theory, the discussion now applies the concepts more directly to the organization of educational partnerships.

The Agency Problem and Educational Partnerships

The issues of efficiency and productivity are very much a part of the language describing educational partnerships. In the *American 2000: An Education Strategy,* the authors argue that this nation cannot continue to compete and prosper in the global arena when more than one-fifth of its children live in poverty and one-third grow up in ignorance. Collaboration is described as a primary strategy by which student learning and economic vitality can be improved. Incited by the commission reports of the 1980s (especially the report, *A Nation at Risk*), the business community believed its competitive edge was dulled by the ineffective efforts of teachers and administrators to improve education. Michael Cohen (1987) argued, as a spokesperson for business, that, "neither government agencies nor the school system alone can solve the educational crisis. But a network of business, labor, education and local communities can" (65). By 1986, a mail survey revealed that 73 percent of Forbes 500 corporations were participating in school/business collaborations. Around the country, state governments have promoted school/business partnerships as a way of improving public education (Greenberg 1991; Gross 1988; McLaughlin 1988).

The heart of partnerships is one of collaboration or teaming. Armen Alchian and Harold Demsetz (1986) describe the process of teaming as cooperative specialization, where resource owners increase productivity through the organization of exchanges between agencies or firms. Partnerships between schools and universities, businesses, and even community members are well described by such language. Cooperative specialization thus represents an effort to organize in ways that enhance the productive interests of all concerned partners: businesses in assuring a qualified work force, universities in qualified students, schools in graduating students, and parents in the welfare of their children.

The potential of partnerships has limits, however. Where owners hire managers to perform jobs, there is the possibility that the managers will not make decisions that maximize the interests of the owners. Where uncertainty about these issues is high and monitoring is difficult, organizations will seek ways of ensuring compliance while minimizing costs. Ouchi (1984) and others have identified trust, interpersonal relations (including family and clans), as an important governance structure where contracting is complex and expensive. In situations where individuals are mutually bound to a common purpose, trust may serve admirably in the resolution of agency problems associated with collaboratives and partnerships (monitoring activities, ensuring fiscal accountability, etc.).

As partnerships evolve beyond minor donations of fiscal resources and begin to command major contributions, the promise of trust does not hold the same currency. If educational partnerships are to emerge as part of a fundamental reform, and a viable alternative to the governance of schools, they will have to ensure the level of accountability that current organizations provide. These new organizational arrangements will have to ensure levels of accountability in an efficient manner. The issue of efficiency is particularly important for understanding the full implication of agency theory: where partnerships expand and the contractual relationships become more complex and subject to greater scrutiny, the cost of monitoring such arrangements will create an influential pressure towards more efficient contractual arrangements. Vertically, integration is one possible solution to these escalating costs; another solution is to disband the organization. In any event, collaborative teams bound by mutual trust and mutually beneficial arrangements are likely to give way to organizational solutions that are able to minimize contracting and monitoring costs while maximizing accountability, a feature about which school bureaucracies are especially good.

AN ILLUSTRATIVE CASE STUDY

The above sections outline the framework for thinking about the organization and behavior of educational partnerships and collaboratives in general. In the following sections, a case study of one partnership is described as an illustrative example of the theory discussed above. The word illustrative is used advisedly because the purpose of the study is not to test agency theory or to assess the effect size of specific variables, but rather, to provide a descriptive context for understanding the presence and influence of agency costs on the evolving structure and organization of the Mathematics Engineering Science Achievement (MESA) partnership.

I have always attributed to Karl Weick the observation that it is not necessarily bad to look for confirmatory data relative to one's theoretical interests, but to do so does not mean that methods are not used to protect from the potential effects of observer bias. Over the course of the last two years, discussions and more formal interviews with members of the MESA Board and Executive Board, as well as with the Advisory and Technical Boards have provided a rich source of data for the case study. Additionally, exchanges with the State MESA Coordinator, as well as university, business, and school representatives supporting the MESA program, have provided additional perspectives. Program records, minutes, and budgetary information were also available for review.

As a participant observer, who had access to all program records (as noted above) and who attended all board meetings, the details of the administrative response to contractual relations relative to a change in funding structure were readily available to me. Such a position enabled me to develop a historical framework by which to examine, question, and interpret the minutiae of program decisions. A number of strategies were implemented to enhance the validity, or merit, of the data collected. First, I started with several possible theoretical explanations for the organization. This strategy allowed me to look for evidence that contradicted my working hypotheses as they evolved over time.

My ideas about the forces shaping the structure of the MESA program changed over time to include variables identified in the theory of agency proposed by Demsetz (1991) and others. Initially, the organization of the partnership appeared driven by a goal-oriented functional rationality. But, despite organizational meeting full of rhetoric about the purposes and goals of the program, the board members and participating teachers all recognized the discrepancy between the grand design of the program and its operation. Compromises between program goals and program operations were frequently based on the amount of work one plan or another required, the least costly to implement and maintain being the one most often chosen. Decisions about how to organize the program seemed more sensitive to the potential relationships of constituent members and the effects of such plans and their operational efficiencies than on program's goals or functionality.

Another alternative explanation for the organizational of MESA and similarly structured programs can be found in the institutional theories of organization (DiMaggio and Powell 1991). These theories suggest that organization is a product of macro social and cultural values that change slowly over time. Agency theory, on the other hand, describes organization as a product of contractual agreements that changes rapidly and at a very micro level. Observation of program responses to a changing environment provided ample evidence that changes occurred rapidly and were sensitive to efficiency issues. To examine this working hypothesis, I used a pattern matching strategy for collecting and organizing data. Five key data categories were identified from agency theory—capital structure, accountability, quality, monitoring, and ownership. The presentation of the data collected over a two-year period is organized around these data categories. The story that follows does not prove one theory or another. Evidence of the influence of agency on organizational decisions does suggest, however, that cultural theories of organization may not provide the only or best framework by which to predict the evolution and structure of educational partnerships like MESA. Thus, while the character of the following description is anecdotal, it is rich and illustrative of the agency problem identified in agency theory.

MESA: The Partnership

Schools have long been organized as relatively simple hierarchies closed to the external environment. In recent years, concerns about the competence of schools have been associated with an opening of school organizations to include numerous other governing constituents. School-based partnerships are one example of such changes.

For example, when the concern about minority representation in the math and science fields emerged as a national issue, school-based partnerships involving university, business, and community representatives found a fertile organizational environment in which to work. The Mathematics Engineering Science Achievement (MESA) program is a specific example of such a partnership. First organized in 1976 at the University of California at Berkeley, this collaborative model has been adopted in other states throughout the country. The goal of the program is to provide academic and social support to student groups who are underrepresented in the science and math career fields. The collaboration of business, community, school, and university members not only contributes additional revenues for program activities directed towards this purpose, it also provides students with role models; real people like themselves that have made it in the academic and corporate/scientific world.

Utah's MESA program was first organized in 1986. Initially formed through efforts of both university and district personnel, the program has grown significantly over the years. Serving only a few hundred students in 1986, Utah's MESA now enrolls more than 2000 students in 7 school districts and operates with an annual budget of more than $500,000.

Utah's MESA organization is headed by a Board of Directors that includes public school, corporate, community, and university representatives. The Board of Directors is supported by two advisory boards, the technical and industrial boards. The daily operations of the program are overseen by a state MESA coordinator. Unlike other MESA programs around the country, Utah's MESA program is not directed by a university administration, but rather, by a true collective of business, university, and public education affiliates.

The MESA program provides students with two types of experiences. The first involves supplementary mathematics courses for students who have the potential for achieving in this area but who need additional instructional support. The second set of experiences is delivered through the MESA Club, which is a peer group support club. The two opportunities are intended to complement one another. MESA Club experiences, for example, support mathematics and science skills through engineering contests and other activities. Club activities are also intended to provide students with support as they cope with the stress of learning math and preparing for entry into college programs.

Funding for the program was initially derived from corporate, public school, and university grants. In 1991, however, the Board (including its business representatives) was able to sell the MESA program to the Utah Legislature, which provided the program with a legislative grant. While the acquisition of state funding was intended to resolve funding uncertainties, there is increasing evidence that the effect has been just the opposite.

The Grant

Organizations are always struggling to cope with the problem of efficiently organizing their internal operations, particularly as they deal with the constraints imposed on them from the external environment. Some of these events, however, are more defining than others. For the MESA program, one of these significant events came when Utah's State Legislature awarded the program state funds ($156,000) in its annual appropriation legislation (Senate Bill 212, 1991).

Prior to the legislative funding, MESA had struggled along with donations from business, the schools, and the universities. Fewer than 700 students in twenty-two schools were enrolled in the program. The explicit purpose of the legislative funding was to support expansion of the program. In the following year (1991–92) program enrollments increased by 68 percent. There is a sense in which this appropriation gave the program a measure of legitimacy that was greatly enjoyed by the program's directors and instructors. At the same time, this public attention required of the program a measure of accountability that previously had not been provided. Issues of accountability underlie a series of program activities that raised questions about the efficiency of the organization as a means by which to provide these services. Indeed, as members amongst the programs leaders began to assess the situation, the question that crossed conversation was whether the program could survive its own success.

State Funding: Implications for MESA

Legislative grants are not, however, simple gifts bestowed in perpetuity. Concerns about accountability and, subsequently, questions about how the organization ought to be structured and which among its many goals ought to hold primacy manifested themselves in numerous ways. The immediate problems that emerged were: (1) questions about how policies designed to ensure accountability could be implemented, (2) how questions of quality could be maintained as the program expanded, and (3) who had authority over the fiscal resources. All of these issues are technical and functional in nature and are fundamental dilemmas that virtually all organizations must resolve in order to survive. The insight of agency theory is not one of revealing a unique set of problems, but rather of drawing attention to the centrality of organizational/contracting solutions to exchange agreements. The problems confronting MESA are not, as Jeffery Pfeffer and Gerald Salancik (1978) would assert, ones of coping with the domination of public school bureaucracies, but rather of developing efficient organizational solutions that are marginally more productive than those available within school bureaucracies. Failure to do so suggests, according to Agency Theory, that partnerships like MESA will be assimilated by schools as a matter of market efficiency, not market domination.

While the above questions can be conceptually separated, they are in practice overlapping. In the following paragraphs, illustrations of these questions or problems are described. For the sake of clarity, the discussion illustrates first accountability, then quality, and finally authority or ownership.

Accountability

Prior to the legislative grant, donations came from a variety of sources (the university, public schools, and businesses) and frequently were donations in kind (services, printing, volunteer work, classroom space, materials, etc.). Accountability for these funds was limited to a single yearly budget report. Provision of state funding required new procedures to be enacted. These requirements were, in part, legal because the grant involved public money distributed through the State's school finance formula and, in part, self imposed because failure to provide clear evidence of accountability was thought by the Board members to hurt chances for future funding.

A consequence of these demands was the hire of an accountant for the MESA program. The accountant implemented a new accounting scheme, which impacted both the State Coordinator and school district program administrators. Concerns about how grant funds were being used led to decisions to implement quarterly financial reports. Where district managers of the MESA program one had considerable autonomy over fiscal and programmatic matters, concerns about accountability required new documentation about how money was being used. These demands required additional accountability from all personnel that before had largely been left as a matter of trust.

Another consequence of the accounting issue is related to the intention of the legislative grant to facilitate program expansion. When the program was comparatively small, the application process for a school was relatively simple. The legislative grant generated sufficient interest in the program that restructuring of the application process as a competitive process was necessary. This required considerably more work on the part of both the board reviewing the applications and the schools making the applications. In particular, schools making application had to carefully document the type and kind of contribution it made to the program, as well as carefully identify the audience targeted by program funds and activities.

The issue of centralization and bureaucratization evident in accounting for fiscal matters was also evident in the activities of the MESA Board of Directors. One of the directors characterized the circumstances by noting that, "We are no longer a mom-and-pop organization." Informal arrangements that had once governed the organization no longer sufficed, particularly if the program was to maintain legislative support. Consequently, as a way of facilitating accountability and communication among participant members, the Board decided to reorganize itself. Several strategies were implemented to achieve a more active Board of Directors. Efforts were taken to eliminate inactive members, make committee assignments, and develop new governance structures to accommodate the new demands placed on the program. While each of these steps represents a rationalization of the governing process, they required more effort from both Board members and field representatives. Rationalization without attention to costs can have the opposite intended effect; rather than promoting effective governance, it can kill initiative and productivity.

There are many specific examples of the issues identified above. The point relative to the theory of agency is that changes in the capital structure (the legislative grant) had important implications for how the program organized, utilized, and monitored its commitment of resources to programmatic purposes. Where once the agency was able to capitalize on the informal arrangements by which program practices and accounts were managed, changes in the funding required changes in organizational structure to assure accountability. If information were perfect and individuals were not opportunistic, such efforts would not be necessary, but frequently accounts have to be audited and rectified to ensure that money for program purposes was not spent on pizza instead (not all infractions are vial and sinister). These insights about the costs associated with ensuring accountability have important implications for the future of the program: if MESA once operated cost effectively outside of school's organization, the program's centralization raises questions about whether that advantage can be maintained.

Quality

Before receiving the legislative grant, district MESA teachers had considerable autonomy over fiscal and programmatic matters. The state MESA coordinator provided administrative support but interfered relatively infrequently in day-to-day matters. Pressures to expand the program's services raised concerns among the Board of Directors about maintaining the quality of program services. These concerns resulted in the implementation of new program activities, such as the statewide training, to ensure program quality.

MESA's program expansion brought in a large number of new MESA aides and teachers. The statewide training represented an effort to maintain and improve the quality of service offered students. While the Board of Directors had a long history of debating questions of assessing program quality, it was only to show the legislators that their funds were being used effectively that action was seriously initiated. Uncertainties about how program outcomes could be measured turned the debate to questions about how to standardize inputs. The statewide training emerged as a means by which both to improve the program and to ensure that program goals are universally recognized.

In a significant way, the statewide training represented a simple means by which to enact an implicit contract between the funders of the program and the managers. The issue of agency costs should not be diminished here. Monitoring the activities of teachers was neither a feasible nor affordable solution to questions about the quality of field activities. The program had already hired an evaluator, but teacher and student questionnaires could not adequately monitor the true activities of the teachers. State-run training, while expensive, was viewed as a reasonable alternative to the problem of monitoring the activities of all teachers.

Questions of quality and accountability are shown here to be directly linked to changes in the governance structure and activities of the MESA program. One could argue that the centralization and rationalization of MESA are nothing more than the process by which emerging organizations respond to an increasingly complex environment. Indeed, to this extent, the observations of organizational theory (Thompson 1967) are very similar to those of agency theory (Alchian and Demstez 1986). The differences, however, are significant. Agency Theory builds a causal explanation for these responses on the aggregated responses of individuals operating within organizations and the response of owners to monitor and regulate the behavior of employees. Efficiency concerns are at the heart of Agency Theory and underlie the theoretical assumptions guiding the theory. Central to these assumptions is the notion of comparative advantage. For MESA, this means that if the cost of governance increases owners (the funding agents: schools, universities, the legislature, and businesses) will begin to seek alternative means. Public school organizations may not be good organizational solutions for all the problems they are asked to address, but they are very good at providing the kind of accountability being demanded of MESA.

Ownership and alternative means of production

The issue of ownership is fundamental to understanding the theory of agency. Ownership can be defined in terms of those who invest in the program (e.g., money, personnel, time, etc.) and carry the risk of losing on their investment. Jacob Michaelsen (1981) described these owners as the de jure (rightful) owners and distinguishes them from managers, or de facto (actual) owners. Agency Theory provides an additional definition of ownership by drawing attention to the question of who has the residual rights to production. In a business where a single owner fronts capital for a project, that person alone has rights to residual profits (the profits above costs). De facto owners (i.e., managers) may attempt to use some of those benefits for their own interests (opportunistic behavior), but, unless specified otherwise, the single original owner (de jure) has sole rights to those profits.

In a public bureaucracy, issues of ownership are less well defined. This is particularly true for the MESA program, where funders include a number of second-party interests (the legislature, business, and universities). Funding is only one aspect of ownership. The MESA Board is ostensibly the contractual owner of the program, even if their equity in the project is limited. With regard to residual rights, the question of ownership is even more problematic because outcomes of the MESA project are related to student graduation and entry into the labor market. Such a focus ignores the many short-term administrative problems that can significantly impact the relative cost effectiveness of different segments or sectors of the program.

This seemingly abstract problem manifests itself in significant and common ways. For example, prior to the legislative grant, districts were largely responsible for collecting student demographic data and submitting it to the MESA State Coordinator. Demands by the MESA board for districts to comply with a new standardized demographic survey was viewed by personnel in some districts as a practice of questionable value that negatively impacted their local operations. Many districts had developed their own data bases that satisfied their local needs as well as those of the MESA program. Requirements to comply with the Board's mandate was largely interpreted as an issue of power and authority. To the state MESA Board, however, the question was how demographic data collected from various sources could be merged easily into a single, consistent, and useful data base. Asking the districts to comply with state MESA survey methods required the district to adjust, at considerable cost (and much complaint), to a system that primarily benefited state MESA administrators. The reluctance of district administrators to comply with state MESA requests reflected a larger issue regarding ownership of the program and rights to make decisions about how the organization would operate.

Ownership emerged as an issue for more than just teachers and administrators operating the program. Historically, MESA activities were represented to the State Education Office by the Office of Equal Opportunity. The legislative grant was assigned, however, to the Special Education Division responsible for at-risk programs. Emerging from these circumstances is a debate between these offices over who has authority for the administration of MESA funds. The issue of who was the responsible fiscal agent for the legislative grant was made particularly salient when the State Education Office announced that $6,000 that previously had been available to the MESA program had been withdrawn. When the state MESA Coordinator questioned who had authority for such a decision, she was informed that she had no authority over the funds.

The dynamic interactions and adjustments among constituent members of the MESA program are not over. The theory of agency, as presented above, suggests that organizational members will continue to seek ways of reducing the costs associated with contracting, exchanging, monitoring, and organizing the program. These efforts will manifest themselves in an evolving system of contractual and organizational adjustments, reflecting changes in the capital structure and characteristics of the market and products being exchanged.

Two issues loom large with regard to the future course for the MESA organization: ownership and comparative advantage. A potential strength of partnerships is collaborative specialization, where two or more parties combine resources in ways that enhance the productive capabilities of their available resources. But the collaborative aspect of the MESA organizations can also serve as a liability, in that the program lacks a clear sense of ownership. Subsequent questions about risk bearing, accountability, and residual rights all complicate the exchange agreements among MESA members. As the cost of collaborative governance structures increases, the tenets of Agency Theory and comparative advantage would predict the emergence of new governance structures.

Eugene Fama and Michael Jensen (1986) note that a wide variety of organizational structures and processes can be used to reduce these agency problems. Indeed, a possible solution to the increasing complexity and uncertainty associated with the governance of the MESA collaborative is that public schools will absorb the organization into their bureaucracies. Organizational theorists, such as Pfeffer and Salancik (1978), might argue that such circumstances are examples of how public schools are able politically and economically to dominate the environment. From the perspective of agency theory, however, the issue is not solely one of domination, but rather, one of costs and market efficiencies. Without a concept of market-caused effects on organizational behavior, one is likely to misinterpret the evolution of partnerships like the MESA program solely in terms of power and institutional domination. The message of Agency Theory is not that such domination does not ever occur, but rather, that underlying the evolution of collaborative and bureaucratic organizational structures is the influence of market efficiencies that cannot long be denied.

CONCLUSIONS

In his paper entitled, *The Power of Paradigms,* William Boyd (1992) suggests that there is no more powerful force than an idea whose time has come. Many educators (e.g., Jones and Maloy 1988; Gross 1988; Beber 1984) have argued that the notion of collaborative partnerships in education is just such an idea. Kenneth Sirotnik and John Goodlad (1988) suggest that the potential of educational partnerships is so great as to constitute a paradigmatic shift in the governance of public education, one that could significantly improve the quality of educational services.

Underlying such claims is an assumption that the organization of educational services through collaborative arrangements promotes production efficiencies through specialization and scale economies. This perspective does not suggest that collaboration is a cheaper way of producing educational services, but rather, a more cost effective method.

The problem of understanding costs is essential to any consideration regarding the future of educational partnerships. The credit that collaboration receives as a cost-effective means of producing and distributing educational services tends to ignore many of the most fundamental costs associated with such efforts. Agency Theory draws attention to how information, monitoring, contracting, and opportunity costs all impact the relative advantage of one organizational structure versus another (including market contracts). Where many theorists such as Sirotnik and Goodlad (1988) seem ideologically committed to collaboration as a means by which to change schools, agency theorists (e.g., Jensen and Meckling 1986) would argue that collaboration is simply one among many structures by which to govern the production of educational services. Within this framework the normative problem for participants is to find contractual and organizational solutions that reduce the cost of exchange relative to their individual calculus. Recognition of the influence of markets and market disciplines on the structure of organizations is one of the insights provided by agency theory and organizational economics in general.

To ignore the influence of the market on organizations is to miss a fundamental message of agency theory. The message is not without its implications for policy. If one accepts that schools operating in isolation can no longer serve the educational needs of society, then attention to the agency costs of collaboratives and partnerships is central to their long-term success. Specifically, issues of ownership, accountability, and monitoring will need to be resolved. The success of resolving these issues lies in generating policy that will create an incentive structure that makes a virtue of self-interest. However, the incentive structure implied by agency theory need not rest on the competitive, individualistic assumptions of neoclassical economics. If Coase (1937) is correct in his assertion that markets and firms are simply alternative means of production, then markets are competition as organizations are to collaboration. Policies promoting collaborative ventures such as partnerships will thus require group, rather than individualistic, incentive structures based on a cooperative, rather than competitive, concept of exchange, production, and efficiency. The future of educational partnerships is not in a commitment to ideology, but rather, to a recognition of the market disciplines influencing the choices and actions of all organizational actors. Only by recognizing the full range of costs can policies be formed that promote and sustain the promise of collaborative ventures.

BIBLIOGRAPHY

Alchian, A., and H. Demsetz. (1986). Production, information costs, and economic organization. In *Organizational Economics,* ed. J. Barney and W. G. Ouchi, 129–155. San Francisco: Jossey-Bass. Reprinted from *American Economic Review* (1972) 6(5):777–795.

Barney, J., and W. G. Ouchi. (1986). *Organizational economics.* San Francisco: Jossey-Bass.

Beber, H., ed. (1984). Realizing the potential of interorganizational cooperation. In *New directions for continuing education.* San Francisco: Jossey-Bass.

Bennett, W. (1993). Is our culture in decline? *Education Week* 9(28):32.

Billis, D. L. (1993) *Organizing public and voluntary agencies.* London, New York: Routledge.

Blank, M. & Melaville, A. (1993). *Together we can.* Washington D.C.: U.S. Department of Education, Office of Educational Research and Improvement.

Boyd, W. L. (1992). The power of paradigms: Reconceptualizating educational policy and management. *Educational Administration Quarterly.* 28(4), 504–528.

Coase, R. H. (1986). The nature of the firm. In *Organizational Economics,* ed. J. Barney and W. G. Ouchi, 80–98. San Francisco: Jossey-Bass. Reprinted from *Economica* (1937) 4:386–405.

Cohen, M. (1987, December). *Restructuring the education system: Agenda for the 90s.* National Governors Association Center for Policy Research.

Davis, P. (1986). *Public-private partnerships.* Proceedings of The Academy of Political Science. 36(2) New York.

Fama, E. F., and W. H. Jensen. (1986). Separation of ownership and control. In *Organizational Economics,* ed. J. Barney and W. G. Ouchi. San Francisco: Jossey-Bass.

Greenberg, A. R. (Ed.) (1991). *High school college partnerships.* Prepared by ERIC Clearinghouse on Higher Education, The George Washington University in cooperation with Association for the Study of Higher Education, ASHE-ERIC Higher Education Report No. 5.

Gross, L. T. (1988). *Partners in education: How colleges can work with schools to improve teachers and learning.* San Francisco: Jossey-Bass.

Hall, R. H. (1991). *Organizations: Structure, process, & outcomes.* Englewood Cliffs, New Jersey: Prentice-Hall, Inc.

Hammack, D. C., and D. R. Young. (1993). *Nonprofit organizations in a market economy.* San Francisco: Jossey-Bass.

Hesterly, W. S., J. Liebeskind, and T. R. Zenger. (1990). Organizational economics: An impending revolution in organization theory? *Academy of Management Review* 15(3):402–420.

Hoenack, S. A. (1983). *Economic behavior within organizations.* New York: Cambridge University Press.

Hoyle, J. (1993). Our children: Dropouts, pushouts, and burnouts. *People and Education* 1(1):26–41.

Jensen, M. C., and W. H. Meckling. (1986). Theory of the firm: Managerial behavior. In *Organizational Economics,* ed. J. Barney and W. G. Ouchi. San Francisco: Jossey-Bass.

Jones, B. L., and R. W. Maloy. (1988). *Partnerships for improving schools.* New York: Greenwood Press.

Kirst, M. (1993). Strengths and weaknesses of American education. *Phi Delta Kappan* 74(8):613–618.

Lawrence, P. R., and J. Lorsch. (1967). *Organizational and environment: Managing differentiation and integration.* Cambridge: Graduate School of Business Administration, Harvard University.

March, J. G. & Simon, H. A. (1958). *Organizations.* New York: John Wiley.

McLaughlin, M. W. (1988). Business and the public schools: New patterns of support. In *Microlevel School Finance: Issues and Implications for Policy,* ed. D. H. Monk, and J. Underwood, 63–80. Cambridge, Mass: Ballinger Publishing.

Michaelsen, J. B. (1981). A theory of decision-making in the public schools: A public choice approach. In *Organizational Behavior in Schools and School Districts,* ed. Samuel Bacharach, 208–241. New York: Praeger Publishing.

Neal, D. C. (1988). *Consortia and interinstitutional cooperation.* New York: American Council on Education, MacMillan Publishing Company.

Otterbourg, S. D., and M. Timpane. (1986). Partnerships and schools. In *Public-private partnerships,* ed. P. Davis. Proceedings of The Academy of Political Science, 36(2) New York.

Pfeffer, J., and G. R. Salancik. (1978). *The external control of organizations.* New York: Harper & Row.

Sarason, S. B. (1979). *The challenge of the resource exchange network.* San Francisco. Jossey-Bass Publishers.

Scott, Richard W. (1992). *Organizations: Rational, natural and open systems.* Englewood Cliffs, N.J.: Prentice-Hall.

Selznick, P. (1966): *TVA and the grass roots: A study in the sociology of formal organizations.* Berkeley: University of California Press. (Originally published in 1949).

Sirotnik, K. A., and J. I. Goodlad, eds. (1988). *School/university partnerships in action.* New York: Teachers College Press.

Thompson, J. D. (1967). *Organizations in action.* New York: McGraw-Hill.

Walsh, M. (1993). Signing up the public: Community at large must help pull lever for change. *Education Week* 9(28):9–14.

Williamson, O. E. (1975). *Markets and hierarchies: Analysis and antitrust implications.* New York: The Free Press.

Williamson, O. E. (1986). *Economic organization: Firms, markets and policy control.* New York: New York University Press.

Chapter 11

Reforming American Education Policy for the Twenty-First Century

Deborah A. Verstegen

During the decade encompassing the current education reform movement in the United States, most aspects of the education system have come under intense scrutiny and debate. However, a paucity of attention has centered on the role of school resources in systemwide change and improvement and in creating equal opportunities to learn for all children and at all schools. This chapter reviews the concept of equal opportunity to learn over time as related to school finance systems; in it are discussions on the current state of education finance; and the need for redesigning funding structures and linking them to upgraded curriculum and equitable school practices, to provide "aligned" education policy aimed at a high quality education. The assumption is that curricular improvements and finance reforms work more effectively together than either would alone.

The second but equally important set of linkages discussed is between aligned education policies, including finance systems, and community services dealing with health, welfare, juvenile justice, and social and rehabilitation services. These linkages would extend the reach of the current reforms beyond the school through interagency collaborations to address the multiple and interlocking needs of many children that create effective obstacles to learning.

These two strategies for reform are mutually reinforcing and inextricably linked. Successful interagency collaborations rest upon aligned education policies aimed at quality education for all children and at all schools. In their absence, joint ventures will be hobbled by attempting to create a seamless web of quality programs and services for children and youths if they attend unequal and inferior schools. Likewise, without interagency collaborations to address the often multiple and interlocking needs many children bring with them to the schoolhouse door, America's children and youth will not be ready to learn an upgraded, world-class curricula that addresses the needs and opportunities of the information age and global economy for the nation and the child.

EQUAL OPPORTUNITY TO LEARN

Equality of educational opportunity has appeared as a normative goal of educational policy in the United States since the beginning of the republic (Butts & Cremin 1953; Rossmiller 1987). In the early nineteenth century, with the onset of the Industrial Revolution and the necessity for training in general skills, public education and an interest in the equality of educational opportunity began to appear in America and Europe. Initially, equality of educational opportunity was defined in terms of access to the common school. The goal was to provide all children free elementary schooling up to a given level that constituted the principal entry point into the labor market; subsequently, this was extended to include free access to secondary schooling.

By the beginning of the twentieth century, equality of access was generally available—but racial minorities and children with disabilities were often excluded or placed in separate educational facilities—and the concept of access to a minimum education program began to emerge. Educational opportunity was defined in terms of a minimum common curriculum that would be available to all children, regardless of background (Coleman 1986); it was intended to enable the child to effectively function in a democratic society and contribute to it. This concept was developed through approaches to financing education by school finance theorists: Ellwood Cubberley (1906) with revisions to the flat grant, Harlan Updegraff and King (1922) through district power equalizing systems George Strayer and Robert Haig (1923) with the foundation school program, and Henry Morrison (1930) through full state funding schemes (see Johns, Morphet, and Alexander 1983). Under these plans, additional local funding beyond the minimum amount needed to finance the basic education program was generally permitted and presumed to buy local, not state or national, benefits.[1]

A second focus in this concept was ushered in by the Cardinal Principles report (National Education Association, 1918). Access to a common curriculum gave way to the assumption of different educational futures for children—vocational and college—that would, in turn, require differentiated curricula. To achieve equal opportunity, schools provided the course of study that ostensibly best met a student's needs. It wasn't until the 1960s, however, that this concept was generally expanded to include supplementary funding for special needs students, whose education imposed higher than average costs—e.g., special, compensatory, bilingual, vocational, and gifted and talented education students.

The origins of the third stage in the evolution of the concept of equal educational opportunity (Murphy and Hallinger 1986) were with the Supreme Court ruling in *Brown v. the Board of Education* (1954). A new and different assumption emerged: even when identical facilities and teacher salaries existed for racially separate schools, separate schooling was not equal because the effects of those schools were likely to be different. The assumption was that "equality of opportunity depends in some fashion upon effects [or] . . . results of schooling" (Coleman 1968, 15). Implementation of *Brown* was painfully slow, however, until passage of the Civil Rights Act of 1964 and subsequent legislation, which also mandated the Commissioner of Education to assess the lack of equality of educational opportunity in schooling among racial and other groups. Five types of inequality were defined,[2] but the emphasis of the examination was to be on the fourth definition, where equality of educational opportunity was defined as equality of results (Coleman 1968).

The Coleman Report (1966) issued the survey results, which found the relationship between inputs and achievement was as follows: facilities and curriculum least, teacher quality next, and backgrounds of fellow students and families, most. Many educators and others however, were unwilling to accept Coleman's conclusions and mounted research efforts to demonstrate that the quality and quantity of schooling does make a difference in student outcomes and that student achievement is not dependent on the student's social and family background. This work yielded a body of literature generally referred to as research on "effective schools"[3] (Edmonds 1982–1983; MacKenzie 1983; Purkey & Smith 1983; Rossmiller 1987; Rutter, Maughan, Mortimore, Ouston, and Smith 1979). It documents the effectiveness of some schools in improving student performance regardless of family or social background characteristics of the child. Its findings were generally taken to mean that schools can make a difference in student outcomes regardless of social and economic circumstances (Rossmiller 1987).

Although one of the main affects of the Coleman Report was to refocus research and debate away from equal opportunity issues to outcomes and productivity concerns, at the same time state school finance litigation emerging over the 1970s, based on the pattern set in *Serrano v. Priest* (1971), continued to define equal opportunity as substantial equality of expenditures among districts within a state, i.e., an input versus output focus. In this, equality of opportunity was consistent with a wealth neutrality standard: the quality of a child's education should not be a function of wealth other than the wealth of the state as a whole. This bifurcated focus has continued into the present.

The genesis of the fourth stage in the evolution of the concept of equality of educational opportunity commenced with the adoption of the national education goals in 1990 and a corollary stream of activity originating from state courts (Verstegen 1991, 1992). Recent decisions emerging from the school finance litigation sweeping the country are, in many cases, like the national education goals, redefining equal educational opportunity in the context of the information age and global economy. In this context, equal educational opportunity is interpreted to mean student access and outcomes consistent with a quality education—not a basic or minimum education. A major issue for the future is how to restructure the education system to achieve long-term, systemic change and improvement consistent with the definition of equal educational opportunity embedded in the fourth generation of equity issues—and how to link directions of the courts with the achievement of the national educational goals.

Restructuring School Finance Systems and Linking Them to Curricular Improvements Through Systemic Reform

> • *To link the directions of the courts to the achievement of national education goals, school finance systems must be radically restructured and linked to curricular improvements to give to the many what has been reserved for the fortunate few: equal opportunities for excellence in education. Equity without excellence is not the goal.**

Recently, the critical examination of education in America has given way to the third wave of the education reform movement (for a discussion of the three waves, see Murphy 1990; Verstegen and McGuire 1991; Verstegen 1993) with its genesis in the historic creation and adaption of the ambitious national education goals by the 50-state governors and the president in 1990 (National Governors'

---

*The italicized statements at the beginning of each major section are propositions to help guide the reader.

Association [NGA] 1990, 1991, 1993). The thrust of the third wave of reform is on systemic change to radically restructure all components of the education system in an effort to achieve a high-quality education for all students and at all schools. It centers on defining what all students should know and be able to do to be competitive in a world-class economy and to achieve the national education goals, and it includes the creation of national standards, curricular frameworks, a renewed emphasis on accountability and assessment, and interagency collaboration on behalf of needy children and youth (NGA 1990, 1991). Key issues propelled by the third wave of education reform include strategies to achieve the national education goals, with the role of federal, state, and local governments in systemic change and improvement as the focus of third wave efforts (Stedman and Riddle 1992).

Generally, five key components are considered critical to systemwide change: (1) the establishment of goals or standards expected of all students; (2) the development of curricula linked directly to those standards; (3) the use of high-quality instructional materials appropriate to the curricula; (4) the institution of professional development programs to enable teachers, administrators, and other school staff to understand the curricula and the most effective ways of instructing students; and (5) the creation and implementation of student assessment systems that are based directly on the curricula (U.S. General Accounting Office 1993).

Notably lacking discussion or debate, however, is the role of school resources in achieving systemwide change and providing equal opportunities to learn. Given the wide variation in the quality and equality of schooling in America, this raises critical questions related to justice and fairness in education: Shall we use the same performance standards and high-stakes tests at all schools and for all children but provide them with different opportunities to learn the material they will be tested on? Shall we hold the schools/children accountable for results and not hold the federal/state governments accountable for resources (Clune 1993)? At issue are ways to provide all children with the resources necessary to learn what they need to know to meet high national performance standards, the means to ensure that students do not bear the sole burden of attaining enhanced outcome requirements, and strategies to encourage assurances that the tools for success will be available at all schools and for all children (NGA 1993).

These issues have been at the heart of the groundswell of school finance litigation that is sweeping the country, which is propelling issues of equity to the top of state policy agendas and providing a competing narrative for the change and improvement of America's educational system. Currently, a majority of states have active or planned challenges to the constitutionality of their school finance systems due to gaps in quality and equality among school systems with a state. Just since 1989, seven states[4] have had their finance systems declared unconstitutional; unappealed lower-court rulings have overturned state financing schemes in additional states.[5] Overall, these courts are calling for an equality of quality programs and services for all children and at all schools. They suggest remedies that would close the gap between the best and the worst financed system in the state, with differences favoring the most needy.

In the New Jersey decision (*Abbott v. Burke* 1990), for example, the court found that disparities in curricular offerings constituted disparities in educational opportunities; this formed a basis for overturning the state finance system. Court-specified objectives for student attainment included the ability of students from poorer districts to compete for jobs with those from wealthier districts and "course offerings resulting in such intangibles as good citizenship, cultural appreciation, and community awareness" (Benson 1991, 414). According to the court, fiscal and programmatic imbalances must favor the least fortunate:

> If the educational fare of the seriously disadvantaged student is the same as the "regular education" given the advantaged student, those serious disadvantages will not be addressed, and students in the poorer urban districts will simply not be able to compete.

In Kentucky, after finding unconstitutional not just the school finance system but the entire education system, the court defined the constitutional requirement for "efficient" education, which linked upgraded program requirements, a redesigned finance system, and elevated outcomes. The court called for all children to have access to an adequate education, one which is uniform and has as its goal the development of the seven capacities, including:

> (i) sufficient oral and written communication skills to enable student to function in a complex and rapidly changing civilization . . . (vii) sufficient levels of academic or vocational skills to enable public school students to compete favorably with their counterparts in surrounding states, in academics or in the job market. *Rose v. Council for Better Education*—790 S.W. 2d 186 (Ky. 1989).

As the courts call for the new equity in education, they are also propelling school finance systems to be restructured and aligned to curricular improvements to give to the many what has been reserved for the fortunate few: equal opportunities for excellence in education. School finance systems can be a powerful tool to raise both the level and distribution of educational outcomes in an information age and global economy and to provide equal opportunities to learn, but there are at least two major obstacles that must be addressed. These are discussed below.

Restructuring the Level of Education for All Children

> • *A major obstacle in using current school finance systems to drive systemic change and improvement in education is that they are obsolete and need radical restructuring if they are to keep pace with today's educational needs and the global economy. Future education finance systems must rest on a conception of a quality education for all children and all schools—not a minimum or basic education.*

When one examines the basic finance structure currently used by the fifty states to equalize educational opportunities for children between more and less affluent localities, two overall findings emerge. First, there have been no new approaches developed or used to equalize state aid to localities since the 1920s. Second, however, there have been substantial shifts in the relative use of finance systems over time, and additional provisions have been added to finance high-cost students and schools, which have increased over time, particularly over the last decade (cf., Tron 1978–1979; Verstegen 1990).

Antiquated School Finance Systems. Despite shifts in the relative use of school finance systems over time,[6] and the recognition of high-cost students and schools, a major obstacle in using current school finance systems to drive systemic change and improvement in education is that they are obsolete and need radical restructuring if they are to keep pace with today's educational needs and the global economy. Antiquated school finance plans rest on a conception of a minimum education—not a quality or world-class education. In the past, once the vision of the basic or minimum education was crystallized through state curriculums, courses and objectives, state accreditation standards, high school graduation requirements or exit exams, it could serve as a basis for the state funding guarantee. This approach, however, resulted in at least two problems.

First, there was no clear consensus on what students should know and be able to do on which to hinge a revenue estimate. Where state curricula or tests could inform this thinking, in many cases, educational programs and school finance were decoupled, i.e., state finance guarantees did not reflect the school curriculum or its costs. The recent school finance court decisions have displayed a keen interest in the linkage between finance and program, however, and this interest is accelerating, encompassing the policy arena as well.

Second, in most cases, the courts are calling for a quality education for all students, not a minimum or basic education, and the national goals have also moved boldly in this direction. The national education goals would bring all students to high levels of thinking and problem solving in English, mathematics, science, geography, and history and have the U.S. rank first in the world in mathematics and science. In contrast, current school finance systems were created to support a minimum level of schooling necessary for an individual to effectively function in an industrial era. However, an information age makes new and more stringent demands on its schools (Drucker 1990), and school finance systems have not changed appreciably over the last seventy years to reflect them.

Thus, school finance systems do not need to be repaired; they need to be radically redesigned and aligned to systemic change and improvement across all facets of the education system in an effort to achieve both excellence and equity for all children and all schools and guide and drive a world-class education system. Redesigned finance systems would rest on a conception of quality education for all children, not a basic or minimum education.

Restructuring the Distribution of Education for All Children

• *A second major obstacle to using school finance systems to drive excellence in education for all children and all schools is that school finance systems are flawed in theory and practice: they drive wide and growing gaps in education quality and equality among schools and school districts. All too often, these differences penalize the poor, condemning them to "inequality under the law" (Kozol 1991).*

Although the goal of state school finance systems is to provide equal opportunities, they have fallen noticeably short of this goal. In more than one-half of the states in the nation, the range of difference in spending among school systems is at least two-to-one; in one-third of all states, spending varies over three-to-one[7] (Riddle 1990). In Illinois, for example, spending for elementary education varies from $1,162 per student in one elementary school to $7,040 in another. In New Jersey, one elementary district spends $2,081 per pupil, and another spends $12,556. In Virginia, wealthy localities have an additional $4,343 per pupil, or almost three times more, to spend on education than do poor localities (Verstegen and Salmon 1989). Interstate variation in education revenue is also extreme. In 1990, state and local revenue (excluding federal aid) averaged $4,464 across the states; it ranged from $2,612 in Mississippi to $6,120 in New Jersey. Thus, New Jersey had nearly three times more revenue available per pupil than did Mississippi, a difference that amounts to over $105,000 for each class of thirty students.

School finance disparities—differences in spending between wealthy and poor schools—arise from the way states finance public schools. This is the essential problem: by requiring students to attend certain schools, but not requiring equity among schools, states therefore fund inequity in schooling. All too frequently, inequities penalize poor children and youths, compounding adverse social and economic circumstances by hobbling them from securing a viable passport out of want and deprivation, from securing a quality education. In essence, then, under current finance systems, poor children and localities are often condemned to inequality under the law (Kozol 1991). And almost of all the states rely on state finance structures that theoretically equalize revenues for education (but only up to a point), but almost all states also finance inequalities when they: (1) fund a significant portion revenue outside the equalizing formula, (2) include provisions that work against the equalizing features of the system, (3) fail to fund the full cost of education—causing inadequacy in the system, both for the regular education program and for children and localities with special needs, and (4) rely heavily on proper taxes raised locally.

To address these shortcomings, some states fund all education programs through the equalizing grant of the finance formula and, in so doing, achieve greater fiscal equity in education. This approach contrasts to an approach that adds on additional funding for new programs and services outside the formula—through a uniform amount of money that is distributed to all localities regardless of local ability to pay for education. Second, states that phase out provisions that provide uniform assistance across all localities—minimum aid, hold harmless provisions, and unequalized categorical aid—increase equity in school finances. Third, states that fully fund the cost of the education program increase fiscal equity. If funding is inadequate, then wealthy districts will raise the difference easily out of local sources—and go beyond them—but poor districts will not be able to afford even a basic education program. Fully funded education programs would also provide extra assistance to high-need students and jurisdictions, when these needs were based on legitimate and justifiable differences in costs and requirements.

Importantly, perhaps the major source of disparity in state finance plans is in the locally raised revenue from the property tax. When localities raise money outside the finance formula through property taxes, wealthy jurisdictions raise more dollars and poor localities less—at the same tax rates—because property tax bases vary widely among localities, thus providing unequal access to revenue for education and unequal dollars for education even when tax rates are equal. This traps less affluent localities in a cycle of deprivation and widens the gaps in spending across the state. Moreover, school finance plans that assume that all localities have a similar ability to increase taxes for public schools subsidize affluent localities, with more disposable income available to raise taxes, and widen disparities between rich schools and poor schools (Verstegen 1991a).[8] Property wealth relates poorly to a locality's ability to pay taxes—all taxes are paid out of income. Therefore, states that pay the full cost of education from state-federal tax sources (including a statewide property tax) eliminate this problem altogether.

In an information age and global economy, given the relationship between education and economic growth (Dennison 1983) and individual opportunity (Card & Krueger 1992; Kaus 1992; Reich 1991), investment in an equality of quality schooling is one of the most promising strategies to truly reform American education, not only for the child, but for the nation. This would require not only investing in the schooling of the poor to provide equal opportunities to learn but would also address fiscal support and focus attention directly at programs to alleviate poverty and its interlocking effects in the community. Necessary linkages to achieve these ends are discussed below.

Creating Aligned School Policy by Enhancing and Linking Program and Finance Equity

• *The first set of linkages to create aligned school policy would connect redesigned school programs, curricula, materials, and incentive and assessment systems to redesigned fiscal structures.*

To interrelate education program reform and education finance reform in an effort to address these issues, at least two overriding linkages are critical. The first set of linkages would align restructured school programs, curricula, materials, and incentive and assessment systems aimed at high-quality education systems to redesigned fiscal structures. The second, but equally important, focus is the linkage between aligned school structures, including finance systems and community services dealing with health, welfare, juvenile justice, and social and rehabilitation services to provide interagency collaboration on behalf of needy children and families (NGA 1991).

Under one approach to link school program reform to finance reform, there must be a common vision of an upgraded education system that would be widely developed and broadly communicated through, for example, a set of goals/state standards consistent with constitutional requirements (Smith and O'Day 1991). All aspects of the education system, including finances, would be aligned to the common set of standards or goals, creating coherent education policy with a systemic focus aimed at improvement and change. State education standards or education goals consistent with constitutional requirements would provide what Kern Alexander (1991) has called "foundational limits" that may be used to guide legislative enactments and serve as a basis for cost estimates. Importantly, they must go well beyond the old equity of basic skills goals of the 1960s, 1970s, and 1980s to reflect the new equity of quality education for all students of the 1990s. Marshall Smith and Jennifer O'Day (1991, 247) assert:

> They must provide standards that challenge the public and the educational system to prepare our youth to grapple thoughtfully with those problems that defy algorithmic solutions and to be skilled and confident learners in schools and later on.

Some goals/standards could address desired changes in the nature or quality of educational inputs, such as the quality of the teaching force or the curriculum used in the schools. For example, a state goal may be to provide curricular equity among schools. Other goals may be related student outcomes (Smith and O'Day 1991).

Content Standards. Goals or standards once developed need to be particularized to indicate what all students should know and be able to do when they leave the education system. These are referred to as content standards/curricular frameworks and include the best thinking in the field about what knowledge, processes, and skills students from K–12 need to know by various stages of their education, i.e., in fourth, eighth, and twelfth grade. They would set out desired intellectual curricular themes, topics, and objectives in sufficiently long-range chunks to allow maximum flexibility at the local level while providing clear goals for the system as a whole (Smith and O'Day 1991). Content standards would be linked to high-quality instructional materials, teacher education programs and inservice, and assessment systems to provide coherent education policy aimed at high-quality outcomes.

Opportunity to learn standards. Importantly, curricular frameworks, once developed, must be aligned to resources to fuel improvement and ensure that equal opportunities are available to reach the elevated standards. Programmatic requirements would be linked to finance systems by affixing cost estimates to them and utilizing the resulting figures as a basis for funding guarantees. Improvements over time have resulted in more refined methods for estimating costs based on programmatic assumptions (Chambers and Parrish 1983; Monk and Walker 1991) and for determining necessary excess costs beyond the general education program for high-cost schools/districts and students with special learning needs (Hartman 1990; Monk 1982, 1990). In this, equal opportunities to learn would require sufficient revenue for comparable programs and services, teachers, facilities and instructional materials, and teaching-learning strategies for all students and at all schools, when the costs of providing them and special student needs were taken into consideration.

Decentralized Approaches. Under a decentralized, bottom-up approach, the "challenge is to design policies that combine the high standards of systemic policy with a broad diversity of curricular options [to reach them] and a powerful local delivery system" (Clune 1993, 234). Thus, high goals and standards would be developed, curricular frameworks would be provided as a guide, while at the same time allowing other curricular options developed locally to match diverse needs and contexts. High-stakes exams would be avoided; the system would primarily rely on professional development and capacity-building school improvement strategies. Attendant finance criteria would be based on a "key school or district" concept: that district providing the highest quality *programs and services* would serve as a benchmark for the programmatic breadth and depth that should be made available to all children and at all schools—although delivery strategies may vary.[9] In this, large, affluent districts may serve as standardbearers for determining what is curricularly possible when small size, geographic isolation, and poverty are inoperative. Alternatively, schools/districts meeting or exceeding enhanced curricular frameworks (including curricular depth and breadth) and assessment targets may function as key schools/districts for cost determination. This would require the identification of a group of exemplary schools or districts across differing student populations and district sizes to determine expenditures, which would serve as benchmarks for the state guarantee(s). This approach was suggested in the seminal research of the National Educational Finance Project in the 1970s (Rossmiller, Hale, and Frohreich 1970). In essence, like the aforementioned approach, it would give to the many what has been reserved for the fortunate few: equal opportunities for financing excellence in education. It would link program and fiscal equity. Differences in funding would favor the least advantaged.

School-linked policies alone, however, while necessary for change and improvement aimed at upgraded educational standards for all children and at all schools, will not be sufficient to transform schooling in America to world-class status consistent with the requirements of the information age and global economy. Importantly, collaboration across extraschool agencies and bureaus on behalf of needy children and families is necessary to address the multiple and interlocking needs many children bring with them to the schoolhouse door that create obstacles to learning. To be effective, however, interagency collaborations must rest on aligned school policies aimed at a high-quality education for all children and at all schools. This would assure that needy children and youth would not be disadvantaged by inadequate and unequal schooling. While aligned school policies would provide a systemic strategy to transform and upgrade schooling in America for all children and youths, interagency collaboration would address the crisis brought on by deteriorating conditions of children and the changing demographics of education.

Integrating Funding Streams on Behalf of Schools, Families and Communities

• *A second, but equally important, focus of redesigned education systems is creating linkages between school services and other community services, such as health, juvenile justice, rehabilitation, and social and welfare services to provide interagency collaboration to meet the multiple and interrelated needs of children and families, which often create obstacles to learning.*

Interagency collaboration would extend the reach of current reforms beyond the school to address the interlocking effects of poverty and economic instability to influences beyond the education system. The need for interagency collaboration on behalf of needy children and families derives from major demographic, social, and economic changes over the past decade that have had profound effects on the lives of the nation's children and families (Edelman 1991; Hodgkinson 1989; Verstegen 1991b). In large part, children and the poor bore the burden of debt and recession that was to accompany the redistribution of wealth and opportunity over the past decade. By 1988, median family income was lower than in 1973, measured in constant dollars, and average weekly earnings were lower than in 1962 (Phillips 1990; Kraus 1992). This affected children directly. The child poverty rate grew from 8.4 percent in 1973, representing 9.4 million children, to 20.4 percent in 1987, when 12.8 million children—one out of every five children, and one out of every four children in preschool—were in poverty. Today, for the first time in the nation's history, children in America are the single largest poverty group and the fastest growing homeless subpopulation—and the interlocking effects of want and deprivation extend into most aspects of these children's lives. Although traditionally measured in terms of income, poverty's true horror extends to all aspects of life: susceptibility of disease, inaccess to most services and information, lack of control over resources, subordination to higher social and economic forces, extreme vulnerability to sudden misfortunes, and utter insecurity in the face of changing circumstances (During 1990). Children in poverty experience the highest incidence of health problems but live in the least healthful environments and have the least access to medical care; they are at the highest risk of academic failure but often attend the worst schools; their families experience the most stress but have the fewest social supports (National Commission on Children [NCC] 1991). Thus, a fundamental mismatch is apparent: while the nation faces a substantially needier school population, the requirements of the information age and global economy call for all youth to leave schools with significantly upgraded and enhanced knowledge and skills.

Although an array of programs, services, and funding arrangements have been developed over the past two decades to address the special needs of children and families, their effectiveness has been limited due to a number of factors—including underfunding or underservice, a focus on remediation rather than on prevention, and service fragmentation (Kirst and McLaughlin 1990; Verstegen 1991b).

The lessons from decades of working with these programs indicate that full funding for all eligible recipients, assistance for programs aimed at prevention in addition to remediation, and interagency collaboration would build on the positive outcomes past initiatives have evidenced (Schorr and Schorr 1989; Schorr 1993; Verstegen 1991b).

Fragmented, Uncoordinated Policy. Currently, aid for needy families and children is scattered across multiple agencies, departments, and offices and consists of hundreds of major federal, state, and local programs and services, each with separate eligibility requirements, provisions for assistance, and administering agencies. For example, in fiscal year 1989 the federal government spent approximately $59.5 billion on programs and services for children, which supported at least 240 programs administered by offices and agencies in eleven cabinet-level departments. State and local governments spent approximately 31 percent of their budgets on children's programs and services, similarly dispersed across numerous state and municipal agencies and offices (NCC 1991). In California, over 160 programs residing in thirty-five agencies and seven departments exist to serve children and youth, an array that is not unique to that state (Kirst and McLaughlin 1990). Often there is a lack of communication across service delivery systems, with four or five agencies working independently with a child or family and each unaware of the other's involvement (Kirst 1992). Eligibility requirements and guidelines are separate; funding streams and accountability requirements differ; services address only one of myriad problems the family and child are experiencing; and often each program and service is provided by a separate office and at a separate location and delivers narrowly defined services to narrowly defined populations with little collaboration across functional lines (NCC 1991). Thus, while children's and family's needs are increasingly horizontal, programs and services are organized vertically (Kirst 1993).

This antiquated structure for the provision of services has led to program fragmentation, costly duplication of programs, and uncoordinated services in a time of limited resources. Moreover, families are forced to navigate this complex structure and overcome countless barriers to access the services they require (Child Welfare League of America 1993). For families and children with multiple and severe problems, the present system fails to provide the broad array of high-quality services and supports that seek to prevent, as well as treat, their problems and that recognize the interrelationships among their

education, health, social service, child welfare, employment, and training needs (NCC 1991). What is lost is a focus on the interrelationships
between multiple problems for any particular individual and family,
the continuity of care for children and youth as they move from one
service provider to another—e.g., from institutionalization to community care, or from home to detention in a juvenile facility—and collaboration between schools and other agencies to deal specifically with
the multiple needs of a set of families and their children (Hodgkinson
1989; Kirst 1992; Kirst and McLaughlin 1990). According to one study:
"Children and families in such a system bounce like pinballs in a
pinball machine—from problem to problem, from one agency to the
next—with little cooperation or follow-up" (Education and Human
Services Consortium [EHSC] 1992).

   To address these problems, some states and localities have begun
experimenting with cooperative or collaborative ventures. Florida's
Department of Education is working with Health and Rehabilitative
Services to develop a strategic plan for creating "full service" schools;
California has added a cabinet-level secretary for child development
and education; the Annie E. Casey Foundation's New Futures Program provides $10 million to each of five cities to address the prob-
lems of at-risk thirteen- to nineteen-year-olds through coordinated
comprehensive services and in-school support teams headed by case
managers (NGA 1991). Increasingly, research has shown that an integrated, collaborative approach for the provision of multiple and
intergenerational services for children and families is most effective
(Kirst and McLaughlin 1990; NCC 1991).

Interagency Collaboration. The concept of interagency collaboration
on behalf of needy children and families would reorient systems away
from the narrow dimensions of single program or agency mandates to
knit a "seamless web of services" focused on the broad-based needs of
children and families (EHSC 1992). Comprehensive service systems
would begin with an assessment of the needs of families and determine the agencies from which they are receiving services as a basis for
collaborative ventures, while helping underserved families and children identify the assistance they need from a menu of core services,
including basic income subsidies, housing, child welfare services, prenatal, health, employment training, and education. The family could
also draw on support services, such as child care, counseling, transportation, literacy and job search skills, recreation, and leadership
development.

To move beyond simple referral of a family from one agency to another, colocation of staff among agencies, interagency teams from multiple human service agencies and education, and "one stop shopping centers" would facilitate the access of families and children to the mix of services and programs they require (EHSC 1992). Thus, staff would be repositioned from one agency to branch offices located at other organizations whose clients they share; either a cross-trained individual with the knowledge, skill, and authority to address a child/family's multiple problems and needs across functional lines or an interagency team would assume the primary responsibility for the multiple needs of specific families or children. The single location or hub would house multiple public and private agencies that provided services, such as education, counseling, health, housing, juvenile justice, social, and welfare services, together with opportunities for families to find productive employment at a decent wage (EHSC 1992). Schools could constitute one of the centers of a collaborative network of comprehensive children's services because they have the most sustained contact with children and families, although they cannot provide the full mix of services that children and families need given their academic responsibilities. This requires a joint effort by all sectors serving needy children and families and the ability to overcome funding limitations that often drives the failure to collaborate.

Most funding for children's services is provided through categorical aid mechanisms and is restricted to specific programs and population groups, with attendant provisions that require separate accounting and auditing trails. In an effort to simplify compliance with fiscal requirements, many states and localities have segregated children's services according to funding channels and have been hesitant to collaborate with outside agencies due to perceived increased administrative burdens and turf questions. However, most categorical aid programs do not require the segregation of services among beneficiaries or "pull out" programs, although in some cases these may be warranted.

An Integrated Service Approach and Cost Sharing. For example, currently the federal compensatory education program (ESEA Title I) allows resources to be used for children identified for compensatory education, that also receive limited English proficiency programs, and special education; However, separate audit trails are required due to excess costs and supplement, not supplant, provisions that prohibit commingling of funds. A child eligible for several categorical programs can, therefore, be furnished with a single integrated program supported from multiprogram funds. The services purchased with categorical funds from several program areas would be combined, but separate tracking of revenue would be maintained. Thus, an integrated service model or cost-sharing model for integrating funding streams on behalf of children would integrate *services* from several categorical programs but would keep financial audit trails separate.

The Mukilteo School district in Everett, Washington, has used such a model since 1982, using funds allocated from a variety of programs including basic education, ESEA, Chapters 1 and 2, state remediation, and state and federal refugee and bilingual programs. The program recognizes that the "supplement-not-supplant issue is best left at the funding level, not the service level. Categorical dollars must be spent on eligible children only, and those dollars must be in addition to basic education dollars" (Felix, Hertlein, McKenna, and Rayborn 1987, 787–788). The decision on how those dollars are spent, however, rests with local districts.

Extending this concept beyond education programs and services, collaborative services across public and private agencies have the potential to harness and combine the substantial funding streams permanently available from multiple agencies beyond education on behalf of children in a time of fiscal stress in education budgets among all levels of government—although expanded investment in needy children and families is necessary if the full range of prevention, treatment, and support services is provided, incentives for fresh ventures created, and gaps in existing service structures filled.

Revenue provided through existing funding streams currently appropriated under several state and federal programs in education, social services, and juvenile justice, such as Medicaid and drug abuse prevention, would follow programs to a "one stop" location to support a tailored set of comprehensive services for children and their families (Kirst 1991, 1993). For example, funding available to support related services for exceptional children enrolled in local public schools currently is disproportionately drawn from local education agencies (LEAs), although the utilization of funding streams drawn from other agencies may be a much better and more effective resource decision, as, theoretically, several federal and state agencies share responsibility for the special education and related service needs of children with disabilities. However, translation of this theory into practice has often resulted in "bureaucratic fragmentation, duplication and retreat." For example, mental health agencies frequently provide psychological or counseling services but they may lack adequate financial and staff capacity to meet the needs of [children with disabilities]. Sometimes these agencies will serve some children [with disabilities] but leave the school district responsible for providing the same services for other [children]. Districts often complain that public agencies that once met some of the needs of [exceptional] students now claim that the schools must pay for all such services for [special education] students because of legal mandates contained in the federal and state law. But federal law intentionally does not prescribe that the education budget bear all the costs of special education. According to P. L. 94–142 [currently the Individuals With Disabilities Education Act], as long as an appropriate special education program is provided at public expense, the local education agency and the state have met their obligation. (Moore, Walker, Holland 1982, 63–64).

Interagency cooperation for the provision of programs and services on behalf of needy families and children would have several benefits for children and families over current practice. It would bring together a broad range of professional expertise and agency services on behalf of children and families, harness and combine substantial funding streams available in several institution's budgets, and reorganize available resources to create integrated programs and services addressing the multiple needs of children and families. However, these initiatives also encompass a number of challenges that must be addressed if the potential of cooperative arrangements is to be attained. For example, interagency cooperation requires the commitment of administrative time and staff to locate, patch together, and create comprehensive services from dozens of revenue sources available through multiple programs. It requires record keeping to maintain the accountability necessary for multiple funding sources and financing to support the new administrative structures it creates.

The Door—a private, nonprofit, comprehensive service agency and pioneer of cost sharing strategies for at-risk youth in New York—illustrates the challenges in purchasing comprehensive services for children and families with categorical funds from multiple human service programs, while providing separate auditing and accounting trails for each.

The Door must mix State Department of Health preventive and prenatal care funds, federal family-planning monies, and community health center dollars, among others. Because each funding source

requires categorical accountability, The Door must separate out exactly how many services were paid for by dollars from each source
funding non-Medicaid clients' clinic visits. The task then becomes
how to subdivide the cost of a single visit into an accurate percentage
of time spent on family planning, AIDS education, or general health
care (EHSC 1992, 13).

A more efficient means to deal with this complexity and the often
time-consuming and conflicting rules and regulations attendant to the
integration of multiple, categorical programs, according to The Door,
would be for lead agencies to develop a multiyear service contract to
guarantee support for comprehensive service providers and to allow
them to subcontract for services that it was not equipped to offer from
cooperating agencies (EHSC 1992). The latter, "glue" money would
allow one agency to subcontract with other agencies to ensure that
children can get services in one place and be assigned a case manager
who could procure resources from other agencies. Additional facilita-
tive provisions for cooperative agencies, would hook a child's or
family's participation in one program to another to eliminate duplicative intake processes through multiple recipient eligibility. Joint ventures would allow several agencies to raise funds for jointly operated
programs or to set aside a portion of the current budget for cooperative undertakings (Kirst 1992, 1993).

Collaborative Models. Once agencies agree to work together on behalf
of children and families, they must decide whether joint programs
will be cooperative or collaborative. According to Education and
Human Services Consortium (EHSC 1992), *cooperative* service delivery
arrangements allow partner agencies to help each other meet their
respective organizational goals without making any substantial changes
in their own basic services or the rules or regulations that govern their
agencies. At the system level, they assess the need for more comprehensive services and recommend strategies to coordinate existing programs, services, and funding streams. *Collaborative* ventures, on the
other hand, establish common goals among agencies to address complex problems that may lie beyond any individual agency's exclusive
purview, rather than focusing on their individual agendas. Resources
may be pooled and new services planned, implemented, and evaluated (EHSC 1992).

Moving beyond the assessment and advisory activities characteristic of most cooperative financial initiatives, collaborative ventures

allow participants to transform goals and objectives while fundamentally altering service delivery through the power to recombine existing resources (EHSC 1992). Foci may change from crisis intervention to preventative services centered on the total needs of the child and family. State-level leadership can facilitate comprehensive ventures through technical assistance—e.g., by developing common definitions, simplifying eligibility requirements across agencies, assisting local institutions acquiring necessary certifications for collaboration (e.g., Medicaid), providing demonstration models, and disseminating promising practices. States can assist in creating and maintaining joint client information banks, confidentiality release policies, and incentive systems to encourage interagency agreements by making funding contingent on interagency involvement. Federal incentives for interagency collaboration for states and localities to plan education programs across multiple domains of youth services would also provide an important impetus for joint ventures at all levels.

Importantly, government initiatives can provide incentives for joint ventures through the provision of funding. This is the critical variable in interagency collaborations because the "availability of resources will determine (1) whether or not the changes in services and service delivery that the joint effort has established will become permanently institutionalized, and (2) the size of the population that will eventually benefit from these changes" (EHSC 1992, 31).

Funding for interagency services may be derived from new policy initiatives and revenue sources; selective decategorization of restricted aid programs that meld existing funding into an overall special purpose grant but, at minimum, maintain antecedent funding levels (NCC 1991); and contractual agreements between agencies that dedicate a fixed percentage of current agency budgets to new collaborative ventures. Ultimately, then, service delivery efforts must be joined by systemwide policy changes to ensure the financing necessary for the continuity of comprehensive services and to facilitate long-term linkages among service providers. Although new resources must be found and/or current resource streams pooled and reconfigured to create new, comprehensive services to warrant continued operations and expanded revenue streams, collaborative efforts must result in direct benefits to children and families that can be demonstrated to funding agencies and must provide information to guide and drive improved service delivery strategies on behalf of children and families (EHSC 1992, 11ff.).

Strengthening Communities

Although improving the delivery of government services on behalf of children and families and aligning school policies aimed at enhanced knowledge and skills for all children and youth are both essential if America's schools are to be upgraded, communities must also be strengthened to prevent and ameliorate problems affecting children and families before they come to agency attention (Raspberry 1991). Because child poverty is the single most powerful risk factor in accounting for high rates of damaging outcomes, higher family incomes are the single most critical need (Schorr 1993). Lowering unemployment rates, raising wages and benefit levels, extending benefit coverage or otherwise increasing income through such means as increasing child support collections, and expanding the earned income tax credit, together with promoting the productive use of the poor's most abundant asset, labor, have been found to provide large impacts on poverty and its interlocking effects (World Bank 1990). Analysts find that policies and programs must lead to full employment, make work pay, and provide job training and supports for the transition from welfare to work. Moreover, economic remedies must be coupled with social supports, including comprehensive health care, safe and supportive communities, quality child care, and services to strengthen families (Schorr 1993).

A strategy that addresses the root causes of poverty and economic instability in communities directly, together with school and community-linked services on behalf of needy children and families, would provide a multifaceted attack on the many faces of poverty with a premium placed on job training and education. This approach is based on the assumption that good education is the most promising passport out of poverty and the foremost means to "prevent the disadvantage associated with poverty from being passed down to the next generation. High skills and an educated workforce are also widely agreed to be the key to higher productivity for the nation" (Schorr 1993, 45).

Thus, the challenge for the future, if continued improvement for children, families, and communities is to be realized and poverty abated, is the provision of decent health care, full employment, fair housing, proper nutrition, and quality schooling. It requires nothing less than closing the gap between the best and the worst educational systems and integrating extraschool programs and services into education systems to address the multiple and interlocking needs many children bring with them to the schoolhouse door. It calls for government policies and programs aimed directly at the alleviation of poverty and its interlocking effects among families and in the community. This, then, is the challenge for American education into the future—and the opportunity.

NOTES

1. Full state funding is an exception, as all revenue is provided by the state.

2. These included differences in (1) input-per-pupil expenditure, school plants, libraries, quality of teachers; (2) racial compositions of the schools; (3) intangible characteristics of the schools—teacher morale, expectations; (4) consequences of the school for individuals with equal backgrounds and abilities, and the exposure of different groups to these factors; (5) inequality defined as the consequences of schooling for individuals of unequal backgrounds and abilities.

3. Characteristics of effective schools identified by Edmonds include (1) a principal who provides leadership and gives attention to the quality of instruction, (2) a pervasive and broadly understood instructional focus, (3) an orderly, safe climate conducive to teaching and learning, (4) teacher behaviors that convey the expectation that all students will obtain at least minimum mastery of the subject, and (5) the use of measures of pupil achievement as the basis for program evaluation.

4. Texas (three times), New Jersey, Kentucky, Arizona, New Hampshire, Massachusetts, Tennessee.

5. For example, Alabama, Missouri.

6. Currently, all but two states apportion revenue for public schools through a foundation school program (33 states), district power equalization approach (4 states), or, more recently, a combination of these plans (9 states). Only one state uses full state funding to apportion school aid, and one state uses a flat grant system—the plan used by a majority of states prior to the 1970s. Currently all states provide additional assistance to supplement basic costs for special education programs, 31 states for compensatory education, 24 states for bilingual education, 31 states for gifted and talented education. Additional funding is provided for sparsity or small schools/districts in 30 states, adjustments for intrastate variations in the cost of education in 5 states, declining enrollment/growth adjustments in 24 states, and grade level differentials in 24 states (see Verstegen, 1990).

7. These are conservative estimates. Due to the lack of data, the estimates do not include, for example, funding for capital outlay, which is generally provided out of local funding. Nor do they include locally argumented revenues

raised through private foundations, activities, and associations. Additional revenue for justifiable differences in costs for pupil or district needs is not excluded. These modifications would show disparities in funding to be larger than the figures illustrate.

8. Changes in federal aid distribution will also be required if interstate variations in education support are to be addressed, but this is beyond the scope of this paper. For a discussion, see Verstegen (1991).

9. The concept of a "key" school district has fallen from use. This phrase designated the highest wealth district, in contrast to the sense in which it is used here: the district with the best curricular program and or most elevated outcomes.

REFERENCES

Abbott v. Burke. (1990). 575 A.2d359, New Jersey.

Alexander, K. (1991). Financing the public schools of the United States: A perspective on effort, need and equity. *Reforming Education in a Changing World: International Perspectives,* 122–144.

Benson, C. S. (1991). Definitions of equity in school finance in Texas, New Jersey, and Kentucky. *Harvard Journal on Legislation* 28(2):401–422.

Brown v. Board of Education of Topeka. (1954). 347 U.S. 483.

Butts, R. F. and L. A. Cremin. (1953). *A history of education in American culture.* New York: Henry Holt.

Card, D., and A. B. Krueger. (1992). Does school quality matter? Returns to education and the characteristics of public schools in the United States. *Journal of Political Economy* 100(11):1–40.

Chambers, J. G., and T. B. Parrish. (December 1983). *The development of a resource cost model funding base for education finance in Illinois.* Final Report of the AEFP School Finance Study for the State of Illinois, Illinois State Board of Education.

Child Welfare League of America. (1993). An urgent call . . . for a national plan for children and their families. Washington, D.C.: Child Welfare League of America.

Clune, W. H. (1993). The best path to systemic educational policy: Standard/ centralized or differentiated/decentralized? *Educational Evaluation and Policy Analysis* 15(3):233–254.

Coleman, J., E. Campbell, C. Hobson, J. McPartland, A. Mood, F. Weinfeld, and R. York. (1966). *Equality of educational opportunity.* Washington, D.C.: U.S. Government Printing Office.

Coleman, J. S. (Winter 1968). The concept of equality of educational opportunity. *Harvard Educational Review* 38(1):7–22.

Cubberley, E. P. (1906). *School funds and their apportionment.* New York: Columbia University Press.

Dennison, E. G. (1983). *Trends in American economic growth, 1929–1982.* Washington, D.C.: Brookings Institution.

Drucker, P. (1990). *New realities for the nineties.* New York: Harper & Row.

During, A. B. (1990). Ending poverty. In *State of the world* ed. A. B. During, 135–153. New York: Norton.

Edelman, M. W. (1991). Children at risk. 295–306. In *Crisis in American Institutions,* ed. J. H. Skolnick & E. Currie. New York: Harper Collins.

Edmonds, R. R. (1982–83). Programs of school improvement: An overview. *Educational Leadership* 40(3):4–11.

Education and Human Services Consortium * Institute of Education Leadership. (1992). *What it takes: Structuring interagency partnerships to connect children and families with comprehensive services.* Washington, D.C.: Institute for Education Leadership.

Felix, N., F. Hertlein, D. McKenna, and R. Rayborn. (June 1987). Combining categorical program services can make a major difference. *Phi Delta Kappan* 787–788.

Hartman, W. (1990). Supplemental/replacement costs: An alternative approach to excess costs. *Exceptional Children* 56(5):450–459.

Hodgkinson, H. L. (1989). *The same client: The demographics of education and service delivery systems.* Washington, D.C.: Institute for Educational Leadership.

Johns, R. L., E. L. Morphet, and K. Alexander. (1983). *The economics & financing of education.* Englewood Cliffs, N.J.: Prentice-Hall.

Kaus, M. (1992). *The end of equality.* New York: HarperCollins.

Kirst, M. W. (April, 1991). Improving children's services: Overcoming barriers, creating new opportunities. *Phi Delta Kappan* 617.

Kirst, M. W. (July 1992). *Changing the system for children's services: Building linkages with schools.* St. Louis, Mo.: Council of Chief State School Officers.

Kirst, M. W. (1993). Financing school-linked services. *Education and Urban Society* 25(2):166–172.

Kirst, M. W., and M. McLaughlin with D. Massell. (1990). Rethinking policy for children: Implications for educational administration. In *Educational*

Leadership and Changing Contexts of Families, Communities, and Schools ed. B. Mitchell and L. L. Cunningham, 69–90. Eighty-ninth Yearbook of the National Society for the Study of Education. Chicago: University of Chicago Press.

Kozol, J. (1991). *Savage inequalities.* New York: HarperCollins.

Lawyers Committee for Civil Rights Under Law. (1980, 1982). *Update on statewide school finance cases.* Washington, D.C.: Lawyers' Committee for Civil Rights Under Law.

MacKenzie, D. E. (1983). Research for school improvement: An appraisal of some recent trends. *Educational Researcher* 12(4):5–16.

Monk, D. (1982). Educational cost differentials and rural schools: A broadened view. *Administrator's Notebook* 30(4):1–4.

Monk, M. D. (1990). Educational costs and small rural schools. *Journal of Education Finance* 16(2):213–225.

Monk, D. H., and B. D. Walker. (April 8, 1991). *The Texas cost of education index: A broadened approach.* Austin, Tex.: Texas Education Agency.

Moore, M. T., L. J. Walker, and R. P. Holland. (1982). *Finetuning special education finance: A guide for state policymakers.* Princeton, N. J.: Education Testing Service.

Morrison, H. (1930). *School revenue.* Chicago: University of Chicago Press.

Murphy, J. (1990). The educational reform movement of the 1980s: A comprehensive analysis. In *The educational reform movement of the 1980s: Perspectives and cases,* ed. J. Murphy, 3–55. Berkeley, Calif.: McCutchan.

Murphy, J., and P. Hallinger. (1986). Education equity and differential access to knowledge: An analysis. Paper presented at the American Education Finance Association, Chicago. In R. A. Rossmiller. (Spring 1987). *Achieving equity and effectiveness in schooling. Journal of Education Finance* 12:561–577.

National Commission on Children. (1991). *Beyond rhetoric: A new agenda for children and families.* A Final Report of the National Commission on Children. Washington, D.C.: U.S. Government Printing Office.

National Education Association. (1918). *The Cardinal Principles Report.*

National Governors' Association. (1990). *Educating America: State strategies for achieving the national education goals.* Washington, D.C.: National Education Association.

National Governors' Association. (1991). *From rhetoric to action: State progress in restructuring the education system.* Washington, D.C.: National Governors' Association.

National Governors' Association. (January 31, 1993). *Strategic investment: Tough choices for America's future.* Backgrounder. Washington, D.C.: National Governors' Association.

O'Day, J. A., and M. S. Smith. (1993). Systemic reform and educational opportunity. In *Designing coherent education policy: Improving the system,* ed. S. Fuhrman, 250–312. San Francisco: Jossey-Bass.

Phillips, K. (1990). *The politics of rich and poor: Wealth and the American electorate in the Reagan administration.* New York: Random House.

Purkey, S. C., and M. S. Smith. (1983). School reform: The district policy implications of the effective schools literature. *Elementary School Journal* 83(3): 427–452.

Raspberry, W. (February 2, 1991). Problems of the poor can be addressed. *Daily Progress.* Charlottesville, Va. A4.

Reich, R. (1991). *The work of nations.* New York: Alfred A. Knopf.

Riddle, W. C. (July 5, 1990). *Expenditures in public school districts: Why do they differ?* Report 90-322 EPW. Washington, D.C.: Congressional Research Service.

Rossmiller, R. A. (Spring 1987). Achieving equity and effectiveness in schooling. *Journal of Education Finance* 12:561–577.

Rossmiller, R. A., J. A. Hale, and L. E. Frohreich. (1970). *Resource configurations and costs.* National Educational Finance Project, Special Study No. 2. Madison, Wisc.: Department of Educational Administration.

Rutter, M., B. Maughan, P. Mortimore, J. Ouston, and A. Smith. (1979). *Fifteen thousand hours: Secondary schools and their effects on children.* Cambridge: Harvard University Press.

Smith, M. S., and J. O'Day. (1991). Systemic school reform. In *The politics of curriculum and testing,* ed. S. H. Fuhrman and B. Malen. 233–268. New York: Falmer Press.

Serrano v. Priest, (1971) 487 P.2d. 1241; (1976) 557 P.2d. 929 Cal.

Schorr, L. B. with D. Schorr. (1989). *Within our reach: Breaking the cycle of disadvantage.* New York: Anchor Books.

Schorr, L. B. (Spring 1993). What works: Applying what we already know about successful social policy. *The American Prospect* 13:43–54.

Stedman, J. B., and W. Riddle. (1992). *The national education goals: Federal policy issues.* Report No. IB92012. Washington, D.C.: Congressional Research Service.

Strayer, G. D., and R. M. Haig. (1923) *Financing education for the state of New York.* New York: Macmillan.

Tron, E. O. (1978–79). *Public school finance programs.* Washington, D.C.: U.S. Department of Education.

Updegraff, H. and L. A. King. (1922). *Survey of the fiscal policies of the State of Pennsylvania in the field of education.* Philadelphia: University of Pennsylvania.

U.S. Congress, House of Representatives. Subcommittee on Select Education (March 16, 1983). *The report of the commission on the financing of a free and appropriate education for special needs children.* ERIC Document Reproduction Service No. ED232400. Philadelphia: Research for Better Schools.

U.S. Congress, U.S. House of Representatives. Committee on Ways and Means. (March 15, 1989). *Background material and data on programs within the jurisdiction of the Committee on Ways and Means.* WMCP: 101–4, 942 Tables 2, 3, 944–945. Washington, D.C.: U.S. Government Printing Office.

U. S. General Accounting Office. (April 1993). Systemwide education reform: Federal leadership could facilitate district-level efforts. Report No. GAO/HRD-93-97. Washington, D.C.: U.S. General Accounting Office.

Verstegen, D. A. (1990). *School finance at a glance.* Denver, Colo.: Education Commission of the States.

Verstegen, D. A. (1991a). Invidiousness and inviolability in state education finance. *Education Administration Quarterly* 26(30):205–234.

Verstegen, D. A. (1991b). The economic and demographic dimensions of national education policy. In *Demographic trends and cultural diversity: Challenges for school finance policy,* ed. J. G. Ward and P. Anthony. 71–96. Newbury Park, Calif.: Sage Publications.

Verstegen, D. A. (April 1992). *Linking the national education goals and education finance.* Paper presented at American Education Research Association Annual Conference, San Francisco, Calif.

Verstegen, D. A. (1993). Financing education reform: Where did all the money go? *Journal of Education Finance* 19(1):1–35.

Verstegen, D. A. and C. K. McGuire. (1991). The dialectic of reform. *Educational Policy* 5(4):386–411.

Verstegen, D. A. and R. G. Salmon. (1989). The conceptualization and measurement of equity in school finance in Virginia. *Journal of Education Finance* 15(2):205–228.

World Bank. (1990). *World development report 1990: Poverty.* Oxford: Oxford University Press.

III

*Evaluation and Critiques
of Coordination as a Reform*

Chapter 12

We're Not Housed in an Institution, We're Housed in the Community: Possibilities and Consequences of Neighborhood-based Interagency Collaboration

Colleen A. Capper

Some educational scholars, practitioners, researchers, and policy makers are increasingly searching beyond the school to communities and families for hope and solutions to the ills of public education (Coleman 1985; Davies 1991; Heath and McLaughlin 1987; Mitchell and Cunningham 1990; Schorr 1988; Seely 1981). The relationships among communities, families, and schools have been conceptualized as overlapping spheres of influence on children's learning (Epstein 1992). This conceptualization yields a six-part typology of relationships among schools, families, and communities: (1) school help for families, (2) school-home communication, (3) family help for schools, (4) involvement in learning activities at home, (5) involvement in school governance, decision-making, and advocacy, and (6) educational collaboration and exchanges with the community. Although the literature on the sixth domain—collaboration and exchanges with communities—is growing, scholars acknowledge this research base to be the weakest link and have called for a focus on this "complex and relatively unexplored research agenda" (Epstein 1992, 1147; see also At Risk Youth in Crisis 1991; Cohen 1989; Davies, Burch and Johnson 1992; Nettles, 1992).

In the literature, collaboration and exchanges with the community are explored primarily with respect to public relations (Kindred, Bagnid, and Gallagher 1990), ways to seek community support (Fantini 1983; Whitaker, King, Lowham, and Norby-Loud 1992), school-business partnerships (Jidrell 1990; MacDowell 1989), and interagency collaboration (Blank and Lombardi 1991; Bruner 1991; Cohen 1989; Crowson and Boyd 1993; Davidson 1976).

Although well intentioned, the interagency collaboration efforts in the 1970s failed to achieve major changes in service delivery (Rogers and Whetten 1982, 46). Some of the reasons for these disappointing results included "the political, constitutional, legal, and technical barriers to coordination [that] have been at least as strong if not stronger than the pressures to coordinate." Coordination also resulted in pursuing safe ventures that did not threaten local control; political comprises that "insure[d] the maximum protection for individual agencies"; power struggles among agencies, which limits cooperation; divided loyalties among members and between their own agency and the collaborative effort; and shortages of time, funds, and personnel that were directed to the cooperative efforts.

Relatedly, J. Kahne and Carolyn Kelley (1993) argue that interagency coordination, in itself, does not necessarily guarantee emancipatory ends. For example, coordinated systems can lead to centralization of services, which can constrain client choices, can result in organizational goals to meet organization rather than client needs, and can decrease financial efficiencies by increasing access and, consequently, demand for services. Other scholars posit that "federal and state initiatives that attempt to improve interorganizational coordination at the community level are simply an attempt by bureaucrats to modify the end of the delivery stream so they can avoid confronting the front-end inequities and inflexibilities" (see Morris and Lescohier 1978; Wildavsky 1979 in Alter and Hage 1993, 89).

In spite of these cautions and limitations, what is clear from the literature is that scholars and practitioners advocate for interagency services (Gray 1985; Gray and Hay, 1986; Hord 1986). Nearly all research, practical examples, and recommendations have focused on informal communications between schools and agencies or *school-based,* interagency services (Dryfoos 1991; Gardner 1992; Jehl and Kirst 1992; Melaville and Blank 1991; Palanki, Burch, and Davies 1992; Payzant 1992; Smylie, Crowson, and Hare 1992). Some scholars, however, are cautious about using the school as a hub of community services (Chaskin and Richman 1992; Kirst 1991; Heath and McLaughlin 1987), and other scholars advocate *community-based* interagency services (Baglow 1990; Wilson 1983) to the extent that some city initiatives have been funded to guide community-based interagency planning for school restructuring (Wehlage, Smith, and Lipman 1992).

R. Chaskin and H. Richman (1992) argue that community- or neighborhood- based integrated services provide multiple access points to children and their families. Advocates of neighborhood-based interagency collaboration argue for the deliberate involvement of traditionally disempowered people in human service processes (Zey-Ferrel 1979). These scholars suggest that agencies, including the school, are on more equal footing in the community than if coordinated services are based in one of the agencies; that services are more accessible to community residents; that residents can have more input on service delivery; and that services are individually tailored to meet the cultural, ethnic, and racial needs of community members. Neighborhood residents and students can be empowered via dialogue and representative participation on the neighborhood teams. Of the few projects thus far that have been community or neighborhood-based (see Nettles 1992), the link with schools has been weak, the scope of services narrow (e.g., a focus on pregnancy issues), and, although interagency councils had been formed, council members did not actually spend time in the community (Kirst 1991).

Specific focus. In my previous work on neighborhood-based interagency collaboration, I have critically examined the macrolevel and microlevel power relationships among participants (Capper and Hammiller 1993a), have used Smylie's (1992) work on teacher participation in decision making to frame resident participation on interagency teams (Capper and Hammiller 1993b), and have juxtaposed critical and poststructural perspectives of neighborhood-based efforts (Capper and Hammiller 1993c). My purpose in this paper is to further explore neighborhood-based, interagency collaboration, focusing on (a) participants' perspectives concerning a neighborhood-based effort versus a school-based effort and (b) possible constraints and consequences of such a neighborhood focus. First, I briefly describe the interagency effort that was the focus of the research.

One interagency effort. In March 1992, a neighborhood interagency team was formed through the impetus of county leaders, agency administrators, and field-based workers in each of two neighborhoods in a Midwestern city. Targeted neighborhoods were chosen because they had high concentrations of low-income people of color and among the highest crime rates in the city. Guided by a 14-member Oversight Committee of agency administrators and agency representatives, each team included a representative of the police department (neighborhood officer), school district (school social worker), human services (social worker), and public health (nurse). The teams began meeting weekly and spending additional time in the neighborhoods in October 1992. Each team served as a coordinator of neighborhood services with each of these agencies.

In relation to schools and education, the interagency teams were seeking to move beyond an "educentric" perspective (in the traditional sense), which placed the school as the locus of control and pedagogy, apart from communities and families. In contrast, taking a longitudinal approach, the teams were seeking to bolster the neighborhood residents and families, including their children, in ways that would support education efforts. In so doing, the teams hoped to channel information concerning family and student needs into the school via the school representative on the teams. The teams viewed these student and family needs within two contexts: the context of social class, race, culture, and ethnicity, and the separate but related context of neighborhood constraints and supports for education efforts. School administrators hoped that this neighborhood, family, and student understanding would translate into more appropriate curriculum and instruction at school. Similarly, team members and agency administrators hoped that school representation on the teams could facilitate school efforts in the community and make services more efficient and effective when several providers, including the school, offer similar services (e.g., after-school programs, immunizations, and work apprenticeship programs). In short, the teams sought to take a global, holistic perspective of the community and family in relation to the student, rather than a narrow perspective that isolates student problems in the school.

Logistically, students in the first neighborhood attended two different elementary schools and a middle and high school. All four schools are beyond walking distance of neighborhood students. Bus transportation to the schools was complicated, with no direct route from the neighborhood to the school; residents must ride a bus that takes them five miles from the school to the downtown area and then makes several transfers before circling back to the schools, which are approximately two miles from the neighborhood. In the second neighborhood, students attended an elementary school located on property adjacent to the neighborhood. Students also attended two different middle schools located about one and three miles from the neighborhood and a high school five miles from the neighborhood.

Qualitative methods guided the data collection. A research assistant and I gathered observation data at all the interagency team meetings in each neighborhood and at all related meetings, such as meetings with the neighborhood association groups; group meetings between parents, community members, and school personnel; and related meetings at the county, city, and state legislative levels. The teams met in each neighborhood once a week for two hours over the first nine months of the project; then each team convened a Resident Advisory Board, which met in two-hour, biweekly sessions to provide neighborhood resident participation. We observed every team meeting since the beginning of the project, observing a total of 110 meetings over twelve months, gathering 220 hours of observation data.

We also interviewed a total of thirty one participants, including all the interagency team members in the two neighborhoods, residents on the Resident Advisory Board, and the administrators of each of the four represented agencies (including four school principals: one elementary, two middle, and one high school). The demographic profile of interviewees included 10 males, 21 females: 23 Caucasian and 8 African Americans; 11 team members associated with public schools; 6 neighborhood residents, and 2 family/community/school liaisons; and 8 members of the Oversight Committee. All of the team members were white, with the exception of two African-American service providers added to one of the teams. Each interview lasted more than one hour, and all interviews were taped and transcribed. Interview protocols and meeting observations were designed to parallel research questions, which were developed with the input of team members at the beginning of our involvement and as result of analyzing eight months of meeting notes.

The data analysis was guided by the constant comparative method (Glaser and Strauss 1967). To examine participants' perspectives of neighborhood-based interagency collaboration versus school-based efforts, I searched for themes in the responses to related interview questions and opinions on the linkages or outcomes of the work of the interagency teams for the schools. For the second research question, I considered possible consequences of such a neighborhood-based effort that emerged from the data, partially shaped by poststructural theoretical perspectives. In reporting the findings, I chose to include many quotations from participants for two reasons, both of which are supported by previous research: to maintain the integrity and voice of the participants, and allow readers to formulate their own interpretations based on the raw data (Anderson 1989; Hammersley and Atkinson 1983; Lather 1991; Lincoln and Guba 1985).

FINDINGS AND DISCUSSION

Participants Perspectives

Twenty-nine interviewees believed that, regardless of school location, the collaborative should be neighborhood based. The other two participants believed that, if the schools were more centrally located in the neighborhood, the collaborative effort should be anchored there. Those who favored the neighborhood focus believed that such a collaboration provided (a) treatment at the core of student struggles (i.e., within their families and communities), (b) shared blame and responsibility for student problems, (c) increased accessibility of services, and (d) personalized services for residents and a vehicle for agency public relations and outreach.

Treatment for Community and Families. The participants believed that a neighborhood-based effort was more appropriate than school-based interagency collaboration because they believed the students' family lives and the influence of their neighborhoods were at the heart of student problems in the school. Participants believed that if (a) the neighborhood and family could be strengthened, (b) have their basic needs met, and (c) organized to empower themselves, students would do better in school. For example, one team member noted,

> If [this project] can do something that can strengthen families, and families have more confidence, then I think were gonna see kids doing better in school . . .

Another team member concurred, "it's imperative that this community get stabilized so that [the school] can be stabilized." This same team member emphasized: "the way I see it, a student . . . is not able to learn unless there's . . . lots of stability at home. They're just not mentally present and emotionally present in the school building unless there's some stability."

Relatedly, many participants believed that neighborhood-based interagency collaboration would help families get their basic needs met more effectively than if specific agencies, including the school, attempted to meet these basic needs independently. One school principal explained, saying that

> a lot of times we are in it trying to do things we really don't have the resources to do. I mean the number of families that don't know how they are going to get food, how they are going to get clothing . . . what do they do about their AFDC [Aid to Families with Dependent Children]. I mean, there are all of those things that no wonder the kids can't come and attend to what's going on here because the family is trying to figure out how they are going to survive the next day, and so I think, if somebody could help take care of a lot of those issues, it would make a big difference.

Third, meeting and working in the neighborhood rather than the school meant more opportunity to engage in what participants' termed "community organizing." One administrator argued,

> we talked about the basic principles that were important to us and that was a broad-brush approach to community empowerment . . . we want our systems to change based on the realities of people's lives, not on administrative convenience.

A school principal agreed on the importance of community organizing, explaining,

> I think it makes sense in the neighborhoods because, you know, the whole idea is built around empowerment and creating better neighborhoods, cooperative neighborhoods, and I think that they really take on a role, a little bit as kind of community organizers?

In sum, participants in the neighborhood-based interagency effort believed that working in the neighborhood would facilitate meeting basic resident needs and would strengthen and empower the neighborhood, leading to increases in student achievement.

Shared blame and responsibility. The team members believed that a neighborhood-based effort meant agencies shared both the blame and the responsibility for students and their families. For example, one school principal noted,

> I think in a more system sense, [the interagency effort] provided an acknowledgment within the city, that this is a city, county, and school

district problem. It is not a problem belonging to any one of those
areas, so it is at least an acknowledgment that this doesn't belong to
one area, that it shouldn't be solved by one area. It has started to help
to eliminate some of the finger-pointing in all directions. . . .

Another school administrator reflected on sharing the blame:

> I do think that one of the things that we've found that is very easy
> to do is blame the school for everything. You know, the kid gets in
> trouble and it's the school's fault. And so I would guess that maybe
> the school being a player on a neighborhood team would lessen that
> maybe a little.

Second, participants believed that a neighborhood-based effort
meant more equal sharing of responsibility. Even though one team
member articulated the strengths of a school-based effort, she believed
a neighborhood-based effort was better. She argued,

> I like the fact that this isn't as directly school-based. I see the school
> as one of many resources in the community. . . . [this] puts the school
> in an equal position with a bunch of other community resources
> surrounding and supporting the neighborhood.

One principal agreed about the importance of sharing responsibility:

> [the interagency effort] has taken the onus off of the schools as far as
> having to do everything: teach, mother, father, clothe, feed, provide
> therapy, deal with kids who should be in treatment, and so on and
> so forth. I mean we still have that there, but at least there is an
> acknowledgment that maybe somebody else needs to be getting in-
> volved, too . . . . And I like taking the focus off of the school . . . not
> because I want to escape responsibility but because I want the com-
> munity to realize this is a community effort. It's not just a school
> effort.

Third, participants believed a neighborhood-based effort meant
not only sharing responsibility, but also resources, among agencies.
One team member suggested,

> I think it's troublesome in that schools have such massive mandates
> to do everything to everybody for every reason that the scope of
> their responsibility is impossibly broad, to the extent that they add to

that whole menu significant initiatives to engage people in neighborhoods . . . that I think it stretches their resources and is too bold and too expansive a responsibility for anyone to have. . . .

A school administrator agreed:

we just continually have limited resources, and it would seem logical that, when you have a number of agencies basically serving the same clientele, that you would have a coordinated effort in what each of those was providing.

In sum, participants believed that a neighborhood-based inter-agency effort, in contrast to a school-based effort, positioned the agencies on equal footing in the neighborhood, sharing blame, responsibility, and resources among each other.

Accessibility. According to the participants, neighborhood-based interagency collaboration meant increased accessibility along a number of lines: (1) Services were more readily available and accessible to residents; (2) The teams were more accessible to residents for resident involvement, and (3) information was more accessible from residents/ neighborhood to the agencies via the neighborhood-based workers.

First, a neighborhood-based interagency effort meant more immediacy for resident concerns. One resident explained:

[the team has] made a difference because sometime you would come to . . . the neighborhood center. You come over and you need someone right away. You may have to wait two or three hours because [the director] is only one person . . . but with [this project], I can come here and say, "[team member's name], I really need to talk." [Team member] makes that work, "Just a second, [resident], I'll be right with you." And after she hangs the phone up, she's right on it, and that helps me a lot . . . and with [this project], they listen to ideas, and they don't put them on the back burner like everybody else. . . . Somebody from downtown might say, "We're going to stick this on the back burner and work with it later." Uh-uh. [This project] don't do that. They work right along with you on the idea. They take it and say, "we're going to work it like this." And, [resident], if you think it'll work, go for it." They don't say, "Wait till next month, or wait until the middle of the year."

Another team member offered a second example of accessibility to resident concerns, noting that residents shared with her that they trusted her to approach her for help.

Second, the teams were also more accessible for resident involvement. For example, one team member explained in detail the importance of residents voices and the teams being the accessible vehicle for those voices:

> this is the reason that I end up committed to this, is that it has to do with access. . . . That I think is the major reason for being out in the neighborhood . . . we're going to do everything we can to make it as easy as possible for that family unit to have access, to be able to say what it is they need to say to the school, to the human services, to health, to police, which pretty much covers your life.

Third, the agencies, including the schools, had a consistent contact person in the neighborhood to answer their needs and concerns, which resulted in the agencies having more information access to the neighborhood. For example, one school principal described the role of her school social worker on the team and the contact she had with the other team members: "Many times, [she] will say let's call [the team member] . . . I'll get her today on that whatever it is." A second school principal provided yet another example of contacts in the neighborhood:

> one of the things that we've been saying . . for along time to human services is it would be much easier for us to deal with a social worker in an area rather than a social worker assigned to a family and a different worker to the family next door and a different worker to the family up on second floor, so that we are not dealing with ten or twelve different workers.

A third principal provided another example of accessibility to the neighborhood via a team worker when he heard of a student who had moved into the neighborhood but did not attend his school. One phone call to the neighborhood police officer encouraged the officer to visit the home of the student, and the student enrolled the next day. The principal noted that, "quite frankly, I don't think had we not gone and had the officer knock on the door and pushed it, I don't think this kid would have surfaced for the whole year."

In sum, participants believed that neighborhood-based interagency collaboration provided increased accessibility among agencies, between the residents and the agencies, and between the residents and the teams.

Personalized Services. Many of the participants believed that neighborhood-based interagency collaboration resulted in close, positive, interpersonal relations with residents. A team member offered an example of community connections:

> you really become a member of the community. The students, the parents, the children in the neighborhood identify with you, who you are and what you do and how you can be helpful. . . .

A second team member reflected on the close, interpersonal relations, a result of spending time in the neighborhood:

> a neighborhood-based [project] . . . has significant advantages because it allows for much more personal, relationship-based involvement. Someone in a school cannot know six hundred kids and twelve hundred parents and an area that covers a bunch of square miles. It's not just physically or practically possible.

Getting to know many residents personally, and interacting with them on a consistent basis in the neighborhood, meant that services could be tailored to meet their cultural, ethnic, and racial needs. One team member explained:

> [we need to do] more outreach about what it is that we do, what can you get through me and who am I connected to and why is this important to you culturally . . . the neighborhoods we serve are largely populated with people who don't have the luxury of worrying about what might happen in the same way that middle and upper middle, upper class populations do. They have to sorry about what is happening, and prevention is worrying about what might happen.

The more personal services within the neighborhood also took away the sting of intimidating agencies. One team member noted,

> In a lot of ways schools are intimidating places to people, especially if they are illiterate or they have had a bad experience in school . . . . The [department of social services] to some is "that place that takes away your kids or that place that doesn't give you your public assistance benefits because you didn't meet some criteria or do some hoop-jumping that they wanted.' So I think it's just real important for that effectiveness of that effort to flow from the community and not from these megasystems that have their own baggage.

Another principal argued that reducing intimidation went both ways; that is, parents could become less intimidated by the school, and school personnel could feel less intimidated by the parents. He explained,

> I think it'll be good for the people who work in the schools to feel more closely connected with the neighborhood and that . . . the parents are more approachable and easier to work with and the parents will see the school as being not so threatening and as something that they can understand and a system they can fit into and that the parents won't feel as uncomfortable about going to school, so I think it'll just help; strengthen the connection and make the school part of the community. . . .

Finally, the neighborhood interpersonal connections provided an opportunity for agency outreach and public relations. One principal described the public relations aspect of the school's involvement:

> I feel like . . . the primary thing is that this provides a vehicle for schools to be visible in the neighborhood, that they aren't isolated in the school building, and it helps to strengthen the connection between the students and what goes on at school and to know that they aren't two separate things. . . .

Similarly, a third principal explained, "I'd like to think that it's increased . . . the image of a more positive image hopefully about this school."

In sum, neighborhood-based interagency collaboration supported positive interpersonal relationships between agency workers and neighborhood residents, which helped workers to be more culturally sensitive. The teams' base in the neighborhood also afforded the agencies an opportunity for public relations and outreach.

Summary. Participants in this neighborhood-based interagency collaboration effort believed that neighborhood-based services, in contrast to school-based services, could treat the community and family by supporting the neighborhood residents, meeting basic needs, and encouraging community organizing. They believed that neighborhood-based services allowed for joint sharing of blame, responsibility, and resources among the agencies; increased resident accessibility to services and agency accessibility to neighborhood information; and resulted in more personalized relationships and services to residents and an opportunity for agency outreach and public relations.

Consequences and Constraints

Even though participants cited many strength of neighborhood-based interagency collaboration, some team members were cautious about it and considered their effort in relation to its historical and social context. For example, when responding to her view on major future road blocks to their efforts, one team member offered,

> I would see the ultimate road block being historical patterns and social norms that classifies people by income, race, and ultimately, in my belief, limits people's opportunities, legitimacy, and access and empowerment to education and opportunity . . . we have an institutionalized underclass that has many deficits and many dilemmas, and I see the kind of intervention required to address problems as being much more global and way beyond a community or an agency or a collaborative project, as being larger and involving economics and history and a bunch of complex and complicated issues.

When addressing institutional barriers in working with parents, another team member concurred and said,

> The institutional problem that affects me is not the one within my agency, it's . . . really society at large, which is the underlying reason that a lot of the folks I see are having problems they are having . . . is poverty and other institutionalized reasons, racism, what have you, that lead them to be in the position that they are in.

A third team member agreed:

> when you start identifying the problem as a neighborhood problem, it's kind of a cop out. They've given up on solutions and they're trying to deal superficially with the end results . . . poverty and racism and education. . . . So this is the Band-Aid approach. Let's make the neighborhood look better rather than elevate everybody for competition and jobs.

To further probe the constraints or consequences of neighborhood-based interagency collaboration, I juxtaposed the data against poststructural theoretical perspectives of power. In contrast to modernist approaches to power, which assume power always emanates from the top of a literal or figurative hierarchy, power from poststructural perspectives is decentralized, plural, complex, weblike—everywhere, which Michel Foucault termed "disciplinary power." In relation to neighborhood-based interagency collaboration, J. Rouse (1987, 220) argues, "The discovery that schools or hospitals needed to understand and regulate the entire family and community environment in order to educate or treat their students and patients" is symptomatic of the strategies of disciplinary power.

Rouse (1987) provides explanations of several strategies through which disciplinary power is exercised, including surveillance and its connection with normalization. In the past, people in power and those upon whom power was exercised were both quite visible. With surveillance, however, the "exercise of power is hidden, while those upon whom it works are increasingly laid open to scrutiny," and architecture is designed to increase this visibility and ability for surveillance (Rouse 1987, 214). Accordingly, these scholars believe that neighborhood-based interagency coordination serves to increase community and family surveillance, which perpetuates power inequities via normalization. That is, constraints and consequences of neighborhood-based interagency collaboration included increased observation and control of neighborhood resident behavior to match white, middle-class norms, which could lead educators to shirk their responsibility for change at the school level.

Surveillance. Spending time in the community—in the form of wandering around the neighborhood, hanging out at the neighborhood center, and attending neighborhood team meetings—and having residents be on teams meant resident lives were more open to scrutiny by team members. As a result, resident space became more controlled. For example, in one neighborhood, the interagency office and the team meetings were held in an apartment next to other resident apartments. One resident team member noted,

> I've mentioned to [team member] that the doors to stay closed down there cause even though it is an office, this is still and apartment building where we have privacy that the apartment people need. . . . [one resident] was getting real intimidated cause . . . she knew that every time someone came or went from her house, people from [the interagency teams] knew whether she was doing anything wrong or not. It was just a matter of her privacy was invaded. . . . [team member] wants an open door policy—well all of us do, which I can see, but like I said, they still have to respect our privacy as tenants of the building . . . .

One team member acknowledged the tension between coming to know the neighborhood and respecting resident privacy. When commenting on the advantages of a school-based versus neighborhood-based effort, he noted,

> A neighborhood person can . . . in a fairly intimate way, come to know essentially everybody either directly or by collateral contact information or access to everybody. Now if that's good or bad, that's another question. People have a right to be private and not have people involved in their lives. . . .

Surveillance went both ways. That is, having agency team members spend time in the neighborhood meant the neighborhood was more open to scrutiny; but it also meant the agency team members and the work of the agencies were more open to scrutiny by the neighborhood residents, and some residents disliked what they saw. For example, one resident noted,

> To me, I don't see nothin' coming out of it . . . . They talk about a lot of good things but I don't know if it's gonna work . . . . Cause a whole lot of talk going on for the last one, two, three meetings I been to and ain't no, I don' see nothing coming out of em. . . . One thing I would like to see in the meeting, though, is something being solved. Everything's been thrown out but I never see a solution to anything you know. . . . There's problems there but nothing's being solved. . . .

Another resident expressed her frustration with the lack of structure at team meetings and felt little was being accomplished. She offered her solution:

> I think what needs to be done . . . they need to have bylaws. Lay out . . . what they think they want to accomplish in six months or in eight months. Maybe not, bylaws isn't the right word for business plan or plan of some sort to where in six months we can look at that plan and say "yes, we did do this. Yes, we did do this. Oh, we have to work on this in our next six months. You know, or maybe three months." But ya, it seemed to me like well, so if all this then, what is [the project] here for?

In sum, surveillance occurred when interagency teams met in the neighborhoods and engaged with neighborhood residents. However, neighborhood-based work also meant that residents could peer into the work of the interagency teams and the agencies themselves (e.g., the school).

Normalization. According to Foucault (Rabinow 1984), surveillance leads to classification, description, explanation, documentation, tracking, recording, and filing. These tracking and sorting strategies serve as a means of identifying what is normal, and what is not, and of shaping the behavior of persons to be "more normal." According to Rouse (1987, 26), the function of normalization is "corrective. It reconstructs the person and her or his behavior by gradual steps and small impositions."

One explicit function of the teams was to "change the norms" of the neighborhoods. The teams' mission statement declared that "the planning team strongly feels that each neighborhood must drive the focus of this effort, which will lead to the development of strategies that address neighborhood behavioral norms. . . ." Neighborhood norms targeted by the teams for change included the existence of drug houses where drugs were used and sold, keeping the neighborhood clean, norms of appropriate child behavior and discipline, and appropriate sexual behavior of neighborhood youth.

One example of the process of normalization occurred when a principal was discussing the role of the interagency teams with neighborhood parents. He viewed the work of the interagency teams as a way to activate parents to adapt to the values of the school. The principal noted that,

> It would also be important to encourage and get support from the other agencies to sort of activate parents that are worked with to get more involved in the kids' education. . . . you know, if you want to look at it as adopted middle-class values, which is something that they're not real accustomed to doing in the past. . . . I'm thinking as the teams work, the family might be swept up more total by all these agencies working with them and um, as a team there might be a little more, ah, motivation, direction.

When offering her views of the neighborhood-based interagency effort, one resident responded,

> I'm hoping that whatever [this project] is, which I am still trying to find out, isn't another one of these agencies that are coming in and trying to control . . . I mean they'll come in and take over and pretty

soon our ideas and dreams and things become theirs and I mean it's like, it's theirs all over again. . .

One possible outcome of agencies, including the school, attempting to normalize the residents to their culture and standards of behavior is denial that change needs to occur within the agencies themselves. One principal explained his enthusiasm for the neighborhood-based effort,

> what I would be interested in as a school person is that this translates to school achievement, improved learning in the classroom, that if health needs are covered, if social service issues are dealt within the family, um, if there's an appropriate line of talk between the service providers and the community and the school, then this makes kids more ready and more capable to learn, and then we see the benefits of that with greater achievement performance at school.

This principal believed that the teams could better prepare the children for school.

Another school administrator believed that the neighborhood-based interagency effort would allow people to examine a number of problem areas, and, if students weren't successful, only then should the school examine its own role. He explained,

> if we're having difficulty with kids learning, and the teachers are saying it's because of their environment, it's because of their social skills, it's because of these other things, and the [project] resolves some of those things, and they still have problems, then we've got to look at what we're doing.

Like surveillance, normalization was not confined to the teams attempting to normalize the neighborhood, but neighborhood residents also attempted to normalize the teams to their culture and beliefs. One team member inadvertently identified the tension between the team's normalization of the neighborhood and the resident's normalization of the teams, noting,

> I think that being out in the neighborhood has its advantages, um, I think it also could have its disadvantages. I think it could get narrow vision. . . . schools are very efficient from a time point of view . . . and neighborhoods are very inefficient from a time point of view . . and what I see is a significant . . . it's sort of like taking on what we might think is, um, the pace of the neighborhood. I think we meet our

clients wherever they are. On the other hand, we don't need to down speed so much that we, you know, join them.

One example of how the residents attempted to normalize team members occurred when one neighborhood resident suggested that she felt that the style of communication in meetings with agency personnel, including the school, should change to reflect, in her view, a way African-Americans communicate in meetings. She explained,

> they'll [school personnel] say "oh, we'll sit down and we'll talk with you" but as soon as the parents start saying, because they've been holding things in for so long. Of course they're upset and, you know, of course they're gonna get real aggressive. They don't want to hear it because then they say, oh, we're getting out of control. Because our voices are raised. Well, when you've been holding things in for years and you're not being listened to, you're going to be upset. Black people always talk loud. I mean, it's just the way we are. We talk big to get our point across to each other. I mean, we can sit and talk loud to one another and know that we're not gonna get violent but to people you know . . . but there's some white people think because we raise our voices that we're getting violent, and we're not gonna go, and they think we're gonna jump up and hit them or something because we're talking loud, but it's when you hold something in for so long, it's gonna come out like that. It's like so much pressure in you that when it comes out it's like an explosion, and they can't handle it. They want us to sit at the table with our hands crossed and go, "oh, yes, and I don't feel."

In sum, being neighborhood-based meant that agency team members spent considerable time in the neighborhoods, within the neighborhood community center, on the streets with the residents, and in their apartments. This allowed team members open access to the personal lives of the residents (surveillance) and subjected the work of the schools and other agencies to the surveillance of neighborhood residents. The information from surveillance was then subject to the expert/normalizing interpretations of both agency team members and residents, which could provide an excuse for agencies not to initiate or to delay self-examination of their own policies and practices.

IMPLICATIONS FOR SCHOOL REFORM

As a school reform initiative, educators want to jump on the bandwagon of interagency collaboration/coordination, believing that it proactively addresses student/family needs beyond academics. These educators may make the assumption that collaboration, in and of it-self, guarantees increased efficiency, effectiveness in schooling, and, in some cases, empowerment of students and families. Indeed, moving beyond the school and positioning agency workers in the community conveys a reform initiative that is self-consciously power leveling and empowerment oriented. It is possible that coordinated, neighborhood-based services may inform what is needed to sustain neighborhood recovery, which, in turn, may contribute to longer term, consistent, community developed educational supports essential for student suc-cess. However, while neighborhood-based interagency collaboration could be considered an empowering strategy for community residents, it could be a way to maintain the status quo.

Based on the findings, several implications and considerations can be made for school reform via collaboration. First, because of some of the merits of neighborhood-based interagency efforts, before initiating school-linked or school-based services, educators should consider neighborhood-based interagency collaboration, regardless of the geo-graphical location of the school.

Second, although the data suggest that neighborhood-based inter-agency facilitates working directly with families and communities, and promotes a shared responsibility among agencies, educators must not shirk their educational responsibility under the guise of collaborative reform. That is, learning to relate more positively with families and neighborhoods is critically important, but educators should not frame their work with families and neighborhoods in terms of "treatment" and should tread carefully in the area of neighborhood development. Further, sharing blame and responsibility with other agencies may signal a respect for neighborhood culture and values, but, again, edu-cators should be careful about shifting blame and responsibility away from educational concerns that need to be addressed at the school-level. Moreover, neighborhoods and families should not be used as a means to further school reform ends (e.g., positive public relations), which could discount neighborhood culture and values.

Third, neighborhood-based interagency collaboration could further school reform efforts because of its built-in accountability system. That is, although, as the findings suggest, neighborhoods and families are privy to increased observation and normalization as a result of neigh-borhood-based work, the agencies, including the school, are also more vulnerable to scrutiny and normalization by neighborhood residents and families. This vulnerability and normalization of the school to neighborhood observation and feedback on school efforts could be used as a vehicle to drive education reform at the school level.

Finally, the caution voiced by several team members that crime and poverty in these neighborhoods are but symptoms of societal racism, classism, and other inequities, and are beyond the reach of interagency collaboration efforts, should serve as a warning to educators to be careful that school reform via neighborhood-based collaboration does not mask or divert attention from the pervasiveness of such inequities.

In short, educational institutions have often been seen as authoritative social control mechanisms; therefore, the assumption that they will quickly and successfully be able to empower others who do not feel a part of their institutional structure may not be a valid one. Before initiating any collaborative efforts, educators need to consider their goals and possible consequences of such efforts.

This article represents a first step toward the articulation of the empowering and constraining aspects of neighborhood-based interagency teams heard through the voices of the stakeholders. Extensive research, including community directed interviews, over the next several years will further evaluate the process and outcomes of such efforts, particularly in terms of minority student outcomes and implications for school reform. In so doing, these findings can significantly inform the work of those who advocate for school/community linkages via interagency collaboration but who have given little attention to neighborhood-based efforts.

NOTE

I would like to thank all the participants in this interagency effort who through their examples of risk and courage, have opened the doors to our involvement; to Ruth Hammiller, doctoral student who collected most of the data, to departmental secretary Pat Nehm, who transcribed many of the taped interviews, and to Sandi Hanson and Rebecca Ropers-Huilman, doctoral students, who critiqued the final version. Portions of the data gathering and analysis were supported by the Graduate School Research Committee, the Arvil Barr Fellowship (sponsored by the School of Education), the Spencer Foundation, and by the Department of Educational Administration at the University of Wisconsin-Madison. The data presented, the statements made, and the views expressed are solely the responsibility of the author.

REFERENCES

Alter, C., and J. Hage. (1993). *Organizations working together.* Newbury Park, Calif.: Sage Publications.

Anderson, G. L. (1990). Toward a critical constructivist approach to school administration: Invisibility, legitimation, and the study of non-events. *Educational Administration Quarterly* 26: 38–59.

At-risk youth in crisis: A handbook for collaboration between schools and social services, Vol. I: Introduction and resources. (1991). Eugene, Ore.: ERIC Clearinghouse on Educational Management.

Baglow, L. J. (1990). A multidimensional model for treatment of child abuse: A framework for cooperation. *Child Abuse and Neglect* 14: 387–395.

Blank, M. J., J. Lombardi. (1991). *Towards improved services for children and families: Forging new relationships through collaboration. The Eighth Annual Symposium of the A. L. Mailman Family Foundation,* White Plains, New York.

Bruner, C. (1991). *Thinking collaboratively: Ten questions and answers to help policy makers improve children's services.* Washington, D.C.: Education and Human Services Consortium.

Capper, C. A., and R. Hammiller. (April, 1993). *Intersections of difference in community-based interagency collaboration.* Paper presented at the American Educational Research Association, Atlanta, Ga.

Capper, C. A., and R. Hammiller. (1993b). *Community-based interagency collaboration: Participation in the context of decentralization.* Unpublished manuscript.

Capper, C. A., and R. Hammiller. (1993c). *Community-based interagency collaboration: A poststructural interruption of critical practices.* Paper presented at the University Council for Educational Administration, October 29, Houston, Tex.

Chaskin, R. J., and H. A. Richman. (1992). Concerns about school-linked services: Institution-based versus community-based models. *The Future of Children* 2(1): 107–117.

Cohen, D. L. (1989). Joining forces: An alliance of sectors envisioned to aid the most troubled youth. *Education Week* March 15, 7–16.

Coleman, J.S. (1985). Schools and the communities they serve. *Phi Delta Kappan* (April) 527–532.

Crowson, R. L., and W. L. Boyd. (1993). Coordinated services for children: Designing arks for storms and seas unknown. *American Journal of Education* 101(2): 140–179

Davies, D. (1991). Schools reaching out: Family, school, and community partnerships for student success. *Phi Delta Kappan* (January) 376–382.

Davies, D., P. Burch, and V. Johnson. (1992). *A portrait of schools reaching out: Report of a survey on practices and policies of family-community-school collaboration.* Report No. 1, The Center on Families, Communities, Schools and Children's Learning, Baltimore, Md.

Davidson, S. M. (1976). Planning and coordination for social services in multiorganizational contexts. *Social Service Review* 117–137.

Dryfoos, J. G. (1991). School-based social and health services for at-risk children. *Urban Education* 26: 118–137.

Epstein, J. (1992). *School and family partnerships.* Report No. 6, from the Center on Families, Communities, Schools, and Children's Learning, Baltimore, Md.

Fantani, M. D. (1983). From school system to educative system: Linking the school with community environments. In *For every school a community: Expanding environments for learning,* ed. R. L. Sinclair. Boston: Institute for Responsive Education.

Gardner, S. L. (1992). Key issues in developing school-linked integrated services. In *The future of children,* ed. R. E. Behrman, (85–94). Center for the Future of Children. The David and Lucille Packard Foundation, Los Altos, Calif.

Glaser, B. G., and A. L. Strauss. (1967). *The discovery of grounded theory: Strategies for qualitative research.* Chicago: Aldine.

Gray, B. (1985). Conditions facilitating interorganizational collaboration. *Human Relations* 18: 911–936.

Gray, B., and T. M. Hay. (1986). Political limits to interorganizational consensus and change. *Journal of Applied Behavioral Science* 22(2): 95–112.

Hammersley, M., and P. Atkinson. (1983). *Ethnography: Principles in practice.* London: Routledge.

Heath, S. B., and M. W. McLaughlin. (1987). A child resource policy: Moving beyond dependence on school and family. *Phi Delta Kappan* 68: 576–580.

Hord, S. M. (1986). A synthesis of research on organizational collaboration. *Educational Leadership* 43(5): 22–26.

Jehl, J., and M. Kirst. (1992). Getting ready to provide school-linked future of children, ed. 2, ed. R. Behrman. *The Center for the Future of Children:* ed. 2 The David and Lucille Packard Foundation, Los Altos, Calif.

Jidrell, S. B. (1990). Business education partnerships: Pathways to success for black students in science and mathematics. *Journal of Negro Education* 59(3): 491–505.

Kahne, J., and C. Kelley (1993). Assess the coordination of children's services: Dilemmas facing program administrators, evaluators, and policy analysis. *Education and Urban Society* 25(2): 187–200.

Kindred, L. W., D. Bagnid, and D. R. Gallagher (1990). *The school and community relations,* (ed. 4) Needham, Mass.: Allyn and Bacon.

Kirst, M. W. (1991). Improving children's services: Overcoming barriers creating new opportunities. *Phi Delta Kappan* 72: 615–618.

Lather, P. (1991). *Getting smart: Feminist research and pedagogy with/in the postmodern.* New York: Routledge.

Lincoln, Y. S., and E. G. Guba. (1985). *Naturalistic inquiry.* Beverly Hills, Calif.: Sage Publications.

MacDowell, M. A. (1989). Partnerships: Getting a return on the investment. *Educational Leadership* (April) 8–11.

Melaville, A. I., and M. J. Blank, (1991). *What it takes: Structuring interagency partnerships to connect children and families with comprehensive services.* Washington, D.C.: Education and Human Services Consortium.

Mitchell, B. and L. Cunningham, ed. (1990). *Educational leadership and changing contexts of families, communities, and schools.* Eighty-ninth yearbook of the National Society for the Study of Education. Chicago: University of Chicago Press.

Morris, R. and I. M. Lescohier. (1978). Service integration: Real versus illusory solutions to welfare dilemmas. In *The management of human services,* ed. R. Sarri and Y. Hasenfeld, (21–50). New York: Columbia University Press.

Nettles, S. M. (1992). Community involvement and disadvantaged students: A review. *Review of Educational Research* 61(3): 379–406.

Palanki, A., P. Burch, and D. Davies. (1992). *Mapping the policy landscape: What federal and state governments are doing to promote family-school-community partnerships.* Report No. 7, from The Center on Families, Communities, Schools, and Children's Learning, Baltimore, Md.

Payzant, T. W. (1992). New beginnings in San Diego: Developing a strategy for interagency collaboration. *Phi Delta Kappan* 74: 139–146.

Rabinow, P., ed. (1984). *The Foucault reader.* New York: Pantheon Books.

Rogers, D. L., and D. A. Whetten. (1982). *Interorganizational coordination: Theory, research, and implementation.* Ames, Ia: Iowa State University Press.

Rouse, J. (1987). *Knowledge and power: Toward a political philosophy of science.* Ithaca, N.Y.: Cornell University Press.

Seely, D. S. (1981). *Education through partnership: Mediating structures and education.* Cambridge, Mass.: Ballinger Publishing.

Schorr, L. B. (1988). *Within our reach: Breaking the cycle of disadvantage.* New York: Doubleday.

Sirotnik K., and J. Oakes (1986). *Critical perspectives on the organization and improvement of schooling.* Boston: Kluwer-Nijhoff Publishing.

Smylie, M. A., R. L. Crowson, and V. C. Hare. (1992). *The principal and school-level administration of coordinated children's services.* Paper presented at the Convention of the University Council for Educational Administration, Minneapolis, Minn.

Smylie, M. A. (1992). Teacher participation in school decision making: Assessing willingness to participate. *Educational Evaluation and Policy Analysis* 14(1): 53–68

Vandercook, T., and J. York. (1990). A team approach to program development and support. In *Support networks for inclusive schooling: Interdependent and integrated education,* ed. W. Stainback and S. Stainback, 95–122. Baltimore, Md: Brookes Publishing.

Wehlage, G., G. Smith, and P. Lipman. (1992). Restructuring urban schools: The New Futures experience. *American Educational Research Journal* 29(1): 51–93.

Whitaker, K. S., R. A. King, J. Lowham, and M. Norby-Loud. (1992). *Essential conditions for creating collaboratives with schools: Perspectives from non-educators.* Paper presented at the University Council for Educational Administration, Minneapolis, Minn.

Wildavsky, A. (1979). *Speaking truth to power: The art and craft of policy analysis.* Boston: Little, Brown.

Wilson, S. H. (1983). Strengthening connections between schools and communities: A method of improving urban schools. *Urban Education* (July) 153–177.

Zey-Ferrel, M. (1979). *Dimensions of organizations: Environments, context, structure, process, and performance.* Santa Monica, Calif: Goodyear.

Chapter 13

Schools and Community Connections: Applying a Sociological Framework

Gail Chase Furman
Carol Merz

INTRODUCTION

The idea of "community" is a central concept in much of the current discussion on educational reform. "Second wave" reforms that focus on addressing the needs of children at risk are based in the widely held assumption that communities, neighborhoods, and families are in decline (Coleman 1985). A primary example is the movement toward interagency collaboration between schools and other human service agencies, the subject of this book. This reform is driven by the assumption that the existing social service system is inadequate to meet children's needs created by community decline and family disintegration. Interagency collaboration is intended to address this problem by linking schools with community agencies to enhance the efficiency and scope of social services. Collaboration is thus an example of a nationwide movement in education toward "community-connections experimentation" (Crowson & Boyd 1983), an umbrella term that includes such reforms as parent involvement programs and site-based management at the school building level.

Yet the concept of community, as it is typically used in discussions of interagency collaboration and other reforms, is ambiguous. Much of this discussion, even when explicitly addressing community linkages, is not informed by a theoretical understanding of community. The appropriate role of schools in relation to contemporary American communities has not been adequately explored, nor has the impact of specific reforms on community linkages been adequately demonstrated. As Lonnie Wagstaff and Karen Gallagher (1990, 92) note, the "ill-defined nature of the relationship [among families, communities and schools] underscores the current dilemma facing politicians, practitioners, professional organizations, and academic researchers."

In this chapter, we are interested in the concept of community, in exploring its meaning as developed through sociological theory in a way that may be useful to educators concerned with reform. Specifically, we are interested in using a theory-based concept of community to analyze interagency collaboration because this reform is intended to directly address needs created by community decline. We approach this analysis in several steps. First, we discuss a framework for understanding the concept of community based on the theories of Ferdinand Tönnies and the more contemporary interpretation of his work by American sociologist Thomas Bender. Next, we use this framework to explore the role of schools in relation to modern community. We then apply this analysis to understanding reform movements in terms of their potential impact on the school/community interface. Finally, we return to the specific topic of interagency collaboration and its potential impact on the role of the school in community.

FRAMEWORK FOR COMMUNITY

What do we mean by "community"? In education, much of the discussion of community is vague and romantic. We seem to have a nostalgic notion of what community means, and we may experience its loss as a lack of belongingness (Mitchell 1990). Educators use the term community with different shades of meaning. We speak of community relations when we mean the management of the local politics of education; of schools located in "dysfunctional" communities when we mean that certain neighborhoods are characterized by social ills; and of schools *as* community when we mean the development of a strong organizational culture. The education literature has given little attention to clarifying these varying notions of community and defining it in a way that is useful.

Sociologists struggle as well with defining community. As Bender (1978) points out, though community has been a fundamental "unit-idea" of sociology for the last century, its definitions vary widely within the field. However, various theoretical schema surrounding the concept of community have endured within sociology and continue to be useful. Our premise in this chapter is that this sociological theory base on community can serve as a conceptual tool to clarify and deepen our thinking in education about current issues related to schools, community, and reform.

The concept of community was a central concern of several nineteenth and early twentieth-century thinkers, including Tönnies, Max Weber, and Emile Durkheim. With society caught up in rapid industrialization and urbanization, these early sociologists were concerned with potential disintegration of traditional patterns of social life. They sought to develop theory to explain the context of social change in which they lived and to predict the future state of society if rapid changes continued. Given the temporality of this early work and problems of translation from the German, it may seem inaccessible and anachronistic to educators and sociologists concerned with the year 2000. Yet, as Bender (1978) points out, this classical sociological work on community, first and perhaps most clearly articulated by Tönnies, provides a paradigm for understanding community that remains viable and useful.

Ferdinand Tönnies (1855–1936) was a German sociologist and professor at the University of Kiel. The son of a prosperous farming family, he was concerned throughout his career with the growing impact of commerce and industrialization on community life in towns and villages. He published his landmark work, *Gemeinschaft und Gesellschaft*, early in his career and continued to develop theory and write about community throughout his life. Tönnies' work, although less accessible in English than that of Weber or Durkheim, persists as foundational in Western sociology.[1]

The central idea of Tönnies' system of sociology is the Gemeinschaft/ Gesellschaft typology for social relationships.[2] Gemeinschaft and Gesellschaft are loosely translated into English as "community" and "society," respectively; however, the English terms lack the full connotations of the German, and the German terms are typically used in discussions of theory. We will follow this precedent here and will use the adjective forms gemeinschaftlich and gesellschaftlich, since, again, there are no appropriate English alternatives.

In Tönnies' system, Gemeinschaft and Gesellschaft are constructs representing different arenas of human interaction. The Gemeinschaft represents human relationships based on neighborliness, kinship, and friendship, while the Gesellschaft represents the public world of commerce and its marketplace relationships. Gemeinschaftlich relationships are characterized by trust, intimacy, and loyalty. Participation in gemeinschaftlich relationships promotes feelings of belongingness and personal security. In contrast, gesellschaftlich relationships are characterized by contractual guarantees of performance, impersonalization, and temporality, that is, they exist only during the period of the contract. Tönnies (1887/1957, 37–38) compared the two types in these words:

> All intimate, private, and exclusive living together . . . is understood as life in Gemeinschaft (community). Gesellschaft (society) is public life—it is the world itself.

and

> In contrast to Gemeinschaft, Gesellschaft is transitory and superficial. Accordingly, Gemeinschaft should be understood as a living organism, Gesellschaft as a mechanical aggregate and artifact. (35)

Central to understanding the Gemeinschaft/Gesellschaft typology are the concepts of "natural will" and "rational will." Tönnies assumed that all social relationships are created by the will of individuals to associate and that this will varied in quality from one situation to another. Gemeinschaftlich relationships are governed by "natural will," which means that one person associates with or responds to another because it is natural to do so. Examples are a parent's response to a child's need for comfort and reassurance, the desire of spouses to provide companionship for each other, or friends offering condolence and assistance at the time of a death in the family. In contrast, the "rational will" of the Gesellschaft means that one person responds to another because they have a contractual agreement to do so. The contractual agreement can be as simple as the improptu barter of eggs for flour or as complex as a legally negotiated 100-year lease on a factory site. Thus, in the Gesellschaft, associating with another is always the means to an end. Tönnies' translator Charles Loomis explains:

> For instance, a group or a relationship can be willed because those involved wish to attain through it a definite end and are willing to join hands for this purpose, even though indifference or even antipathy may exist on other levels. In this case rational will . . . in which means and ends have been sharply differentiated . . . prevails. On the other hand, people may associate themselves together, as friends do, because they think the relation valuable as an end in and of itself. In

this case it is natural or integral will which predominates. (Tönnies 1887/1940, xv)

In Tönnies' system, Gemeinschaft and Gesellschaft are constructs of ideal types that do not exist in pure form.[3] Rather, as Tönnies pointed out, all social systems are a mix of gemeinschaftlich and gesellschaftlich relationships. Systems differ, however, in the relative dominance of one type or the other and, therefore, in the quality of the experiences of individuals within the system. In a system dominated by Gemeinschaft and natural will, individuals will experience more belongingness, permanence, and a sense of security. In a system dominated by Gesellschaft and rational will, individuals will experience more isolation, transience, and relative insecurity.

Tönnies saw an inevitable shift in Western society from the Gemeinschaft to the Gesellschaft. Although he was concerned with the costs of this shift in terms of human experience, he saw it as a productive and natural maturing process for society. However, at the core of Tönnies' theory is the idea that both Gemeinschaft and Gesellschaft were permanent aspects of social life. He wrote, "the force of Gemeinschaft persists, although with diminishing strength, even in the period of Gesellschaft, and remains the reality of social life" (Tönnies 1887/1957, 232). In other words, Tönnies held that Gemeinschaft was an irreplaceable aspect of human experience and would never be totally subsumed by Gesellschaft. Thus, individuals in modern society live in a bifurcated social world and must learn to participate in both Gemeinschaft and Gesellschaft relationships.

Later social theorists tended to overlook this key aspect of Tönnies' theory, focusing instead on the inevitable shift in society to Gesellschaft. This led to the dominance of the linear "community breakdown theory" in twentieth-century American sociology and the related idea of the need for social control. In this view, as local communities (Gemeinschaft) inevitably decline, their moral influence disintegrates, leading to social chaos and unrest. To prevent his, society's leaders (Gesellschaft) need to use formal institutions (e.g., the schools) to control and socialize the population. In Bender's words, "With the erosion of all traditional or communal forms of social cohesion in modern urban society, it was essential . . . to develop artificial or formal institutional mechanisms of social control" (1978, 35).

In summary, Tönnies' theory offers a definition of community that is still useful: community (Gemeinschaft) is not tied to a specific place but is an enduring form of social interaction based on natural will. It is "a network of social relations marked by mutuality and emotional bonds" in which "there is the expectation of a special quality of human relationship" (Bender 1978, 6–7). It is characterized by experiences of belongingness, intimacy, and trust. Although the balance between participation in authentic community (Gemeinschaft) and participation in the larger society (Gesellschaft) has shifted to the Gesellschaft pole, community persists as an essential aspect of our lives.

Tönnies' theory suggests an analytical framework for studying the social world. Since we live in a bifurcated society of Gemeinschaft and Gesellschaft, the focus of study becomes the interaction of these types of relationships in our lives. As Bender states, "The focus of analytical interest becomes . . . the interaction and interplay of communal and noncommunal ways in the lives of all" and the "changes in salience toward either pole of the continuum" (1978, 43). In other words, based on this sociological perspective on community, we are interested in the balance of Gemeinschaft and Gesellschaft in our lives and in our social institutions.

THE ROLE OF SCHOOLS IN COMMUNITY

Institutions, like individuals, exist in a bifurcated social world in which the values of the Gemeinschaft and of the Gesellschaft interact. For schools, the tension between Gemeinschaft and Gesellschaft values has always existed, especially in the perennial debates over centralization or decentralization. In the following paragraphs, we argue that this tension is exacerbated in an era of reform and is related to the school's role, or mission, in relation to community.

Historically, the identity of the school was as a bridge between two social worlds, the Gemeinschaft and Gesellschaft.[4] Schools were firmly linked to traditional local communities, which were gemeinschaftlich in character. Whether urban or agrarian, the local community was typically homogeneous and stable and marked by close kinship and neighborhood ties. The school was to serve the local community by educating children in the ways of society at large (the Gesellschaft), instilling in them the skills of communications and commerce needed for social and economic success. But, as the first social system beyond the family and church, schools were also asked to support the values and mores of the local community. Thus, "local control" referred, not only to the political arrangements through which schools were governed, but also to monitoring by the local gemeinschaftlich community of the bridge function of the school—

socializing children into the behaviors and values needed for successful participation in the larger, gesellschaftlich society. This worked reasonably well because the local community believed the school was a necessary supplement to the family and that education was the key to success in the larger society. More important, it worked because the local community supported the perceived values of the Gesellschaft— the ideals of democracy, individualism, and free enterprise that supposedly governed the larger society. Thus, while a tension between Gemeinschaft and Gesellschaft values in the school was inevitable, a workable balance was the norm. Throughout the twentieth century, however, several trends have eroded this balance and changed the relationship among local community, schools, and the larger society.

First, schools as organizations have become more bureaucratic, and governance of schools has become more centralized. Raymond Callahan's work (1962) and David Tyack and Elizabeth Hansot's (Tyack 1974; Tyack and Hansot 1982) histories of American education clearly document the origins of the corporate, bureaucratic model for school organization and the gradual shift to state-level, centralized governance. Regardless of the number of efforts at decentralization over the years, and regardless of the continued rhetoric about local control, the education system in general has become ever more centralized (Wise 1988). Political reform of local school boards at the turn of the twentieth century contributed to bureaucratization and the erosion of local control. As Tyack (1974) explains, under the guise of "getting the schools out of politics," reform led to election of a few "successful men" to local boards. These persons represented the elite class of business and professionals rather than the largely working classes who were served by neighborhood schools.

> As men who had perfected large organizations, they had national reference groups and thought in cosmopolitan rather than merely local terms. Successful in their own careers, they assumed that what was good for their class and private institutions was good public policy as well. . . . These leaders were impressed with the newly developed forms of corporate structure which had revolutionized decision-making in vast business organizations. (130–31)

Thus, the culture of the elite leaders of business, largely white, Anglo-Saxon and Protestant, came to dominate the schools. In terms of the Gemeinschaft/Gesellschaft continuum, bureaucratization and centralization shifted the school away from its close ties to local Gemeinschaft values. In essence, the perceived mission of the school gradually changed from serving the needs of the gemeinschaflich local community to serving the interests of the larger society. Schools assumed a cultural assimilation role; they were to teach children the values, attitudes, and behavior of the dominant culture and liberate them from the bonds of class or ethnicity and the provincialism of rural life, which limited their social and economic mobility. The role of the school shifted toward the Gesellschaft pole of the continuum.

Second, the nature of the local community changed—the decline so often noted in recent literature. Changes in families have been well documented (Hoffer and Coleman 1990; Coleman 1987) Communities have changed as people work farther from their homes. The number of face-to-face contacts with neighbors has decreased dramatically in America since World War II. Interchangeable suburbs have replaced individually identifiable neighborhoods; some traditionally ethnic neighborhoods have disappeared (Coleman 1985; Wagstaff and Gallagher 1990). Families and neighborhoods have become less coherent and exhibit fewer of the traditional gemeinschaftlich qualities. Children go to day-care centers, people shop at supermarkets, life assumes a more anonymous, interchangeable, or gesellschaftlich quality. Although Gemeinschaft may persist (Bender 1978), it is in a more fragmented form and lacks a coherent voice to influence the schools.

Third, the ideals of democracy and free-enterprise in the larger society have become tarnished (America's Parasite Economy 1992). There seems to be little consensus in the late twentieth century around national goals or a national ethic for the Gesellschaft. Instead, the values of the corporate world—profit and competition—have come to dominate the larger society, to crowd out the traditional ideals of democratic participation, individualism, and free-enterprise opportunity. We tend to be disillusioned with our political and institutional leaders and regard with cynicism the business-dominated values of the Gesellschaft. G. Kreyche (1993, 98) calls the disillusionment with national leaders "the demise of moral authority":

> Perhaps even more important in the current value crisis is the ongoing demise of moral authority, which implies having a natural measure of control or influence over another. Presidents such as George Washington and Abraham Lincoln not only were the nation's civic authorities, but also were seen as moral leaders. . . . Moral authority is not bestowed, but is based on right conduct and the depths of one's character and personal commitment.

The disillusionment with leaders and the values of the larger society is particularly acute for persons in poverty and for persons whose access to the economic mainstream is impeded by cultural and language barriers. Cornell West (1993) has documented this phenomenon among African Americans. He describes the hopelessness and despair of African Americans today as the greatest threat to Black America. He sees economic and social conditions feeding a growing nihilism that becomes increasingly devastating and leads to a disregard for life and property among African Americans. The result of this disillusionment with societal values is that many people no longer aspire to participate successfully in the larger society, the Gesellschaft. As the school has traditionally been perceived as the bridge to the Gesellschaft, many people no longer see the common school as the path to upward mobility or social and economic success, that is, they no longer trust the bridge role for schools. Wagstaff and Gallagher (1990, 94) state:

> It is a long-recognized bond between schools and parents to turn children into productive citizens. Yet many American families in the 1980s are either unable or *unwilling* to shape, support, stimulate, or encourage their children in the traditional ways schools expect" (emphasis added).

Educators frequently interpret this cynicism regarding the school's traditional mission as a lack of parent support, a symptom of a dysfunctional community, or a student motivation problem Thomas Hoffer and James Coleman (1990, 129) state, "the single most important problem that American society faces in its effort to educate children is that young people have become segregated from the structure of responsibilities and rewards of the productive adult society" and lack "a sense of purpose in their schooling." We are suggesting that this motivation problem is related to something more disturbing than segregation from productive adult society. It is related, we believe, to rejection of the values of the "productive adult society" (the Gesellschaft) by large segments of the population. Since schools represent a bridge to the Gesellschaft, and success in school means acceptance of these values, the result can be low levels of voluntary participation in the school's program among large segments of the population.

In summary, the trends of bureaucratization and centralization, changes in community structure, and erosion of the ideals of a democratic society have altered the role of the school in relation to community. Schools have become more alienated from the fragmented local community in governance and structure and more in resonance with the marketplace values of the Gesellschaft, at the same time that these values are being discounted by a growing segment of the population. In essence, the perceived mission of schools has undergone a subtle transformation—from educating for participation in a democracy to educating for work roles in a corporate-dominated technocracy—and this transformed mission is viewed with cynicism by many. But the ability of the fragmented gemeinschaftlich local community to resist this change in the role of the school has all but vanished. Thus, the role of the school in relation to community has become troubled and ambiguous. The school's identity as the perceived bridge to a better life has been undermined.

Clearly, this analysis surfaces a number of complex issues. Can schools, for example, shape a new mission that will both serve the larger society and be understood and accepted by local communities? Might this mission be to educate children for participation in a *multicultural* democracy, as Maxine Greene (1993) has suggested? In so doing, could schools be instrumental in regeneration of a national civic morality based in democratic ideals? While most of these important issues exceed the bounds of this chapter, we will focus here on one critical aspect of this problem, namely, the link between the role of the school in the community and current reform efforts to improve school-community ties, particularly through coordinated services.

REFORM AND THE CONCEPT OF COMMUNITY

Certainly there have been perennial tensions surrounding the role of the school in community and the appropriate direction for school reform (Bacharach 1990; Hawley 1988; Wise 1988). These tensions have been exacerbated in recent years by public dissatisfaction with the schools, leading to the current context of simultaneous and often conflicting reform agendas. Indeed, the current reform climate resembles, not so much the metaphorical pendulum swing from one reform to another, but a fast-paced metronome. Educators find it impossible to stay in time.

We view the current reform climate as interactive with the issue of the school's role in relation to community, discussed in the previous section. The school's "identity crisis" drives many current reform proposals, which, in turn, exacerbate the confusion over the school's role. In other words, the clamoring for school reform arises from dissatisfaction with the school's current role in a bifurcated society—dissatisfaction with the declining ability of the bureaucratized, gesellschaftlich school to relate to the gemeinschaftlich local community, and dissatisfaction with the school's ability to serve as an effective bridge to economic success in the larger society. This dissatisfaction drives specific reform movements, which address one of these areas of dissatisfaction over the other, that is, which address either gemeinschaftlich or gesellschaftlich values. And these sometimes conflicting reforms further the confusion and debate over the appropriate role of the school.

K. Hoyt (1991, 450–53) states that "every education reform proposal of the 1980s was rooted in the need to increase America's ability to compete in the international marketplace." Hoyt is referring to "first wave" reforms (Hawley 1988), those that arose in the wake of the original 1980s reform reports. The first wave focused primarily on improving student achievement and technical skills to ensure the nation's economic and military competitiveness. These reforms addressed the presumed deficiencies in the delivery of educational services, that is, the structure of schools and the quality of the teaching force. To do this, first wave reforms targeted such educational issues as incentives for teaching (e.g., career ladders), the quality of the curriculum (e.g., curriculum alignment), and standardization of student assessment practices (e.g., minimum competency exams). To the extent that first wave reforms were indeed implemented, they resulted in greater centralization, regulation, and standardization (Wise 1988).

While we need not agree with Hoyt's narrow conceptualization of the purpose of reform, his view clearly illustrates that many reforms are identified with gesellschaftlich values, that is, they are intended to better prepare students to participate in the workforce and to contribute to the nation's economic prosperity. Indeed, Hoyt beautifully summarizes the gesellschaftlich perspective on the link between student achievement, school reform, and national economic competitiveness:

Other nations with which America currently *competes in the world marketplace* have education systems that already produce higher levels of *measured achievement* than ours. If we continue on our present course, the situation will surely get much worse. Thus the need for education *reform* is clear. (1991, 453, emphasis added)

In contrast, a number of reforms, often identified as part of the "second wave" (Hawley 1988), target the needs of children and families rather than deficiencies in the school system. These reforms reflect a growing concern with addressing the problems of children "at risk" (e.g., poverty, poor physical or mental health, family instability) and with the need for stronger links between school and community. Reforms of this type include a variety of "community-connections experiments" (Crowson and Boyd 1993) such as interagency collaboration, parent involvement programs (Epstein 1992; Mannan and Blackwell 1992), and James Comer's model for urban schools (1980), as well as reforms that attempt to return some governance powers to local communities (e.g., site-based management, schools of choice).

The central focus of these second wave reforms on a child-centered approach and on involvement with local community is reflected in recent writings by Brad Mitchell and Coleman. Mitchell (1990) analyzes the themes of "loss, belonging and becoming" as they relate to the role of schools. He states, "A sense of belonging seems to be at the epicenter of cultural and individual transformation" (p. 61) and argues that school reform should focus on enhancing the belongingness of students in school. Coleman (1985) defines "intergenerational closure" as a key element for success in school. Intergenerational closure means, "A child's friends and associates in school are sons and daughters of friends and associates of the child's parents" (529). Such closure facilitates communication among parents about school activities and the ability to "establish and enforce norms of behavior for their children" (530). Coleman suggests that schools be associated with existing functional communities, such as the workplace, in order to recreate intergenerational closure.

In terms of the Gemeinschaft/Gesellschaft continuum, these child-, family-, and community-centered reforms address the issue of weakened linkages between the school and the local gemeinschaftlich community. Seen from this perspective, these reforms attempt either to shore up the local community by taking over some of the functions typically associated with the Gemeinschaft or improve communication and relationships between the school and the existent, but fragmented, local community. This category of reforms, then, tends to pull the role or mission of the school back to the Gemeinschaft end of the continuum.

It is important to note that first wave reforms continue to influence educational policy, often in competition with second-wave, child-centered reforms. As Willis Hawley (1988, 419) states, "This does not mean that the energy of the first wave is spent. Indeed, it is precisely because the two waves overlap, and sometimes move in different directions, that the potential benefits of the reform movement are so problematic."

In summary, the Gemeinschaft/Gesellschaft continuum is useful in understanding the current reform climate in education. From this perspective, reforms are viewed as addressing current dissatisfactions with the role of the school in a bifurcated society. Reforms differ in reflecting either Gemeinschaft or Gesellschaft values for the school and conflict because they imply different roles for the school in relation to local community. In essence, current reform agendas are pulling schools in opposite directions along the Gemeinschaft/Gesellschaft continuum, with some intended to recreate links with the Gemeinschaft and some intended to better serve the interests of the Gesellschaft. The core issue, we believe, in the current reform climate is the role of the school in relation to the local community. Policy makers need to recognize this issue. They need to recognize that choosing a reform agenda or direction has important implications regarding the school's mission. In terms of the theoretical framework on community, the choice involves attempting to recreate authentic links with the gemeinschaftlich local community or continuing to gravitate to the Gesellschaft by serving the interests of a corporate-dominated economy.

An important question that arises from this analysis is how a specific reform, such as interagency collaboration, impacts the role of schools in community. By adopting a specific reform, what choice is being made regarding the "mission" of the school? In the next section, we consider these questions in regard to interagency collaboration.

INTERAGENCY COLLABORATION

Interagency collaboration is a reform receiving increased attention in the literature and in the field. The movement responds to a universally recognized need to improve social conditions for children and youth, a concern of the second wave of reforms as discussed previously. Harold Hodgkinson (1989), Michael Kirst and Milbrey McLaughlin (1990), and others have presented demographic data that graphically illustrates the extent of this need. Advocates for collaboration argue persuasively that collaboration will address several problems with the existing system of social services for children, including: (a) existing services focus on crisis intervention rather than prevention (Melaville and Blank 1991); (b) existing service delivery is fragmented and fails to recognize the interrelated nature of children's problems (Gardner 1990; Kirst and McLaughlin 1990); and (c) the existing multiagency system wastes scarce resources by, for example, duplicating services across separate agencies (Kirst and McLaughlin 1990).

To date, the emergent and limited education literature on inter-agency collaboration has addressed several strands: (a) defining what is meant by true collaboration, usually in contrast to simple coopera-tion (Appley and Winder 1977; Boyd et al. 1992; Hord 1986); (b) mak-ing the case for collaboration (Hodgkinson 1989; Melaville and Blank 1991; Kirst and McLaughlin 1990); (c) describing promising early ef-forts at collaboration (Crowson and Boyd 1993; Gardner 1990; Kirst and McLaughlin 1990; Melaville and Blank 1991); (d) identifying bar-riers to successful collaboration (Guthrie and Guthrie 1991; Heath and McLaughlin 1987; Kirst 1991); and (e) offering practical guidance on doing it (Gardner 1993; Liontos 1990). With few exceptions (e.g., Boyd et al. 1992; Crowson and Boyd 1993), the literature reports little re-search on implementation and impact of interagency collaboration involving schools. Robert Crowson and William Lowe Boyd (1993, 152) state:

> Despite widespread interest, there have been few in-depth evalua-tions, to date, of coordinated-services experiments. As might be ex-pected, the rapidly expanding literature . . . abounds with testimonials and anecdotal claims to success. However, little hard evidence exists documenting significant gains in either education or child and family welfare as a consequence of service-integration investments.

Gardner (1993, 141), for example, claims that "the development of school-linked services has progressed to a point where we can begin to distill the most effective approaches to planning and implementing these programs" but offers no evidence of a data base on which to base his recommendations. Despite this paucity of research as to its effectiveness, interagency collaboration receives little opposition in the literature. Clearly, the need for improved social services for children is so compelling, and school involvement in interagency collaboration is such an apparently valid response to the need, that there is no evident argument against it as a reform.

We will not dwell here on these background issues, which con-tinue to receive much discussion in the literature, including the chap-ters of this book. We will focus, instead, on analyzing this reform movement through the lens of the sociological framework on commu-nity and the role of schools in community, which are the main themes of this chapter. In other words, we are interested in how the inter-agency collaboration reform fits with the Gemeinschaft/Gesellschaft continuum.

As we explored this issue, we identified several key questions to address: (a) What is the primary purpose of the collaboration reform, and does this purpose reflect Gemeinschaft or Gesellschaft values for schools? (b) What structures, strategies, and processes are proposed to implement the reform, and do these structures and processes fit with the purpose? (c) How might interagency collaboration impact over time the role of schools in relation to community? We address these questions in the following sections.

The Purpose of the Reform

The core purpose of interagency collaboration is to improve social conditions for children and families. Indeed, the case for collaboration is based on dire social needs, which are not adequately addressed through the existing fragmented social service system. Hodgkinson (1989), for example, cites data related to low-income housing shortages, inadequacy in health care and transportation systems, and growing crime rates to support the case for collaboration. And, in practice, collaborative efforts have targeted such basic social problems as teen pregnancy, youth unemployment, low rates of immunizations and other basic health care deficiencies, drug and alcohol abuse, and inadequate child care programs (Kirst and McLaughlin 1990; Melaville and Blank 1991). The explicit purpose of collaboration, then, is to improve social conditions by improving the delivery of social services to children and families in need.

A related purpose is to enhance the opportunity for school success for at-risk students, that is, those students whose lives are impacted by various social problems. The causal logic is that students' readiness to learn is negatively affected by these basic social problems. Schools cannot solve these problems alone but, in collaboration with other agencies, can mitigate these problems to allow at-risk students to profit from the school's program. A recent initiative in Washington State illustrates this assumed linkage between social service needs and school achievement. Washington has provided grant funds to support the development of "consortia" consisting of school districts and local social service agencies. The mandated purpose for each consortium is to identify local needs that interfere with children's readiness to learn and to address these needs through collaborative delivery of services, with the ultimate goal being to ensure children's success in school (Readiness 1993). This example illustrates that, for some advocates of collaboration, improved student achievement is an important goal. It further suggests that political support for collaboration often hinges on this assumed linkage.

How do these purposes of interagency collaboration fit with the framework for community? Clearly, the purpose of collaboration, to improve social conditions for children and their families, which frequently concerns such intimate issues as pregnancy, nutrition, and substance abuse, places the reform at the Gemeinschaft end of the continuum. Essentially, collaboration intends to provide basic maintenance functions traditionally associated with families. In this sense, schools involved in social service collaboration purport to *become* part of the gemeinschaftlich local community by providing essential nurturance usually associated with the natural will of the Gemeinschaft. Although a related purpose, to some stakeholders, is to improve academic achievement, this is a desire by-product of collaboration, rather than a targeted primary outcome.

In sum, the core purpose of interagency collaboration is to meet needs traditionally met within the family and gemeinschaftlich community. In terms of our analysis of reform movements, interagency collaboration is directed toward the Gemeinschaft pole. It may be assumed, then, that successful collaboration between schools and local community agencies would strengthen the links between school and community and enhance the belongingness of students ins schools. Yet, as we discussed earlier, the Gemeinschaft is characterized by more than basic maintenance care; it also involves natural will, trust, and intimacy in relationships. Whether interagency collaboration promotes these qualities of the Gemeinschaft has to do more with its structure and the style of its processes than its core purpose.

Structures and Processes of Collaboration

Identifying typical structures and processes for the implementation of interagency collaboration is difficult for two reasons. The research literature to date is too sparse to lead to generalized conclusions, and, in any event, structures and processes adopted for collaboration depend on the local context. G. Guthrie and L. Guthrie (1991, 17) state:

> Just as all politics are local, so will improved services for children develop in the contexts of particular communities, schools, and service agencies. The strategy that helps collaboration in one community may not apply in the next; and the set of agencies involved, or how they connect with schools, may differ from community to community.

However, educators who write on collaboration have suggested a number of common models and have offered sets of guidelines for collaboration and examples of collaborative efforts.

The proposed models for collaboration include (a) agencies housing "branch offices" within schools and other agencies; (b) schools serving as "brokers" for services provided by collaborating agencies; and (c) "case managers," perhaps housed in the schools, coordinating services provided by multiple agencies to children and their families (Boyd et al. 1992; Crowson and Boyd 1993; Guthrie and Guthrie 1991, Melaville and Blank 1991). In practice, collaborative efforts vary widely along a number of dimensions. Crowson and Boyd (1993) cite a number of exemplars that differ in locus of initiation (e.g., state-level or local, government or private foundation), scope of involvement of agencies (multisite or single site), and specificity of targeted services and clients.

Guidelines for collaboration are in the style of "avoid-these pitfalls" (Crowson and Boyd 1993, 152) and are typically based in anecdotal reports of implementation problems. Guidelines direct would-be collaborators to (a) map the territory, gathering as much information as possible regarding needs of clients, available services, and providing agencies; (b) engage in in-depth strategic planning, which involves all stakeholders, including clients; (c) obtain long-term funding commitments and allocate adequate resources within agencies for planning and implementation; (d) clarify participating agencies' roles and responsibilities; (e) create new managerial/professional roles that emphasize mediation and coordination skills; (f) provide for cross-training of agency personnel to learn each others' vocabularies and procedures; (g) ensure "line worker buy in" to collaborative efforts; (h) develop efficient information-sharing systems; and (i) stress prevention in provision of services to clients.[5]

From these models and guidelines, we can glean some essential features of the structure and processes typically involved in interagency collaboration. First, collaboration requires the development of new roles or the expansion of existing ones in the organizations involved. For example, for the suggested case manager and broker models, new organizational (or cross-organizational) roles are created that require additional training and resources. As A. Melaville and M. Blank (1991, 10) state: "With training and sufficient resources to support a broadened set of responsibilities . . . carefully selected social workers, counselors, or interdisciplinary teams can facilitate high quality, comprehensive service delivery" as case managers. Crowson and Boyd

(1993) carry this theme further by suggesting the formalization of these roles into new professions, perhaps requiring specialized training and certification.

Second, collaboration requires additional resources to support the extra organizational burdens, new roles, and responsibilities involved. For example, collaboration requires in-depth, strategic planning on the part of personnel from each collaborating agency. This planning burden goes beyond the typical work assignment for individuals within the organization, and adequate time must be allocated to it. Collaboration "imposes extraordinary time demands in the work life of the enterprise" (Cunningham 1990, 16). To support these additional responsibilities and new positions that are generated, new sources of money are needed. Often, collaboratives are begun only when seed money is provided through grants. Kirst and McLaughlin (1990, 15) state:

> Our understanding of the ingredients to successfully initiate local service coordination suggests that flexible initiative money through foundations has been crucial in generating effective local child-resource policies . . . Consequently we believe that federal and state government should provide seed money [for] integrated children's services.

A lack of adequate additional resources has been cited frequently as a barrier or cause of failure of collaborative efforts (Hord 1986).

And, third, the language used throughout the collaboration literature reflects the bureaucratic perspective of "professionals" providing "services" to "clients" (Hodgkinson 1989). Frequent references are made to identifying the "clients" to be "targeted" for services, and, as mentioned above, service coordinators may be seen as constituting a new "profession."

These three themes reflect what has been traditionally understood as the bureaucratic response to solving problems. Bureaucratic organizations respond to new demands in their environment through growth and increased specialization (Perrow 1970). Increased specialization typically involves new personnel and expansion. Budgets grow as specialized personnel and programs are added and new funding sources are needed. Thus, the structures and processes identified with interagency collaboration may be seen as bureaucratic in character and interagency collaboration, in general, as the response of bureaucratic organizations to environmental demands. The idea of expansion of bureaucracies through which "professionals" serve "clients" is hardly resonant with gemeinschaftlich values of intimacy, trust, and belongingness. Rather, it is disturbingly resonant of social control, which we discussed in the section on Tönnies' theory. That is, it reflects the assumption that Gesellschaft-dominated bureaucratic institutions need to train and control the less-privileged classes to ensure social stability as local gemeinschaftlich communities disintegrate.

At the same time, guidelines for implementing interagency collaboration frequently mention the importance of a sense of personalization in provision of services. This is stated in a number of ways. According to the Education and Human Resources Consortium (cited in Boyd et al. 1992, 5), a successful collaborative involves "a commitment to empowering families, actively involving them in identifying services they need." Similarly, Kirst and McLaughlin (1990, 82) argue for integrating children "as active participants into the community of services and resources. It is not integration if we simply move to integrate services that continue to talk *at* rather than *with* children; or that continue to do *to* and *for* children rather than plan and work with them." Yet, there is nothing built in to interagency collaboration per se (which essentially consists of bureaucratic arrangements) to guarantee this focus on personalization. And the pervasive mindset of professionals serving clients implies status differences, which interfere with personalization. Further, should an individual case manager succeed in personalizing services, this does not mean that the school environment in general will be personalized for the client. Boyd (1992) and his colleagues report research supporting this latter point. They concluded that after three years of operation the Center Project, a nationally recognized collaborative, had a greater impact on the individuals involved than on the participating organizations. Similarly, D. Cohen's (1991) report on collaborative efforts in a number of cities found little change in "the way schools work" under collaboration.

In summary, the structure and processes of collaboration reflect the characteristics of bureaucratic responses to problems. In our view, these bureaucratic arrangements are not likely to promote the gemeinschaftlich qualities of intimacy, trust, and belongingness in the school environment. While some early research findings support our view, much more research is needed to evaluate the long-term impact of collaboration on the school environment.

Impact of Interagency Collaboration on the Role of Schools in Community

Exploring the potential impact of interagency collaboration on the role of schools in relation to community is highly speculative. To date, research on the impact of interagency collaboration has not focused on this specific question. But, given the forgoing analysis, we would predict a minimal impact on the role of the school in the community. Our earlier analysis of the weakened linkages between the school and the local Gemeinschaft community surfaced two issues: (a) the bureaucratic, centralized school organization is alienated from the governance and influence of the local gemeinschaftlich community; and (b) the school's perceived mission reflects the values of the Gesellschaft, which are increasingly viewed with cynicism. We would argue that interagency collaboration alone will not have significant impact on these two issues.

First, the modest reorganization, expansion, and specialization required within the school organization to accomplish collaboration will have little impact on the overall operation and governance structure of the school district, which is likely to remain highly bureaucratic and centralized. With collaboration for social services in place, governance decisions regarding the operation of the school district in general will still emanate from elite school boards, which, as we argued earlier, reflect the values of the Gesellschaft. The local gemeinschaftlich community is not likely to be drawn in to increasingly meaningful involvement with school governance. Individual children and families, the clients of interagency collaboration, may benefit from services and be more comfortable in the school environment, if, for example, they work closely with a case manager housed in the school. And school personnel involved in collaborative services may develop and enjoy closer relationships with client families. However, as Boyd and his colleagues report (1992), these positive outcomes for individuals seem to have little impact on the school as an organization. In sum, interagency collaboration alone is not likely to have significant impact on the alienation of the local gemeinschaftlich community from the school's structure and governance.

Second, although the school will be involved in social maintenance functions associated with the Gemeinschaft, this will have limited impact on the overall perceived mission of the school. For individuals, as stated above, there may be positive outcomes, including a heightened sense of belonging in the school environment. It is possible that, over time, as more clients are served through collaboration, the school's image as a welcoming, nonthreatening institution may be enhanced. In this limited sense, the school's perceived role might shift to include a social support function. But a more central issue is the school's perceived mission regarding its technological core, the educational program. Here we would expect little impact. As we argued earlier, the school's mission in this regard reflects the Gesellschaft values of the elites. With collaboration in place, this would still be the case. The educational program and its perceived purpose would still be determined through the centralized, bureaucratic governance structure that reflects Gesellschaft values. The issue of cynicism regarding this mission would not be addressed. The school might become a more welcoming environment to individual community members, but the school still expects "buy in" to the values guiding its educational program.

Summary

Interagency collaboration as a reform reflects gemeinschaftlich values for schools. Yet the structures and processes of collaboration are clearly bureaucratic, and collaboration is likely to have little impact on the basic issue of the school's role in relation to local community. Essentially, collaboration means improvement in the bureaucratic efficiency of professionals providing services to clients. Collaboration may improve linkages with certain segments of the local community through moderate personalization of the school environment but not in a way that alters the governance structure or perceived mission of the school's technological core. This sense that collaboration has value but is a stopgap, bureaucratic response to meeting human needs is captured by Luvern Cunningham (1990, 16): "[Collaboration] has to occur pending the reconstitution of public and private institutions that will bring them into closer correspondence with human need."

CONCLUSION

We return to the main theme of this chapter. Sociological theory of community offers a conceptual tool that is useful in understanding the current reform movement in education. Our analysis suggests that a central issue underlying this reform climate is the school's identity crisis in relation to local community. Reform agendas conflict in their assumptions regarding the school's identity or mission, pulling schools toward opposite poles of the Gemeinschaft/Gesellschaft continuum. Further complicating the picture is the paradox that individual reforms, which may be intended to strengthen school-community ties, such as inter-agency collaboration, are actually elaborations of the school bureau-cracy and may have little impact on school-community linkages.

While the prescription of alternative policy solutions for strength-ening links between schools and community exceeds the bounds of this inquiry, some implications for policy can be drawn from this analysis. We would argue that continued exploration and analysis from a variety of perspectives is needed regarding the fundamental prob-lem of the school's role and mission in respect to local community. We suggest that policy makers and educators take a critical look at the pervasive influence of Gesellschaft values in the schools and what this means for building authentic linkages with the local community. Per-haps it will be necessary for educators to take on the burden of defin-ing a mission or multiple missions for the school that is attractive to, and consonant with, local Gemeinschaft values. This is not to say that reforms such as interagency collaboration are not valuable but that they are limited in their impact on this central problem. These limita-tions need to be recognized. The risk is that individual reforms, such as interagency collaboration, may consume the school's reform energy over the next several years with disappointing results and to the ne-glect of more central issues. We have attempted here to highlight one of these central issues—the school's role in community—by applying the conceptual tool of the Gemeinschaft/Gesellschaft continuum.

NOTES

1. Tönnies wrote in old German diction, which was difficult even for his contemporary German readers. Charles Loomis, Tönnies' translator, comments: "Many reviewers have bemoaned the difficulty of style and wording which carried the profound thought of its author" (Tönnies 1940, ix).

2. The discussion of Tönnies' work is based on several sources: Bender 1978; Cahnman and Heberle 1971; Lutz and Merz 1992; and Tönnies 1940, 1957. We are not able to do justice to Tönnies' complex theory of social rela-tionships here; rather, we are attempting to summarize its most salient features.

3. Tönnies' use of antithetical ideal types is similar to the theoretical concepts of several other sociologists, including Emile Durkheim's mechanical and organic solidarity, Charles Horton Cooley's primary and secondary groups, and Howard Becker's sacred and secular societies.

4. This discussion draws from Tyack's (1974) and Tyack and Hansot's (1982) work on the evolution of the American school system and Bender's (1978) work on the evolution of American communities.

5. See, for example, Crowson and Boyd 1993; Gardner 1993; Guthrie and Guthrie 1991; Liontos 1990; and Melaville and Blank 1991.

REFERENCES

America's parasite economy. (1992). *The Economist* 325:21–24.

Appley, D. G., and A. E. Winder. (1977). An evolving definition of collaboration and some implications for the world of work. *Journal of Applied Behavioral Science* 13: 279–291.

Bacharach, S. B., ed. (1990). *Education reform: Making sense of it all*. Boston: Allyn and Bacon.

Bender, T. (1978). *Community and social change in America*. New Brunswick, NJ: Rutgers University Press.

Boyd, B., B. Dunning, R. Gomez, R. Hetzel, R. King, S. Patrick, and K. Whitaker. (1992). *Impacts of interagency collaboration on participating organizations*. Paper presented at the Annual Meeting of the American Educational Research Association, April 20–24, San Francisco.

Cahnman, W. J., and R. Heberle, eds. (1971). *Ferdinand Tönnies on sociology: Pure, applied, and empirical. Selected writings*. Chicago: University of Chicago Press.

Callahan, R. E. (1962). *Education and the cult of efficiency*. Chicago: University of Chicago Press.

Cohen, D. L. (1991). Reality tempers "New Futures" optimism. *Education Week*, September 25:1, 12–15.

Coleman, J. S. (1985). Schools and the communities they serve. *Phi Delta Kappan* 66:527–532.

Coleman, J. S. (1987). Families and schools. *Educational Researcher* 16(6):33–38.

Comer, J. P. (1980). *School power: Implications of an intervention project*. New York: The Free Press.

Crowson, R. L., and W. L. Boyd. (1993). Coordinated services for children: Designing arks for storms and seas unknown. *American Journal of Education* 101:140–179.

Cunningham, L. L. (1990). Educational leadership and administration: Retrospective and prospective views. In *Educational leadership and changing contexts in families, communities, and schools: Eighty-ninth yearbook of the national society for the study of education*, Part II, ed. B. Mitchell and L. L. Cunningham, (1–18). Chicago: University of Chicago Press.

Epstein, J. L. (1992). School and family partnerships. *The Practitioner* 18(4):1–8.

Gardner, S. L. (1990). Failure by fragmentation. *Equity and Choice* 6(2):4–12.

Gardner, S. L. (1993). Key issues in developing school-linked integrated services. *Education and Urban Society* 25:141–152.

Greene, M. (1993). The passions of pluralism: Multiculturalism and the expanding community. *Educational Researcher* 22(1):13–18.

Guthrie, G. P., and L. F. Guthrie. (1991). Streamlining interagency collaboration for youth at risk. *Educational Leadership* 49(1)17–22.

Hawley, W. D. (1988). Missing pieces of the educational reform agenda: Or, why the first and second waves may miss the boat. *Educational Administration Quarterly* 24:416–437.

Heath, S. B., and M. W. McLaughlin. (1987). A child resource policy: Moving beyond dependence on school and family. *Phi Delta Kappan* 69:576–580.

Hodgkinson, H. L. (1989). *The same client: The demographics of education and service delivery systems.* Washington, D.C.: Institute for Educational Leadership.

Hoffer, T. B., and J. S. Coleman. (1990). Changing families and communities: Implications for schools. In *Educational leadership and changing contexts in families, communities, and schools: Eighty-ninth yearbook of the national society for the study of education,* Part II, ed. B. Mitchell and L. L. Cunningham, 118–134. Chicago: University of Chicago Press.

Hord, S. M. (1986). A synthesis of research on organizational collaboration. *Educational Leadership* 43(5):22–26.

Hoyt, K. (1991). Education reform and relationships between the private sector and education: A call for integration. *Phi Delta Kappan* 72:450–453.

Kirst, M. W. (1991). Improving children's services: Overcoming barriers, creating new opportunities. *Phi Delta Kappan* 73:615–618.

Kirst, M. W., and M. McLaughlin. (1990). Rethinking policy for children: Implications for educational administration. In *Educational leadership and changing contexts of families, communities, and schools: Eighty-ninth yearbook of the National Society for the Study of Education,* Part II, ed. B. Mitchell and L. L. Cunningham, 69–90. Chicago: University of Chicago Press.

Kreyche, G. F. (1993). The demise of moral authority. *USA Today* 122(2580):98.

Liontos, L. B. (1990). *Collaboration between schools and social services,* Washington, D.C.: Office of Educational Research and Improvement. (ERIC ED 320197).

Lutz, F. W., and C. Merz. (1992). *The politics of school/community relations.* New York: Teachers College Press, Columbia University.

Mannan, G., and J. Blackwell. (1992). Parent involvement: Barriers and opportunities. *The Urban Review* 24:219–226.

McLaughlin, M. W., and J. Talbert. (1990). Constructing a personalized school environment. *Phi Delta Kappan* 72:230–235.

Melaville, A. I., and M. J. Blank. (1991). *What it takes: Structuring interagency partnerships to connect children and families with comprehensive services.* Washington, D.C.: Education and Human Services Consortium.

Mitchell, B. (1990). Children, youth, and restructured schools: Views from the field. In *Educational leadership and changing contexts in families, communities, and schools. Eighty-ninth yearbook of the national society for the study of education,* Part II, ed. B. Mitchell and L. L. Cunningham, 52–68. Chicago: University of Chicago Press.

Perrow, C. (1970). Organizational Analysis: A sociological view: Belmont, Calif.: Wadsworth.

Readiness to learn grant application. (1993). Olympia, Wash.: Office of Superintendent of Public Instruction.

Sergiovanni, T. J. (1992). *Moral leadership: Getting to the heart of school improvement.* San Francisco: Jossey-Bass.

Tönnies, F. (1940). Fundamental concepts of sociology (gemeinschaft und gesellschaft). Trans. C. P. Loomis, (Original work published 1887.) New York: American Book.

Tönnies, F. (1957). Comunity and society (gemeinschaft und gesellschaft). Trans. C. P. Loomis, (Original work published 1887.) East Lansing, Mich.: Michigan State University Press.

Tyack, D. B. (1974). *The one best system: A history of American urban education.* Cambridge: Harvard University Press.

Tyack, D. B. and E. Hansot. *Managers of virtue: Public school leadership in America,* 1820–1980. New York: Basic Books.

Wagstaff, L. H., and K. S. Gallagher (1990). Schools, families, and communities: Idealized images and new realities. In *Educational leadership and changing contexts of families, communities, and schools: Eighty-ninth yearbook of the National Society for the study of Education,* Part II, eds. B. Mitchell and L. L. Cunningham, 91–117. Chicago: University of Chicago Press.

West, C. (1993). *Race Matters.* Boston: Beacon Press.

Wise, A. E. (1988). Legislative learning revisited. *Phi Delta Kappan,* 70, 328–333.

Chapter 14

Connecting Schools and Communities Through Interagency Collaboration for School-Linked Services

Debra Shaver
Shari Golan
Mary Wagner

Cross-agency collaboration among providers of education and human services is a reform idea that has received much attention across the sectors of human services. Many believe that, by working together, service-providing organizations can address the complex needs of children and families in a holistic and integrated way. Particularly as concerns rise over the inadequacies of the current system to effectively address the multiple and often overlapping needs of children and families in poverty, cross-agency collaboration appears to be a promising approach to service delivery.

Linking health and human service organizations with schools is one approach to integrating services. However, like "school restructuring" and other reform labels, "integrated school-linked services" is a concept that often has vague and varied meanings to policy makers, scholars, and practitioners. Usually, it means bringing multiple agencies and schools together to jointly address the needs of the community; however, little is known about how this collaboration works. For example, how do schools and outside agencies work together when they have different service philosophies, different professional cultures, and different norms and standards? From the literature on

349

interorganizational relations, we know that interagency collaboration is not easy; it often requires new skills, new procedures, and new ways of doing business for those participating in the collaborative venture. To move toward an integrated service system, human service agencies and institutions must cross their organizational boundaries and develop new ways of working with other service providers. This chapter uses empirical data from an evaluation of a statewide integrated school-linked services initiative to provide concrete information about interagency collaboration among schools and community agencies working together to improve the way services are provided to children and families.

In this chapter, we investigate interagency collaboration in thirty seven communities that received funding under California's Healthy Start initiative (Senate Bill 620) to provide comprehensive and integrated school-linked services to children and their families.[1] Our examination of collaborative processes has two major objectives: to describe how communities have put the concept of collaboration for school-linked services into operation, and to identify factors associated with early indicators of successful collaboration. For the purposes of this research, we define success in terms of good working relationships among collaborative members and the ability of collaboratives to resolve major obstacles to collaboration and service integration. Specifically, this chapter addresses the following research questions:

(1)   What is the organizational and political context of collaboration for school-linked services, and how is the context related to the effectiveness of collaboratives?

(2)   What is the structure of their interorganizational relations, and how is the structure related to collaborative success?

(3) What efforts are collaboratives for school-linked services making to increase and enhance connections between member organizations, and how are these efforts associated with measures of collaborative effectiveness?

(4)   How are measures of collaborative success related to each other—specifically, are some types of collaborative success associated with success in other areas?

The answers to these questions will provide valuable information to policy makers, practitioners, and consumers about how collaboratives for school-linked services can be successfully supported and implemented.

Although we believe that collaboration with families and community members is a critical piece of integrated school-linked service reform, we focus here on collaboration at the organizational level, examining the way schools, human service agencies, and other organizations work together. Connections among families, schools, and providers of school-linked services are the focus of other chapters in this book, as well as of other research.[2]

Our examination begins with a discussion of the theoretical framework guiding this research. Next, we discuss the methods used for conducting the study, followed by the results section of the chapter, which is organized by the four research questions outlined above. The chapter concludes with a summary of the major findings of the research and their implications for policy and practice related to integrated school-linked services.

THEORETICAL PERSPECTIVE

The theoretical foundation for our research assumes that organizations forge partnerships with other organizations as a way of controlling their environments. Research on formal organizations notes that, to capitalize on valuable resources and minimize environmental forces that may negatively affect them, organizations often choose to connect their activities with those of other entities, engaging in such practices as bargaining, joint ventures, mergers, and other coordinating strategies (Thompson 1967; Scott 1987). Thus, interorganizational relations represent important ways in which social organizations, such as schools and community agencies, respond to outside forces, such as decreased funding opportunities, increased community needs, and other factors affecting the organization's ability to fulfill its objectives.

With this basic assumption in mind, we use research on interorganizational relations to conceptualize how schools and human service agencies work together to provide integrated school-linked services. On the basis of previous research, we postulate that the way an interorganizational group is structured and how it functions are important determinants of the group's effectiveness in achieving its goals. We examine such factors as the context of interorganizational relations, the structure of interorganizational relations, and the attention paid to increasing group members' capacities to work across institutional boundaries as predictors of the effectiveness of collaboratives for school-linked services.

For this research, we use two indicators of collaborative effectiveness: the extent to which the relationships between collaborative members are positive, and the degree to which interagency groups are able to resolve major obstacles to their collaborative work. Although the ultimate measure of the success of collaboratives for school-linked services is whether or not consumer outcomes improve, we believe that good working relationships and the ability of collaboratives to resolve obstacles are important interim indicators of their success.

This research begins with a look at the concepts relevant to the first research question: what is the political and organizational context in which collaboratives for school-linked services operate, and how is it related to the success of the collaborative? In particular, we investigate the political climate supporting or hindering collaborative efforts, the types of organizations involved, and the length of time the group has been working together. On the basis of the work of P. Mattessich and B. Monsey (1992), A. Melaville and M. Blank (1993), and others who have investigated collaboratives for school-linked services, we hypothesize that collaboratives that have strong support from the community and from decision makers within the participating organizations will be more able than other collaboratives to resolve problems when they occur. In addition, we expect that the types of organizations involved in the partnerships help determine the interorganizational group's ability to achieve its goals. For example, we believe that high levels of participation from the public sector will bring to the collaborative the necessary political resources for resolving such public policy issues as conflicting requirements regarding who receives services, who can provide services, and how information about service consumers can be shared. Finally, researchers and policy makers note that the length of time that organizations have worked together is an important feature of their organizational context (e.g., Aiken and Alford 1970). We hypothesize that the longer organizations have been working together, the more effectively they will work together and resolve serious challenges to their collaborative work. Thus, for this study, we examine these contextual factors and their relationships to collaborative success.

The second research question reveals our interest in the structure of interorganizational relations among collaboratives for school-linked services. Research has found that important dimensions of interorganizational structure include its degree of formality and the degree to which authority is concentrated or dispersed (Mulford 1984; Pfeffer and Salancik 1978). The level of formality in interorganizational relations tells us how much collaborative groups rely on formal procedures, rules, and documents to carry out their collaborative work. Investigations of dyadic relationships between health and social welfare organizations, where the resources being exchanged are intangible ones such as client referrals and information, have found that relations are often characterized by a low degree of formality and standardization (Marrett 1971; Van de Ven and Walker 1984). We hypothesize that, as collaborative ventures expand beyond a few organizations, they will need a more formal structure to support their work, including such elements as memoranda of understanding, written bylaws for the collaborative, and an organization chart. How the level of formality is related to the working relationships and the resolution of collaborative challenges will be explored in the analyses.

The concentration or dispersion of authority represents the second dimension of interorganizational structure that is of interest for this study. Jeffrey Pfeffer and Gerald Salancik (1978) and others theorize that the degree to which authority is concentrated in one or a few organizations or dispersed over a large number of organizations predicts well the nature of relations among the organizations working together. Specifically, when authority is dispersed, trust among members is expected to be higher, and members are expected to have a greater sense of ownership of the collaborative venture than in groups in which authority is heavily concentrated. Citing some of the dangers of concentrating authority in a single person or organization, Melaville and Blank observe that "continued reliance on a single voice, however, will ultimately stanch the flow of new ideas, under-utilize the pool of available talent, and undermine the growth of interdependence central to joint efforts" (1991, 25). Thus, we expect that how collaboratives for school-linked services are led and how decisions are made affect the collaborative process, with more democratic forms of leadership and decision making contributing to better working relationships among members and easier resolution of challenges.

For the third research question, we investigate the efforts that collaboratives for school-linked services make to increase the connections between members and improve those connections through training on interagency collaboration and coordination. How well connected organizations are to each other has been cited in other research as an important factor determining the success of collaborative work (e.g., Pfeffer and Salancik 1978).

For the purposes of this research, we define interconnectedness as the amount of communication between organizations involved in the collaborative. As one theorist notes, through frequent communication, individuals involved in interorganizational relations develop collective meanings that enable the group to function effectively (Olsen 1978). On the basis of this theory and other research (e.g., Mattessich and Monsey 1992), we hypothesize that more frequent communications will lead to better working relationships among collaborative members and the ability to resolve collaborative difficulties when they arise.

How well members of collaboratives can communicate with partners and work across institutional boundaries will depend on the skills that members have for working collaboratively. This research assumes that effective collaboration among schools and public and private service organizations requires members to break out of institution-specific traditions, habits, and norms and embrace new ways of doing business—a process that does not come easily for many people. Therefore, we expect that the more attention collaborative groups give to helping members through this process, the more successful they will be in working together to achieve common goals. Specifically, we hypothesize that involvement in activities such as cross-training on other agencies' procedures and norms, training on how to work collaboratively, and efforts to develop new joint procedures and eliminate conflicting ones will enable partners to work together effectively. Furthermore, we hypothesize that these efforts will help in the resolution of obstacles to collaboration such as turf battles between partners or conflicting policies and procedures, which often result from misunderstandings or policies that can be changed easily (Melaville and Blank 1991).

For the final research question, how measures of collaborative success are related to each other, we investigate the associations between working relationships and the resolution of obstacles, hypothesizing that collaboratives with better working relationships among members will be better able to avoid and resolve collaborative challenges. In addition, we explore whether the resolutions of some obstacles are associated with the resolutions of other obstacles.

We will investigate the hypotheses outlined above with data from the research study described below.

METHODS

The results of this research describe interagency collaboration in thirty-seven programs that received funding as part of California's Healthy Start initiative in 1992, the first year of the initiative. The initiative provides grants to public educational institutions (serving grades kindergarten through 12) to encourage and support local programs for integrated, school-linked services for low-income children and families. Grantees are engaged in self-generated collaboratives to plan and implement programs they have determined will meet the needs of their students and families. Many programs involve single schools or a small cluster of schools, some are districtwide, and a few are countywide systems change efforts.

Data come primarily from semistructured phone interviews and mail surveys of members of Healthy Start collaboratives, conducted in February through April 1993. The findings presented here are based on descriptive statistics and bivariate analyses (e.g., Pearson correlations and cross-tabulations) of survey data. To provide a context for the quantitative findings, we also present qualitative information from phone interviews and visits to several of the programs, highlighting interagency collaboration in three diverse Healthy Start collaboratives. The three example collaboratives and the survey samples are described below.

Sample and Data Sources

Interview and Survey Samples. To identify collaborative members, the coordinator of each program was asked to provide a roster of the members of the collaborative for school-linked services, including the program's contact person at each organization. Telephone interviews included the coordinator of each program and the contact people at three to five agencies participating in each collaborative, for a total of 180 completed interviews and a response rate of 90 percent. The mail questionnaire was sent to the contact people at all the public agencies (e.g., departments of health and social services, and offices and programs administered by county agencies) who did not participate in a telephone interview, and we received one hundred completed questionnaires, a response rate of 68 percent. The contact people were typically administrators, although some respondents were direct service providers.

Example Collaboratives. The three illustrative collaboratives were selected to represent the diversity in the context, structure, and interorganizational connections in collaboratives for school-linked services. Smalltown Family Resource Collaborative[3] is located in a relatively small suburban community and serves primarily elementary students and their families, focusing on their academic, social, and emotional needs. The County Services Collaborative features a team of professionals, primarily from public agencies, who serve children and their families across a large rural county. The Family and Adolescent Services Collaborative features family resource centers located at two elementary schools and one high school where families and individuals can come for a variety of health, education, and social services. We will use these examples throughout the chapter to illustrate the diversity of collaboratives and to further explain the findings from the quantitative analyses.

Indicators

The variables used for the analyses of the relationships between collaborative characteristics and indicators of collaborative success are described in Table 14.1. As evidenced in the descriptions of variables, the collaborative for school-linked services operating at each Healthy Start program is the unit of analysis for the findings reported in this chapter. Thus, for measures obtained from multiple respondents, responses were combined to form a mean value for the collaborative.

Regarding the last entry on Table 14.1, the resolution of obstacles, the analyses include factors most frequently identified by respondents as obstacles to collaboration and integrated services. These include problems with county- and local-level policies, lack of buy in from top administrators, barriers to information sharing, turf battles among collaborative members, conflicting professional cultures and norms, and state and federal policies, including restrictions on categorical funding.

RESULTS

In this section, we present findings on the context of interorganizational relations among collaboratives for school-linked services, the interorganizational structure, the efforts made to develop and improve connections between collaborating organizations, and the interrelationships among indicators of collaborative success.

Context of Interorganizational Relations

We begin our analyses by describing the organizational and political context in which collaboratives for school-linked services operated and by examining how this context is related to indicators of the collaboratives' success. We look first at the number and types of organizations involved in collaboratives for school-linked services.

TABLE 14.1

Operational Definitions of Variables Used in Correlations

Variable	Source	Measure
Context		
History of collaboration	Coordinator	Number of years since the organizations involved in the collaborative began working together on school-linked services.
Composition of collaborative	List of current members of the collaborative provided by coordinator	Each organization was assigned a code designating the type of organization it was. Four variables were used in analyses: the percentages of organizations on the collaborative member list that were public agencies (not including schools and school districts), educational organizations, private agencies, and nonprofit community-based organizations.
Level of support	All respondents	Program-level mean of reported levels of support from front-line staff, top administrators, business, and families. Responses included "not very supportive (1)," "somewhat supportive (2)," and "very supportive (3)."
Structure		
Degree of shared authority	All respondents	A 4-point variable with the following ordinal categories: single leader and low levels of consensus decision making (1), single leader and high levels of consensus decision making (2), shared leadership and low levels of consensus decision making (3), and shared leadership and high levels of consensus decision making (4). Scale uses two variables: whether the program was led by one officially designated leader or multiple leaders, according to the coordinator; and the program-level mean of responses to the statement, "Decisions about the project are made by consensus."
Degree of formality	Coordinator	A 6-point scale indicating the number of the following mechanisms in place: interagency memoranda of understanding, a statement of philosophy or mission for the school-linked services program, an organizational chart for the collaborative, minutes of collaborative governance or subcommittee meetings, and bylaws for the interagency group (the last indicator of formality, bylaws, was weighted twice as much as the other indicators in the scale).

continued on next page

TABLE 14.1 (continued)

Variable	Source	Measure
Connections		
Formal communications	All respondents	Program-level mean of frequency with which respondents reported that they or other representatives of their organization attended meetings about the program for school-linked services.
Informal communications	All respondents	Program-level mean of frequency with which respondents reported that they or other representatives of their organization talked to other members of the collaborative outside of regular meetings.
Participation in training on collaboration	All respondents	Proportion of respondents from each program who indicated that they or other representatives of their organization had participated in training on collaborative skills.
Participation in developing procedures for information sharing	All respondents	Proportion of respondents from each program who indicated that they or other representatives of their organization had participated in developing procedures for sharing information across agencies.
Working Relationships	All respondents	Program-level mean of two variables: "What is the level of trust among collaborative members?" (using a 4-point scale from "very low" to "very high") and the level of agreement with "Most organizations involved in the project have a real sense of ownership of it" (using a 4-point scale from "strongly agree" to "strongly disagree"). Items are correlated with each other at $r = .72$, $p < .001$.
Resolution of Obstacles	All respondents	Program-level mean on degree to which a particular obstacle (e.g., turf issue) was resolved (responses include "not at all resolved," "partially resolved," and "fully resolved"). Includes only respondents who indicated that a particular issue was an obstacle. Measure of overall ability to resolve obstacles averages the resolution score across all obstacles.

One of the few stipulations of the Healthy Start grant was for programs to have a collaborative group composed of "representatives of each public or private agency that will provide or is anticipated to provide services under the program" (Honig 1992, 11). Therefore, all Healthy Start programs have a collaborative group that governs or advises program operations. Table 14.2 summarizes the characteristics of these collaboratives.

TABLE 14.2
Characteristics of Collaboratives for School-Linked Services

Context

Mean number of years working together	3
Median number of member organizations	14
Percentage of member organizations that were:	
Public	60
Private	11
Nonprofit/community-based	27
Percentage of collaboratives whose members reported that group was "very supportive":	
Top administration	97
Line staff	87
Business	65
Families	74

Structure

Percentage of collaboratives with type of authority structure:	
Single leader and low levels of consensus decision making	32
Single leader with high levels of consensus decision making	11
Shared leadership with low levels of consensus decision making	27
Shared leadership with high levels of consensus decision making	30
Mean level of formality*	3.5

Connections among Organizations

Mean amount of formal communication	monthly
Mean amount of informal communication	weekly
Mean percentage of collaborative members who attended training on collaboration	58
Mean percentage of collaborative members who participated in developing procedures for information sharing	64

*Values range from 0 (low level of formality) to 6 (high level of formality).

Across the thirty-seven collaboratives included in the study, more than six hundred organizations were represented. Collaboratives ranged in size from five to sixty-nine member organizations, with a median of fourteen organizations. As revealed in Table 14.2, 38 percent of participating organizations were private or nonprofit community organizations, such as private health providers, businesses, youth-serving organizations like the YMCA, family counseling centers, agencies offering child-care or recreational services, and community advocacy groups. Thus, considerable private resources were available in these public-private partnerships. About 60 percent of member organizations were from the public service sector, with about 27 percent of members representing educational organizations (e.g., schools, school districts, county offices of education, postsecondary institutions). The remaining public-sector members consisted primarily of county and city agencies. For example, the vast majority of collaboratives for school-linked services included the county departments of health and social services, and most programs, particularly those serving adolescents, involved the justice system. Thus, the typical collaborative for school-linked services involved fourteen organizations, about five of which were from the private or nonprofit sector and nine from the public education, health, or human service sector.

Some of these collaborative groups represented new inter-organizational arrangements; others represented groups whose members had been working together on school-linked services for a number of years. Slightly more than half of the collaborative groups (twenty) were formed in the year preceding the Healthy Start initiative, perhaps at least partly in response to the availability of Healthy Start funding. Among the remaining groups, thirteen collaboratives reported having worked together for two to five years, and four collaboratives reported having worked together for more than five years. Three years was the average length of time collaborative members had been working together. Therefore, for the members of the majority of groups, working together to design and implement school-linked services was a new venture; for the others, it represented more established ways of doing business.

We use collaborative members' perceptions of the level of support for the program from various groups as a measure of the political context of collaborative efforts. Table 14.2 shows that members believed that, overall, support for the program was high, with respondents from the vast majority of collaboratives (more than 74 percent) reporting that top administrators, front-line staff, and families were very supportive of the program. Perceptions of high levels of business support were less pervasive—respondents from 65 percent of collaboratives reported that businesses were very supportive. Higher levels of perceived support from business were reported in programs with larger proportions of private organizations, such as private medical clinics, counseling centers, and other private business, involved in the collaborative ($r = .39$, $p < .05$).

Table 14.3 shows the characteristics of the three example collaboratives. These examples illustrate the vast range in the collaboratives' history, composition, and political support. As shown in the table, the Smalltown Family Resource Collaborative was a small group of public and nonpublic organizations that had worked together for fifteen years and enjoyed very high levels of support for the program from all levels. By contrast, the County Services Collaborative was a very large collaborative that was heavily dominated by public organizations, most of which were the schools served by the program. County agencies in this community came together about three years before the Healthy Start initiative to coordinate their efforts in the face of declining county resources. With the exception of support from top administrators, this collaborative reported relatively low levels of political support for the program. The third example, the Family and Adolescent Services Collaborative, was made up of many public and community-based organizations. Efforts to coordinate services were led by the school district and several county agencies during the year before the Healthy Start initiative. Support for the program among professionals (i.e., top administrators and line staff) was high, but the collaborative had yet to garner the support of the community.

We now turn to identifying which aspects of the organizational and political context of collaboration were related to measures of collaborative success, beginning with factors related to good working relationships.

The top part of Table 14.4 displays the correlation coefficients for the relationships between contextual factors and measures of collaborative success. As the table illustrates, neither the organizational context (i.e., the types of organizations involved) nor the historical context of previous interorganizational relations was related to working relationships among collaborative members. In fact, the only contextual factor related to working relationships was the perceived level of support from families: the higher the perceived level of support from families, the better the working relationships between collaborative members ($r = .44$). We are not sure whether the involvement or support

TABLE 14.3

Characteristics of Example Collaboratives for School-Linked Services

	Smalltown Family Resource Collaborative	County Services Collaborative	Family & Adolescent Services Collaborative
Context			
No. of years working together	15 years	3 years	1 year
Composition of membership			
No. of organizations	7	42	30
Types of organizations	Majority are nonpublic, community-based agencies	Almost entirely public county agencies and schools	Half public, the rest private and nonprofit community agencies
Level of support from*:			
Top administration	High	Medium high	High
Line staff	Medium high	Medium	Medium high
Business	High	Low	Low
Families	High	Low	Low
Structure			
Level of shared authority	Shared leadership and high levels of consensus decision making	Single leader with low levels of consensus decision making	Shared leadership with low levels of consensus decision making
Formality	Medium low	Very high	Medium
Connections among Organizations			
Formal communication	A few times a month	Less than monthly	Almost weekly
Informal communication	Weekly	Monthly	Weekly
Level of training on collaboration*	Very low	Medium high	High
Indicators of Effectiveness			
Working relationships*	Very good	Poor	Fairly good
Resolution of obstacles	Fully resolved most obstacles	Fully resolved policy obstacles, not able to resolve other obstacles	Partially resolved some, but not able to resolve problems with categorical funding

*In this table, we characterize the scores of collaboratives on several variables (level of support, level of training, and working relation-ships) relative to those of other collaboratives. For example, "low" here means that a collaborative's mean score was lower than those of most other collaboratives.

TABLE 14.4

Correlations between Collaborative Characteristics and Indicators of Success

				Resolution of Obstacles			
	Working Relationships	State/ Federal Policy	Local Policy	Lack of Buy in From Top	Barriers to Information Sharing	Turf Issues	Conflicting Group Cultures
Context							
Number of years working together	-.10	-.07	-.50*	-.16	.32	.32+	.47*
Proportion of organizations that were:							
Public	-.08	.47*	.55*	-.06	.08	.17	-.14
Private	-.10	-.04	-.21	.23	-.16	.04	.32
Nonprofit/community-based	.14	-.53*	-.62**	-.29	-.18	-.35+	-.06
Level of support from:							
Top administration	.25	.00	.16	.01	.34+	-.11	.14
Line staff	.05	-.17	.06	.00	.52**	-.02	.20
Business	.21	.13	-.04	-.52	.05	.08	.28
Families	.44*	.18	.12	-.03	.06	.06	.41
Structure							
Level of shared authority	.49**	-.45*	.21	.79*	.34+	-.06	.03
Formality	.10	.37+	.23	-.09	-.15	.21	-.12
Connections among Organizations							
Formal communication	.33*	-.14	.29	-.37	.06	-.04	-.04
Informal communication	.31+	-.31	.07	.32	.17	-.02	.31
Training on collaboration	.09	-.22	.06	.19	.23	-.29	-.01
Developing procedures for information sharing	.17	-.13	.38	-.07	.45*	-.07	.42*

+ p < .10.
* p < .05.
** p < .01.

of families helps collaboratives develop better working relationships or whether collaboratives that are more inclined to involve and earn the support of families are also the types of collaboratives that have good relationships among members. In any case, these two factors are related.

The context of interorganizational relations, particularly the composition of collaboratives, seemed to be more important when it came to resolving obstacles or challenges to collaboration and service integration. For example, collaboratives that were heavily dominated by public agencies were better able to resolve state and federal policy issues, including problems with categorical funding ($r = .47$), and they had fewer problems resolving challenges with county, local, and school district policies, such as requirements for staff hiring and training, than did collaboratives that had fewer agencies from the public sector ($r = .55$). These findings suggest that having strong representation of public agencies, including school districts, can provide collaboratives with the resources necessary to deal effectively with obstacles relating to local and state policies and with power struggles among collaborating agencies—issues that can impede the progress of collaborative efforts to provide integrated school-linked services. As an example, the coordinator of Smalltown Family Resource Collaborative, which is run mostly by community-based and private organizations, commented on the difficulties his collaborative experienced in resolving problems with school district policies, stating simply, "We don't have the power to make things happen in the school." Representing another perspective, members of the County Services Collaborative reported initially having problems with turf battles between county agencies that were serving the same clients. These issues were fairly easily resolved, largely because of the high level of involvement of county agencies on the collaborative and their commitment to resolve the conflict.

The findings about the history of collaboration and the resolution of obstacles were mixed. On one hand, the longer that collaboratives had been in existence, the better able they were to resolve problems with professional culture clashes between organizational members ($r = .47$). On the other hand, a longer history was related to greater difficulty in solving problems with local and county policies, such as requirements for staff hiring, procedures for purchasing materials, and paperwork and reporting requirements ($r = -.50$), a finding that contradicts our expectations about the relationship between collaborative history and success.

Political support for the program was not generally related to the resolution of collaborative obstacles; however, the support of the front-line staff who worked directly with service consumers was positively related to the resolution of problems with information sharing procedures ($r = .52$).

In summary, several of our hypotheses about the relationship between the context of collaboration and the success of collaboratives were supported, and others were not. First, contrary to our hypotheses, with the exception of the level of support from families, the context of collaboration was not related to working relationships among collaborative members. In addition, the finding that political support was not generally related to the resolution of obstacles was unexpected. Supporting our hypotheses, however, was the finding that the types of organizations involved in the collaborative were a factor relating to the resolution of collaborative challenges, with stronger representation by public agencies being related to the easier resolution of several state- and local-level policy issues. Finally, having a longer history of working together appeared to help collaborative members work through conflicts in professional cultures and norms, whereas a shorter history was better for resolving local policy issues.

Features of Interorganizational Structure

As stated in the theoretical framework, we believe several aspects of the interorganizational structure of collaboratives to be important in understanding how organizations work together. In this section, we describe collaborative leadership, decision making, and the level of formality of relations, and we investigate how these factors are related to measures of collaboratives' effectiveness.

To learn about leadership arrangements, we asked coordinators of the school-linked services programs to describe how the collaboratives were led. They reported that fewer than half of the collaboratives (43 percent) were led by one official lead agency. In all these cases, the official lead agency was the local education agency (e.g., school district, school, or county office of education) that initiated the Healthy Start grant application. Hence, these schools, districts, and county offices of education led the development of the grant proposals and continued their leadership role in the collaboratives for school-linked services after the grants were awarded.

The remaining collaboratives (57 percent) shared leadership between two or more collaborative members; however, how leadership was shared between multiple leaders differed from program to program. For example, some programs had a rotating leader, others had several designated leaders, and still others reported that they did not have any designated leaders because leadership was shared across all collaborative members.

Whether or not official leadership was shared was one indicator of the degree to which power was dispersed in the collaboratives; how decisions were made about the collaborative and its school-linked services project was another. We assumed that the more collaboratives made decisions by consensus, the more power and authority were dispersed across members. Table 14.2 illustrates how authority was structured in collaboratives for school-linked services, in terms of leadership and the prevalence of consensus decision making.

We found that consensus decision making was relatively rare among the collaboratives led by one officially designated leader—only four of these collaboratives had high scores on the consensus decision making variable. On the other hand, collaboratives with shared leadership arrangements were about equally divided between those with high levels of consensus decision making (11) and those with low levels (10). Thus, collaboratives with an officially designated lead agency usually had decision-making authority centralized in that one agency, whereas collaboratives with multiple leaders varied in the extent to which decision making was concentrated or dispersed, with some groups giving authority to all members via consensus decision making and other groups having decision-making authority reside with a subset of members.

Whether or not groups made decisions by consensus was not related to the size of the group. Therefore, although we suspect that consensus decision making may have been easier in smaller collaboratives, both large and small groups were able to use it. For example, one relatively large collaborative (not one of our example sites) with twenty-one member organizations decided that most decisions about the program, from major policy decisions to decisions about the day-to-day operation of the program, would be made by consensus. The leaders of this collaborative believed that, although participatory decision making required a great deal of patience, it was critical to obtaining the buy in and commitment of all of its members and to the ultimate success of the collaborative.

Going back to our three illustrative programs (Table 14.3), the three cases represent the diversity in how authority was structured. The County Services Collaborative was led by the county office of education, and, although the coordinator of the program (from the office of education) worked very closely with several other county departments, her agency had the ultimate authority and responsibility for making decisions about the program. At the opposite end of the spectrum was the Smalltown Family Resource Collaborative, which was administered by a nonprofit, community-based organization; however, all members of the collaborative had an equal voice in decision making. In between these two programs in terms of authority was the Family and Adolescent Services Collaborative, which was facilitated by the school district but several organizations had leadership responsibilities. This program actively solicited the input of all collaborative members; however, final decisions were usually made by the various leaders of the collaborative's activities.

With regard to the level of formality in interorganizational relations, our survey results demonstrate that the collaboratives for school-linked services had relatively formal interorganizational structures. Three-fourths of the program coordinators characterized their collaborative as a formal, structured group. In addition, large majorities of collaboratives reported having established memoranda of understanding among partners to guide their work (94 percent of collaboratives), a vision statement to codify their shared intentions (89 percent), and an organizational chart of the collaborative group and the participants (64 percent). A relatively small proportion of collaboratives had established formal bylaws (15 percent). Table 14.2 reveals that the average collaborative had between three and four of these formal elements in place. The size of the collaboratives was related to the level of formality, with large collaboratives (in terms of the number of member organizations) having more formal structures than smaller collaboratives ($r = .33$, $p < .05$). This pattern held true for our three example collaboratives, with the smallest collaborative (Smalltown Family Resource Collaborative) having the least formal structure and the largest collaborative (County Services Collaborative) the most formal.

Our analyses focus next on investigating relationships between the structure of interorganizational relations and indicators of collaborative success, and we return to Table 14.4.

Table 14.4 reveals that the degree to which authority was shared was associated with collaborative success, whereas the level of formality was not related to indicators of success. Regarding authority, we found that the more dispersed the authority was among collaborative members, the better the working relationships ($r = .49$), lending some support to our hypothesis that more democratic forms of leadership yield higher levels of trust and perceptions of shared ownership among collaborative members. The case of the Smalltown collaborative, however, leads us to question the direction of the hypothesized causal relationship. This collaborative had very good working relationships, according to our measure. In talking with Smalltown's collaborative members, we learned that relationships have always been characterized by high levels of trust and shared ownership in this tightly knit community. According to respondents, their democratic form of authority came about very easily because of good working relationships. Thus, in this case, shared authority seemed to result from good working relationships, not vice versa as we had hypothesized. Similarly, we do not know if poor working relationships in the County Services Collaborative resulted from authoritarian leadership or if this form of leadership came about because of a lack of mutual trust among collaborative members. We will revisit this issue in the discussion section that concludes this chapter.

Collaboratives with more shared authority also had a much easier time resolving problems with buy in among collaborative members ($r = .79$) than did collaboratives in which authority was more centralized. On the other hand, shared leadership and decision making was related to greater difficulty in resolving state and federal policy issues ($r = -.45$), suggesting that concentrated authority brings some benefits to resolving collaborative issues.

Therefore, as we expected, the degree to which authority was dispersed was associated with working relationships among collaborative members and the resolution of some obstacles, although the relationship was not in the expected direction for the resolution of state and federal policy issues. The fact that the level of formality was not related to working relationships or the ability to resolve collaborative obstacles suggests that both informally and formally structured collaboratives can develop good working relationships among members.

Efforts to Establish and Improve Connections among Organizations

School-linked service programs seek to achieve goals that cannot be easily attained by any organization acting alone. Success thus requires establishing methods for interorganizational communication and increasing collaborative members' abilities to work collaboratively. We examine here the extent of formal and informal communication taking place among collaborating organizations. In addition, we consider the amount of participation by collaborating organizations' staff members in activities designed to establish better coordination across agencies.

Finally, we discuss how the amount of communication and level of participation in training activities are related to indicators of collaborative success.

As shown in the lower part of Table 14.2, collaborative members reported communicating formally through attending meetings on school-linked services (e.g., executive committees, advisory groups, working groups, or case review meetings) about monthly, on average, and they reported having informal communication (dialogue outside of meetings about school-linked services) about weekly. The level of informal and formal communication varied considerably from program to program, with some collaboratives reporting meeting only four times a year or less often and talking informally only monthly or less and others reporting weekly meetings and almost daily conversations outside of meetings. The level of communication varied for collaboratives with different characteristics. For example, members of collaboratives with greater shared authority talked more frequently with other collaborative members outside of meetings ($r = .49, p < .05$). Similarly, members of collaboratives who reported higher levels of support from front-line staff—those who worked directly with service consumers—also reported having informal communications with other collaborative members more frequently ($r = .51, p < .05$). Finally, the amounts of communication that occurred through meetings and outside of meetings were positively related to each other ($r = .40, p < .05$).

Our three example programs follow these patterns to some degree (see Table 14.3). For example, County Services Collaborative, which had the least shared authority and the lowest level of support from front-line staff among the three collaboratives, also had the least frequent formal and informal communications, meeting less often than monthly and talking informally only monthly, on average. The other two example programs had several different work groups and committees, requiring members to meet several times a month. Additionally, members of these two collaboratives found it necessary to talk with each other informally at least weekly to coordinate their activities.

In addition to the frequency of interorganizational communication, we were interested in the efforts collaboratives made to improve the quality of these contacts. We asked respondents whether they or anyone in their agency had participated in various types of trainings or meetings, including such activities as training or conferences on collaboration or service integration, cross-training on other agencies' norms and procedures, and meetings to develop new procedures for sharing information about service consumers across organizations.

We found that about 58 percent of respondents at the average project reported that they or another representative from their organization had attended a training session on interagency collaboration or cross-training on other agencies' services and procedures. In addition, 64 percent of respondents at the average project said that they or a colleague had participated in interagency development of new confidentiality procedures to allow for more information sharing among agencies.

The amount of involvement in these activities was not the same across all the collaboratives. Members in collaborative programs with shorter histories of working together were more likely to participate in cross-training on other agencies' norms and procedures and developing new confidentiality procedures ($r = .33$ and $.35$, respectively, $p < .05$) Furthermore, collaborative members were more likely to be involved in developing new procedures for sharing information across agencies if the collaborative had high levels of support from top administration and line staff ($r = .42$ and $.35$, respectively, $p < .01$ and $.05$), and placed an emphasis on establishing formal guides (e.g., memoranda of understanding and organizational charts) for their interactions ($r = .35$, $p < .05$). Finally, collaboratives whose members were more involved in cross-training and developing information-sharing procedures were also more likely to communicate more frequently with each other outside of meetings ($r = .42$ and $.45$, respectively, $p < .01$).

The figures presented at the bottom portion of Table 14.4 provide only a little support for our hypotheses concerning the relationship between efforts to develop and maintain good interorganizational connections and collaborative success. Supporting our hypotheses was the finding that more frequent meetings were associated with better relationships among collaborative members ($r = .33$). Contrary to our hypotheses, the level of participation in efforts to improve connections between collaborating organizations through training was not related to working relationships. We learned from our qualitative interviews that often the intensity of these training sessions was not sufficient to affect partners' working relationships; many of the training sessions were short, one-time attempts to improve collaborative skills. As a rare example, the Family and Adolescent Service Collaborative held a yearly 2-day retreat focused on how to understand and work with other organizations. Members of this collaborative believed that these retreats and other training activities were instrumental to improving working relationships among the collaborating partners. Therefore, if

our measures of participation in capacity-building activities had captured the intensity and quality of these activities, we might have found
a significant relationship between training activities and working relationships. Since we did not have data on these aspects of training
sessions, we were not able to adequately test our hypotheses about
their association with working relationships.

Our hypothesized relationship between interorganizational communications and the resolution of obstacles also was not supported
empirically; the amount of communications, formal or informal, was
not correlated with the resolution of collaborative obstacles. Furthermore, the level of participation in training on collaboration and the
resolution of obstacles were not associated with each other, a result
perhaps explained by the limitations of our measures noted above.
Only participation in developing new procedures for sharing information across organizations was related to the resolution of obstacles,
with participation in this activity being positively related to the resolution of barriers to information sharing and problems with conflicting professional cultures ($r = .45$ and $.42$, respectively).

Interrelationships among Indicators of Success

In this section, we examine how indicators of collaborative success
were related to each other. Specifically, we are interested in whether
collaborative projects with better working relationships resolved certain obstacles more easily and whether the resolution of certain obstacles was tied to the resolution of other obstacles.

Using a measure of the degree to which collaboratives were able
to resolve all the obstacles that confronted them (described in Table
14.1), we found that collaboratives with better working relationships
among members were better able to resolve many obstacles than were
projects without that advantage ($r = .52$, $p < .01$). Table 14.5 demonstrates that better working relationships were especially important in
the resolution of people-oriented obstacles, such as problems with lack
of commitment from top administration ($r = .75$) and turf issues among
different partners ($r = .36$). In addition, good working relationships
seemed to help collaboratives resolve problems with county and local
policies, such as rigid school district regulations and conflicting policies across county agencies ($r = .66$). Citing the importance of good
working relationships, the coordinator of the Smalltown collaborative
stated that, because of such high levels of trust and shared ownership
of the program, he could go to partners for help and get immediate

TABLE 14.5
Correlations between Indicators of Success

Indicator of Success	Working Relationships	State/ Federal Policy	Local Policy	Resolution of Obstacles			
				Lack of Buy in From Top	Barriers to Information Sharing	Turf Issues	Conflicting Group Cultures
Working relationships	1.0						
Resolution of obstacles:							
State/federal policy	.02	1.0					
Local policy	.66**	.53*	1.0				
Lack of buy in from top administrators	.75*	.66	.71+	1.0			
Barriers to information sharing	.09	-.05	.37	.95**	1.0		
Turf issues	.36*	.51*	.51*	.66	.28	1.0	
Conflicting group cultures	.22	.02	.19	.78+	.58**	.47*	1.0

+ $p < .10$.
* $p < .05$.
** $p < .01$.

attention and resources toward solving problematic issues. He had observed other collaboratives that did not have the luxury of good working relationships struggle with partners who failed to follow through on commitments and who were absent when it came to resolving collaborative difficulties.

Concerning the resolution of obstacles to collaboration, we found that some were connected to one another. For example, collaboratives that better resolved their federal and state policy problems were more likely to report more fully resolving the obstacle of county and local policies ($r = .53$) and turf issues among agencies ($r = .51$). Similarly, the resolution of people-oriented problems such as turf issues among agencies and conflicting professional cultures were related ($r = .47$).

Another set of problems that affected many collaboratives were barriers to information sharing about clients (present in about three-fourths of collaboratives). Resolution of this problem appears to be heavily tied to resolving both within-agency and across-agency people-oriented problems. Specifically, resolving barriers to information sharing was tied to increasing buy in from top administrators ($r = .95$) and reducing conflict between professional cultures of different involved agencies ($r = .58$).

These findings demonstrate that, as we expected, working relationships were strongly related to the ability to resolve collaborative obstacles. Furthermore, successful resolution of some obstacles appeared to be tied to the resolution of others.

DISCUSSION

Our descriptive analyses revealed that collaboratives for school-linked services come in many different shapes, sizes, and ways of operating, from small informal groups to large formal ones, from groups involving mostly schools and public agencies to those involving mostly private and nonprofit community agencies, from those with authoritarian leadership to those with democratic leadership, and from groups whose members communicate daily to groups whose members go several weeks without talking to each other.

In addition to describing collaboratives for school-linked services, we tested hypotheses about the factors that would lead to more successful collaboration. Using parts of our four research questions to organize our comments, we summarize below what we learned about the relationships between collaborative characteristics and collaborative success.

How is the organizational and political context of collaboration related to collaborative success? We found that the context of inter-organizational relations was not generally related to working relationships among partners, but several contextual factors were related to the ease with which collaboratives were able to resolve obstacles. We found that stronger representation by public agencies was related to the easier resolution of policy issues such as restrictive client eligibility requirements and reporting requirements. Also providing some support for our hypothesis, we found that a longer history of working together was related to the easier resolution of problems with conflicting professional norms, but a longer history was also related to more difficulty in resolving local policy obstacles. We believe that the latter finding may mean that collaboratives with a longer history face more severe challenges with local policies than collaboratives that are at the beginning phase of their work together and that this finding does not reflect poor problem-solving abilities of older collaboratives.

We were surprised that the amount of support for the program was not related to collaborative success. This may be due to insufficient variation on our measures of political support, since perceptions of support from various groups were generally quite high across all programs. Alternatively, measuring collaborative members' perceptions of the level of political support may not have been a good indicator of the political climate in which collaboration occurs. Thus, methodological factors may explain why this hypothesis was not supported.

How is the structure of interorganizational relations related to collaborative success? The level of formality was not related to working relationships or to the resolution of obstacles, suggesting that formality is not a factor that facilitates or inhibits collaborative success; however, our analyses provided some support for our hypothesis that the level of shared authority is an important factor determining collaborative success. We found that greater shared authority was related to better working relationships, as we had expected; however, information from our qualitative interviews cast doubt on the direction of our hypothesized relationship. Although we did not purport to test the causality of this relationship in this study, we had believed that more shared authority led to better working relationships. We now believe that this relationship may be reciprocal—that shared authority yields better working relationships, but that better working relationships also lead to the willingness of collaborative members to have authority shared across members. What is clear from our research is that these factors are strongly associated with each other.

With regard to the resolution of obstacles, our findings demonstrated that collaboratives with dispersed authority were much more likely to resolve problems with buy in among collaborative members, a finding that supports our hypothesis; however, shared authority was related to more difficulty in resolving state and federal policy issues, a finding that contradicts our hypothesis. From the latter finding, we conclude that problems that originate outside the collaborative, that is, those that come from the state or federal policy level, are more easily resolved when one organization is responsible for running the collaborative and its program. Thus, democratic forms of leadership may help organizations become committed to the collaborative's objectives and may improve working relationships, but the democratic process seems to get in the way of solving at least some policy obstacles.

How are collaboratives' efforts to increase and enhance connections between member organizations associated with collaborative success? Contrary to our hypotheses, these efforts were generally not associated with our measures of collaborative success. The exception was the positive relationship between the amount of formal interorganizational communication and working relationships. We did not find support for our hypothesis that collaboratives' efforts to improve connections through capacity-building exercises would contribute to collaborative success. Based on our qualitative findings, we conclude that because our measures of capacity-building exercises did not capture the intensity or quality of these activities, we did not sufficiently test this hypothesis.

How are indicators of collaborative success interrelated? The findings supported our hypothesis that good working relationships among partners contributed to the ability to resolve problems, including problems with a lack of commitment from top administrators, turf battles, and local policy issues. Furthermore, the resolution of some obstacles, such as barriers to information sharing, was related to the resolution of others such as problems with obtaining buy in from top administrators and conflicting professional cultures.

The fact that several of our hypothesized relationships between collaborative characteristics and indicators of success were not supported empirically suggests that many different types of collaboratives can enjoy success. This research demonstrates that success can be achieved by both large and small and old and new collaboratives, collaboratives with various types of members, those with formal structures and those with informal structures, and collaboratives with various levels of interorganizational communications.

Nonetheless, our findings suggest that certain characteristics contribute to effective collaboration. For example, factors associated with better working relationships include high levels of support from families, shared authority for the project, and frequent interorganizational communications. Characteristics associated with the resolution of policy issues, such as requirements attached to categorical funding and other regulations of state and local programs, include shared authority and high concentrations of public agencies as collaborative members. Similarly, the successful resolution of barriers to sharing information about service consumers appears to be tied to high levels of support from front-line staff involved in service delivery and a high concentration of schools and other educational organizations represented on the collaborative, while having shared authority appeared to contribute to resolving problems due to lack of buy in from top administrators. Finally, good working relationships among collaborative members appeared to be an important factor in the resolution of several collaborative obstacles.

The three collaboratives that we highlighted in this chapter illustrate the differences in collaborative outcomes for different types of collaboratives. The most successful collaborative, in terms of working relationships and the resolution of obstacles, was the Smalltown Family Resource Center, which had high levels of political support for the program, democratic leadership, and high rates of interorganizational communication. The least successful collaborative, the County Services Collaborative, with its relatively poor working relationships and inability to resolve some obstacles, had relatively low levels of political support, authoritarian leadership, and very low levels of interorganizational communications. The one advantage this collaborative had was a high concentration of public agencies, which appeared to have paid off in the resolution of local and state policy obstacles. The third example, the Family and Adolescent Services Collaborative, was partially successful with relatively good working relationships and some obstacles partially resolved; this collaborative was in between the other two programs in terms of the level of shared authority, political support for the program, and amount of interorganizational communications.

Collaborative members at all three of these programs agreed that good working relationships and smooth functioning at the collaborative level were critical to effective operations at the service delivery level. For example, one collaborative reported having to wait until an agency director retired before they could get services from one public program because relations with this person were so bad. Consequently, these particular services were not available to consumers of the program for school-linked services. Furthermore, according to collaborative members, when the collaborative functions well, service providers can cut through the red tape that often accompanies service provision. Thus, although we have looked only at success at the collaborative level, we believe that success at this level will ultimately affect the quality of services provided to consumers.

With this research, we have shown how schools and community agencies come together to provide school-linked services to children and families. Our bivariate analyses have identified factors related to several measures of collaborative success; however, this research does not answer every question about how to develop successful collaboratives for school-linked services. For example, we were not able to look at the independent effect of each collaborative characteristic on indicators of collaborative success; consequently, we do not know if one factor is more important than another in explaining collaborative success. We hope that research and policy attention continues to focus on how interorganizational collaboration for school-linked services works, so that researchers, practitioners, and policy makers can learn from the experiences of those who have put this reform movement into practice.

NOTES

1. SRI International is evaluating the Healthy Start initiative under contract to the California State Department of Education and the Foundation Consortium for School-Linked Services. The 3-year evaluation examines the collaborative processes at the state, county, and local levels, their impacts on participants and service delivery, and the outcomes of school-linked services for children, families, schools, and communities.

2. See, for example, Shaver and Newman (1994) and Smrekar (1994).

3. Pseudonyms are used to represent actual programs.

REFERENCES

Aiken, M., and R. Alford. (1970). Community structure and innovation. *American Sociological Review*, 35:650–665.

Honig, B. (1992). *SB 620/Healthy Start grant application materials*. Sacramento, Calif.: California State Department of Education.

Marrett, C. B. (1971). On the specification of inter-organizational relations. *Sociology and Social Research* 56:83–99.

Mattessich, P. W., and B. R. Monsey. (1992). *Collaboration: What makes it work. A review of research literature on factors influencing successful collaboration.* St. Paul, Minn.: Amherst H. Wilder Foundation.

Melaville, A. I., and M. J. Blank (1991). *What it takes: Structuring interagency partnerships to connect children and families with comprehensive services.* Washington, D.C.: Education and Human Services Consortium.

Mulford, C. L. (1984). *Interorganizational relations.* New York: Human Sciences Press.

Olsen, M. E. (1978). *The process of social organization.* New York: Holt, Rinehart, and Winston.

Pfeffer, J., and G. R. Salancik. (1978). *The external control of organizations.* New York: Harper & Row.

Scott, W. R. (1987). *Organizations: Rational, natural, and open systems.* Englewood Cliffs, N.J.: Prentice-Hall.

Shaver, D., and L. Newman. (April 1994). *The role of families in school-linked services.* Paper presented at the annual conference of the American Educational Research Association, New Orleans, La.

Smrekar, C. (1994). The missing link in school-linked social service programs. *Educational Evaluation and Policy Analysis* 16(4).

Thompson, J. D. (1967). *Organizations in action.* New York: McGraw-Hill.

Van de Ven, A. H., and G. Walker. (1984). The dynamics of interorganizational coordination. *Administrative Science Quarterly* 29:598–621.

Chapter 15

Beyond Consensus: Mapping Divergent Views of Systems and Power in Collaboratives

Maureen W. McClure
Bruce A. Jones
Eugenie Potter

INTRODUCTION

No Consensus? Need Maps to Find Each Other

Without shared understandings about how authority and legitimacy is distributed, how formal and informal incentives and sanctions are assigned, and how success or failure should be identified and evaluated, people with shared intentions may find it difficult to "hear," translate, and "speak" each others' "languages," let alone create a working consensus (Bickel and Hattrup 1991–92; Hattrup and Bickel 1993).[1] Within institutions, work practices many develop into cultural frameworks which help people focus their attention, resources and moral judgment. Collaborative members may simply accept these frameworks without reflection, because they "work."[2] Across institutions, however, work practices can conflict, so collaborative members who cannot show others "where they are," may unknowingly talk past their clients, their supporters, and each other.[3]

"Collaboration" usually connotes teamwork, mutual goals, a shared world view, and a willingness to labor together towards an agreed-upon end. What happens, however, when any or most of these critical elements are missing? For example, what if the goals are neither clear nor equally beneficial? What if the stakeholders have world views and interests that cannot be fixed by programs or techniques? Can a collaborative effort succeed to the levels anticipated when the work began?

One Foundation, Two Frameworks

We originally intended for two frameworks to be structured along classic adversarial lines, under the assumption that truth would emerge from mutual challenges. Eugenie Potter offered a more compelling argument that we needed to formally recognize that we stood on common ground. Thus we began by acknowledging that we were constructing two different ways of approaching the foundational question of "doing good." We called it a moral space onto which we would map our diverging views.

We also debated what it meant to use multiple frameworks. As expected, we could not reach a consensus. Maureen McClure saw them as aesthetic practices with public consequences.[4] Potter thought of them as philosophical traditions to be learned and appreciated. Bruce Jones thought of them as approaches to evaluation. We did agree that it was useful to try to see if, by working together, we could learn more than we might by working alone. We explored two claims: one that based collaborative policies on the efficiencies of systems, the other on the conflicted alliances of people. McClure and Potter collaborated on the introduction and conclusion. The original Jones report was summarized without altering its language. McClure then added her critique. Jones then responded to the critiques by McClure. Readers are invited to see how two well-meaning scholars used the same information to reach quite different conclusions. We used reporting styles that tried to give the reader direct access to our language by limiting our use of quotations by other scholars. Our conclusions reflected an acknowledgment that our own collaboration using dissensus practices was far more difficult than we had imagined because we had to construct translatable language just to speak to each other. In the process we discovered that, in this one case, even the best intentions did not render a collaborative effort simple or the underlying assumptions clear and unproblematic.

Potter's foundation: doing good as the basic problem. There is a common phenomenon that social scientists of all types, as well as philosophers and theologians, have long struggled with: Why do people do good? Why do people want to do good? What constitutes "doing good"? Robert Bellah (1992) says that we live through institutions. However, morality as such does not—indeed cannot—reside in institutions; morality resides in and is expressed by individuals. Individuals who engage in moral efforts may believe they act from shared values, beliefs, and understandings, so they do not take the time to identify, reflect on, or disclose their own fundamental assumptions. Important conflicts may thus be masked, weakening both systems and alliances. The participants in the dropout prevention collaborative in this study may have believed they were there to do good, but their goodness may not have a unified interpretation. Jones used a structuralist framework to argue that the collaborative produced a number of "good" outcomes. He assumed that systems have quality which require inspection and adjustment. McClure used a critical framework to argue that the collaborative lacked moral credibility because they did not acknowledge their own conflicts of interest. She assumed that personal not community interests shaped, perhaps determined, collaborative work practices.

Our participation in a collaborative form of inquiry led us to rethink issues of autonomy and community. On the one hand, each of us had a scholarly duty to be forthright in our analyses (and be willing to subject our work to each other's scrutiny), and, on the other, we accepted an ethical duty of "no harm" to support the efforts of our colleagues in such a way that they were enhanced, not diminished. This latter responsibility derives from a commitment to the idea expressed by Walter Lippman: "We are in truth members of one another, and a philosophy which seeks to differentiate the community from the persons who belong to it, treating them as if they were distinct sovereignties having only diplomatic relations, is contrary to fact and can only lead to moral bewilderment" (Lippman [1937] quoted in Bellah 1992, 280). Perhaps this can be as good a starting place as any—and better than most—for any kind of collaborative effort, whether among colleagues or members of a more extended community.

We chose the Crawford City project because it tackled complex community issues that required cooperation across agencies, races, and classes. We assumed that all those engaged in the Crawford City Collaborative (CCC) brought with them their own interpretations of how they meant to do good for children who might drop out of school. We now turn to two analysts who, like many of today's scholars, so deeply assumed they were doing good, that they had no need to formally reflect on the issues of their goodness with readers.

Framework one: summary of Jones' original report using a systems' approach. Crawford City was a grantee of the Traveler Foundation Dropout Prevention Urban Collaborative Program. A team of researchers, of which Jones was a member, served as documenters of he program for three years. "Crawford City" is, of course, a pseudonym, as is "Traveler" for the funding foundation. Located in the southeast, Crawford City had a population of 285,720, according to the 1990 census. In 1987, the per capita income was $12,536. The median household income was $24,695. Approximately 43.6 percent of the residents were African American, while approximately 55.3 percent were White (Barlow and Wassermann, 1992). A major university and the government were the two major sectors that provided employment. This fact left a significant portion of the population unemployed because it lacked the skills to work in either sector. Small businesses were the third leading sector to provide employment; however, these jobs generally provided minimum wages.

An estimated 32,528 students were enrolled in the school system. The largest cluster of students (9,174) was enrolled at the elementary level. The average student dropout rate of the city was 3.1 percent, which was slightly lower than the state average of 3.2 percent. As of 1991, the percent of students enrolled classified as non-White was 74.9 percent. Fifty-three percent of the total school enrollment was eligible for the free or reduced price lunch program (Barlow and Wassermann 1992). The numbers revealed a difficult problem: few jobs, high dropout rates. The city appeared to the Traveler Foundation to be a good candidate for a collaborative effort created by business and educational leaders.

Over the past decade, thousands of education-related collaborative ventures have sprung up across the nation. The Crawford City project was not atypical. The growth and development of these ventures is well recorded by Shirley Hord (1986), Ann Lieberman (1986), Byrd Jones and Robert Maloy (1988), S. Otterbourg and D. Adams (1989), the U.S. Department of Education (1989), and Bruce Jones (1989; 1991; 1992; 1993a; 1993b). A common belief today is that the many student needs in our urban centers can be appropriately addressed only by joining the limited human, fiscal, and material resources of institutions in the community that interface with students.

Collaboration has thus come to mean multiple institutional alliances (e.g., schools, universities, businesses, religious groups, social services agencies, and parent and student constituencies) coming together to address common educational concerns. What motivates institutions to become involved with a collaborative initiative? How does this involvement diminish or sustain itself? What policies emerge from a collaborative that is dependent upon multiple institutional involvement? How should they be documented and evaluated?

Documentation, according to Clark (1991; et al. 1989), is a mechanism for systematically capturing the events which facilitate and or hinder the accomplishments of major educational innovations. The focus of documentation is typically on process implementation and the effectiveness of those processes. The primary goal of documenting the Traveler program was to provide a record of the planning and implementation process. Additionally, documentation was to assist the Foundation and grantees to shape the program as it evolved. Site visits to each city occurred at least one time each month. Prior to the visitations, documenters established interview schedules with approximately five to twenty collaborative members. Each interview ranged between thirty and sixty minutes. During this period, documenters observed collaborative steering committee meetings, collaborative executive and public sessions, and collaborative-related activities and events for children and parents.

Interview, observation, and event information logs were used by the documenters as a guide for all interviews and observation recordings in each city. The interview logs contained structured and open-ended questions that focused on obtaining information relevant to the broad goals and objectives for collaboration. These goals and objectives were established by the Travelers Foundation and each city. In this way, the primary data collected under the rubric of the documentation strategy was collected in a consistent manner by all documenters. The study is largely limited to a study of the collaborative process, as opposed to outcomes relative to student achievement and attendance. This limitation coincides with the definition of documentation—which focuses on process.

The basic conceptual framework for the Crawford City evaluation draws on David Easton's (1965) systems analysis of process through a "dynamic response model." With this model, a series of institutional demands and supports is directed toward a particular political entity. These demands and supports influence the political entity as it develops policies and programs around a particular issue. Once inside of the political entity, the demands are converted. This conversion leads to the formation of policy outputs. Reactions to the outputs occur from institutions (e.g., interests groups) that are housed in the outer environment. These reactions are funneled in a circular fashion along a feedback loop to the demand element.

The political entity evaluated was the collaborative organization. It housed the goals and objectives of the community's collaborative efforts. (See Figure 1.) The first source of institutional demands and supports is referred to as the "external funding source," that is, the Traveler Foundation, which provided the principal funding support for the collaborative and stipulated conditions for continued funding. The second source of demands and supports was local. This "local institutional impact" included schools, businesses, and community-based and religious groups. In this case, the local institutional impact on collaboration fluctuated according to three levels of institutional involvement: primary, intermediary, and peripheral.

Local institutions involved at the primary level were institutions serving in collaborative executive roles. These institutions were a part of the decision-making "inner circle." The intermediary level included involvement by those institutions that served on steering committees not involved with the decision making of the inner circle. They were, however, frequently consulted with and solicited for general advice on setting general directions. The peripheral level included those institutions that helped facilitate collaborative activities by supplying data but did not serve directly on the executive or steering committees. Institutions in the outer environment were not involved with the collaborative at any level (directly or indirectly). Throughout each phase of the project, levels of institutional involvement changed as they jumped in and out of the collaborative process. This jumping in and out was affected by whether or not the collaborative process was viewed with legitimacy from the standpoint of the community and whether or not institutions stood to gain something by involvement. Moreover, fluctuating levels of involvement were affected by the leadership needs of the CCC and the perceived types of institutional involvement that would maximize financial and community support.

The school and university sectors were perfectly matched for the tasks of the exploratory phase of the collaborative process. The school system housed student achievement data. The university possessed data analysis tasks. The dean of the school of education chaired the steering committee. At the planning phase, the Parent Teachers Association (PTA) and business communities were brought onto the steering committees. This movement was deliberate and strategic. The dean believed "there is recognition that down-the-road the CCC will need the business community to spearhead the implementation of the dropout plan. Therefore, they must be solicited now." The parents, she reported, "will be critical to planned student at-risk intervention strategies." (Jones, 1993, p. 21)

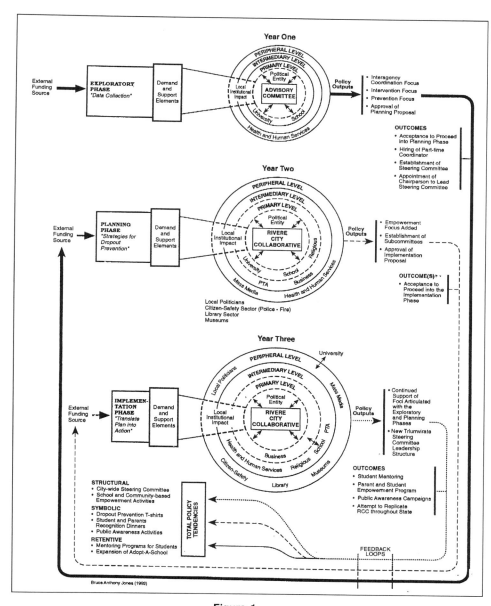

Bruce Anthony Jones (1993)

Figure 1
THE "FLUID" NATURE OF THE RIVERE CITY COLLABORATIVE (RCC)
Levels of Institutional Impact and Policy Tendencies
CENTRAL ISSUE: THE DROPOUT CRISIS

By year three of the implementation phase, the business community dominated the center, while all other institutions moved toward
the periphery. What contributed to these shifts?

Several members of the CCC steering committee recognized the
importance of the role of business and the need for the school, according to one steering committee member, to "take a backseat," during
implementation (Jones, 1993, p. 21). According to a member of the
Chamber of Commerce, when the school board voluntarily integrated
the school system, its credibility in the eyes of the community at large
diminished. The controversy became so intense that: (a) the business
community pulled out support for the public schools; (b) the schools
received negative media coverage ("there is nothing that the school can
do right"); (c) real estate agents directed Whites out of the areas where
the public schools are housed; and (d) the school system received mixed
audit reports. According to the interviewee, with this history, the CCC
was well aware that it was "fine and necessary" for the school sector to
take the lead in the earlier phases of planning (Jones, 1993, p. 23). The
implementation phase, however, would entail selling the plan to the
entire community. The key seller, he reported, "must have credibility in
the community. The school system does not have credibility. The business community has credibility." (Jones, 1993, p. 23)

The integration issue described above serves as an example of
how a set of unique political idiosyncrasies of the local setting can
have an impact on the process of implementing collaborative strategies. The positive perception of the business community is deeply
rooted in this issue. According to one interviewee, the business community was responsible for resolving a substantial amount of the community conflict that surrounded integration. In the early years, it
established an organization to deal specifically with the conflict.

Toward the end of CCC dropout prevention study, the school sector was brought back into the collaborative in a symbolic way. The
superintendent was named one of the three cochairs of the CCC steering committee. He never, however, attended meetings or participated
in the activities. The business cochair truly directed the fate of the
CCC.

The evaluation established that a number of positive outcomes
occurred. These included: (a) the establishment of a program for
empowering parents; (b) the establishment of five Youth-Speakouts
for the purposes of empowering students; (c) the expansion of a
mentoring program to develop student leadership skills, jobs, and
employment marketability; (d) the development of a massive public

awareness campaign around issues of dropout prevention; and (e) the initial effort to replicate the CCC as a model for collaboration throughout the state.

In closing, basic questions remain. How can collaboration help stakeholders' groups learn about each other? How can institutions overcome organizational differences in order to work together on critical issues? Some CCC institutions had prior experience working together. Some of these experiences, unfortunately, were negative. Given deep historical divisions, how can collaboration lead to mutual understandings across groups of individuals divided by race, social class, gender, and ethnicity? Finally, what specific policies emerge from comprehensive urban collaboration? Does collaboration lead to symbolic and/or structural change? Each of these represents questions for further study as collaboration continues to grow as an important mechanism for policy strategies and urban community change.

Framework two: McClure's critique. This critique of text builds on earlier work that examined the usefulness of multiple perspectives (Capper 1993; McClure 1990, 1994; Merchant 1993). Working from a postmodern economic framework, I drew on both critical and poststructural approaches. Critical theory was used to focus on conflict and community power relationships (Blaug 1987; DeYoung 1989; Foster 1987; Giroux 1983; Klees 1986, 1990) within a context of aesthetic practice (Tillich 1963; Van Reijen 1992) for the common good (Bryson & Crosby 1992). Poststructural theory was used to analyze this conflict in terms of language use (Brown 1992; McCloskey 1985). I analyzed Jones' text to map assumptions, framing metaphors and omissions (Foucault 1988; Gottlieb 1987; Mathew 1995; Paulston 1990).

I assumed economic relationships had a substantive, but invisible, impact on discourse and behavior; and I predicted that members of the business community would rationally pursue their economic and cultural self-interest by controlling the framing of the problem, turning it over to public sector professionals to fix and then rushing back in to take credit for it. By framing the poor as a problem to be fixed by expert techniques, leaders did not have to face the unsettling possibility that dropouts were rational actors, investing efficiently in education for a part-time, minimum wage work world with no health-care benefits. The experts had no reason to challenge a framework that created relationships of dependency and profitable control. I assumed that some businessmen were making good money by paying minimum wages, and they would not want those revenue streams threatened either by public scrutiny or by a pool of better-educated workers. I also assumed these issues would be frozen in profitable silence because leaders had no incentives to face them and sources of dissent had been crushed by discredit. Is it a coincidence that integration brought with it White flight, media disconfirmation and bad audits? The businessmen and the White community pull out the resource rug, blame the district for failing without resources, and then demand control to ensure legitimacy. Cheeky, perhaps. But the far more troubling issue is that no one seems to notice the effective "blame the victim" strategy. This is not a Southern problem. It is an American problem.

A man may want to do good by improving education for the poor, but his piety may conflict with another, equally valid view of the poor as his own children's future competitors.[5] This is a dilemma that few will face publicly. Indeed, community leaders may generously reward professionals who avoid broaching this terrible reality. Who benefits from a collusion of silence about the direct or indirect benefits community leaders might have received from preserving low wage scales, few benefits, and high unemployment rates? Might not employers ensure loyalty and profits by offering protection to relatively uneducated workers who are afraid of a labor surplus?

As long as the community leaders control not only the sources for economic legitimacy but those for social legitimacy as well, they may be unlikely to publicly face embarrassing questions about how their wealth was accumulated or is sustained. Many company towns juxtaposed divide-and-conquer intimidation of labor against highly visible, benevolent, awe-inspiring generosity, thus fostering both economic and cultural dependence. Today, the mills and mines are gone, and some of these towns lack a cultural capacity for resilience (Serrin 1993). Does Crawford City fit this pattern to some extent?

We shall never know. There are, however, indications that affirm this metaphor. The very use of the term *dropout prevention* labels it as a tactic to fix poor people, not help neighbors. The CCC stumbled about, defined the problem and then hired an expert to help fix it. This may appear to be a natural, efficient solution to an ordinary organizational problem, but it created dependent power relationships in every direction. It shut off upward channels of communication to businessmen because experts are still only employees to those who control their wages. It shut off channels outward into the community because experts have priviledged positions and are not necessarily good neighbors. The simple act of organization probably reproduced a hierarchy of conversations among those who were in charge, those who were in service, and those who were being helped. Peer relationships were left outside the formal structure. Without the legitimizing force of peers, however, the language of those in service to those in charge may have foreclosed the raising of potentially embarrassing moral questions or issues (Duignan and Macpherson 1993).

The traditional language of those in service is conveniently objective, which to me means that the user prefers to turn into an object rather than face Machiavelli's painful moral contradictions of power in practice. By vesting quality in systems not moral relationships, the metaphor eliminates cultural conflict through oxymorons and anthropomorphisms. For example, systems lack volition, and they don't initiate institutional alliances, involvement or motivation. This systems anthropomorphism conveniently forecloses consideration of other relationships of power, such as cronyism, by connecting the leadership solely to the legitimacy of the organization, rendering all other relationships invisible. Leaders and systems become substitutes for each other, and all other volition is suppressed in the assumption that the person in charge can speak with a single voice that perfectly represents all those in service or being helped.

Jones' metaphors and language of systems quality used oxymorons, which, though not intended, conveniently resolved the internal contradictions created by the community leaders' needs to be seen in public as dispensing benevolent legitmacy, but ensuring dominance in private. How could someone use a systems language and not see these dilemmas? First, his language associated leaders with their institutions, thus foreclosing discourses about the impact of other political and social relationships such as race, socio-economic status (SES), or personal dominance. It encapsulated thinking, which "keeps people from making meaningful connections to the real world" (Noreen Garman 1994, pp. 43–49). Second, the collaborative appeared to interpret legitimacy as sustained, reliable access to social acceptance, not valid proximity to student experience, substantive achievement, or community economic and social development. Potential conflicts of interest created by personal, cultural, or community interests in legitimacy and access were assumed away. Jones merely used the language he was taught. It is so encapsulating, and it can be passed on intact from teacher to pupil without reflection on its use.

Questions of extrainstitutional power relationships were thus masked by systems thinking in the evaluation. We do not know who is related to whom. We do not know their political affiliation, what exclusive schools they want their children to attend, what clubs give them exclusive access to legitimacy and resources, which neighborhood housing values they want to protect, where their money is invested, and what they have to lose if the collaborative succeeds. Should such scrutiny be mandated? No. But the burden of power is public accountability for it. Systems thinkers bear no responsibility for these omissions, since their sight is defined by systems' territorial boundaries and not by concerns for public accountability. Finally, these utilitarian views of mechanistic systems contrast sharply with N. Garman's emphasis on moral alliances of people:

> "Collaboration" describes the nature of the involvement between or among the people working in an educational alliance. An "educational alliance" includes at least four [sic] levels of involvement: nonworking involvement; working involvement; working-acceptance involvement; involvement with genuine participation; and involvement with organic participation. . . . These, too, are characteristics of supervision as the moral scenario presented. (1982, 42)

Without description of collaborative participants, their agendas, and their personal, political, and cultural interrelationships, systems thinkers must assume that the road to Crawford City's success was paved with good intentions on the part of all parties. Jones' census data, documents, and interviews with leaders do not address what might be the collaborative's most serious threat: How would a larger cadre of well-educated poor people threaten the community's existing economic and social relationships? How might the threatened respond? The business community is presented as THE legitimating group, and its social acceptance became the surrogate for substantive performance. I must assume that social acceptance by local businessmen was an inadequate measure of improvement in poor people's returns to their educational investments.

Legitimacy, not authenticity or strategic competence, appeared to drive access to this collaborative. There was no serious representation from community groups, which might have been close to the dropout experience, but not part of the established community. The documentation does not show that dissidents were sought out for interviews. Community leaders may have had all the best intentions to help the poor people, but they could not see how they protected their interests by treating poor people like dependent patients in need of technical care instead of rational investors in need of more just options. The bitter reality in many communities is that students who finish high school find no better opportunities than those who do not (Gillette 1991). Dropping out can be an economically rational choice because it simply makes more hours available for working in a dead-end job. What does it say about a conservative community and its liberal funders that no one noticed they had framed poor Black people as problems to be fixed by nice White people?

The Crawford City study makes a useful comparison because it was well designed from a systems perspective. The evaluation process was formative, embedded right into the planning and implementation processes. This allowed the systems ongoing feedback from outside observers, which, in the past was often not available until after the process has been completed. Its structure allowed the outside evaluators to observe the extent to which each of the communities in the study was complying with the general constraints designed by the foundation. I do not critique the methodology, I merely reject its framing premises. The foundation treated the collaborative like a charity, as something that helped the poor. Charities too often divide communities into patrons who feel purposive by naming problems, program experts who feel competent in solving them, and dependents who are supposed to be grateful for the help. Charitable thinking rarely frames the poor as peers or neighbors investing in sustaining their communities. No one mapped the impact of alternative dropout policies on the region's economic assets and relationships, yet regional workforce quality lay at the core of the effort. There appeared to be little sense of economic purpose beyond institutional self-interest, as though institutional good were a perfect substitute for community economic development. Institutions seemed to sell programs as educational talismans, inherently good commodities, which, if acquired, would attract good jobs. Education is not a religious relic or an indulgence for purchase; it is our mutual investment in safe, creative futures. It is to this world of interdependent investment and compassionate self-governance that I now turn.

What then might an evaluation look like from a critical perspective? It would ask questions such as, What were the consequences of the collaborative's efforts for the community's primary economic and social structures? It would be unwise to judge silence as moral failing without giving leaders a fair hearing. It would be important to know how participants saw themselves as moral actors trying to do good. I would have first asked them to reflect on their efforts and to map their community's interdependent economic and social relationships. Second, I would have asked people to juxtapose their maps with others, looking for the common moral ground. Third, I would have asked them to consider the effects of language that reframed patrons, experts, and the poor as regional peers, neighbors, and fellow investors in a sustainable quality of life. Fourth, I would have asked for a public accounting of their priority-setting and decision-making rules. Finally, I would have asked for demonstrations of how they tested the validity of their claims and actions.

I would have used the following techniques to map a mapless world: (a) inventories of economic and social assets and liabilities; (b) maps of regional economic and social assets and relationships; (c) descriptions of how decision makers view their expectations, attributions, and choices as rational; (d) story finding about how the community really gets things done; (e) documentation of participants' predictions of policy consequences for those directly or indirectly involved, with specific regard for flows of resources; and (f) creative expressions by constituents that convey what it really means to be themselves, how they view their relationships with the community, and how they frame their own issues. These documents would then serve to guide the collaborative's map making as its members charted the impact of reform on existing structures and relationships. This complex and contradictory information could be available to constituents who want to learn to enter the experience of others in order to assess the potential for long-term alliances across a community deeply divided by race and class. This process would not be done once; it would be updated regularly. The foundations would be invited to be active partners at the community-building table and not left in the shadowy background of charitable patrons represented by outside observers.

Finally, collaboratives, like other areas of the economy are too complex to be thought of as mechanisms to fix things, efficiently planned for and guided by the benevolent hands of charitable patrons. Collaboratives may be better construed as investments in our unique, colorful, creative marketplace communities teeming with struggles for territory and glory, often splendidly constructed to appear as confident as destiny—normal and legitimate. As in all investments, caveat emptor.

Jones' Response to McClure's Critique. McClure draws attention to a critical gap in the literature on collaboration and how it is practiced. The Crawford City study was only one of several that I have documented, but many of the same issues arise elsewhere. In support of

McClure's earlier statements, I have observed that the emphasis is to avoid conflict and push toward consensus. Despite the fact that there are often diverse constituencies involved with these collaboratives, issues of race, gender, class, and integrally related social, political, and economic inequities are seldom discussed. These issues may surface privately or in brief public outbursts; however, they are rarely discussed systematically in terms of the implications for human relations and policy development.

The long-term survival and credibility of collaboration as a way to bring about structural change in education rests on addressing these issues. Potter and McClure rightly point out the need to emphasize and understand the human relations and moral dimensions of collaboration. This means academicians, practitioners, and policy makers need to understand the human, as well as the technical, dimensions of collaboration.

From a conceptual standpoint, micropolitical theory (Blase 1989) supports the analytical group approaches suggested by McClure. This theory allows for developing an understanding of the importance of individual roles, past histories and motivations for becoming involved with collaboration. The theory also allows for an understanding of institutional traits from a historic standpoint that might affect current human relations. In this regard, McClure's critique leaves out the possibility that an institution may develop these traits independent of the individuals who inhabit the institution at a particular time. These institutional traits may be grounded in past actions by individuals who are dead and gone. Regardless, these traits may affect current collaborative practices and require understanding.

What We Learned From Each Other. This chapter used a collaborative approach to frame an evaluation of an urban collaborative on dropout prevention in a Southeastern city. We examined, compared, and learned from two distinct collaboratives—the text describing and evaluating the project, and our own process of coauthorship. We became caught up in our unanticipated interactions as members of our own scholarly collaborative. What began as a relatively straightforward attempt to apply new ideas in multiple perspectives and conceptual geography (Capper 1993; Paulston 1990, 1994a, 1994b), turned into a Sisyphean struggle to create language. We anticipated differences in ideas but assumed it would not be difficult to create ordinary language for reporting. We tried to avoid the precise, but often arcane, language of philosophical and critical scholarship; yet, when we tried to translate our ideas into a common, ordinary language that could be understood by a broader audience in educational administration, we found we had distinct languages. In other words, we found in ourselves the same conflicts of meaning and purpose we found in the collaborative we studied.

We learned that the melting pot notion of a single voice in the authorship of policy analysis and evaluation, while useful, had limits. Once we relaxed our traditional scholarly assumptions of a unified, collective consensus of identity in writing, however, we discovered that our training in different fields, our ideologies, and our temperaments contributed to distinctive, but incommensurable, voices. We also found that we could not distill this complexity into a consensus that assumed a common language based on common beliefs and experience. To write this chapter, we had to design a different, divergent approach to creating our text.

In the course of our efforts to frame and respond to our own differences, we also realized that our efforts placed us in a different relationship with readers. It became our responsibility, not to guide readers towards solutions proposed through a collective identity, but rather to converse with those who are also struggling with their own sense making and expectation mapping. We spoke separately as objective scientists revealing our truth, and as impassioned advocates teaching our truth, but together as scholarly artists and cartographers (Paulston 1990; Borradori 1994, 1–25), creating and sharing our interpretations of the world as best we could while remaining rivals.

As artists we were obligated to design a conceptual space large enough to situate the juxtaposition of differing viewpoints. We agreed with Colleen Capper (1993) and William Foster (1986) that both policy analysis and evaluation can be enriched by multiple perspectives. We had to admit, however, that, in many respects, our separate perspectives could only give us small understandings, and adding the images together could not determine clearer solutions. Our hope lay in our moral choices to affirm creative tolerance for each other's struggles for new meanings and understandings (Sergiovanni 1992).

In our own collaboration, we learned that we needed translatable language to nurture and sustain our alliances. At the outset we lacked the language we needed to work together. We had no map. We thought at first we would define ourselves in opposition to each other, but our positions were not comparable. Potter then created the foundational moral space for doing good so McClure and Jones could map frameworks relative to it. It was a long and tedious struggle to create shared meaning. Jones' systems perspective was based on evaluation theories and professional concerns for objectivity and rational obligation, which suppressed the subject so the systems could operate efficiently. McClure's critical perspective, based on economic and sociological theories of volitional power relationships, focused on the conflicts that arise in social hierarchies. Her professional concerns centered on meaningful participation in a community. The systems language generated from Jones' perspective was incommensurable with McClure's language of volitional struggles for autonomy, meaningful self-governance, and fair labor markets. In other words, from a systems' view, critical language appeared to be personal, not professional, whereas, from a critical view, systems language appeared to be instrumental, not moral. Both have strong academic, linguistic traditions rooted in moral philosophies (Kreisberg 1992; Potter 1988; Rader 1976). By focusing on the common ground of our desires to do good, we were able to identify and juxtapose our separate frameworks to highlight the complexities of collaborative evaluations. We believed that is was important for readers to see how our individual language and moral values were embedded in our personal understandings of what it meant to be a scholar within a field of practice. The creation of this conceptual geography allowed us to work together, keep our space, and not be conscripted into a command for consensus.

We rejected the notion that institutions act independently of the people who represent them. We did not, however, have a consensus as to how those connections were made. We wrote as scholars concerned about educational administration who believe that institutional objectivity is an insufficiently complex concept to describe community collaboratives. We all agreed that the future of our communities rests on our ability to put aside the class lines that divide us into the experts and the needy who depend on the vision of patrons. A language of "need," "vision," and "leadership" for education in a market democracy must visibly demonstrate that it encourages community self-governance and economic self-reliance, not dependence.

We concluded: (a) that the construction of ordinary language was far more arduous than we had imagined; (b) that our generational, iterative, and cumulative approach to the text, critique, and response was effective for our work with each other, and (c) that those studying, working in, or evaluating collaboratives might benefit from postmodern techniques of mapping multiple perspectives through text juxtapositions and cumulative critique. We also concluded that, for a collaborative to succeed, members should consider spending time at the beginning examining their assumptions of common intent in order to develop ways of accommodating inevitable differences in these critical underpinnings.

Finally, we concluded that stories and other narrative material could help a group determine, first, whether a collaborative effort had a chance to succeed and, second, the degree to which translatable beliefs, values, and assumptions could be constructed to build its own good polyphonic society (Paulston 1994c). Market democracies help us hear and mediate our different interpretations of systems and power. A collaborative that requires or assumes a consensus or a common vision cannot account for the conflicted power relationships inherent in a participatory democracy. Without mutual recognition and a fair hearing, the transaction costs for social and economic exchange rise. The cultural capital of democracies—respect for the other's freedom and civic responsibility—is at least as valuable as its economic capital.

In closing, we learned that collaboratives may help us redefine what we mean by efficiency. Efficiency is not simply a means for obtaining goals; it is also a means for sustaining political and social differences through responsible liberty. These alliances need to tap the strengths of our heterogeneous society. It will be important for collaborative members to listen to each other's stories, to map ways of seeing and being with each other by, hopefully, learning each other's languages. The struggle to do good is always a struggle because we lead lives of conflicted interests. We may yearn for the completeness of efficient solutions, but history has too often shown us the high cost of total solutions. Shared common ground must be created and recreated, moment by moment, one word at a time, by each generation. Paradoxically, divergent, not convergent, public and universal education may better help us learn how to constructively and creatively mediate our differences with our neighbors.

NOTES

The authors would like to thank Noreen Garman, David Plank and Rolland Paulston for their helpful comments. We would particularly like to thank Rolland Paulston for his willingness to read and skewer multiple drafts.

1. Differences in understandings created by differences in work practices may also be exacerbated by differences created by other cultural territories such as religion, ethnicity, or class.

2. Expectational maps or schema are deeply embedded in your thinking so you can function without thinking about them (Huff 1994). Imagine you have been invited to join an educational collaborative in your community. You walk into an office building for your first meeting, take the first right turn, and open the second door on the right. What might you expect to find behind the door to the next room: four walls, a floor, someplace to sit, lights, clever people, etc.? Let's suppose, however, that you open the door, peek in, and there, sitting around the conference table, are a cast of cartoon characters engaged in spirited conversations. They look up at you curiously. Your first thought might be disbelief. No expectational map prepared you for this moment. You might feel disoriented and start looking around the room for more familiar cues. Perhaps only now might you see the lamps and the floor.

As a collaborative participant or as a reader, you may not be aware of all the expectations and attributions that you have to help you make sense of your world. If you are from a bureaucratic culture, for example, you might expect both community collaboratives to be made up of and scholarly papers to be written by people who agree with each other and write in a single objective or professional voice. You might also expect all reports to be unified in their construction and held together by a logical, deductive, organized hierarchical system of topics and subtopics. These expectations, however, could not prepare you to work with people who do not share your map. What do you do if you must work with people with different expectational maps? We invite you to consider, at least for the duration of this chapter, that multiple perspectives can help lower the costs of learning to navigate shared power worlds. Learning what to do without maps begins with the realization that they frame our experience and sense of well-being. Being in a space without them was very discomforting for us.

3. Transcultural differences may render consensus both impossible and undesirable (Bryson and Crosby 1992). Under these pluralist conditions, dissensus practices (Capper 1993, 23) may help people learn to consciously reflect on their own cultural practices so they can map, acknowledge, and negotiate each others' frameworks. This means that people may need to take the time to learn what it means to come from a different work culture so they can speak to someone working out of a different aesthetic. For example, corporate executives may think it natural and good to place only one person in charge of a task and all others in service to him or her. Corporate-oriented thinkers may also think it is efficient to encapsulate thinking so that all activities and people not directly connected to the collaborative's stated behavioral objectives are legitimately excluded.

In contrast, school board members with democratic, community-oriented work practices may think it natural and good to include as many people as possible in the deliberation process in order to hear a rich texture of conflicting, but authentic, constituent voices. From this framework, everyone may be nominally in charge because they are citizens, and none is in service to the other. This inclusive deliberation may be long and involved because it is intended to build good will and to ensure cooperative working relationships among members of the community. This approach may be seen as a good way of preserving community values and sustaining peaceful social relationships across generations. How then, will the executives and the school board members decide such basic questions about the collaborative as how to decide how to decide?

4. Aesthetics refers to people's practices in the world (Tillich 1963). Theodor Adorno, a student of Paul Tillich's at Frankfurt, considered aesthetics as practices that reached beyond cognition and reason into more intuitive, creative, and complete psychological understandings of the meaning of experience (Van Reijen 1992).

5. Without mutually understandable ways of listening, speaking, and acting, a dilemma of attention may emerge. This dilemma of attention suggests that the very act of focusing may eliminate the necessary. Those who focus on consensus may obliterate valuable dissent. Thus a collaborative effort, so united by common goals and practices that members speak with one voice, may simply not be possible.

6. A systems expert, for example, could assume that these wretched work structures were the result of deterministic natural forces such as global market competition and thus outside the system studied. I dismiss this view at best as naive, at worst as immoral. People create markets. People set wages. People drive home to large homes in the suburbs paid for out of the profits they made by bullying people into part-time jobs without health-care benefits.

REFERENCES

Barlow, D., and S. Wassermann. (1992). *Moving and relocation sourcebook: A reference guide to the 100 largest metropolitan areas in the United States.* Omnigraphics.

Bellah, R. N. (1992). *The good society.* New York: Vintage Books.

Beneveniste, G. (1989). *Mastering the politics of planning: Crafting credible plans and policies that make a difference.* San Francisco: Jossey-Bass.

Bickel, W. E., and R. A. Hattrup. (Winter 1991–1992). A case study of institutional collaboration to enhance knowledge use: Restructuring practitioner-researcher dialogue in education. *Knowledge and Policy: The International Journal of Knowledge Transfer and Utilization* 4(4): 56–78.

Blaug, M. (1987). *The economics of education and the education of an economist.* New York: New York University Press.

Blase, J. (1989). The micropolitics of the school: The everyday political orientation of teachers toward open school principals. *Education Administration Quarterly* 25(4): 377–407.

Borradori, G. (1994). *The American philosopher: Conversations with Quine, Davidson, Putnam, Nozick, Danto, Rorty, Cavell, MacIntyre and Kuhn.* Chicago: University of Chicago Press.

Brown, R. H. (1992). *Society as text: Essays on rhetoric, reason and reality.* Chicago: Chicago University Press.

Bryson, J. M., and B. Crosby. (1992) *Leadership for the common good: Tackling public problems in a shared power world.* San Francisco: Jossey-Bass.

Capper, C. A. (1993). *Educational administration in pluralist society.* Albany, N.Y.: State University of New York Press.

Clark T. (1991). Evaluation: The key to reflective management of school reform for at-risk students. *Urban Education* 26(1): 105–117.

Clark T., S. Ham, B. A. Jones, and K. Thomas. (1989). *School-community urban dropout prevention collaboratives: Information, survey, and inventory.* Paper prepared for the Ford Foundation Urban Dropout Prevention Collaboratives program. New York: Education Resources Group.

DeYoung, A. J. (1989). *Economics and American education.* New York: Longman.

Duignan, P. A., and R. J. S. Macpherson. (1993) Educative leadership: A practical theiry. *Educational Administration Quarterly* 29(1): 8–33.

Easton, D. (1965). *A systems analysis of political life.* New York: John Wiley & Sons.

Foster, W. (1986). *Paradigms and promises: New approaches to educational administration.* Buffalo, New York: Prometheus Books.

Foucault, M. (1988). *Politics, philosophy and culture: Interviews with other writings 1977–1984.* New York Routledge.

Garman, N. B. (1982). The clinical approach to supervision. In *Supervision of teaching,* ed. T. Sergiovanni, 35–52. Alexandria, Va.: Association for Supervision and Curriculum Development Annual Yearbook.

Garman, N. B. (1995). Andragogy and professional education: When adults come together to learn about practice. *Australian Administrator* 6(1): 1–4.

Gillette, L. (April, 1991). *Gatekeepers and scouts.* Paper presented at the annual conference of the American Educational Research Association, San Francisco.

Giroux, H. (1983). *Theory and resistance in education: A pedagogy for the opposition.* South Hadley, Mass.: Bergin and Garvey.

Gottlieb, E. (1987) Development education: Discourse in paradigms and knowledge. Unpublished doctoral dissertation. Pittsburgh, Pa: University of Pittsburgh.

Hattrup, R. A., and W. E. Bickel. (1993). Teacher-researcher collaborations: Resolving the tensions. *Educational Leadership* 50(6): 38–40.

Hord, S. M. (1986). A synthesis of research on organizational collaboration. *Educational Leadership* 43(5): 22–26.

Huff, A. S. ed. (1990). *Mapping strategic thought.* Chichester, England: John Wiley and Sons.

Jones, B. A. (1989). Factors related to effective community-based organization intervention in dropout prevention. Unpublished doctoral dissertation. New York: Columbia University.

Jones, B. A. (1991). Parent empowerment through collaboration. *Partnerships in Education Journal* 5(2): 10.

Jones, B. A. (1992). Collaboration: The case for indigenous community-based organization support of dropout prevention programming and implementation. *Journal of Negro Education* 61: 496–508.

Jones, B. A. (1993a). Advancing an adolescent focused agenda: The collaborative role of school, family and the community. *The School Community Journal* 3(1): 13–22.

Jones, B. A. (1993b). Urban collaboration and the nature of institutional involvement. Unpublished manuscript. University of Pittsburgh, Department of Administrative and Policy Studies. Pittsburgh, PA.

Jones, B. A. (Fall, 1995). School-community based organizational collaboratives. *Educational Research Quarterly: Journal of Learning Improvement.*

Klees, S. J. (1986). Planning and policy in education: What can economics tell us? *Comparative Education Review.* 30: 111–119.

Klees, S. J. (1990). The economics of education: A slightly more jaundiced view of where we are now. In *The future of educational planning,* ed. F. Caillods. Paris: International Institute of Educational Planning, UNESCO.

Kriesberg, S. (1992). *Transforming power: Dominations, empowerment and education.* Albany, N.Y.: State University of New York Press.

Lieberman, A. (1986). Collaborative work. *Educational Leadership* 43(5): 4–6.

Mathew, B. (1994). Structure and power in information technology environments: A geneaology of organizational systems. Unpublished doctoral dissertation. Pittsburgh, Pa: University of Pittsburgh.

Merchant, B. (1993). *Conversations and notes about multiple perspectives in Native American Indian communities.* School of Education. Unpublished manuscript, Champagne-Urbana: University of Illinois.

McCloskey, D. N. (1985). *The rhetoric of economics.* Madison: University of Wisconsin Press.

McClure, M. W. (1990). Adieu Victoria? Reform and critical strategy in the Brimelow-Hickrod debates. *Journal of Education Finance* 15: 534–557.

McClure, M. W. (1994). The reform that wasn't: The lighthouse strategy of local control. In *Investing in U.S. schools: Directions for educational policy,* ed. B. A. Jones and K. M. Borman. Norwood, N.J.: Ablex Publishing.

Otterbourg, S. D., and D. Adams. (1989). Partnerships in education: Measuring their success. Fla.: InfoMedia.

Paulston, R. (1990). Toward a reflective comparative education. *Comparative Education Review* 34: 248–255.

Paulston, R. (1994b). Comparative education: Paradigms and theories. In *International Encyclopedia of Education,* ed. T. Husen and N. Postlewaithe, 923–933. Oxford: Pergamon Press.

Paulston, R., and M. Liebman. (1994a). An invitation to postmodern social cartography. *Comparative Education Review* 38: 215–232.

Potter, E. (1988). The linguistic turn in philosophy of education: An analysis of historical factors affecting an academic field. Unpublished doctoral dissertation. Tucscon, Ariz.: The University of Arizona.

Rader, M. (1976). *The enduring questions: Main problems of philosophy.* New York: Holt, Rinehart, and Winston.

Serrin, W. (1993). *Homestead: The glory and the tragedy of an American steel town.* New York: Vintage Books.

Sergiovanni, T. (1992). *Moral leadership: Getting to the heart of school improvement.* San Francisco: Jossey-Bass.

Tillich, P. (1963). *Systemic theology: Vol. 1. Life and the spirit: History and the kingdom of God,* 62–68. Chicago: University of Chicago Press.

U.S. Department of Education (February, 1989). *Education partnerships in public elementary and secondary schools.* Washington, D.C.: National Center for Education Statistics.

Van Reijen, W. (1992). *Adorno: An introduction.* Philadelphia: Pennbridge Books.

Conclusion:
Toward an Interpretation of School, Family, and Community Connections: Policy Challenges

James G. Cibulka

INTRODUCTION

As William Kritek indicated in the introductory chapter, this book reflects the reemergence of an interest in improving the working relationships among schools, families, and communities. At the moment, the principal strategy in these efforts is the development of coordinated services for children, although other approaches such as parent education are also receiving renewed attention. Chicago's school reform (Hess 1991) represents still a different political approach to empowering parents and community advocates. School choice also is an effort to strengthen the role of families in the educational process (Coons and Sugarman 1978), but from quite a different angle than coordinated services, and it continues to receive much debate.

Obviously then, this effort to link schools, families, and communities in a tighter working relationship is a broadly gauged movement with numerous strands. Once one gets to specifics, its advocates do not always share a great deal else in common. Their conception of the problem they are addressing, for instance, varies considerably. Among those who advocate coordinated services, the perceived problems usually mentioned are the declining condition of children in our society and the inadequacies of services to children and families. By contrast, for Chicago's school reformers it has been opposition to the educational bureaucracy and the desire to replace it with greater accountability by school principals and by local school control. Choice advocates also see the problem as lack of bureaucratic accountability, but they depart from Chicago school reformers in their effort to replace bureaucratic controls by giving families consumer power.

Given this diversity of perspectives among those who wish to strengthen school-community linkages, what we have is a reform movement only in the broadest sense, one animated by a shared disdain for the status quo rather than a common ideological vision. Indeed, advocates of one or another reform vision sometimes have engaged in acrimonious disputes, eager to discredit one another's views. While particular reforms may exist side by side in certain school systems, their coexistence is more a reflection of pragmatic compromises than the logical compatibility of the reforms.

In short, coordinated services for children is part of a broader movement to rethink school, community, and family connections, a movement that shares in common primarily what it opposes (the status quo) rather than what it stands for.

Nonetheless, despite its amorphous quality, this movement reflects an important watershed in the tradition of school-community relations that has been dominant throughout much of this century. The professional-technical model of schooling was first advocated by American Progressive reformers early in the century, won ascendancy and reigned nearly supreme in America during the immediate post-World War II period, but has been in steady decline since the 1960s. That model was built upon the idea that professional educators know best how to educate children, that the requirements for successful education primarily involve the technical application of resources and skills by these educators, that parents and communities should play a secondary, supportive role behind these educators. The family and neighborhood were presumed to be a stable (if sometimes provincial and therefore inadequate) influence within this educative process, and community resources would be easily available when educators called upon them in carrying out their professional goals.

Most of these assumptions, if they never held completely, were sufficiently credible for many decades that they sustained a remarkably stable set of institutional relationships linking schools with their families and communities. It is the unraveling of the credibility of these assumptions that has led to the social movement for reform of schooling. The historical causes of this questioning were touched on briefly in the introductory chapter.

Recognizing that there is a long (and frustrating) history of efforts to improve school-family-community linkages in American public schools, the approach to be taken in this concluding chapter will be to place the present reform efforts in a broad policy perspective. I will highlight the major public policy issues raised by these reform efforts toward coordinated services. Specifically, I shall call attention to four broad tensions in the American political system for which historically there has been no clear resolution. As a consequence, these tensions complicate and confound the task of achieving a tighter coupling between schools, families, and communities.

First, there has been a long struggle in American society over the proper role of the public school. This debate has had many facets, but one in particular stands out when we consider the school's relationship to families and communities. It is, by one construction, the choice of schooling as principally academic or social in its goals. The idea that schools should address the problems and needs of families and communities inevitably takes us into that contested terrain.

Second, the chapter addresses the role of the lay citizenry in service provision, especially vis-à-vis professional authority and autonomy. Progressive educators tipped the scales toward professional control earlier in this century, but, in so doing, they hardly resolved the matter once and for all. Like other reform movements, the efforts toward coordinated services are caught up in this conundrum.

A third problem that will be examined here is the conflict over the nature of the modern welfare state and the specific protections that should be offered for children and families. There are many facets to this debate, not all of which I shall attempt to cover in this chapter. Among our concerns, however, is the question of how broad a safety net should be extended to children. A second question is the specific institutional characteristics such as public versus private provision, as well as the tradition of structural autonomy for schools that the Progressives created to protect schools and the children they serve from overt political influences.

Fourth, there is the long-standing tension among competing values in the American political culture and how they influence policies and programs for children. Should efficiency be a prime goal in organizing services, or should equality of opportunity or outcome be a paramount goal? How much should responsiveness to local interests weigh, as against national conceptions of the community's interests? These fundamental values inform our ideas about the relation among the state and civil society, and, in particular, they shape our thinking about how schools, families, and communities should interact.

Each of these problems will be addressed in turn, albeit briefly in this concluding chapter. The discussion includes examples of how particular chapters in the volume illustrate one or another angle or perspective on the problem.

SCHOOLS AS ACADEMIC OR SOCIAL INSTITUTIONS

The current effort to reintegrate schools and communities and the closely parallel effort to make schools a vehicle for addressing the problems of the poor (particularly the urban underclass) rekindles an old battle in the history of American schooling. Should the schools' role be defined as principally the advancement of literacy and necessary cognitive skills for effective functioning in our society? Alternatively, should they be a vehicle for confronting a variety of social ills that are directly or indirectly linked to education but that have their origins, at least in part, independent of schools?

Both within the educational establishment and outside it, there always have been advocates for each view. For example, when the social movements of the 1960s were pressed upon the schools, it was not uncommon to hear teachers and administrators bemoan the improper use of the schools to solve social problems. From this view, such things as providing breakfasts to poor children are a distraction from the school's real responsibility of conveying knowledge. Similarly, in the 1960s, efforts to introduce "community control" were seen by critics as nothing more than crass ethnic and racial politics that would radicalize the curriculum, politicize hiring, and dilute professional standards (Fein 1970).

The idea that schools should address social problems is most widely associated with the Progressive movement. Reformers such as Jane Adams were alarmed at the lifestyles and living conditions of the poor and sought to enlist the schools, as well as other institutions, to rehabilitate the poor and improve their standard of living. Both in the curriculum, with its problem-centered approach to learning associated with John Dewey, and more broadly in the organization and control of schooling, Progressives sought to strengthen the school's ties to advancement of the "public interest," as they variously viewed it. Progressivism eventually ran its course and officially expired in the early 1950s, but, as Lawrence Cremin (1961) points out, the precepts of Progressivism still enjoyed wide acceptance in public opinion at the time of his writing, despite the collapse of the official movement.

Several decades later, the same issues that surrounded the con-flicting assessments of Progressivism continue to be waged. The Chris-tian right has mobilized to challenge a long list of presumed evils of modernism and relativism that supposedly infect our schools, among them anything that potentially condones alternatives to traditional fam-ily values, such as distribution of condoms in schools, the inclusion of information about nontraditional families, information about sexual practices and values, outcome-based education, and so on. This seg-ment of the American public views schools as too progressive.[1] They seek to narrow the curriculum to basic skills and purge any focus on social problems or values.

While the Christian right has not yet directed a full-scale attack upon the concept of coordinated services, if the concept is ever ex-tended to deal with needs of middle-class communities, the mobiliza-tion of the Christian right to oppose such reforms could be expected.

Regardless of whether the Christian right attacks coordinated ser-vices per se, its importance lies in what it symbolizes about the grow-ing attack on "modernism" in our schools and the attempt to replace social goals with narrowly academic purposes. Since the 1980s, the Christian right has broadened its attacks on the educational establish-ment, which initially were directed at the issues of school prayer and objectionable library books. More recently, all manner of values have come under attack.

The growth of the radical right at the present time is one manifes-tation of the "culture wars" that rage around our schools (Hunter 1994). The insistence that schools dedicate themselves to academic rather than social ends directly contradicts simultaneous demands being placed on the schools to expand their responsibilities. Indeed, it is ironic that, while some are advocating the expansion of the school's social functions in response to the decline of the family, the radical right, vexed by the same problem, advocates a narrowing of that role. Both sides have mobilized nationally to advance their positions, the former through professional networks and foundations, the latter through grassroots pressure tactics and electoral politics at the school board level.

At the same time, we see other echoes of the old debate about the social purpose of the school. In their day, Progressives were attacked from the left as largely conservative in their aims, seeking to preserve middle-class, nativist, small-town values as a response to the urban-ization and industrialization of America (Hogan 1985; Tyack 1974). A more moderate view from the left is that Progressivism embraced several noble ideals that as a movement it never fully embodied—the use of the school to strengthen community service, identity, and pride; individualization of instruction and dealing with the needs of those children least prone to success in school; and teaching the "whole child" by attending to a student's physical, social, emotional, or moral development (Sedlak and Schlossman 1985, 371–383).

Given the parallels between the coordinated services movement and many of the aims of the old Progressive movement, it can be anticipated that current efforts to link schools and communities will receive a skeptical response from much of the political left. From this perspective, Progressive ideals either are a hoax or they do not go far enough to embody the changes sought by these critics. In this volume, Gail Chase Furman and Carol Merz offer just such a skeptical assessment, pointing to the gap between a "romantic Gemeinschaft" view of local communities in much of the current rhetoric alongside what amounts to "bureaucratic/Gesellschaft" solutions embodied in proposals for coordinated services. Thus, depending on one's political perspective, current efforts to expand the role of schools to deal with social needs either go too far or not far enough.

Even within the academic establishment, there has been a very equivocal and qualified acceptance of the broadening of the schools' mission. When the demands for educational reform multiplied in the 1980s following the publication of *A Nation at Risk*, educators were among the first to lay responsibility on society's inclination to ask the schools to do too much and solve all our nation's problems. Critical studies of American schooling (e.g., Grant 1988; Powell et al. 1986) pointed to the lack of focus and the myth of "value neutrality" in American public schools. Accordingly, in the 1980s, critics (Cusick 1983; Goodlad 1984; Sizer 1984) decried the fragmentation and dilution of content knowledge within the academic program. Mainstream reformers such as Ernest Boyer (1983) advocated that state policy makers narrow the focus and expectations for public schools through top-down goal setting. To be sure, this more moderate attack on the wide-ranging functions that public schools have assumed in recent decades has in no way represented an attack on the concept of coordinated services. Some of the same reformers are now backing this reform nostrum. Perhaps it is possible to sharpen the curricular focus of the school on the one hand, while simultaneously widening the school's attention to the social support needs of its pupils. Yet, if this is the case, such a balancing act has received remarkably little attention or debate. More likely, the fact that both points of view are being advocated simultaneously illustrates the ambivalence and even logical contradictions concerning the role of the school that are at the heart of today's reform advocacies.

In short, within the broad movement to reform our schools, it is possible to find conflicting advocacies as to the envisioned academic and social requirements of our schools. Just as the Progressive movement embraced and sought to reconcile apparently conflicting ideologies, values, and interests, this confluence of tensions is at work in today's often contentious efforts to save our schools.

While many would characterize the choice between academic and social purposes as a false and misleading dichotomy, such simplifications do not deter critics who seek to protect the academic role of schools. Even if the academic and social purposes of the school are not always in conflict, they sometimes are in tension. This is illustrated by the chapter on homeless children by Rebecca Newmann and Lynn Beck. Attending to the basic needs of these children often appears to take precedence over the academic program they receive. Indeed, the school plays a secondary role in the child's life, as long as the children's parents choose to limit their cooperation with school authorities, fearing retribution from other public officials. In attempting to offer an academic program to these homeless children, the school is constrained by the web of circumstances and limited options of the families it serves. In this sense, the social circumstances outside the school are potential barriers that must be addressed before any sustained teaching and learning can occur for these children. While the homeless may provide an extreme example of this dilemma, it is, in many respects, no different than the same problem that most educators face. They must address the social needs that stand in the way of their pupils' learning. In this sense, the choice between an academic or social role for the school is not a choice at all but a necessity, given the changing social fabric of American life. Within this context, to be sure, more can be done to strengthen the academic focus in the curriculum, but the latter is not a substitute for a more ecologically based role for the school.

A second example, drawn from the chapter by Shirley Brice Heath and Milbrey McLaughlin, suggests how high a price high schools have paid by ignoring the *positive* social forces within communities that can provide some basis for informal learning. Knowing little about the community or the personal lives of their students, many teachers see only negative forces in the students' personal lives. They point to the factors that interfere with learning so that the school may proceed with its academic role. More broadly, the academic role may have to accommodate in more direct ways the social context of youth's lives, particularly for youth in central cities who find the school in its present form hostile or irrelevant to their life circumstances. Clearly, the complex relationship between academic and social roles for our schools, a problem that preoccupied Progressive educators early in this century, is equally a puzzle and challenge at the end of the century as we seek to redefine school-community-family ties.

CITIZEN ROLES AND PROFESSIONAL AUTHORITY

Efforts to rethink the relationship between schools, families, and communities cannot escape the issue of what role citizens should play in the schools, and how they should properly relate to the professionals who are hired to run these schools.

This is, of course, far from a new problem. Therefore, there is a considerable body of literature pointing to the tensions between parents and communities on the one side and the schools on the other. At one level, this tension appears between teachers and parents (Waller 1932) who may have different perceptions about the child's strengths and needs. Parents are concerned mainly for their own child's welfare, not those of an entire class for whom a teacher bears responsibility. Parents have special knowledge about their child that may be unavailable to the teacher, and vice versa. Teachers claim special knowledge in pedagogy and content, which some parents are inclined to challenge. This tension between teachers and parents also applies to the other professionals who make claims to possessing expertise, such as guidance counselors, psychologists, reading specialists, social workers, and school administrators.

The lay-professional tension extends beyond the classroom. It also has been given much attention at the governance level (e.g., Boyd 1976; Gittell 1969; Zeigler, Jennings, and Peak 1974). School board policy making typically is heavily influenced, if not dominated, by superintendents, and citizens find difficulty gaining access to board and administrative decision making. In recent years, school boards have functioned even less effectively than in the past, due to a combination of factors (Danzberger, Kirst, and Usdan 1992) that include problems of recruitment and narrower electoral districts and constituent pressures. At the same time, this reduced effectiveness may reflect an increase in lay citizen influence and school board influence because of the proliferation of one-issue candidates who have been elected to boards, the growth of special-interest groups influencing school boards,

and the responsiveness of school board members to narrower constituencies from which they are selected. In general, it appears that
the autonomy once enjoyed by superintendents and school boards in
setting educational policy has been greatly diminished in recent years.
This also reflects growing public concern about school quality, business mobilization (Jackson and Cibulka 1992), and criticism of school
spending by mayors who must cope with taxpayer resistance.

An important subtheme in the literature on citizen participation
and lay-professional roles is the unequal access to school officials
enjoyed by citizens of different races, social classes, and gender. School
boards continue to be dominated by individuals of relatively high
social standing in the community (Wirt and Kirst 1989), although less
so than in the past because of the problems of recruitment. Even in
large cities with substantial African-American and Hispanic populations, many school boards underrepresent these groups (Jackson and
Cibulka 1992). Some argue that the domination of school boards by
the most socially advantaged members of a community preserves
professional domination because of a presumed harmony of interests
between the two.[2]

Whenever there is debate over how much direct influence citizens
should have over school policy, the discussion inevitably turns to the
causes of poverty. Some ask how, if the poor have caused their own
predicament through incompetence and irresponsibility, they can be
expected to make valid judgments about their children's education.
This "deficit" model for analyzing the poor has gained considerable
political ground since the Reagan years, and critics like Charles Murray
(1984) initially blamed the growth of an underclass on the Kennedy-
Johnson Great Society programs that supposedly undermined personal
responsibility. Recently Herrnstein and Murray (1994) have expanded
this analysis of class structure to include the issue of intelligence differences among individuals and groups in American society. On the
other side, it is argued that this approach to analyzing poverty places
all the responsibility for being poor on the poor themselves, in effect
blaming the victim, rather than addressing the differences in social
opportunity structures that create unemployment, crime, school dropouts, and so on. As the next section of the chapter shows, this line of
analysis constitutes a frontal assault on the American welfare state
itself. In this specific context, however, many professionals use a similar, if less extreme, version of the deficit argument to cast doubt on the
efficacy of involving the poor. If the poor, regardless of race, are characterized increasingly by dysfunctional families, so the logic runs, there

is even less hope that this strategy of empowerment will be effective than three decades ago when the War on Poverty was launched. In short, the discussion of lay-professional roles has been much affected by this argument over whether to characterize poverty as *primarily* caused by individual deficits (and misplaced government programs) or by societal structures.

Not all professionals share this dim view of the efficacy of *parental* involvement, as distinct from *community* involvement. There is a considerable body of literature that suggests that involving parents in the education of their children is effective in raising student achievement levels (For a review of this research, which covers some negative findings as well, see McAllister 1991). And while parental involvement is to some degree threatening to professionals, it can be channeled and controlled more readily than participatory strategies that attempt to empower the entire community.

A number of authors in this book give attention to this lay-professional tension and the related problem of unequal access and influence to school decision making. Claire Smrekar, for instance, highlights the complexities of implementing the Kentucky Family Resource Centers (FRC) so that teachers have a broader awareness of student's personal lives, beyond what students voluntarily and selectively share, and the difficulty of shifting the school's orientation toward problem solving, not mere problem identification. The FRCs sometimes find it necessary to distance themselves from the schools in order to achieve community legitimacy but thereby limit the close working relationship with the schools, which is a precondition for changing teachers' roles and school orientations. While very early in the implementation stages, the FRCs, in this and other examples cited by Smrekar, illustrate that structural reforms do not quickly change historically rooted norms and values both in the school's language and procedures.

Bruce L. Wilson, Jaci Webb, and H. Dickson Corbett show the tension between professional perceptions and those of parents and other community members. Teachers tend to view the family lives of children in largely negative terms and to portray the community as beset by problems, while community members see the same phenomena differently. On the other hand, these authors hold out hope that these different perceptions can be overcome.

I have discussed this same tendency to stereotype the community and to underestimate the educative potential existing within peer and community networks, which is addressed by Heath and McLaughlin. The image of schools that emerges from their study is that of alien institutions that may be in the community but stand apart from it, particularly those features of communal life that offer constructive possibilities. Their chapter suggests the resistance that can be found within schools to including parents and community persons in school programs, quite apart from any role they might play in governance.

Several of these papers, then, illustrate that the problem of linking schools, families, and communities is rooted in tensions between lay-persons and professionals. At one level, it is a tension born of conflicting knowledge bases about children, families, and communities, and the different understanding of the "problem" that flows from those separate angles of vision. At another level, it is a problem rooted in the professionals' membership in public schools, an institution with its own traditions and organizational interests. (The same could be said for social workers, health officials, and others with their particular organizational loyalties.) In addition to the role interests of professionals, there are the ever-present problems of race and social class that influence the way professionals and laypersons view one another and complicate their ability to work together effectively.

It follows that this multilayered aspect of the lay-professional tension is unlikely to be ameliorated effectively through any one strategy. First, it is so fundamental to the problem of building better linkages among schools, families, and communities that it approaches a dilemma that will never be entirely solved, only managed with more or less skill and sensitivity by leaders who understand the value choices underlying their actions.

Second, putting parents or community persons in control of a governance board or sharing power with professionals will not necessarily close this large gap unless ways can be found to address the differences of status and power that divide the two groups. The experiment described by Paul E. Heckman, W. Reed Scull, and Sharon Conley stands as one example of a coalition-building approach that seeks to forge closer ties between school officials and the community. Indeed, this coalition's basic aim is to build bridges to the broader community's resources, not merely to strengthen lay-professional ties, although this may be an important by-product of the experiment.

Similarly, the reform efforts described by Wilson et al., with their emphasis on shared goals for children, are intended to create some common ground between school professionals and laypersons, from which greater mutual understanding and respect might evolve. While these are modest beginnings, they speak to the importance of normative rather than merely structural responses to this complicated problem.

This is not to underplay the role that new structural responses might play in addressing the problem. Clearly, Kentucky's Family Resource Centers, as described by Smrekar, have the potential for reshaping school-community relations by bringing within mutual reach heretofore separate spheres of influence and information outside and inside the school. But new structures can often be undermined when they fail to address head-on other aspects that reinforce this divide—mutual suspicion, limited conceptions of the way roles should be defined or reshaped, structural rigidities within schools that teachers and administrators, and even parents and community leaders, fail to challenge because they are so deeply ingrained by tradition.

While the lay-professional tension is a fundamental dimension of the task of linking schools, families, and communities, it has often been ignored in the recent discussions about coordinated services for children. The latter reform movement has been framed quite a bit more narrowly, concentrating on the array of services available to families and children (particularly for those most at risk) and how those services are to be delivered. Much of the impetus for this reform has been led by professionals and their allies in foundations and concerned interest groups. It has not come from a groundswell of populist sentiment, although public opinion has followed with strong support in public opinion polls for expanding services to children.

By contrast, demands for more parental and community influence over schooling come from different voices and coalitions, frequently based in local neighborhoods or in social service advocacy organizations, as well as among supporters of school choice and charter schools and the like. These groups do seek to alter the balance of power in favor of parents, and their image of an effective school may have little to do with coordinated services. This should caution us that lurking behind the efforts at reform in this area are quite different groups and agendas. Those who favor coordinated services frequently seek to improve the effectiveness of the welfare state, not to shift its locus of control to lay citizens.

While the ideal of political equality in American culture symbolically encourages citizen participation through a variety of channels, the involvement of the poor in self-governance was not conceived of as national policy until the Kennedy Administration. The War on Poverty, however, was less than an unqualified success, partly because of underfunding in the Johnson Administration years as the Vietnam War began to reduce expenditures on the ambitious programs of the Great Society and partly because sharing power with the poor proved unpopular with America's mayors (Greenstone and Peterson 1973). Moreover, involvement of the poor not surprisingly led to many abuses to the tradition of "good government" as jobs and contracts were brokered by the new leadership such programs created. In a period of civil rights ascendancy, much conflict also attended efforts to empower the poor, and, when criticism was directed at established authorities, they became less enthusiastic about political egalitarianism. In short, efforts to involve the poor led to widespread criticism (Moynihan 1969). While federal domestic policy continues to encourage citizen participation in a variety of federal programs, there has been little interest in extending political power too far. Moreover, the larger number of African-American elected officials at the local level today has reduced to some degree the pressure that once existed to bring African Americans into the political system, to counteract a century of post-Reconstructionist exclusion. Thus, any discussion about a strong role for lay citizens in the fledgling coordinated services movement is bound to confront these historical impediments.

Those who seek to increase political involvement ordinarily assume that it will lead to positive policy outcomes. The chapter by Deborah Shaver and colleagues suggests a more complicated scenario. Projects run by community-based organizations were less effective than those run by public agencies in gaining legitimacy, an important political asset for negotiating the complex interorganizational relationships embedded in coordinated service projects. However, it is too early, based on the preliminary evidence presented, to conclude that this flaw will prove to be fatal.

Whatever the political obstacles, however, the need for some participatory strategies has never been greater, particularly in urban neighborhoods where persistent poverty is most prevalent and where neighborhood organizations and institutions have weakened rather than strengthened in recent decades. A neighborhood-based strategy of urban development has its critics (Lehmann 1994), but some new channels of democratic participation seem to be needed desperately to address the exclusion and despair of growing segments of the American population with the unresponsiveness of the political system. Coordinated services, if it is to realize its potential as a reform vector, must be more than a professionally driven and controlled reform movement.

This unresolved tension in the American political system concerning the role of citizens, particularly the poor, in governing services brings us to the larger debate about welfare statism as a model of defining the relationship between the individual and society, to which the next section turns.

PROTECTING CHILDREN IN THE WELFARE STATE: A STRONG OR A WEAK ROLE?

It is a common observation that the welfare state in America, quite unlike its European counterparts, is a patchwork lacking any semblance of comprehensiveness. Instead, it is an "amalgam of ideologically disparate programs" that reflect no coherent social vision (Karger and Stoesz 1993). The relative incoherence and weakness of America's welfare state policies reflects a deep ambivalence about individual versus collective responsibility and the dangers to individual liberty potentially posed by a strong or activist government. In addition, other explanations for its weakness, compared to European counterparts, include the absence of a feudal tradition, the development of democracy prior to the emergence of a working class, relative prosperity, and so on (Wilensky 1975).

This American welfare state was built over a very long period, even if its origins are usually attributed to Franklin Roosevelt. Insofar as children and families are concerned, one can reach back to the Progressives in the early twentieth century and, indeed, to reform efforts in the nineteenth century. Juvenile courts, juvenile correctional institutions, foster care for dependent children, and a variety of reforms emerged from this period. While such reforms often did not match the rhetoric of those who proposed them (Cuban 1984; Sedlak and Schlossman 1985), they did constitute improvements over the what was in place at the time. Among the evils Progressives sought to eradicate was the replacement of service provision by private charities with public institutions, arguing that they alone would overcome the gaps and abuses in this loose system of voluntary charities. In this crusade, they were not wholly successful, of course, because the system of voluntary agencies and services remains intact alongside the public sector to this day, although more closely regulated, partly as a result of Progressive efforts as well. Public schools were not excluded from this reform platform, but schools were quite successful in accommodating reforms such as the public health nurse and municipal recreation movement while essentially marginalizing their impact.

The last major expansion in the scope of welfare state services came with the Great Society programs of President Lyndon Johnson (Koppich 1994), despite some individual programs in the 1970s and even 1980s. In education few of these initially had a strong community or family focus. Even Head Start, which was not even entrusted to the educational establishment, only slowly evolved into a family-oriented intervention (Valentine and Zigler 1983).

The ascent of Richard Nixon to the presidency represented the beginning of a mounting attack on liberal welfare-state policies, coming from intellectuals and public opinion, fueled by political and social conservatives. In the late 1970s President Jimmy Carter created an Office of Families and in 1980 convened a White House conference on Families, but these fledgling efforts were stillborn through the 1980s. Despite myriad programs at federal, state and local levels that purport to address family concerns, there is no overall national policy to coordinate these efforts. Part of the problem Carter faced was the political mobilization of the Moral Majority against the development of any governmental policy in this "private" sphere (Kagan, Klugman, and Zigler 1983).

At the risk of some oversimplification, it is possible to divide the attacks on the welfare state into two groups, one coming from the political left and the other from the right. Those on the left worry about the welfare state as a new form of social control, particularly over society's most vulnerable members, but reaching to nearly all spheres of the population touched in some manner by the widening embrace of social welfare policies.[3]

Those on the right attack the welfare state, particularly the major welfare program Aid to Families with Dependent Children (AFDC) in contrast to the major social insurance program, Social Security, as encouraging illegitimacy, dependency, cheating, to name only several problems (Murray 1984). Michael Joyce (1994) argues that the discredited Progressive state was nothing less than a frontal attack on civil society itself and on the mechanisms of voluntarism that are an essential feature of civil society.

In between these polar attacks are the rather tortured defenses of the welfare state by liberals (e.g., Ellwood 1988; Katz 1989), which some accuse of being "backward looking" (Berkowitz 1991, xiv). Neo-Marxists argue that the state in capitalist societies cannot address human needs because these conflict with the constraints of the capitalist economic system (e.g., Gough 1979). These perspectives focus first on social class (Carnoy 1989). Undeniably, however, the analysis of poverty in the United States is complicated by radical prejudice (West 1993), which is partly economic.

By 1995, the political center in America had shifted dramatically to the right, and a Republican-controlled Congress announced its intention to achieve welfare reform, a balanced budget, and other important policy changes outlined in the Republican Party's "Contract with America." Many Republicans, partly those newly elected, appeared to endorse a classical liberal view of the welfare state (e.g., Ruggie 1984 with fewer individual entitlements, smaller government, a weaker role for the federal government in particular, and a stronger place for markets.

How does the current effort to coordinate human services fare within this historical debate about the role of the welfare state? There is no straightforward answer to this question. Those on the left who see government efforts as largely driven by a social control perspective will no doubt find ample evidence in new reforms to support their claim. Consider the Clinton Administration's efforts to create a national network of job centers, where the jobless receive welfare checks and job training under one roof. The state-run Job Service offices and private and public job training programs are housed alongside welfare and basic adult education programs. For instance, a model center in Kenosha, Wisconsin, was described in glowing terms by one official: "In the past, you went and applied for AFDC at the Department of Social Services. Now you apply for AFDC at the Job Center. We think that gives a message philosophically to anyone who comes through the door just what our mission is." (*The Milwaukee Journal,* April 3, 1994). Participating agencies work together, sharing staff, financing, and responsibilities rather than duplicating efforts, officials say.[4] Clearly, the political agenda underlying the efforts to coordinate services, in this case, is the Clinton Administration's welfare-to-work proposals. However laudable on its face, powerful antiwelfare-state assumptions seem to be inherent here—the idea that many on welfare prefer not to work, that jobs abound for the taking or will be created by an expanding economy, and so on. As to the former, there is much evidence to dispute the characterization of the poor as lazy and unmotivated to work (Katz 1990). Nor is it clear that the new jobs that would be created by an expanding economy, should that come to be, would rise above the plethora of low-skill, low-pay "junk jobs" created by the American economy in the 1980s.

Concern about the status of children in American society, which undergirds the broad-gauged efforts to improve services to children and their families, has enjoyed bipartisan support at the center of the political spectrum in American politics. In particular, approaches such as coordinated children's services have had the enthusiastic support of the more cosmopolitan wing of the business class, represented by the Committee for Economic Development, and by many foundations.

It is by no means self-evident, however, that this moderate approach will prevail. Following the 1994 midterm elections, Republicans argued that their electoral sweep indicated that the American people endorsed sweeping changes. House Speaker Newt Gingrich called for more orphanages built on the model of Boys Town U.S.A., which Democrats dismissed as a cruel and absurdly unrealistic proposal that would harm many children. A similar debate surfaced over work requirements and time limits for welfare recipients; what safety net, it was asked, would protect children? In short, at this writing it is far from clear that the coalitions that have generated demands for improvement in childrens' services to children will prevail over other coalitions primarily concerned with reducing the welfare state and the costs of government. Those who are optimistic might see in this situation an opportunity to rationalize and expand the American welfare state, long lamented for its inadequacies by many intellectuals and students of the welfare system. Pessimists might read the opposite into the coordinated services movement, which has so far shown a reluctance to frame its proposals in broad social policy terms. Clearly, by 1995 the efforts to expand childrens' services faced a new and powerful challenge from the political right, which claimed broad public support for its radical proposals. Faced with dramatic political rhetoric from its opponents, who claimed a higher moral ground, the fledgling childrens' services movement was for the first time challenged to defend its basic assumptions and to build a broad-based movement at the political center. How it will choose its political allies and what political agendas it will select will be important to its survival as a viable political movement.

In this regard, the success of the coordinated services movement will depend at least partly on which political forces have the greatest staying power. The Pew Charitable Trust, one of the most enthusiastic and generous benefactors of the concept, announced in June 1994 that it would withdraw its funding support from the Children's Initiative, a projected $60 million commitment over a 10-year period. Foundation officials cited uncertainty that its projects in five states could actually improve outcomes in child health, child development, school readiness, and family functioning of sufficient magnitude to warrant an entire replacement of existing services (Cohen 1994). While at least four other large foundations, and scores of others, remain committed to the coordinated services movement, the announcement was perhaps most important for what it symbolized about the potentially mercurial support the movement will receive from the top.

One concern expressed by Pew officials is that the outcomes envisioned under the Children's Initiative depended on even broader reforms in other areas such as housing and jobs. Put differently, can the coordinated services movement succeed without a more comprehensive overhaul of the welfare state? And from a political perspective, is the movement likely to enjoy greater success if it takes a high profile position on reshaping public policy in complex and controversial areas such as welfare, housing, and drugs?

Those who advocate a more comprehensive array of services to children may be right in trying to disassociate this movement from the move to overhaul the welfare system. The latter is surely more overtly political, but it also carries far greater interest by the broad public than the children's services movement, about which the general public is vaguely aware but generally supportive, if one gives any credence to public opinion polls. As a consequence of public concern, much of it misinformed, there is likely to be action on welfare reform in the 1990s, but the prognosis for improving childrens' services, and thereby strengthening the American welfare state, is far less certain.

The tendency to frame the problem of childrens' services through an inordinately narrow lens is illustrated by the funding problem. Deborah Verstegen puts this point nicely in her chapter. The coordinated services movement will not realize its potential as a reform movement if it is only a patch on a threadbare system. The funding of public education remains a formidable challenge, despite several decades of legal decisions and legislative reforms. State funding systems are, in many cases, archaic and almost everywhere peppered with inequality. They are only rarely used by states as a tool to achieve other education reforms. Beyond this, their relationship to other human services remains a black box. Meaningful reform will require a comprehensive look at funding structures that are controlled and provided in different policy domains.

The ability to wed school finance reform to the larger effort toward more comprehensive services for children would be an important victory for the idea of a stronger social welfare state. Education is deemed a fundamental right in many state constitutions, while in others it is not. Even where it is, practice lags behind constitutional protections. And the federal constitution provides no fundamental right to an education. In such circumstances, the right to an adequate education may have to be wedded to some wider definition of social need.

Embedded within this issue of the nature of services available to children is the problem of organizational dysfunction. It is identical to the attacks made on the welfare system from the political right, now eagerly embraced by centrist Democrats. According to the organizational dysfunction thesis, public service bureaucracies are inefficient, unresponsive, self-aggrandizing, and/or duplicative of one another. The most conservative of these critics of public bureaucracies argues for dismantling them altogether, giving clients/customers vouchers, and letting market forces rather than bureaucracies, which requires overhauling their regulatory environments. Included in this diagnosis is a need to overhaul governance of these separate, fragmented bureaucracies. For example, at the federal level, myriad Congressional committees oversee the vast array of disjointed programs affecting children. Accordingly, these reformers in the political center call for reorganization from the top, both in Congress and in the management of programs. It is within this frame of reference that much of the discussion of coordinated childrens' services takes place.

Many on the political left, particularly critical theorists, see these organizational issues as secondary to the danger that these social welfare bureaucracies will use their authority for social control of the poor and those served by them. They view service bureaucracies as all too effective, despite their lack of formal integration or even coordination.

Which of these views of organizational dysfunction thesis is right? As we address the organizational issues surrounding coordinated services, choices among these competing views cannot be avoided. Robert L. Crowson and William Lowe Boyd are quite right in viewing such organizational issues as highly political in their origins, reflecting both interest of particular organizations as well as larger political forces at work in our society. At the same time, Crowson and Boyd are convinced that there are important issues of management to be discovered in the experiments and innovations now underway. They make an argument for the usefulness of this managerial knowledge, if it can be developed, to help improve the likelihood that coordinated services can be made to succeed.

The public schools have a great deal at stake in this effort to link them to other human services in a new model of the welfare state. For many decades school officials have fought off the political integration of schools with other human services. As Crowson and Boyd (1993) point out, public schools have been able to rebuff or assimilate such demands. This strategy of marginalization may already be at work, as Smrekar's chapter, discussed above, offers evidence to support. At the same time, the forces advocating change in the

institution of schooling, from its governance to the content of the
curriculum, are far more pervasive than they have been for many
decades. Thus, following institutional theorists, we can characterize
the present moment as one in which the basic institution of public
education is undergoing a fundamental transformation. One facet of
this reformulation may be a less autonomous pattern of organization
and control. Another facet, equally speculative at the moment, is a
trend toward public-private forms of organization and control, represented by vouchers and/or charter schools.

This latter scenario does not make a managerial view of the problem incorrect. An institution under transformation may be managed
through that transition with more or less competence. But it does argue that political forces, not technical problems of organization, are at
the core of the volcanic forces now erupting. The more insightful leaders of the public school institution seem to understand that such a
fundamental transformation is underway and that the old strategies of
stalemate and accommodation that preserved public schools from their
challengers will no longer do.

Crowson and Boyd's attention to managerial issues is a reminder
that leadership is a core ingredient of successful innovation. However,
it is a very different kind of leadership than has typically been required of school leaders in the past. For many decades, the basic structural framework for organizing teaching and learning processes was
static, notwithstanding efforts at experimentation and innovation. Since
the 1960s, the basic organizing framework for public schooling has
been subject to escalating debate, even though until recently school
principals had little autonomy to adjust structure. With the advent of
school-based management, and demand for more fundamental change
in management and school organization, the expectations for principals have escalated dramatically. Leadership now requires not merely
the use of structure (administration) but also its origination and inter-
polation. Consequently, a number of new theories and models of leadership are being discussed in educational administration, such as moral
leadership (Sergiovanni 1992), transformational leadership (Leithwood
1994), educative leadership (MacPherson 1993), and so on. These newer
theories of leadership emphasize variously the leader's role in promoting change and the ability to work collaboratively with a range of
actors. We would add to this the idea that leadership at the school
level now requires leaders to invent new structures and processes for
collaborative decision making that involve working with a wide variety of actors.

Mark A. Smylie, Robert L. Crowson, Victoria Chou and Rebekah A. Levin's analysis shows how difficult this leadership adjustment can be. Given the range of expectations and demands with which principals must cope, there is the tendency to minimize the disruptive impact of a reform and to make certain that it can be controlled. This prudential orientation to avoid conflict, which is a well-known norm in educational administration (and among middle-managers generally), sharply constrains the potential for fundamental reform to occur. In the Chicago schools experiment Smylie, Crowson, Chou, and Levin examine, school principals were operating under very different pressures and expectations from those that university personnel brought to the project and, accordingly, moved to confine the reform within much narrower boundaries than university personnel envisioned the project. While this disappointing development can be analyzed on a number of levels, one aspect of the implementation problem clearly involves different conceptions of leadership that the two institutions brought to the experiment. Any attempt to institutionalize a reform of this magnitude requires some willingness to reexamine and possibly redefine traditional structures, processes, and roles.

Patrick F. Galvin's examination of a university-based collaborative program in Utah illustrates that, as collaborative programs mature, they face painful choices, perhaps organizational imperatives, which force organizational actors to weight the costs of collaboration against the benefits. Galvin's finding that collaboratives are more cost effective than traditional forms of organization, but not necessarily cheaper, is a reminder that this new form of organization will surely be disappointing to some. Further, partnerships face not merely often-cited obstacles of power and institutional domain, but also the calculation of costs and market efficiencies.

While these institutional impediments can be powerful, Hanne B. Mawhinney uses an institutional framework to analyze reforms at a Canadian high school. Although the experiment she chronicles is still quite new, she shows how skillful leadership makes it possible to get collaborative innovations underway, despite powerful institutional norms and structures. Indeed, she employs institutional theory to explain how such collaboration can occur despite a host of obstacles.

In closing this section on the relation between coordinated services and a reconception of the role of the welfare state, I want to stress several points. First, one of the central political issues for the remainder of the 1990s is likely to be this question of how to make the welfare state more effective. This theme swept Margaret Thatcher and Ronald Reagan into office on similar platforms, and it brought Bill Clinton to the White House with a very different centrist reform strategy. His inability to articulate a convincing alternative to the discredited tax-and-spend "big government" legacy of the old Democratic coalition appeared to lead to his party's rebuke by the voters in 1994. Apart from its partisan implications, this required reconceptualization goes to the heart of the operation of a federal system of government.[5] This larger struggle will continue to be played out in national, state, and local politics, and it will have an important impact on the status of children generally and, more specifically, on the coordinated services movement.

A second point is that it is difficult to anticipate, much less predict with any precision, the nature of these broader political impacts on coordinated services efforts. Ambitious reforms such as the redesign of the welfare system would create important ripples and perhaps even tidal waves felt by activists seeking to implement coordinated services. Failure to make major reforms would also have an impact, likely in the direction of reducing the success which coordinated services can document.

A third point is that, given the diverse nature of the coordinated services movement, its advocates will have difficulty speaking politically as one voice on matters pertaining to reform of the welfare state. Maintaining a low profile has its advantages, to be sure, since it shields the movement from some of the harsher partisan political winds, but it also makes that movement a largely reactive force vulnerable to changing electoral political considerations at each level of government.

In sum, several important questions must be addressed concerning the welfare state as we know it and as it relates to the movement for coordinated services to children and families. First, the size of the safety net, as it used to be called, will be an important part of the debate. Will the coordinated services movement succeed in strengthening the array of services available to address problems children and families are confronting? While the young coordinated services movement has some potential to influence the otherwise conservative social and economic politics of the 1990s, it also will be impacted by these larger political forces, which are more powerful. A second question is whether coordinated services will contribute to a fundamental transformation of the institution of schooling away from the old ideal of structural and professional autonomy, helping to reshape education and schools into more open and multilateral forms of organization, so that schools are linked to and depend upon a variety of other social and human resources.

If this transformation takes place, surely one aspect of the debate will be about school choice. In its extreme version, a theory of markets represents a post-Fordist view of the state's role with radical assumptions for restructuring government authority.[6] Coordinated services could be adapted to fit this market-oriented model, particularly in view of the fact that many social services and community organizations are private and voluntary. If choice advocates have their way, a reconceptualized welfare state would have a greater mix of public-private forms of control and delivery.

The coordinated services movement may be the new form, or at least one form, contributing to a reconceptualized welfare state. There are competing ideologies about what the welfare state should be. So far, coordinated services has been situated at the ideological center of this debate. Whether new political coalitions will redefine it's meaning and what lasting power coordinated services will have as an approach to protecting children cannot be predicted.

WHICH LEGITIMATING VALUES?

The fourth and final tension to which I wish to call attention is the competing values in our political culture that are likely to exert a profound influence on the success of the coordinated services movement. These values have variously been called liberty or choice, equality, efficiency or productivity, and responsiveness (Guthrie, Garms, and Pierce 1988). Any policy can embrace more than one of these values. Historic periods seem to be shaped by the dominance of one or at most two such values; for example, the politics of equality dominated federal education policy from the mid-1960s until Ronald Reagan's election as president signaled a new interest in efficiency and productivity.

A "competing values" framework is helpful as we attempt to understand the values at work in the current social movement to redefine school, family, and community ties. Each of these values is a driver of the effort to strengthen school-community ties.

For example, the value of equality can be seen in the argument that children, and particularly poor children, have become victims of our society's neglect and that this group of our citizens must be treated more fairly. It may seem self-evident to some that this value is primary, while other values ought to be of secondary importance. For example, liberty and choice are values that spur proposals to decentralize educational decision making to local schools and to expand the role of teachers and community members. Similarly, the idea that reforms in coordinated services will be shaped by local communities through self-help efforts, rather than by the states, federal government, and foundations, is part of the same value of liberty. Closely related to that is the idea that such decentralization will be more responsive to citizens. The logic of efficiency and productivity undergirds the human capital perspective on our children, who are described as a national asset that we cannot afford to squander. The idea that schools should be more responsive to citizens and other human service providers also drives much of the reform impulse, and some enthusiasts for greater responsiveness are strong advocates for opening up the system. In other words, the confluence of a variety of these values legitimates the call for stronger school-community linkages. This diversity of legitimating values at work here helps explain the strength of this social movement. In particular, the concept of coordinated services calls upon all the core values of our political culture mentioned above, whereas some other education reforms are more difficult to defend in terms of these core values. For example, critics of school choice argue that it would reduce equality of educational opportunity, despite arguments by its advocates that choice could improve opportunities for the poor who lack resources to move to wealthy communities with fine schools.

This ambiguity of the movement to coordinate schools with other human resources is not, however, an unqualified benefit. What is a political asset in gaining widespread support can also be a political problem if there is no one dominant value orientation but, instead, many impulses pushing and pulling in different, sometimes contradictory, directions. As these different values clash in specific proposals, it will not be possible to honor all of them. Consequently, the current effort to link schools and community may be no more coherent than the Progressive movement was.

The tensions among these core values are likely to play themselves out in several ways. One manifestation of the struggle was covered already in a previous section, namely, the choice as to whether lay citizens or professionals will play a key role in the reforms. Another potential conflict is between equality and efficiency, which can express itself on a number of levels. Will the movement emphasize reorganizing and expanding services so that they are more comprehensive, or will it address relatively narrow political and program priorities including cost-control? Will the movement emphasize access to services or, more fundamentally, their adequacy?

How important a value should liberty play as the central political value as we think about ways of protecting children, in contrast with strategies centering on either efficiency or equity? State and local officials may pass legislation that is quite prescriptive in its impact on local participants. Despite much rhetoric about deregulation, particularly during the Reagan-Bush presidencies, much of the reform activity in education and social welfare has had centralizing tendencies rooted in economic imperatives. This would be quite in line with a long-standing trend toward centralization in our intergovernmental system, with its emphasis on broad and therefore efficient enactment of goals through law and regulation (Chubb 1985). By 1995 Republicans were promising to finish the revolution begun by Reagan through less government, decentralization, and fewer entitlements, among other things. Some of the allies in the coordinated services movement may welcome devolution of authority because they prefer local self-help to outside assistance and regulation. However, many on the political left who support coordinated services for children focus on the need for clear entitlements alongside this devolution. In other words, how much the value of liberty should be allowed to gain ascendancy over other values such as equity and efficiency is a debate for which there is no clear resolution in sight.

Responsiveness is an important value in our political culture. Yet what exactly does it mean when we say our political system should be more responsive to children? Coordinated services may lead to a more responsive system for parents and communities, or it may also serve to further strengthen an unresponsive bureaucratic state. Furthermore, even within communities, it cannot be expected that coordinated services would benefit all of the individual families within these communities, both the middle class and poor, both Whites and people of color.

A lack of clear resolution to these tensions within and among our fundamental political values will not necessarily doom the coordinated services movement to failure. Most likely, however, it would engender criticisms from all sorts of enthusiasts who later discover that the reforms have not achieved what they had anticipated. And it is an opportunity for the movement's detractors to later say, "I told you so, the movement has not achieved what it promised."

This is not a new problem for social reform. Legislation seeking to change public policy frequently represents a compromise among diverse interests necessary to secure its passage. It is then left to those who implement policy to reconcile the contradictions or outright gaps in the logic of the policy settlement embodied in law (Palumbo and Calista 1990). In other words, whether the coordinated services movement emphasizes efficiency, or greater funding equity for children, or responsiveness to clients, or so on will depend very much on each individual policy settlement and on the implementation politics that follow passage of the reform legislation. Given the rather amorphous goals of coordinated services the pluralistic character of our political system, with its competing core values, opens the possibility, perhaps likelihood, that no one dominant focus will emerge.

In the third section of the book, four chapters addressed the problems associated with evaluating coordinated services. This dilemma is rooted in the incompatibility among core political values that coordinated services symbolically represents. Colleen A. Capper warns that increased social control of the citizenry may be an intended outcome of coordinated services, and this perspective illuminates her evaluation of a coordinated services experiment. In their chapter, Gail Chase Furman and Carol Merz see the rhetoric of coordinated services supporting the gemeinshaftlich conception of community, with its focus on local voluntary action and control, whereas they see many of the elements of coordinated services as actually strengthening bureaucratic conceptions of efficiency.

There are other evaluation issues that must be considered as well, which touch on the tension among these core values. How much should evaluation studies focus on management and organizational issues, which often are rooted in the core values of efficiency and responsiveness? This certainly is the focus of the preliminary evaluation of the California's experiments conducted by Debra Shaver, Shari Golan, and Mary Wagner. Yet not everyone accepts such a narrowly constructed approach to evaluating program effectiveness. The chapter by Maureen W. McClure, Bruce A. Jones, and Eugenie Potter takes the issue of evaluation focus head on. Jones' process approach to evaluating an experiment is challenged by McClure, who argues that it fails to address directly whether such experiments will really improve equality of life chances for all children. She sees hidden economic and other power relationships as standing in the way of true success, even though these remain latent in the course of the experiment. This raises a challenge. To be sure, the management issues about how to effectively organize services must be addressed in evaluating coordinated services (Shaver et al.), as well as the issue of what degree of control is preserved for citizens, not just professionals (Capper chapter). But these must be supplemented by longitudinal analyses of the actual status of children in our society to determine if progress really is being made.

CONCLUSION

This chapter has emphasized that the drive toward coordinated educational services is one wing of a much broader movement to rethink school, community, and family connections. This movement has diverse social and political foundations. It may well be that other aspects of this movement to strengthen school, community, and family ties, such as the interest in family choice, will prove to be more politically popular or have greater potential for fundamentally transforming public schools as we know them today. While there is much that is promising in the coordinated services movement, it is only prudent to view it with a skeptical eye, given the many impediments it faces and the frustrating history of coordinated services efforts, both in education and other social policy arenas.

In this chapter, I have tried to capture the many deeply rooted tensions inherent in the effort to achieve closer coordination between schools and their environments. These debates touch on the role of the school in our society, the influence of laypersons and professionals, the scope of the welfare state, and the competing values in our political culture. While the context here has been principally the coordinated services efforts, many of the same tensions appear in varying degrees and manifestations when other school-community-family connections are discussed, such as family choice arrangements and school-to-work programs. Thus, it is by no means certain which of these branches of this amorphous social movement will grain hegemony, or if any will, since they are all beset by significant political challenges.

What does seem clear is that dramatic change is needed in the attention our society gives to the needs of its children and families. A transformation of many of our social institutions is needed, and schools must be reshaped as part of this transformation. Some continue to believe that schools are primarily created to address academic rather than social concerns. While this simplistic dichotomous view of schools is misguided (they are surely *both* academic and social by necessity), the idea still has many fervent adherents, as the discussion earlier in the chapter underscored. Schools cannot solve all social problems, to be sure, but neither can they hope to define their mission narrowly and be effective, given the decline of other institutions such as families and neighborhoods.

The growth of poverty among children and the attendant problems of families call for a new approach to the welfare state. For

fundamental change to occur, there must be more than marginal adaptation to the status quo. In order for schools to serve their academic
and social goals more effectively, the welfare state must change also.
As we have seen, coordinated services is one response to this required
redefinition. The problem is, as has been shown, that coordinated
services lacks any clear vision and is still being invented. It may never
have a sharper image than it does now. By contrast, simpler solutions
to the welfare problem will have tempting appeal to politicians looking for short-term, politically flashy answers, such as cutting costs,
"ending welfare as we know it," and other dramatic pronouncements.
The coordinated services movement cannot fully escape this political
conflict, and one hopes that school and community leaders advocating
progressive changes will add their voices to the public debate on behalf
of a conception of children and family services that is more comprehensive, democratic, and effective than the patchwork available at
present. One also hopes that the movement will find a place for citizens and clients, not merely professionals, to help shape these reforms. Also, if the movement for coordinated services is to have any
significant impact on ameliorating these problems, it will have to focus quite single-mindedly on how to improve the lives of children and
the health of families, not the narrower goal of making the delivery of
services more economical or efficient, although these benefits might
well be important by-products.

Designing a new system will require action from the top of the
political system, as well as from the bottom. Governance reforms in
the legislative and executive branches are needed, since much of the
fragmentation among programs begins at that level. Yet top policy
makers cannot prescribe how such collaboration should occur. Collaborative models, which are heavily infused with private and voluntary efforts, do not lend themselves to standardized, one-size-fits-all
solutions. This top-down, bottom-up problem has been a major theme
in the education reform movement. It also has important ramifications
in this reform context as well.

The effort to reconnect schools, families, and communities through
coordination of services is perhaps not the final answer to the problems we have reviewed in this book. As we have seen, it is not a single
experiment, and it draws on diverse impulses. However, the social
movement on behalf of childrens' services is an important beginning
if it does open a much needed dialogue within our schools and communities. Indeed, the concepts of coordination and collaboration could
not be better metaphors for the kinds of discussions that need to occur

in our society, as an antidote to the culture wars that are a growing threat to our democratic fabric (Hunter 1994). Any idea that encourages citizens and professionals to talk together about common problems, despite their differences, is an empowering one. The best hope that the coordinated services movement will have a lasting impact on our nation's political landscape is that it will open a dialogue. What coordination and collaboration are needed in order for us to rebuild our schools, communities, and families, and how can we accomplish this task working together?

NOTES

1. This challenge to American schools from the right has its supporters in the academy. An example is Diane Ravitch (1983).

2. Another view held by pluralist scholars of school boards and other electoral bodies was that, while citizen participation is not equal, such unequal representation does not lead necessarily to unequal services. According to the argument, elected officials, however privileged their status, may be forced to respond to a variety of constituencies to remain in office, they may do what is right regardless of pressure (trusteeship), or they may be dominated by professionals who are more evenhanded or fair in their approach. This has been the argument, although some evidence indicates that school boards with higher minority representation are more inclined to support programs and services benefitting minority pupils.

3. Despite criticism of social control as a concept, this line of attack on the welfare state has been particularly strong among social historians of welfare. One of the best known analyses is by Frances Fox Piven and Richard A. Cloward (1971), which has been subjected to numerous analyses and critiques (e.g., Trattner 1983). For a discussion see Van Krieken (1991).

4. "Kenosha center reflects goal of Clinton plan for unemployed." (1994). *The Milwaukee Journal* April 3, p. 3.

5. The federal government has played a central role in promoting social redistribution in our governmental system, and this is the place of higher-level government in a federal system (Peterson 1981).

6. According to Geoff Whitty (1994), some observers interpret the ideology of markets as an attempt by elites to change modes of regulation from the sphere of production to other arenas, such as education and social welfare services. Whereas a Fordist approach to government sought to structure government in order to justify mass production and consumption, a post-Fordist approach seeks to downplay this in favor of flexible specialization arising from differentiated consumption (Ball 1990; Kenway 1993).

REFERENCES

Ball, S. (1990). *Politics and policy making: Explorations in political sociology.* London: Routledge.

Berkowitz, E. D. (1991). *America's welfare state: From Roosevelt to Reagan.* Baltimore: Johns Hopkins University Press.

Boyd, W. L. (1976). The public, the professionals, and educational decision making: Who governs? *Teachers College Record* 77: 539–577.

Boyer, E. (1984). *High school.* New York: Harper & Row.

Carnoy, M. (1994). *The state and political theory,* Princeton: Princeton University Press.

Chubb, J. (1985). Federalism and the bias for centralization. In *The new direction in American politics,* ed. J. E. Chubb and P. E. Peterson, 273–306. Washington, D.C.: Brookings Institution.

Cohen, D. L. (1994). Demise of Pew project offers lessons to funders. *Education Week* (June 1): 1, 15.

Coons, J. E., and S. D. Sugarman. (1978). *Education by choice: The case for family control.* Berkeley, Calif.: University of California Press.

Cremin, L. (1961). *The transformation of The School; Progressivism in American education 1876–1957.* New York: Random House.

Crowson, R. L., and W. L. Boyd. (1993). Coordinated services for children: Designing arks for storms and seas unknown. *American Journal of Education* 191(2): 140–179.

Cuban, L. (1984). *How teachers taught.* New York: Longman.

Cusick, P. (1983). *The egalitarian ideal and the American high school.* New York: Longman.

Dankly, M. (1993). *Solving the maze of federal programs for children and families.* Washington, D.C.: Institute for Educational Leadership.

Danzberger, J. P., M. W. Kirst, and M. D. Usdan. (1992). *Governing public schools: New times, new requirements.* Washington, D.C.: Institute for Educational Leadership.

Ellwood, D. T. (1988). *Poor support: Poverty in the American Family.* New York: Basic Books.

Fein, L. J. (1970). Community schools and social theory: The limits of universalism. In *Community control of schools,* ed. H. J. Levin, 76–99. Washington, D.C.: Brookings Institution.

Gittell, M. (1969). *Limits to citizen participation: The decline of community organizations,* Volume 109. Beverly Hills, Calif.: Sage Publications.

Goodlad, J. (1984). *A place called school.* New York: McGraw-Hill.

Gough, I. (1979). *The political economy of the welfare state.* London: Macmillan.

Grant, G. (1988). *The world we created at Hamilton High.* Cambridge: Harvard University Press.

Greenstone, J. D. and P. E. Peterson. (1973). *Race and authority in urban politics: Community action and the war on poverty.* New York: Russell Sage Foundation.

Guthrie, J. W., W. I. Garms, and L. W. Pierce. (1988). *School finance and education policy: Enhancing education efficiency, equality, and choice.* Englewood Cliffs, N.J.: Prentice-Hall.

Herrnstein, R. J., and C. Murray. (1994). *The bell curve: Intelligence and class structure in American life.* New York: The Free Press.

Hess, G. A., Jr. (1991). *School restructuring: Chicago style.* Newbury Park, Pa.: Corwin Press.

Hogan, D. J. (1985). *Class and reform: School and society in Chicago 1880–1930.* Philadelphia: University of Pennsylvania Press.

Hunter, J. D. (1994). *Before the shooting begins: Searching for democracy in America's culture wars.* New York: The Free Press.

Jackson, B. L., and J. G. Cibulka. (1992). Leadership turnover and business mobilization: The changing political ecology of urban school systems. In *The politics of urban education in the United States,* ed. J. G. Cibulka, R. J. Reed, and K. K. Wong, 71–86. New York: Falmer Press.

Joyce, M. S. (1994). The legacy of the "Wisconsin Idea" Hastening the demise of an exhausted progressivism. *Wisconsin Interest* 3(1): 9–14.

Kagan, S. L., E. Klugman, and E. F. Zigler. (1983). Shaping child and family policies: Criteria and strategies for a new decade. In *Children, families, and government: Perspectives on American social policy,* ed. E. F. Zigler, S. L. Kagan, and E. Klugman, 415–438. New York: Cambridge University Press.

Karger, H. J., and D. Stoesz. (1993) Retreat and retrenchment: Progressives and the welfare state. *Social Work* 38(9): 212 ff.

Katz, D., and R. L. Kahn. (1978). *The social psychology of organizations,* ed 2. New York: John Wiley & Sons.

Katz, M. B. (1989). *The undeserving poor: From the war on poverty to the war on welfare.* New York: Pantheon Books.

Kenway, J. (1993). Marketing education in the postmodern age. *Journal of Education Policy* 8(1): 105–122.

Koppich, J. E. (1994). The politics of policy making for children. In *The politics of linking schools and social services*, ed. L. Adler and S. Gardner, 51–62. New York: Falmer Press.

Lehmann, N. (1994). Rebuilding the ghetto doesn't work. *The New York Times Magazine* (January 9): 27–31, 50, 54, 56.

Leithwood, K. (1994). Leadership for school restructuring. *Educational Administration Quarterly* 30(4): 498–518.

MacPherson, R. J. S. (1993). Administrative reforms and the antipodes: Self-managing schools and the need for educative leaders. *Educational Management and Administration* 21(1): 40–52.

McAllister, S. (April, 1991). *Can parent involvement lead to increased student achievement in urban schools?* Paper presented at the Annual Meeting of the American Educational Research Association, Chicago, IL.

Moynihan, D. P. (1969). *Maximum feasible misunderstanding: Community action and the war on poverty.* New York: The Free Press.

Murray, C. (1984). *Losing ground: American social policy 1950–1980.* New York: Basic Books.

Palumbo, D. J., and D. J. Calista. (1990). Opening up the black box: Implementation and the policy process. In *Implementation and the policy process: Opening up the black box*, ed. D. J. Palumbo and D. J. Calista, 3–18. Westport, Conn.: Greenwood Press.

Piven, F. F., and R. A. Cloward. (1971). *Regulating the poor: The functions of public welfare.* New York: Pantheon Books.

Powell, A. G., E. Farrar, and D. K. Cohen. (1986). *The shopping mall high school: Winners and losers in the educational marketplace.* Boston: Houghton Mifflin.

Ravitch, D. (1983). *The troubled crusade: American education, 1945–1980.* New York: Basic Books.

Sedlack, M. W. and S. Schlossman. (1985). The public school and social services: Reassessing the Progressive legacy. *Educational Theory* 35(4): 371–383.

Sergiovanni, T. (1992). *Moral leadership.* San Francisco: Jossey-Bass.

Sizer, T. (1984). *Horace's compromise.* Boston: Houghton Mifflin.

Valentine, J., and E. F. Zigler. (1983). Head Start: A case study in the development of social policy for children and families. In *Children, families, and government: Perspectives on American social policy,* ed. E. F. Zigler, S. L. Kagan, and E. Klugman, 266–280. New York: Cambridge University Press.

Trattner, W. I., ed. (1983). *Social welfare or social control? Some historical reflections on regulating the poor.* Knoxville, Tenn.: University of Tennessee Press.

Tyack, D. (1974). *The one best system: A history of American urban education.* Cambridge: Harvard University Press.

Van Krieken, R. (1991). The poverty of social control: Explaining power in the historical sociology of the welfare state. *Sociological Review* 39(1): 1–25.

Waller, W. (1932). *The sociology of teaching.* New York: Russell and Russell.

Whitty, G. (August, 1994). *Consumer rights versus citizen rights in contemporary education policy.* Paper presented to a conference on Education, Democracy, and Reform, University of Aukland, New Zealand.

Wilensky, H. L. (1975). *The welfare state and equality.* Berkeley: University of California Press.

Wirt, F. L., and M. W. Kirst. (1989) *Schools in conflict.* Berkeley, Calif.: McCutchan.

Zeigler, L. H., Jennings, M. K. and G. W. Peak. (1974). *Political interaction and local school districts:* North Scituate, Mass.: Duxbury.

About the Editors and Authors

LYNN G. BECK is Assistant Professor of Education at the University of California, Los Angeles. Her work focuses on the principalship, ethics and educational administration, and preparation of educational leaders. She authored *Reclaiming Educational Administration as a Caring Profession* (Teachers College Press, 1994).

WILLIAM LOWE BOYD is Distinguished Professor of Education at Pennsylvania State University. He specializes in the study of educational administration, policy, and politics, including cross-national comparisons of education reform, coordinated services, and urban education. He wrote (with Robert Crowson) "Coordinated Services for Children: Designing Arks for Storms and Seas Unknown." (*American Journal of Education,* February, 1993).

VICTORIA CHOU is Professor of Education and Associate Dean for Academic Programs at the University of Illinois at Chicago. Her research focuses on teacher education, coordinated children's services, and reading. She has written (with M. Bay and S. H. King) "Children's Services and Urban Teacher Education: Beginning the Conversation." In R. Levin (Ed.), *Comprehensive Children's Services and Urban Teacher Education: Beginning the Conversation.* (American Association of Colleges for Teacher Education, in press).

COLLEEN A. CAPPER is Associate Professor of Educational Administration at the University of Wisconsin-Madison. Her research addresses school administration, school-community-interagency relationships, as well as multiple perspectives of organizations and administration, particularly focusing on nontraditional theories. She edited the book, *Educational Administration in a Pluralistic Society* (SUNY Press, 1993).

JAMES G. CIBULKA is Professor and Chair of the Department of Education Policy, Planning, and Administration at the University of Maryland at College Park. His research focuses on educational polities, policy, and finance. Several recent book chapters and journal articles have addressed urban school reform and the state's role in education reform. He is completing a textbook, *School Politics and Policy Making: A Crisis of Governance* (McGraw-Hill).

SHARON CONLEY is Associate Professor at the University of California, Santa Barbara. Her research specializes in organizational behavior in education and the managerial work environment of teachers. With R. Levinson she wrote, "Teacher Work Redesign and Job Satisfaction," *Educational Administration Quarterly* (November 1993).

H. DICKSON CORBETT is Codirector of the Applied Research Project at Research for Better Schools in Philadelphia. His research interests include educational policy, qualitative research, and school reform. He authored (with G. Rossman and W. Firestone) *Change and Effectiveness in Schools: A Cultural Perspective* (SUNY Press, 1988).

ROBERT L. CROWSON is Professor of Education at Vanderbilt University. His research addresses urban school administration, the politics of education, and organizational theory. He is the author of *School Community Relations, Under Reform* (McCutchan, 1992).

GAIL CHASE FURMAN is Assistant Professor in the College of Education at Washington State University. She specializes in policy analysis, with a focus on education reform, as well as qualitative research methodology. Her article, "Outcome-based Education and Accountability," appears in *Education and Urban Society* (in press.)

PATRICK F. GALVIN is Assistant Professor in the Department of Educational Administration at the University of Utah. He specializes in school finance and the economics of organization. He authored the chapter, "A Proposal for Including Data from Economic Theories of Organization in a National Data Base for Organizations," in *Advances in Theory and Research on Administration and Policy*, ed. R. Ogawa and S. Bacharach (JAI Press, in press).

SHARI GOLAN is an Educational Policy Analyst at SRI International. Her research addresses school-based health/mental health prevention and intervention programs, as well as assessment. She authored "Assessing the Effects of Standardized Testing on Schools," in *Educational and Psychological Assessment*, 54 (2), 469 ff.

SHIRLEY BRICE HEATH is Professor of English and Education at Stanford University. She is an anthropological linguist whose research interests have centered on the language and culture of subordinated populations in various parts of the world. Her book (coedited with Milbrey McLaughlin), *Identity and Inner-city Youth: Beyond Ethnicity and Gender* (Teachers College Press, 1993), brings together perspectives on the lives of urban youth.

PAUL E. HECKMAN is Assistant Professor in the College of Education at the University of Arizona. His research interests include educational restructuring and education of poor children of color whose first language is not English. His article "School Restructuring in Practice: Reckoning with the Culture of a School" appeared in *International Journal of Education Reform* (July 1993).

CAROLYN D. HERRINGTON is Associate Professor of Educational Leadership in the College of Education, Florida State University. She studies the politics of education, intergovermental relations, and the politics of integrating children's services. She has edited *Condition of Children in Florida* and *Condition of Education in Florida*.

BRUCE A. JONES is Assistant Professor and Coordinator of Educational Administration at the University of Pittsburgh. His research interests include schools, communities, partnerships, and collaboration. He coedited (with Kathryn M Borman) *Investing in U.S. Schools: Directions for Educational Policy* (Ablex Publishing, 1994).

WILLIAM J. KRITEK is Associate Professor and Chair in the Department of Administrative Leadership at the University of Wisconsin-Milwaukee. He is Senior Associate Editor of *Educational Administration Quarterly*. He specializes in urban education and program implementation. He authored "Effecting Change in Urban Schools," in P. B. Forsyth and M. Tallerico (Eds.), *City Schools: Leading the Way* (Corwin Press, 1993).

REBEKAH A. LEVIN is Visiting Assistant Professor and Coordinator of Research Programs at the Center for Urban Educational Research and Development, University of Illinois at Chicago. Her research interests are urban education evaluation and experiential education. She edited the volume, *Greater than the Sum: Professionals in a Comprehensive Services Model*, published by the Association of Colleges for Teacher Education (1994).

MILBREY MCLAUGHLIN is Professor of Education and Public Policy at Stanford University. Her research interests include planned change/policy implementation, contexts of teaching and learning, and community-based youth organizations. In 1994 she published (with M. Irby and J. Langman) *Urban Sanctuaries* (Jossey-Bass).

MAUREEN W. MCCLURE is Associate Professor in the Department of Administration and Policy Studies at the University of Pittsburgh, where she also is Associate Executive Director of the Tri-State Area School Study Council. She conducts research on finance, strategy, collaboratives, and information systems. She contributed the chapter, "The Reform that Wasn't: The Lighthouse Strategy of Local Control," in *Investing in U.S. Schools: Directions for Educational Policy*, ed. Bruce A. Jones and Kathryn M. Borman (Ablex Publishing, 1994).

HANNE B. MAWHINNEY is Assistant Professor at the University of Ottawa, where she also is Director of Masters of Education and Professional Development. She studies the politics of education, interagency collaboration, and school-community relations. She wrote "Discovering Shared Values: Ecological Models to Support Collaboration" in *The Politics of Linking Schools and Social Services*, ed. L. Adler and S. Gardner (Falmer Press, 1994).

CAROL MERZ is Professor and Dean of the School of Education at the University of Puget Sound, where her research has focused on the politics of education, as well as the relationship between communities and school funding. She published (with Frank Lutz) *The Politics of School Community Relations* (Teachers College Press, 1992).

REBECCA L. NEWMAN is Research Associate in the Graduate School of Education at the University of California, Los Angeles. Her work addresses homeless students and families, children of poverty, and bilingual education. With Lynn Beck she wrote "Caring in One Urban High School: Thoughts on the Interplay Among Race, Class, and Gender" in *Caring in Context: Negotiating Borders and Barriers in Schools,* ed. D. J. Eaker and J. VanGalen (SUNY Press, in press).

EUGENIE POTTER is Heinz Assistant Professor for Religious Studies in Education at the University of Pittsburgh. She specializes in ethical issues in education and religious influences on U.S. education. She wrote "Privatization and Technology: Twin 'Gales of Creative Destruction' Affecting Public Schools and the Potential Role of Educational Philosophers," *Philosophical Studies in Education* (1992).

W. REED SCULL is a doctoral candidate in the College of education at the University of Arizona, where his research focuses on organization theory, leadership and policy studies, and multicultural education. With S. Conley, he wrote "The School as a Workplace: Making Sense of Multiple Frameworks," in *International Journal of Education Reform* (in press).

DEBRA SHAVER is Social Science Researcher at SRI International, where she studies parental involvement in education, program evaluation, and family support programs. She has written "Educating Homeless Children," in S. Dornbush and E. Barclay (Eds.), *Stanford Studies of Homeless Families and Youth,* published by Stanford University Press (in press).

CLAIRE SMREKAR is Assistant Professor at Vanderbilt University. Her research interests include family-school-community relationships, school choice, and the social context of education. She has published recently *In the Interest of Families and Schools: The Impact of Choice and Community* (SUNY Press, 1995).

MARK A. SMYLIE is Associate Professor of Education at the University of Illinois at Chicago. His research expertise includes educational organizations and leadership, coordinated children's services, and work redesign and change. He published "Redesigning Teachers Work: Connections to the Classroom" in *Review of Research in Education* (1994).

DEBORAH A. VERSTEGEN is Associate Professor of Education Policy and Finance in the Curry School of Education at the University of Virginia. Her research interests include federal and state education policy, equal opportunity, education reform, and education finance and litigation. Her article, "Financing Education Reform: Where Did All the Money Go?" appeared in the *Journal of Education Finance* (1993).

MARY WAGNER is Program Manager, Education and Human Services Research, at SRI International. Her research interests include family support, program evaluation, and disability policy research. She authored "Revisiting the Issues: School-linked Services," in *The Future of Children, 3* (3), 1993 (Los Altos, CA: Center for the Future of Children).

JACI WEBB is Research Associate at Research for Better Schools in Philadelphia. Her research interests include school reform, school contexts, and policy research. She authored (with D. Corbett and B. Wilson) "Restructuring Systemically for Students: Is It Just Talk?" in *Restructuring Schooling: Learning from Ongoing Efforts,* ed. J. Murphy and P. Hallinger (Corwin Press, 1993).

BRUCE L. WILSON is Codirector of the Applied Research Project at Research for Better Schools in Philadelphia. His research interests focus on school reform, educational policy, and the sociology of education. His most recent book (with G. B. Rossman) is *Mandating Educational Excellence: High School Responses to State Curriculum Reform* (Teachers College Press, 1993).

Author Index

443

Subject Index